Tourism Social Science Series
Volume 26

Fashion and Tourism

Tourism Social Science Series

Series Editor: **Jafar Jafari**

University of Wisconsin-Stout, USA
Email: jafari@uwstout.edu

Volume Editor: **Juergen Gnoth**

University of Otago, New Zealand

The books in *Tourism Social Science Series* (TSSSeries) are intended to systematically and cumulatively contribute to the formation, embodiment and advancement of knowledge in the field of tourism.

The TSSSeries' multidisciplinary framework and treatment of tourism includes application of theoretical, methodological, and substantive contributions from such fields as anthropology, business administration, ecology, economics, geography, history, hospitality, leisure, planning, political science, psychology, recreation, religion, sociology, transportation, etc., but it significantly favors state-of-the-art presentations, works featuring new directions, and especially the cross-fertilization of perspectives beyond each of these singular fields. While the development and production of this book series is fashioned after the successful model of *Annals of Tourism Research*, the TSSSeries further aspires to assure each theme a comprehensiveness possible only in book-length academic treatment. Each volume in the series is intended to deal with a particular aspect of this increasingly important subject, thus to play a definitive role in the enlarging and strengthening of the foundation of knowledge in the field of tourism, and consequently to expand the frontiers of knowledge into the new research and scholarship horizons ahead.

Published TSSSeries Titles:

Volume 25: Space Tourism: The Elusive Dream, *Erik Cohen and Sam Spector*
Volume 24: Authenticity & Tourism: Materialities, Perceptions, Experiences, *Jillian M. Rickly and Elizabeth S. Vidon*
Volume 23: Social Conflict and Harmony: Tourism in China's Multi-ethnic Communities, *Liping Cai*
Volume 22: Tourism Research Paradigms: Critical and Emergent Knowledges, *Ana María Munar and Tazim Jamal*
Volume 21: Tourism Education: Global Issues and Trends, *Pauline J. Sheldon and Cathy H. C. Hsu*
Volume 20: Tourism Research Frontiers: Beyond the Boundaries of Knowledge, *Donna Chambers and Tijana Rakić*
Volume 19: Geographies of Tourism: European Research Perspectives, *Julie Wilson and Salvador Anton Clavé*
Volume 18: Tourism Social Media: Transformations in Identity, Community and Culture, *Ana María Munar, Szilvia Gyimóthy and Liping Cai*
Volume 17: Culture and Society in Tourism Contexts, *A-M. Nogués-Pedregal*
Volume 16: The Discovery of Tourism Economics, *Larry Dwyer*
Volume 15: The Study of Tourism: Foundations from Psychology, *Philip Pearce*
Volume 14: Modern Mass Tourism, *Julio R. Aramberri*
Volume 13: The Discovery of Tourism, *Stephen L. J. Smith.*
Volume 12: The Sociology of Tourism: European Origins and Developments, *Graham M.S. Dann and Giuli Liebman Par.*

In this publication, the convergence of fashion and tourism is explored from an academic perspective, shedding light on the intricate linkages and reciprocal influences between these two vibrant industries. By delving into their shared history spanning over two centuries, the different authors present a compelling hypothesis that unveils the profound impact they have had on each other. Through parallel analysis in the different chapters, readers gain a deeper understanding of the symbiotic relationship between fashion and tourism, and how their collaborative actions shape and reflect contemporary societies worldwide. This insightful work is a must-read for anyone seeking a comprehensive exploration of the dynamic interplay between these global influential forces.

Eduardo Santander, PhD
Executive Director
European Travel Commission

The topics of fashion and tourism have many traits in common. The academic world has yet studied them mostly separately. The important contribution of this volume lies in its ability to show their joint effect on social life. Both fashion and tourism seek to sell dreams and both rely on brand image in order to gain recognition and attract the attention of consumers. The "parallel stories" that are carefully told in this volume constitute a significant understanding of how two big industries have shaped our taste and behaviour for the last two centuries.

Paula von Wachenfeldt, PhD
Associate Professor in Fashion
Studies Stockholm University

Tourism Social Science Series
Volume 26

FASHION AND TOURISM

Parallel Stories

MARIA GRAVARI-BARBAS
Université Paris 1 Panthéon-Sorbonne, France

NADZEYA SABATINI
Gdansk University of Technology, Poland and USI-Università della Svizzera italiana, Switzerland

emerald
PUBLISHING

United Kingdom – North America – Japan – India – Malaysia – China

Emerald Publishing Limited
Emerald Publishing, Floor 5, Northspring, 21-23 Wellington Street, Leeds LS1 4DL

First edition 2024

British Library Cataloguing in Publication Data
A catalogue record for this book is available from the British Library

ISBN: 978-1-80262-976-7 (Print)
ISBN: 978-1-80262-975-0 (Online)
ISBN: 978-1-80262-977-4 (Epub)

ISSN: 1571-5043 (Series)

Printed and bound by CPI Group (UK) Ltd, Croydon, CR0 4YY

Contents

List of Figures and Tables

About the Contributors

Konstantina K. Agoraki is an Adjunct Lecturer of the Department of Tourism Studies, University of Piraeus (Greece). Dr Agoraki holds a PhD (2017) from the University of Piraeus, Department of Business Administration, and a Master's Degree (2011) in International Economics and Finance from the Athens University of Economics and Business, Greece. Her research interests include various areas of business management, such as knowledge management, technological innovation, competitive advantage, organizational performance, sustainability, and change management.

Sandra Biondo, a PhD candidate at University of Paris1 Panthéon-Sorbonne, is a Lecturer and an academic advisor at Sciences Po Paris (France). Her research interests, based on transnational luxury fashion brands, include public–private partnerships, systems of urban governance, territorial marketing, and urban branding policies. Her works are at the crossroads between cultural and urban geography. Sandra's academic research specifically focuses on the links between cultural and creative industries and urban heritage policies.

Lorenzo Cantoni graduated in Philosophy and holds a PhD in Education and Linguistics. He is a full Professor at USI – Università della Svizzera italiana (Lugano, Switzerland), Faculty of Communication, Culture and Society, where he is Director of the Institute of Digital Technologies for Communication. His research interests are where communication, education, and new media overlap, ranging from computer-mediated communication to usability, from eLearning to eTourism and digital fashion, and from ICT4D to eGovernment. He is USI's Pro-rector for Education and Students' experience.

Erina Cavalli is a stylist for photography and an educator in fashion and luxury based in Paris. Her experience of teaching at international level spans more than 10 years. Cavalli consistently intersects fashion, luxury, art, design, and architecture. She currently teaches in Paris at Paris1 Panthéon-Sorbonne, Sup de Pub where she coordinates a Master in Luxury and Marketing, the Paris School of Luxury, ESMOD, INSEEC, and ISG. She has previously Lectured at Istituto Marangoni in Paris, the Amırkabır University of Technology of Tehran, the Istituto Europeo di Design in Rome, and the European Communication School in London.

Georgios A. Deirmentzoglou is a Lecturer in Business Administration at Neapolis University Pafos. He holds a PhD degree in Business Administration from the University of Piraeus, a Master's degree in Business Administration – Total

Quality Management (MBA-TQM), and a Bachelor's degree in Industrial Management and Technology from the University of Piraeus. In addition, he has studied film and music production. His research interests include entrepreneurship, strategic management, sustainable development, creative industries, culture, and e-commerce.

Triana Rosalina Dewi is a Lecturer at Trisakti Institute of Tourism Jakarta, Indonesia. She gained a Bachelor's degree in Economics at Universitas Dr. Moestopo and a Master's degree in Management at Muhammadiyah University, Jakarta, Indonesia. Her research focuses on leveraging human capital in the hospitality industry and developing tourism products in tourism villages. In addition, she is involved in several community development projects in Indonesia and conducts studies on employee well-being, the leisure industry, and local and regional entrepreneurship.

Gianluigi Di Giangirolamo holds a PhD in Contemporary History. He is an Adjunct Professor of Social History of Fashion at Paris1 Panthéon-Sorbonne and at the University of Bologna. His research interests are history of contemporary society, history of cultural policies and institutions, fashion heritage, and tourism. He is member of the EIREST – Interdisciplinary research team on tourism at the University of Paris 1 Panthéon-Sorbonne and of the international research center, Culture, Fashion Communication, at the University of Bologna.

Maria Gravari-Barbas is an architect and social geographer. She is a Professor at Paris 1 Panthéon-Sorbonne University. She is the Director of the EIREST, a multidisciplinary research team dedicated to tourism studies, with main focus on cultural heritage, development, and urban-tourism evolutions. Since 2009, she is the Director of the UNESCO Chair of Paris 1 Panthéon-Sorbonne University and the coordinator of the UNITWIN network, Tourism, Culture, Development. She is the Chair of the Self Steering Committee of Cultural Heritage of Una Europa and of the Joint Doctoral Committee of the PhD on Cultural Heritage of the European University Alliance Una Europa.

Ulrike Gretzel is a Senior Fellow at the Center of Public Relations, University of Southern California (USA) and serves as Director of Research at Netnografica. She received her PhD in Communications from the University of Illinois at Urbana-Champaign. She is a fellow of the International Academy for the Study of Tourism. Her research focuses on technology-mediated communication and persuasion in digital media. Her expertise spans the design and evaluation of intelligent systems, as well as the development and implications of artificial intelligence. Dr Gretzel has published over 100 peer-reviewed journal articles.

Faruq Ibnul Haqi is a PhD candidate in Urban and Regional Planning at the University of South Australia. His research focus is the role of urban political leadership in the formulation of urban policy in Indonesian metropolitan cities. Faruq holds a Master's of Urban and Regional Planning from the University of South Australia, Adelaide, Australia, and he has a BEng in Architecture from

UII Yogyakarta, Indonesia. His professional and research interest is in urban development and policy, and in urban leadership.

Sandra Krim is a PhD researcher and Lecturer in marketing and communications at Sorbonne School of Management and is a member of the PRISM Research Center from Paris 1 Panthéon-Sorbonne University. Her PhD thesis explores the influence of high culture on the symbolic value of luxury fashion brands, with a focus on their artification strategies. Her research and teaching interests lie in luxury brand management and the brand culture of luxury fashion houses. Sandra studied at the Sorbonne University and holds an MBA in Global Fashion Management from the Institut Français de la Mode (Paris, France).

Sophie Kurkdjian got her PhD in History from the University of Paris1 Panthéon-Sorbonne. She is currently an Assistant Professor at the American University of Paris where she teaches social and cultural history of fashion, and Associate Researcher at the IHTP-CNRS. In 2021, she published *Géopolitique de la mode* (Ed. du Cavalier Bleu) and co-published *Au cœur des maisons de couture. Une histoire sociale des ouvrières de la mode (1880–1950)* (Ed. de l'Atelier).

Fitri Utami Ningrum is an Indonesian cultural activist. She currently pursues a Master's degree in Archeology at the University of Indonesia. She focuses on assisting the community in developing and promoting tourism potential in rural areas through Pesona Desa Nusantara. She also initiated CAVENTER Indonesia (Culture, Art, Community Development, and Ecotourism Center) together with tour operators around Indonesia. She obtained her Bachelor's degree in Marketing Management at University of Indonesia. With the experiences gained from the community empowerment activities, she created coaching initiatives for community/village focusing on heritage, culture, and rural development.

Andreas Papatheodorou is a Professor in industrial and spatial economics, with emphasis on tourism at the University of the Aegean, Greece, where he also directs the MSc program in Strategic Management of Tourism Destinations and Hospitality Enterprises and the Laboratory for Tourism Research and Studies. He is the Editor-in-Chief of the *Journal of Air Transport Studies* and an Associate Editor of *Annals of Tourism Research*. His research interests include aviation and tourism, tourism and regional development, and economics of cultural tourism.

Mario Paris is a researcher in the field of urban planning and a Lecturer at the Università degli Studi di Bergamo. He studies the conditions of the European urban regions and the role of services in their evolution, together with the impact of luxury in the social, economic, and spatial transformation of the city. He is the Editor of the book *Making Prestigious Places* (Routledge, 2018) and of the chapter "Luxury as a Driver for New Urban Identities in Milan: Spatial Practices, Geographics, and Open Questions".

Puspita Ayu Permatasari is of Indonesian origin. She is a Lecturer/researcher in digital transformation in cultural tourism at Breda University of applied sciences (BUas), The Netherlands. She obtained a PhD degree in 2022 from USI-Università della Svizzera italiana in Switzerland by conducting research focusing on the linkage and the communication model of UNESCO intangible heritage of Indonesian Batik textiles with global fashion and tourism. She has a Bachelor's degree from the University of Indonesia, majoring in Chinese Studies and Master's degree in the Management of Natural/Cultural Heritage from IREST – Paris1 Panthéon-Sorbonne, France.

Nadzeya Sabatini holds a PhD in Communication Sciences. She is an Assistant Professor in Digital Transformation at Gdansk University of Technology (Gdansk, Poland). Nadzeya is a Senior Lecturer and academic coordinator of MSc in Digital Fashion Communication, double degree between USI-Università della Svizzera italiana, Switzerland, and Université Paris 1 Panthéon-Sorbonne, France. She is a group leader in Digital Fashion Communication Research at the Institute of Digital Technologies for Communication (USI). Nadzeya's research interests are in the digital transformation of communication in tourism and fashion.

Claudio Visentin is a professional journalist. He mainly investigates the history of Italian tourism, package tours, and international guidebooks. On this topic, he has published *Il Canton Ticino visto dagli altri. L'immagine del territorio nelle guide turistiche internazionali* (2007) and *Il turismo contemporaneo. Cultura e mondo dell'impresa – Visentin C. (2002).* Claudio is the Lecturer of the course, Cultural History of Tourism, at the Università della Svizzera italiana in Lugano, Switzerland. He has been General Secretary of the International Commission for the History of Travel and Tourism, affiliated with the International Committee of Historical Sciences.

Eirini Vlassi is a Lecturer in Neapolis University Pafos in the field of management and marketing of tourism business and tourism destinations. She is also an Adjunct Lecturer, teaching Strategic Tourism Management, in the MBA in Aviation and Tourism Management offered by the Frankfurt University of Applied Sciences, Germany, in collaboration with the University of the Aegean. She holds a PhD from the University of the Aegean. Her research interests include destination marketing and branding and collaborative initiatives in destination marketing.

Daniel William Mackenzie Wright is a Senior Lecturer in tourism. He has a wide interest in the study and research of tourism. His career research began with a PhD exploring the role of tourism in post-disaster situations. More recently, he has turned his attention to the tourism futures field. The study of tourism futures has the potential to engage wider audiences. Importantly, highlighting tourism's potential role in the face of many global challenges and opportunities, Dr Wright has presented at international conferences and continues to be an active educator and publisher in tourism-related subject areas.

Acknowledgments

We are immensely grateful to Jafar Jafari, for his confidence and his tremendous support in meticulously editing the volume. We are also deeply grateful to Juergen Gnoth, who provided valuable advice on how to improve the volume. Our thanks also go to Lorenzo Cantoni, Tekila Harley Nobile, and Elide Garbani-Nerini for their help in polishing our introductory chapter. We thank our authors, colleagues, and friends who joined us during this journey of exploring multiple inspiring connections between fashion and tourism, the two domains we are passionate about.

SETTING THE STAGE

Chapter 1

FASHION AND TOURISM
Parallel Stories of Two "Dream Marvels"

Maria Gravari-Barbas
Paris 1 Panthéon-Sorbonne, France

Nadzeya Sabatini
Gdansk University of Technology, Poland and USI-Università della Svizzera italiana, Switzerland

INTRODUCTION

Fashion and tourism are two social, cultural, and economic phenomena that have both numerous connections and surprising similarities. These are not new: they have been built and developed since the beginnings of tourism as a modern social phenomenon, emerged in Europe in the context of the industrial revolution. They consolidated in the first decades of the 21st century, in a context where both phenomena have completed their "mass" cycle and are currently seeking alternative ways of expression and development. This collaborative nature of fashion and tourism represents the guiding thread of this chapter and, beyond, of the collection of 14 texts gathered in this book.

The chapter analyzes first the common characteristics of these two phenomena, fashion and tourism, as well as the challenges they are facing in the beginning of the 21st century. What can one learn from these proximities? What does the evolution of the practices, policies, and space planning of one phenomenon say about the other? Further, what does their parallel analysis suggest about people, their desires, their wishes, their dreams, and their practices? But also what about the environmental or ethical concerns? The parallel analysis of these two vistas allows one to grasp just that: today, dreams still work well and even better. However, practices are changing, and

Fashion and Tourism: Parallel Stories
Tourism Social Science Series, Volume 26, 3–17

ISSN: 1571-5043/doi:10.1108/S1571-504320230000026001

massification is giving way to differentiated individual practices that integrate sustainability concerns.

The analysis of the state of the art in a cross-cutting manner shows that, surprisingly, very little work has considered the striking parallel developments between the fashion and tourism. Few researchers have sought to better understand the tourism system by examining the functioning of fashion, and vice versa.

FASHION AND TOURISM AS COLLABORATIVE PHENOMENA

The literature suggests several parallels between fashion and tourism.

Global Economic Importance. The considerable economic weight of the two phenomena makes them unavoidable regulators of the world economy, as it was demonstrated, for example, for tourism during the COVID-19 pandemic. Both are important business sectors globally, where tourism accounts for 10% of the global gross domestic product (GDP) (WTTC, 2019), and fashion amounts to 2% of the worldwide GDP (Fashion United, 2021).

Global Consumption. Both fashion and tourism rely on the international production and consumption of their respective products. In the fashion domain, garments are mostly produced abroad, sold, and used in other countries. The same can be said about the international tourism market, where people come from abroad to access tourism products in the destination country.

Importance of the Global Brand Image. Both fashion and tourism rely heavily on brand image, the building and consolidation of which requires significant and continuous efforts. The former has historically relied on designers with a strong identity, often built around their persona, allowing for product differentiation, and creating a distinctive identity. Tourism destinations also develop a strong brand identity to stand out in an increasingly competitive global context.

Dream Industries. Fashion is more than just clothing, and tourism is conceptually constructed as mobility driven by desire. Fashion and tourism are central components of the "Dream Society" (Jensen, 2001). The development of each is based on a transformational narrative capable of radically changing everyday life. Both fashion and tourism are becoming more and more core elements of the global experience economy (Pine & Gilmore, 1999), as well as constitutive parts of the construction of the self and the lifestyle around it.

Traveling for Fashion, Fashion for Travel. According to McKinsey (2020), 20–30% of fashion industry revenues are generated by consumers making luxury purchases abroad. Asian shoppers buy luxury goods outside their home countries not only to benefit from lower prices in Europe but also because shopping has become an integral part of the tourism experience. Buying a brand in its country of origin or where the garment was made comes with a sense of authenticity and excitement.

Destinations Boost Fashion Brands, Fashion Boosts Destinations. Tourism destinations are being used by fashion houses as recognizable shooting locations, as places to stage fashion shows, and to build up their flagship stores. At the same time, fashion designers get their inspiration from certain geographical areas and dedicate their collections to them while then encouraging their fans to visit those locations in the future.

The interdependence of fashion and tourism has been clearly seen since 2020 and the outbreak of the pandemic when international tourism was almost frozen. Fashion companies could no longer rely on foreign tourists coming to Europe's shopping streets to boost their sales (Financial Times, 2022). Before the pandemic, many luxury retailers defined the shopping experience around foreign tourists. Their unexpected absence forced Europe's luxury fashion retailers to rethink their business strategies in working with the tourism industry.

After the pandemic, both fashion and tourism are facing new challenges that will have a lasting impact and call for reinvention. Voices are being raised increasingly to remind both that a paradigm shift is needed. Fashion and tourism have been historically characterized by seasonality, which plays an important role in how industries are structured, namely a clear differentiation between winter and summer destinations and two major seasons in the fashion industry with fashion weeks staged around them. However, in the last decade, the situation changed considerably. On the one hand, fast fashion companies have evolved the traditional seasonality of garment production from twice a year into a continuous delivery of new collections. On the other hand, the increasing importance of low-cost airlines offers cheaper tourism opportunities, consumed more often, by a higher percentage of the market in any season. This, however, has considerable social and environment impacts. Fashion and tourism are among the highest polluting industries globally. The latter produces 8% of the world's carbon emissions (Sustainable Travel, n.d.). The former is responsible for 10% of annual global carbon emissions, more than all international flights and maritime shipping combined (World Bank, 2019).

Fashion and tourism are undergoing major transformations to adapt to changing markets and new sustainable, ethical, and digital paradigms.

Breaking with "Fast" *Fashion and* "Fast" *Tourism.* In both sectors, there is a shift toward "slow tourism" and "slow" or "local" fashion production and consumption (Štefko & Steffek, 2018). The rise of fast fashion (Binet et al., 2019; Niinimäki et al., 2020), which relies on cheap manufacturing, frequent consumption, and short-lived garment use, has become a worldwide problem. "Fast tourism" or "hit and run" tourism (Ruoss & Alfarè, 2013), highly visible in cities that are cruise or day trip destinations, has also became a major issue. Such discussions were strongly expressed in the 2010s with the rise of tourismophobia (Ghidouche & Ghidouche, 2019; Simas, Oliveira, & Cano-Hila, 2021) in several destinations worldwide.

Rethinking the Working Conditions. Both industries have harsh labor conditions. They are not the easiest ones to work in, and ethical issues are increasingly emerging (Miotto & Vilajoana-Alejandre, 2019). Today, there are roughly 40 million garment workers, 85% of whom are women; many of these are among the lowest paid workers in the world, and they do not share the same rights or protections as workers in Western societies. Conditions are also poor for workers in tourism and hospitality in terms of pay, working hours, gender equality, and sexual harassment (Baum & Hai, 2019; Poulston, 2009).

Take the Digital Turn. The digital shift is crucial for both fashion and tourism. In Europe, they are two main product categories currently being sold online. Fashion and tourism are adapting themselves to digital transformation (Buhalis, 2020; Buhalis & Law, 2008; Kalbaska, Sádaba, & Cantoni, 2018), particularly seen in the COVID and post-COVID contexts. Digital transformation in both sectors implies innovative knowledge management (Fuchs, Fossgard, Stensland, & Chekalina, 2021), a human-oriented approach to the e-dimension of fashion and tourism based on ethics, societal impacts, sustainability, and human value dimensions (Gretzel et al., 2020; Nobile, Kalbaska, de Oliveira, & Cantoni, 2021). This transformation is not mainly about technology but about people who consume them, as well as ethics, values, and social structures (Cantoni et al., 2020; Pesonen, 2020).

Fashion and tourism impact people and businesses, but also culture, art, and the whole lifestyle ecosystem. They are closely linked with the latest trends, social practices, and innovative and disruptive technologies. As dynamic industries, in constant evolution, they need critical understanding, particularly concerning influence and independence. Few studies, as discussed below, analyze the emergence, evolution, and current transformations of these two fashion and tourism in a joint and articulated manner.

The Relationship Between Fashion and Tourism

Until recently, studies of fashion and tourism have been suffering from a blurred identity, which is typical for subjects "searching for a discipline" (Tseëlon, 2001). There are striking similarities in how academic research approaches these two topics. Both are wide-ranging and diverse fields of study, which are infused not only with contributions from various domains of inquiry within the "traditional" disciplines like sociology, communication, marketing, and digital media (Cantoni et al., 2020; Rocamora, 2017) but also with more closely related areas such as hospitality, leisure, art and dress history, fashion design, and museum and curatorship (Blaszczyk, 2008;

Kirilenko & Stepchenkova, 2018). In fashion and tourism research, there is no common and unique set of ideas, single conceptual frameworks, or unique methodologies with which they might be defined, analyzed, and critically explained. Despite the interdisciplinarity of tourism and fashion, disciplinary paradigms remain dominant.

Sporadic academic studies in different fields, such as event management, place branding, geography, and communication, were undertaken to understand and explain the interconnectedness of fashion and tourism. In the two main volumes that research the history of vacationing and modern tourism (Löfgren, 1999; Zuelow, 2015), the clothing of travelers and fashion-related practices and how the two are interconnected were noted. However, this discussion has been marginal.

Several scholars have investigated the role of fashion in the destination choice by tourists (Lewis, Kerr, & Burgess, 2019; Lysikova, 2012). They suggest that tourism is an industry in which fashion and the desire for novelty play a major role. Corneo and Jeanne (1999) similarly confirm that the choice of holiday destination is an example of behavior affected by the fashion industry.

The role of fashion as city branding has been investigated in several studies (Bada, 2013; Jansson & Power, 2010; Skivko, 2016). Denissa, Widodo, Adisasmito, and Piliang (2015) discussed city rebranding in Jember (Indonesia), from the production of tobacco to a city that hosts catwalks for fashion carnivals. Capone and Lazzeretti (2016) analyzed the perception of Florence as a fashion city among the tourists visiting this well-known Italian destination in 2015. The study results demonstrate the significant role that fashion plays in the attractiveness of Florence as a fashion city. Lazzeretti, Capone, and Casadei (2017) focused on the role the fashion industry plays in cultivating the image of the city while fostering local competitive advantage, improving its reputation, and increasing its appeal as a destination.

Martinez (2007) presented the case of Antwerp whose status as a fashion capital was created not by hosting traditional fashion weeks, as in cities like Paris or London, but within the logic of organized tourism and mega-cultural events. The intertwining of both public and private networks of influence resulted in fashion becoming absorbed by the local institutions and it has created Antwerp's most characteristic creative industry, which is now extremely attractive for international tourists.

Tourism destinations have been extensively used as recognizable shooting locations (Jung & Childs, 2020). At the same time, fashion companies have recently started developing printed guidebooks and mobile apps about tourism places. The tourist guides produced by fashion houses (Jacquemus, Louis Vuitton, Yves Saint Laurent, and more) became a compelling example of possible cobranding and comarketing activities between fashion houses, city attractions, and tourism destinations (Biondo, 2021).

Indeed, fashion is inextricably associated with urban spaces that mark history and society (Frisch, Sommer, Stoltenberg, & Stors, 2019). This includes the evaluation of the places and spaces of fashion (Breward & Gilbert, 2006; Potvin, 2009), the role of luxury fashion players in city development (Paris, 2018, 2020), or the understanding of the activities of fashion players, such as independent fashion designers, in the development of a fashion city (Heim, Ferrero-Regis, & Payne, 2021).

The impact of fashion weeks on tourism development and destination branding has been studied as well. Liberato, Mendes, Liberato, and Alén (2022) investigated the effects of the realization of a fashion week on the sustainable development of a city and a tourism destination. They discuss the case of the city of Porto in Portugal. The main conclusion of their empirical research shows that Portugal fashion adds value to the city of Porto and contributes to sustainable development both from the economic and socio-cultural perspectives.

Online connections between fashion weeks and tourism destinations have also been examined. Kalbaska et al. (2018) investigated four primary destinations holding major fashion weeks: New York and "New York Fashion Week," London and "London Fashion Week," Milan and "Milan Fashion Week," and Paris and "Paris Fashion Week." Their research identified the role of destinations in the online presence of the four primary "fashion weeks." Two converging analyses were carried out. On the one hand, the websites and online presence of the fashion weeks were analyzed to assess tourism-related content; on the other hand, the websites of the destination management organizations at the city level were inspected, to assess the presence and relevance they provide to fashion weeks. This research suggests that the four destinations do not leverage enough in their online communication practices on the potential such popular events as fashion weeks could bring.

Jennifer Craik in 2013 did the first structured exploration of the linkages between fashion and tourism, while presenting a historical overview and illustrating this through the case of Louis Vuitton. In the same work, she proposed 10 different forms of fashion tourism, some closely related to fashion and others more generic, but they all aimed at demonstrating how fashion exists within tourism, be it through the adoption of national dresses or the purchase by tourists of garments in local designer boutiques or souvenir fashion. However, the sphere analyzed by Craik leaves the cultural part uncovered. For instance, fashion museums or exhibitions, archives or fashion foundations, and creative tourism are represented by intangible cultural heritage offers, which also play an important role in fashion tourism and are crucial to attract tourists.

According to Calinao and Lin (2017) and Laing and Frost (2013), fashion exhibitions, especially those presenting contemporary designers, attract an audience that generates a significant entrance revenue and a high number of tourists, including those visiting museums. As soon as fashion events are staged in a city, they become a unique communication opportunity for the destination (Noris & Cantoni, 2022; Rocamora, 2009).

A recent interest by academics in the topic of communication within tourism and fashion has been observed. The research by Acuti and colleagues in 2018 evaluated how user-generated content (UGC) affects the process of place branding by identifying leading associations of various actors related to London and Florence, both traditionally linked to the fashion industry. Permatasari and Cantoni (2019) studied how Batik is communicated through mobile apps regarding their contents, functionalities, tourism-related content, and their alignment with UNESCO's safeguarding narratives. However, a critical evaluation of parallel developments of communication practices in fashion and tourism is undoubtedly missing.

Few publications explore more specifically the relationships between fashion, heritage, and tourism, as the case of the special issue of the *Almatourism* journal (2018) on "Fashion between Heritage and Tourism," which was a good start to explore this emerging topic.

Fashion tourism, discussed and described as a form of shopping, creative and cultural tourism, which changes social practices and boosts tourism development at the destinations, has attracted attention from researchers in different parts of the world. Farsani and Jamshidi (2021) presented the Iranian case of the positive impacts of traditional fashion tourism on economic, sociocultural, and environmental levels. Hepburn (2000) discussed the impact tourism and foreign visitors had on the local population in Nepal and the way they were dressing.

Finally, the case study of the city of Lagos in Nigeria presented by Bada (2013) focuses on the emerging role of fashion tourism in the city. The researcher concludes the study with a request for a clear development strategy, which a city like Lagos needs to have to be positioned in the future as a new fashion capital. Such a strategy should include better coordination between the sectors (tourism and fashion), better governance, and better marketing and promotional efforts.

Most of the studies in literature review represent different research fields and academic schools and use various research approaches and methods of investigation. They all underline the importance of the practical relationships between fashion and tourism for both industries and their future development. This implies the better understanding tourism and fashion researchers need to have for each other's fields of knowledge. It is clear that holistic overview of the convergences, overlaps, and crossovers between fashion and tourism from an academic perspective is still limited.

Inspiration could come from the study of other connections and reciprocal influence of two phenomena, like Fashion and Music (Strähle, 2018); Fashion and Architecture (Quinn, 2003); Fashion and Museums (Melchior & Svensson, 2014); Architecture and Tourism (Specht, 2014).

This book represents a further step in the direction of critically explaining two phenomena and their interconnectedness. It will broaden readers' understanding of the existing linkages between tourism and fashion research communities and how both fields influence each other. This emerging subject can attract the attention of academics actively researching the topic: master's and PhD students and professionals working in the field of fashion heritage (in fashion museums, fashion galleries, and foundations) or in tourism branding and destination advertising. Can tourism help to understand fashion better? Can fashion contribute to the understanding of tourism? What are the connections between the two domains? This book is set to address these questions.

STRUCTURE OF THE BOOK

Part I. "Dressed for Tourism"

Historical Foundations. Clothing came into travel as a means of personal cultivation and a sign of distinction, where mostly British young men were traveling to continental Europe on the so-called Grand Tour in the 17th–18th century. Clothes during those times were visible emblems of social standing. It was documented in literature and in art pieces, for instance, in "The Grand Tourist" by the painter Pompeo Batoni in 1778. In order to fit in abroad, British men were advised to dress appropriately wherever they traveled. During these cultural trips, they also learned the way others were dressed and brought this knowledge back to Britain.

With the growing economic prosperity, the advent of leisure time and the cars that started to be produced in large quantities, travelers finally got greater autonomy. This also boosted the production of the gadgets and tools a person needed to have in order to travel. Massive production of luggage, valises, and hat boxes has started. The case of Gucci's luggage, which Guccio Gucci produced, represents well the interconnection of travel and fashion. Other luxury brands, like Hermès or Louis Vuitton, joined the high-fashion industry as they started to produce traveling items before becoming the most prominent international fashion brands as we know them today.

Fashion designers started producing clothing pieces specifically for travelers and their comfort and convenience on the road, up to the designers constructing clothes for flight attendants or specific travel groups, such as adventure tourists (Buckley, 2003; Cater, 2006). Swimming suits (from the ones invented in Brighton at the end of the 18th century to the bikinis of the 1960s) were invented for and by tourism.

The contribution of Claudio Visentin (Chapter 2) will discuss the parallel historical developments of fashion and tourism during the last century, starting from the impact of the industrial revolution on society. He will critically discuss the introduction of new seasons in tourism, paid vacations, and new leisure practices, up to the appearance and evolution of the swimsuit. Visentin will propose an in-depth analysis of how the shape of the swimsuit was changing over the years and how it was related to the new requests of society toward the female body. He will discuss the relationship between fashion and tourism domains from a historical and sociological point of view.

Shared Communication Practices. Shared communication practices between the two industries might be the least developed among all the parallel connections discussed in this book, but they are the ones in which we can see interesting potential both in terms of research and industry applications, as fashion and tourism are (also) forms of communication. The way we dress and where and how we travel is a major channel through which we, humans, express ourselves and communicate our identity to others.

Chapter 3 by Nadzeya Sabatini and Lorenzo Cantoni will propose a first attempt at classifying the connections between the two domains starting with the person, his or her body and the relationship this body has with fashion and tourism, and within contemporary society at large. Four layers of such connections will be comprehensively exemplified. The study will be concluded with an introduction to the notion of a "selfie," as an emblematic (digital) communication object, typically and extensively used in both domains. Its iconic, indexical, and symbolic functions will be discussed.

Communication practices help support the nature of both sectors as experience-based. Digital transformation is profoundly impacting fashion and tourism and the communication practices around them. eTourism and digital fashion are pushing fashion brands and tourism companies to also become media companies (Kalbaska et al., 2018; Marchiori & Cantoni, 2011), hence further stressing their communication roles. Digital technologies indeed are beneficial in anticipating the experience, of both travel and fashion. Images, videos, virtual reality, online applications, and websites help start the dream, share experiences, set trends, and launch new styles. This is true for tourism destinations and attractions, as well as for fashion items and trends.

Bloggers and other social media influencers are particularly relevant in both sectors. Let us think, for instance, about the case of Chiara Ferragni (Italian blogger), who has moved from being a popular fashion blogger to launching her own fashion brand, and staging marketing campaigns for museums, hotels, restaurants, and tourism destinations (Sanderson, 2018).

Ulrike Gretzel in Chapter 4 will discuss in depth the role of social media influencers who increasingly determine what is fashionable and what is not in tourism and fashion contexts. Social media influencers by creating and sharing primarily visual content via Instagram platform shape what social media users see and aspire to. This research argues that their visuals also represent emerging visual practices and styles that are typical of influencers and transcend fashion and tourism contexts. Using a netnographic approach, the research presented in the chapter examined Instagram posts of 20 travel and fashion mega-influencers. It finds common practices across all influencers but also identifies differential ways in which fashion and travel visuals are constructed. The chapter highlights how intertwined tourism and fashion have become, especially when it comes to influencers, and provides insights into a phenomenon that has significant ramifications for traditional advertising and consumer behavior in both fashion and tourism.

Part II. Fashion(able) Destinations

Several destinations focus on fashion to create a distinctive tourism product. This implies the cooperation of fashion and tourism stakeholders, independently of whether they are state and local authorities or private actors. This may concern the tour packages and offers, which feature and promote local fashion productions (shopping, fashion shows and other events, tourism visits of local fashion producers), the tourism marketing of labels (such as UNESCO's "creative cities for fashion"), and the organization of the local producers (traditional know-how). Cities, regions, or countries can be labeled and targeted as fashion destinations.

The analysis of the relationship between tourism destinations and fashion allows us to draw attention to the systems of actors (local, national, and international) who work to ensure that the meeting between these two sectors is beneficial to both. Indeed, the creation of a "fashion" destination is not a matter of chance. On the contrary, it is the result of very thorough work on the part of the actors who wish to develop one, the other, or both sectors in an articulated and interconnected manner.

For some countries, the development of these sectors may represent a national priority. This is the case in France, for example, where the fashion sector is very systematically constructed by the central state apparatus as a crucial sector for the national economy. Gianluigi Di Giangirolamo shows in Chapter 5 that political and even nationalistic considerations can also prevail in the political decision to support the sector. It is notable that in the case of France, the state supports both sectors in parallel but without putting in place support or promotion policies that combine them. It was above all the private players (both in tourism, such as hoteliers, and in fashion, such as designers) who consolidated the image of France, particularly Paris, as an essential fashion destination. From the postwar period, Christian Dior's New Look not only asserted Paris' place as a fashion capital but also made a considerable contribution to Paris as a tourist city. It is, therefore, important to remember what Parisian tourism owes to its aura as the capital of fashion, which is undoubtedly more effective than several very costly tourism communication campaigns.

The relationship between fashion and a destination may also rely on a specific, local, and distinctive fashion production. This is undoubtedly the case for Indonesia, which is closely linked in the tourist imagination with Batik. However, for a centuries-old tradition to become an element of the destination's current attractiveness, effort is required. Puspita Ayu Permatasari and colleagues in Chapter 6 show how actors at different territorial and decision-making levels have managed to reaffirm Indonesia as a global Batik and fashion heritage destination.

If tourism benefits from fashion and its "dream capital," it goes without saying that fashion actors can use tourist destinations to promote their collections. The shooting of collections in well-known tourist destinations is based on a basic assumption: the collection piece filmed in Santorini or Tinos (Greece) is associated with a meta-message: that of the life that goes in the shown destination.

It is no coincidence that brands launch collections named after these destinations. For example, in the Louis Vuitton boutique in Mykonos (Greece), the articles on display are designed exclusively for and sold only in the island's boutique. This creates a global geography of holiday and resort destinations, where the affluent global nomads, who are also the customers of major fashion brands, are concentrated. These are places such as Marbella, Bahamas, Palm Beach, San Juan, San Barth, the Mustique Islands, Bali, Mykonos, or Ibiza. According to Lussault (2017), the "hyper-places" are places where the cohabitation of individuals takes shape, and is experienced in all its richness, creativity, and intensity of the lived experience. These "hyper-places," where humans and material and immaterial realities converge, are increasingly differentiated by their greater integration into globalization. The "hyper-tourism-places" are perceived by those that visit them as both exclusive tourist destinations and lifestyle places distinguished by the clothing style of other visitors. Eirini Vlassi and colleagues in Chapter 7 demonstrate this interdependence between fashion brands and tourist destinations by analyzing inflight and fashion magazines. The researchers demonstrate such interdependence through a comparative qualitative analysis of *Blue* magazine (Aegean Airlines *Inflight* magazine) and *Vogue Greece*. This chapter provides insights that may help tourism destinations and fashion partners in Greece and beyond inform their future campaigns and extend their collaboration at various levels.

The interdependence between fashion and tourism can go further than traditional fashion shows staged twice a year in the major fashion capitals or the so-called "Big Four" – Milan, London, Paris, and New York. It can be seen through the case of certain special collections, such as the "cruise collections." Originally (since the 1920s) an interseason or preseason line was produced by a fashion house in addition to the recurrent biannual seasonal collections. They were meant for wealthy customers vacationing in the Mediterranean during the winter months; cruise collections offer summer clothing when the weather at the main points of sale calls for winter clothing. Cruise collections have become a cross-cultural style that signifies relaxation and affluence. This "resort wear" is a specialized year-round clothing style and fashion season. Sandra Krim in Chapter 8 pertinently shows this exclusive global geography of iconic fashion brands and tourism destinations.

As we see, the relationship between tourist destinations and fashion is complex and dynamic. It is certain that fashion contributes greatly to the affirmation of tourist destinations. The latter are putting in place a whole range of tools in this respect: fashion events (sector-based such as fashion weeks or cultural events linked to museums or design centers) or infrastructures (places that showcase fashion creativity: museums, foundations, ateliers, and incubators open to the public).

Part III. Fashion, Tourism, and the City

Literature (Breward & Gilbert, 2006; Bide, 2020; Gilbert & Casadei, 2020; Kurkdjian, 2020) tends to demonstrate that the relationship between cities and fashion is interdependent. Fashion is in essence about display: a display of style and status, character, and commerce, while the city itself provides both a backdrop and an audience for this display. Fashion needs a stage, and cities need spectacles (Mustafa, 2001). The city is historically a site for both the production and the display of fashion, from shops and factories to museums or streets (Beard, 2011).

This fashionable side of the city attracts and encourages tourism. Major fashion cities, e.g., London, Paris, New York, Milan, Rome, and Florence are also major urban tourism destinations and have developed specific tourism-fashion products. The interdependence between cities, fashion, and tourism are multifaceted: fashion is exposed in the permanent collections of museums and galleries. Museums are important vessels and messengers for fashion. They are attractive both for their heritage dimensions (related to the extraordinary collections of clothing, fabrics, accessories, etc., in several dedicated to fashion museums) and for their creative dimension since many of them are also places of production and creation of contemporary fashion.

Several urban tourism destinations have unique museums such as the Galliera Museum, the Yves-Saint-Laurent Museum, the Galerie Dior in Paris, and the MoMu museum in Antwerp. Fashion is also exhibited in flagship temporary exhibitions attracting thousands of visitors, as it was the case for the "Savage Beauty" exhibition of the British fashion designer Lee Alexander McQueen. The exhibition attracted 1,154,552 visitors at the New

York's Museum of Metropolitan Art and London's Victoria and Albert museum in 2015 (Abrams, 2015).

Cities also attract international tourists as shopping destinations. Department stores such as Galeries Lafayette in Paris are historically major tourist destinations, managed as such, with not only services offered to tourists who come to buy but also offer tourist tours of the department stores themselves. For example, Printemps and Galeries Lafayette in Paris are currently offering such tours to their visitors (Rabbiosi, 2015).

Sophie Kurkdjian in Chapter 9 demonstrates how Parisian department stores helped consolidate Paris's place as the capital of fashion and luxury. Through her study, which is based not only on the monographs and primary sources of Parisian department stores but also on the assortment of ephemera produced by department stores (postcards, almanacs, diaries, posters, etc.), Sophie shows how the department stores became over the years one of the symbols of the city and a necessary element in the "Parisian experience."

Certain districts are identified as shopping districts, whether they cater for big brands, such as the "Golden Triangle" in Paris or via Montenapoleone in Milan with the concentration of Haute Couture houses, or for more specialized fashion, whether for women or men with certain districts, such as Saville Road in London, specializing in men's fashion. Both are very popular with tourists.

Erina Cavalli in Chapter 10, while using concepts drawn from cultural theory, economic theory, and anthropology, analyses the flagship shops of certain brands (such as Louis Vuitton, Channel, Prada, or Hermès). Designed by renowned architects and decorated by the most excellent decorators, they became an integral part of the tour circuit in major urban destinations. Cavalli is analyzing how tourists on a shopping spree search for forms of authenticity, how this type of travel is similar in many respects to a religious quest, and, finally, how the design of luxury outlets in European capitals conveys religious overtones.

Fashion is also about events, where fashion weeks are key elements of major fashion destinations not only for business tourism but also for leisure one. They create a great magnet attracting international visitors. After COVID-19, thousands of visitors visited Paris in September 2022 to discover the women's spring–summer 2023 collections. The explosion in internet searches for short-term tourist accommodation on platforms such as Airbnb during Paris Fashion Week is symptomatic of the increase in visitor numbers during this event. Such a number of short-term requests have a crucial impact on the changing structures of the geographies of cities. Mario Paris in Chapter 11 explores the spatial distribution of luxury tourism infrastructure in Milan and how it is connected to the distribution of luxury fashion-related entities. Through a critical reflection on this alternative geography, the researcher discusses the dynamics identified in these neighborhoods and how the actions of luxury operators affect spaces, their quality, and their livability for both inhabitants and tourists.

Sandra Biondo analyses more specifically the relationship between a great fashion designer and "his" or "her" city: indeed, a powerful association is sometimes created between the image of the city and a fashion designer who produced most of his work there. This is the case with Yves-Saint-Laurent in Paris, Salvatore Ferragamo in Florence, Prada in Milan, or Fendi in Rome. The last two Italian "national" brands in particular, Prada and Fendi, are analyzed in terms of their relationship with the city where they are based – respectively Milan (Chapter 12) and Rome (Chapter 13). The researcher pertinently discusses (new) tourism dynamics they create in the cities, especially in districts that were not touristic until recently. These two chapters show the repercussions of the construction of iconic infrastructures in urban peripheries (the EUR district in Rome and the Navigli and Porta Romana districts in Milan).

Maria Gravari Barbas in Chapter 14 discusses the development of "alternative" and "off-the-beaten tracks" fashion visits in more marginal urban areas (such as the cosmopolitan/recent immigration area of Chateau Rouge in Paris). This chapter contributes to drawing new urban geographies of fashion tourism, from the most centrally located touristic areas to the emerging neighborhoods of alternative fashion.

The conclusive chapter of the book, Chapter 15 by Daniel Wright, presents and discusses collaborative fashion drops, their importance for the tourism industry and related communication practices. The author looks into the future and explains how tourism destinations can become part of the fashion drops experience and promote themselves as the "place for dropping" collaborative fashion products and experiences.

CONCLUSION

Fashion and tourism are major indicators of economic and political systems, cultures, values, and imaginaries. Their analysis, conducted in parallel, allows one to better understand not only what one owes to another but also, more broadly, how their parallel action both shapes and reflects contemporary societies. These two fields of study have not been fully explored by the researchers in their common dimensions: the importance of social, cultural, and symbolic capital, the role they play in personal distinction (in Bourdieu's approach), or their strong identity dimensions.

This book tries to fill this gap. It broadens readers' understanding of the existing linkages between tourism and fashion industries, as well as how both industries impact each other. It shows how these two modern "collaborative" phenomena have been reciprocally influenced during the last two centuries, since the beginning of tourism as a modern phenomenon. It explores different facets of the complex and dynamic relationship between tourism and fashion. This book supports an interdisciplinary and diachronic approach, including empirical work, case studies, and conceptual articles.

More than a systematic and exhaustive analysis of all the parallel developments that can be drawn between these two social phenomena, the book presents itself as a series of "open windows" between fashion and tourism, inviting researchers to further complete the picture. The prospects of this cross-analysis are fascinating, given the fact that more and more transversal relations are emerging between the two sectors. Surely several other works will complete the first panorama drawn by this book!

PART I
"DRESSED FOR TOURISM"

Chapter 2

INVENTING THE SUMMER
Evolution of Swimsuit in the 20th Century

Claudio Visentin
USI-Università della Svizzera italiana, Switzerland

Abstract: The close link between fashion and from a historical and sociological point of view is the focus of this chapter. Since the Industrial Revolution, these two industries have been part of the path toward modernity in Western Europe. The new industrial society created a different relationship with leisure time and bodies. On the other hand, fashion tourism accelerated and intensified this process toward unforeseen outcomes: new social relations and the loosening of traditional morality constraints. The swimming costume represents the point of encounter and overlapping between these two spheres: a significant element of novelty despite its ever-shrinking dimensions. **Keywords**: Modernity; sport; tourism; beach; swimsuit; bikini

INTRODUCTION

Between the 19th and the early 20th century, the increasing availability of leisure time favored the development of sport and tourism, two distinct aspects of modernity. These activities required new, more comfortable, and informal clothes. The adoption of sportswear was easier for men, while the female condition was different. The change of clothes called into question matters of taste and decorum, morality, control of impulses, and the visibility of the body in social life.

The case of the swimming costume and its evolution connected with the development of tourism and sport is fascinating. The interwar period is especially interesting, as a new seaside culture was spreading on the beaches of the French Riviera, starting from Antibes. In the mid-1920s, two wealthy Americans, Gerald and Sara Murphy (portrayed as Dick and Nicole Diver in

Fashion and Tourism: Parallel Stories
Tourism Social Science Series, Volume 26, 21–32

Published under exclusive licence by Emerald Publishing Limited
ISSN: 1571-5043/doi:10.1108/S1571-504320230000026002

Fitzgerald, 1934), *invented the summer* in their Villa America (Löfgren, 1999). It was a new way to experience summer by the sea: informal, fast, and fun. Many artists and writers of later fame (Ernest Hemingway, John Dos Passos, Pablo Picasso, Cole Porter) legitimized and spread these new practices.

All along the second half of the 20th century, the beach concept was exported in different territories and histories, with surprising similarities. It started as a French story, to spread throughout Europe and quickly became a global phenomenon. The beach, which until then was a natural, liminal space, became the setting for new social interactions. Tan was the new craze, exposing the body to the sun and other people's eyes.

At the beginning of the twentieth century, women used to wear heavy swimsuits, far below the knee. In the 1930s, they adopted lighter and more adherent fabrics; movements in the water were now more natural and effortless. The turning point in this path was the creation of the bikini, officially presented by the designer Louis Reard in Paris in 1946. At first, the new swimsuit faced strong resistance. However, in the 1950s, it was adopted by several Hollywood movie stars and eventually accepted, becoming fully popular in the 1960s (Alac, 2002).

Tourism is constantly moving in two directions. On the one hand, it is a product of modernity; it is closely connected to significant transformations such as the Industrial Revolution, the Transport Revolution, and a new esthetic linked to Romanticism. At the same time, tourism is a powerful force for modernization; it encourages tourists to have new experiences, it spreads new forms of mobility, and promotes new social interactions and a different relationship with one's body (Zuelow, 2015).

The seemingly trivial history of swimsuits is entirely a part of this broader context and closely intertwined with fashion, leisure, and sport. The analysis in this chapter will adopt a historical point of view. A sociological perspective will be helpful, too, as tourism is, by its very nature, a collective and social phenomenon where the masses are the main protagonists.

FASHION AND TOURISM

The starting point of the narrative is the increased availability of leisure time in the second half of the 19th century. Sport and tourism reached their maturity in the same years, so they competed for workers' attention. This was clear in the case of cycling, with the distinction between racing and cycling tourism. However, despite their apparent rivalry, sport and tourism also had many points in common. For example, both promoted a different relationship with the body and, consequently, more practical, comfortable, and informal clothing.

The beach was the arena for these new practices. Until then, it had been a little-regarded space, but from the interwar period onward, it acquired a new relevance. However, as the case of the swimmer Annette Kellerman shows, the issue acquired a specific significance in the case of women because of morality concerns.

The "invention" of beach life was a revolution for tourism. Moreover, it accelerated the evolution of clothing, increasingly reducing the size of swimming costumes. The outcome was the introduction and the slow social acceptance of the bikini after World War II. This process has different timescales and can be divided into three phases, following the usual periodization of tourism history. During the first phase, tourism evolved gradually from around 1830 until World War I, significantly accelerating during the Belle Époque (Zuelow, 2015). Then, during the second phase, for almost a century, international tourism flourished, thanks to peace, freedom of movement (no passports!), and stable exchange.

On the other hand, the period between the two wars was short and tormented: peace treaties, the rise of dictatorships, and the Great Depression, followed one another in the third phase and happened in about 20 years. Inevitably, tourist flows were reduced, yet this was a period of innovation: seaside resorts, winter sports, cruises, and camping. The most important novelty, however, was the change in seasonality; if initially, international tourists mainly frequented the sea in winter, in the interwar period summer became its primary season.

After World War II, mass tourism changed the scale in terms of numbers. The beach holiday model, developed by the elites in the interwar period, was exported globally. A vast market in northern Europe had access to Mediterranean destinations, thanks to air transport, with Spain becoming the most prominent one. Eventually, tour operators replaced travel agencies.

A Time for Oneself

In the first decades of the 20th century, workers' availability of free time increased, thanks to the unions. This battle was gradual, with a different rhythm in each country. It started with the Bank Holiday Act (1871) in the United Kingdom, which granted bank employees four days of vacation a year (Zuelow, 2015). The model also extended to Canada and the United States. In Germany, paid holidays were introduced in 1905 (in 1910 in Austria) and were later expanded under the Weimar Republic (from 8 to 12 days). In France, the first experiences date back to 1853, under Napoleon III. Still, the topic acquired new importance in the political agenda when in 1936, the Popular Front of the Left seized power in France. Immediately, the weekly working hours were reduced from 48 to 40, and workers were granted two weeks of paid vacation a year, which was crucial for tourism development.

Many studies show that dictatorships were even more concerned with tourism than liberal governments. Fascism, Nazism, and Communism focused heavily on workers' free time from a propaganda perspective. In Italy, the *treni popolari* (trains for the people), which were introduced in 1931, were the first mass tourism experience (Berrino, 2011). Between 1931 and 1939, the state railways, with the support of the fascist regime, transported almost nine million travelers at highly reduced prices. The initiative was extraordinarily successful, especially with workers and employees in big cities. On weekends or during *Ferragosto* (August 15th), massive tourist groups would visit the cities of art, seaside resorts, and spas.

Nazism followed the same pattern after 1933. Holidays were extended from two to three weeks a year by the Nazi leisure organization, Kraft Durch Freude (Semmens, 2005). The organization had a fundamental role in catalyzing support for the regime, proposing tourist experiences once reserved only for the middle class. At the same time, the intangible nature of tourism made it possible to gratify the masses without diverting resources from industrial preparation for the impending war (Baranowski, 2007). Despite the ideological differences, Communism also developed its complex tourism organization. The Soviet idea of tourism was similar to other regimes. The emphasis was on individual self-improvement within the framework of the collective (Gorsuch & Koenker, 2006; Koenker, 2017).

All these stories show how the theme of free time took on new importance in the public debate in the twentieth and 1930s of the twentieth century, building on the significant precedents of the Belle Époque. Sport and tourism (the focus of this chapter) benefited from this favorable context. Sport, played or watched, took advantage of the reduced weekly working hours; tourism took over the longer summer holidays.

From Games to Professional Sports

Between the end of the nineteenth and the beginning of the twentieth century, the most popular sports were introduced or adopted new and more modern rules. Football, for example, was defined ("Cambridge Rules") in 1848. In 1904, the Fédération Internationale de Football Association was established in Zurich, Switzerland. Basketball was invented in Springfield (Massachusetts, USA) in 1892 and became an Olympic sport in 1936. Ten years later, the National Basketball Association, the American professional basketball league, was founded. The invention of volleyball dates to 1895, in the YMCA college in Holyoke, Massachusetts. The origins of tennis can be traced back to the Middle Ages, but modern rules were established in 1874 (Vamplew, 2021).

The history of cycling is of particular interest, because the practice/discipline oscillated between sport and tourism for a long time. After a few decades of experiments, the bicycle assumed its definitive design in 1885 (Rover Safety Bicycle) and it has remained the same to this day. In the following decade, the cycling world was already experiencing a split between the world of sporting races (on the track or the road) and tourist trips (even demanding ones). Before the car, and for a fraction of the cost, the bike gave travelers unprecedented and almost intoxicating freedom of movement (compared with the 1950s of railway routes).

Sport spread rapidly in society before and after the Great War. Compared to traditional games, its rules and timing were better defined, and intensity was greater than ever. Soon the need for lighter, more elastic, close-fitting clothing emerged to allow the body complete freedom of movement. For men, it was easier to replace the formal attire with the new sportswear. After all, it was mainly a matter of taste and habit. Over time, sportswear was also adopted for other occasions, which is still the case today. The female condition was different. The change of clothes called into question matters of taste and decorum, morality, control of impulses, and the visibility of the body in social life. Therefore, women's sports developed more slowly.

Similarly, tourism also radically innovated the old tradition of travel. By the first decades of the nineteenth century, tourism was already significantly different from its illustrious predecessor, the Grand Tour, in terms of audience, practices, and destinations. It was therefore no coincidence that a new word was coined, "tourism," to mark the break from the past. The combination of three innovations – rail transport, "bourgeois" tour guides (Murray, Baedeker), and travel agencies (Thomas Cook) – created a new experience. The beach, which was considered by nearly no one before, was brought to the stage of this new transformation.

From Liminal to Social Space

The summer beach is a riot of colors: striped deck chairs, bright umbrellas, and beach towels. Music blares from the bars. Everything is on the move. Adults play, children build sandcastles along the shoreline, and street vendors shout out their wares. Amid this confusion, each family recreates a space for itself in the shadowy circle of beach umbrellas. It is an intense but short animation, lasting a few summer months. Then all the equipment is put away to wait for the next summer. What could be sadder than a beach out of season? The wind blows some paper; a few chilly walkers along the sea line; a sense of desolation weighs on the heart. Nevertheless, right then, the beach is closer to its *longue durée* history.

Beach tourism is not even 100-years old. For centuries, the beach was perceived as a border space between land and sea, with nothing to offer. Moreover, it was a hostile space because of the heat and the lack of shelter from the sun. Without specific equipment (water, creams, and beach umbrellas) in summer, staying on an unequipped beach, even for a few hours, is challenging. Not to mention that, in the past, danger was coming from the sea, first from the frequent pirate raids. Even Rimini, a symbol of Italian seaside life, turned its back on the Adriatic for most of its history, trusting its river port along Marecchia.

However, precisely in these inhospitable spaces, a revolution in customs took shape. A new interest in the seashore emerged in the first decades of the nineteenth century (Corbin, 2018). The Côte d'Azur (France) was the laboratory for these pioneering experiments. True, the beginnings were very timid. The English tourists favored Nice, which became the first destination in the world. In this small coastal town, tourism made its first experiences. Here the locals had to cope with the unusual demands of *les hivernants* (winter tourists) without any model to follow. The first tourists benefited from the clean air and mild winter temperatures for vague curative purposes; they spent their time in society or on long walks along the sea on the famous Promenade des Anglais (since 1844). Then, in their quest for the perfect constant temperature, they moved to Switzerland or to central Europe's spas in summer.

During the nineteenth century, the sea and the beach were just a *panorama*, a view, the backdrop to a highly social experience. Attempts to dive into the water in summer were timid and uncertain. As early as the last decades of the nineteenth century, some tourists plunged into the brackish waters for curative purposes, something close to a spa experience. However, these remained sporadic experiences, without meaning or continuity. There was no structured practice, no socially recognized sense.

The beach was often avoided. Women particularly preferred to use wheel cabins, hand-pushed or pulled by horses. Ladies could dive into the water through an opening in the floor, protected from the male gaze, at a convenient distance from the shore. These strange vehicles appeared in Munich, Viareggio, Ostend, Scheveningen, San Sebastian, and Blackpool. In other cases, cabins were built on stilts in the sea, and one could go directly from the dressing rooms to the water, bypassing the beach.

The lack of specific clothing also favored these choices. The first swimsuits were knitted garments not too different from everyday clothes. However, it was almost impossible to move freely and swim. The creation of modern swimsuits originated at the intersection of sport and tourism.

The Mermaid

Sport and tourism, the two innovations in the use of leisure time in the twentieth century, found fertile ground for their development in Australia. Even today, a widespread practice of sport at all levels goes hand in hand with a lively beach culture: to mention one, Bondi Beach, near Sydney, is one of the most iconic beaches in the world. As early as 1940, Charles Meere's famous painting, "Australian Beach Pattern," showed how quickly the new role model had established itself on the other side of the world.

Annette Kellerman's personal story intertwines sport and tourism in original ways. She was born in 1886 in the Sydney suburbs into a family of musicians. At six, she began swimming to strengthen her weak legs. After her recovery, she continued to train and became a champion swimmer. The fragile child turned into an attractive woman, very skilled in attracting media attention. In 1905, for example, she tried to swim across the English Channel, but had to give up after three unsuccessful attempts. She also caused a scandal with her "daring" one-piece swimsuits, which today would seem relatively chaste. Nevertheless, they were audacious enough to strike the imagination of her contemporaries, because they adhered to the body, supporting (and therefore revealing) the female forms.

By 1907, Annette Kellerman was already well-known in America. She performed an aquatic dance in a pool in the gigantic Hippodrome Theater in New York on Sixth Avenue, an event considered the origin of synchronized swimming. Nevertheless, she was arrested on a Massachusetts beach for an offense against decency that same year. She was wearing form-fitting sleeveless one-piece knitted swimming tights that covered her from neck to toe. It was the last straw for traditional morality. Thanks to this unintentional publicity, her costumes became more popular, and the actress transformed her intuition into a commercial product.

In Stockholm, in 1912, female swimmers were admitted to the Olympics for the first time. This decision led to the acceptance of the one-piece swimming costume. Two Australians from Sydney starred in Stockholm, Sarah *Fanny* Durack and Wilhelmina *Mina* Wylie. Annette Kellerman did not participate in that competition; she was already looking in other directions. Fame opened the door to Hollywood. She would become the first in a long line of mermaids (her fictional life is told in a 1952 film, "The Million Dollar Mermaid") (Gibson & Firth, 2005). Annette Kellerman came to the creation of the one-piece swimsuit through sport, through swimming. Subsequent developments were seen in tourism.

Inventing the Summer

> On the pleasant shore of the French Riviera, about halfway between Marseilles and the Italian border, stands a large, proud, rose-colored hotel. Deferential palms cool its flushed façade, and before it stretches a short dazzling beach. Lately, it has become a summer resort of notable and fashionable people; a decade ago, it was almost deserted after its English clientele went north in April.

These are the opening lines of "Tender is the Night," the novel by Fitzgerald (1934). At the center of the scene, a group of wealthy American expatriates gathered around Dr. Dick Diver and Nicole, a patient who later becomes his wife. The drafting of the novel began in 1925 after Fitzgerald's extended stay in Cap d'Antibes, on the French Riviera. It is easy to guess the real people behind the two characters: Dick and Nicole Diver are openly inspired by Gerald and Sara Murphy. Gerald was an artist, and Sara was a wealthy heiress (Vaill, 1999). In 1921, they moved to Paris to put an ocean between them and their families, dissatisfied with their marriage. They soon moved to the French Riviera, and in their Villa America at Cap d'Antibes, they *invented*... summer.

The two Americans overturned the usual seasonal pattern established in the second half of the nineteenth century. The sea was a characteristic winter destination until then. Therefore, in summer, the hotels on the Côte d'Azur used to close. Their managers moved to the spa resorts or Switzerland, where the primary tourism season was the summer (later winter sports, also introduced in the interwar period, reversed seasonality in Switzerland and more widely in the Alpine countries). In 1923, the Murphys persuaded the owner of the Hotel du Cap to stay open for the summer to host their friends. It was the beginning of a new era. With the help of their guests, the two Americans imagine a new summer by the sea: informal, fast, and fun. Time is spent with bathing, beach games, swimming, afternoon cocktails, jazz on the gramophone, terrace meals and love affairs, car drives along the "corniche," and so on (Löfgren, 1999).

All this would have remained confined to a personal and familiar esthetic experience had it not been for the important guests of the wealthy American couple. Indeed, taking advantage of the contacts established in Paris, Gerald and Sara Murphy hosted for long periods a large circle of artists, musicians, actors, and writers of the "Lost Generation" destined for future fame: Pablo Picasso, Cole Porter, Rodolfo Valentino, Jean Cocteau, Ernest Hemingway, John Dos Passos, Dorothy Parker, among others. These tourism companions made an essential contribution to spreading and, above all, legitimizing these new practices.

Exceptionally provocative was the choice to spend long hours on the beach, freely exposing the bodies to the sun's rays and, inevitably, to the gaze of others. Until then, elegant foreign tourists on the Côte d'Azur had protected their skin from the winter sun in various ways, with gloves, veils, hats, and umbrellas. Poets associated "moon skin" with female beauty. On the contrary, tanning was traditionally associated with people working in the open air, and poverty (Triani, 1988). In the 1920s, however, an increasing number of workers were employed in factories and offices; their delicate pallor turned into a sad greyness due to the long hours indoors. On the other hand, tanning took on a new meaning. It became a symbol of health, almost a privilege reserved for those who could suspend their daily occupations and business to spend time outdoors on the seashore on holiday.

From the 1920s onwards, Western society "changed its skin." A body in motion is a body that discovers itself. The long, chastened women's dresses of the nineteenth century – with corsets, busts, hats, and gloves – were unthinkable. Instead, the new fashion called for informal clothes, sandals and shorts, and light evening dresses. As early as 1923, fashion designer Coco Chanel flaunted her tan on returning from the French Riviera. At the beginning of the following decade, a new industry was born to produce tight-fitting swimwear and dresses that highlighted tanned skin. In 1927, Jean Patou invented Huile de Chaldée, the first tanning oil, followed by L'Oréal's Ambre Solaire in 1935 (Barbery-Coulon, 2012).

World War II interrupted the development of beach life for a few years but, simultaneously, created the conditions for the definitive rise of mass tourism. As early as the 1950s, a large market interested in this new form of vacation emerged in northern Europe. In the same years, the development of air transport radically shortened travel times and, therefore, distances.

Spain was the laboratory of the new seaside civilization, this time for everyone and no longer just for a small circle of wealthy esthetes. Tour operators exported the beach concept to different territories and histories in the second half of the twentieth century, with surprising similarities. The beach, until then a natural, liminal space, became the setting for new social interactions, a place on the margin where the usual constraints on behavior are suspended, however provisionally (Walton, 2000).

Tourists adopted a set of new, shared rules: the occupation of the space with one's towel, the distribution of time, the exposure of bodies (which, however, cannot be looked at directly, but only behind sunglasses), and the relationship between people (Löfgren, 1999; Urbain, 1996). With its new sociability, the beach increasingly attracted the young generations of the economic boom. Every summer had (and still has) its song, its soundtrack, heard on the beach, from the jukeboxes in the bars. The songs of the 1960s told the story of the discovery of holidays by the sea: the beaches, the bodies exposed to the sun (and the gaze of others), the games, the evening choirs on the beach, and the flirtations. In the case of Italy, to mention one, almost all the 1960s hits have a seaside theme, from "Tintarella di luna" (Mina in 1959) to "Azzurro" (Adriano Celentano in 1968).

"Itsy Bitsy Teenie Weenie Yellow Polka-Dot Bikini"

The one-piece, body-hugging swimsuit was socially accepted in the interwar period. At first, it was only adopted in swimming competitions, but its use was soon extended to beach life. However, the one-piece swimming costume conflicted with the new tanning fashion. The imperative was to expose as much skin as possible, even within socially acceptable limits. At first, the one-piece swimsuit was rolled up at the edges, pulled on all sides to reveal as much skin as possible. Then, already by the end of the 1930s, it was split into two pieces. Necklines plunged at the back, and sleeves disappeared. Swimsuits became more comfortable and form-fitting thanks to new, lighter, and adherent fabrics (*Rayon, Lastex*). Wool was finally abandoned in favor of cotton. Movements in the water were now easier. The new swimsuits were often matched with light and colorful cover-ups and stylish caps.

Many actresses, such as Jayne Mansfield, routinely wore the two-piece, even though always vigilantly covering the navel because its exposure was inappropriate. It was a prohibition familiar to many cultures, which has now completely disappeared and whose meaning one struggles to understand fully today. For example, in the United States, the Motion Picture Production Code, applied after 1934, prohibited female navel exposure in movies. Only in the early 1960s was the ban was softened.

In 1946, for the first time, a coral atoll in the Marshall Islands called "Bikini" became (in)famous because of the atomic bomb tests conducted by the United States. The bomb that was dropped in July 1946 was named "Gilda" (after Rita Hayworth's character in the 1946 film). The test was the first to be publicly announced beforehand and observed by an invited audience, including a large press corp. In June 1946, French designer Jacques Heim dusted off an earlier model of the swimsuit and launched the two-piece "Atome" (with the navel still covered), with the slogan "The smallest swimsuit in the world." However, an automotive engineer, Louis Réard, soon stole the show.

Cleverly exploiting the advertising effect, Louis Réard debuted the skimpy garment bikini only four days after the nuclear test, on July 5, 1946. Réard created the new swimsuit using only four triangles of printed fabric, a scant 30 inches, so that he could promote his creation as "smaller than the world's smallest bathing suit." This claim was somehow justified, even though, compared to later models, Réard's bikini still covered a lot. However, the navel was in full view this time, and this caused a long history of resistance and mistrust. Already for the first public presentation, on the edge of the Molitor swimming pool in Paris, Réard could only rely on Micheline Bernardini, an exotic dancer at the Casino de Paris, as other models had refused his proposal. Moreover, the bikini challenged codes of morality and decency. Many commentators condemned the look, and plenty of communities banned it. The new costume was considered too daring by the censors and most women (Alac, 2002).

The bikini made a fleeting appearance in the awards ceremony of the first Miss World contest (1951). However, it was soon necessary to return to the traditional evening gown due to protests. The Swedish Kiki Håkansson, for a long time, remained the only Miss World to have been crowned in a bikini. The bikini was a very revealing and, therefore, demanding costume, requiring self-confidence, poise, and ease. In 1960, Bryan Hyland was still singing stories of shyness in "Itsy Bitsy Teenie Weenie Yellow Polka-Dot Bikini": the young girl is nervous and afraid to come out of the locker, as she wears bikini for the first time. The extraordinary success of the song – number one on the Billboard Hot 100, a million copies sold in the United States and a worldwide hit – proves, however, that curiosity about the new swimming costume was at least as great as fear. Furthermore, in the 1960s, the desire for transgression and modernity was more substantial than the remnants of modesty.

As with tanning, innovation asserts itself when influential public figures, "legitimators," support it. The last resistance to the bikini dissolved when famous actresses fully adopted it. The list could start with Brigitte Bardot, who starred in "Manina, the Girl in the Bikini" (1952), when she was only 17-years old: the film was controversial for the scanty bikini worn by the young Bardot, one of the first appearances of such costume in a film. Other actresses, including Rita Hayworth, Ava Gardner, and Lana Turner, also received the attention of the press when wearing bikinis.

In 1962, Swiss Ursula Andress played the Bond girl Honey Rider in "Dr. No" (1962). She establishes herself as a diva in the scene where she comes out of the sea wearing a white bikini, accessorized with a belt and a hunting knife. After that, even the last resistance faded away, and bikini sales skyrocketed.

In 1964, the popular American magazine *Sports Illustrated* dedicated a special issue to swimwear, inaugurating a tradition that continues today. Hundreds of indignant readers unsubscribed, but just as many took their place. After that, the bikini was no longer under discussion, and it launched the careers of many supermodels, including Elle Macpherson (Schmidt, 2012). The 1960s marked a turning point in the history of bikini, as they already hinted at the subsequent transformations – more often "reductions" – of the bikini, including the topless version of the 1980s (Kaufmann, 2007).

The bikini is more than a swimsuit; it is first and foremost a new way of experiencing the beach, summer, holidays, and life. In the progress of time, the bikini became a symbol of female sensuality, liberation, play, and fun. Moreover, the costume revolution, which began in the suspended time of the beach holiday, when women were more open to experimentation, often continued after returning at home. In different ways, the emancipation of swimwear is intertwined with the emancipation of women.

Recently, the one-piece swimming costume has registered a revival of interest in fashion, a perpetually changing industry. The question is whether bikini has exhausted its transgressive potential over time. All in all, the bikini fortunes are linked to the baby boomer generation. In 2021, "the world's smallest swimsuit in the world" turned 75-years old and possibly went from the news to history: the story told in this chapter (Alac, 2002).

CONCLUSION

In its two centuries of development, tourism has paved the way for more practical and informal clothing, fit for an active life in the open air. The use of these clothes, first adopted at the time of holidays (or in sport), was later extended to other moments of daily life. The history of the bikini is just one example of this, albeit a prominent one. The body is at the center of the stage. The prolonged and almost complete exposure of bodies in beach life had the effect of redrawing the relations between the sexes and even the ever-shifting boundaries of morality. Especially for women, it was a revolution.

The new rules of holiday life should have remained confined to that particular time (Enzensberger, 1996). However, the holiday quickly became a time of experimentation, and some new behaviors were then permanently adopted in everyday life. For a long time, swimming costumes caused scandals and heated discussions. Nevertheless, in the new millennium, at least in the West, their subversive, disruptive potential seems to have been replaced by widespread acceptance.

The evolution of swimwear shows how the history of fashion and tourism are intertwined in complex ways. Intersections and crossings are frequent, far beyond this particular example. For instance, tourists follow a different dress code when traveling than at home (therefore, they are often easily recognizable). Moreover, they sometimes adopt typical (or deemed so) clothes of the places they visit, favoring a worldwide circulation of different fashions. History continues.

Chapter 3

LINKING FASHION AND TOURISM
From Body to Clothing and Lifestyle

Nadzeya Sabatini
Gdansk University of Technology, Poland and USI-Università della Svizzera italiana, Switzerland

Lorenzo Cantoni
USI-Università della Svizzera italiana, Switzerland

Abstract: There are many profound links between fashion and tourism. This chapter provides a critical reflection, mainly from a philosophical, historical, and linguistic perspective, on the dynamic relationship and parallel evolution between these two sectors. It explains how their interconnectedness form and mirror contemporary society. This chapter classifies the connections between the two, starting with the person, her body, and the relationship the latter has with fashion and tourism, and with the contemporary society at large. Four layers of such connections are exemplified. It also discusses a selfie, as a symbolic (digital) communication object and a complex phenomenon facilitated by changing technological affordances and societal functions as an excellent case of the complex relationships between fashion and tourism. **Keywords**: Fashion communication; tourism communication; lifestyle; selfie; tourism clothing; fashion tourism

INTRODUCTION

Fashion and tourism share many common traits, both as experiences as well as related market fields. One might explore such convergences in several directions: by exploring the role of fashion within tourism, by studying fashion destinations or dedicated attractions (such as fashion exhibitions in museums), by examining the role of tourism within fashion and designed collections, or branding through

Fashion and Tourism: Parallel Stories
Tourism Social Science Series, Volume 26, 33–46

Published under exclusive licence by Emerald Publishing Limited
ISSN: 1571-5043/doi:10.1108/S1571-504320230000026003

the places where fashion items are produced. Fashion and tourism are also means of communication. The way people dress and where and how they travel to are major channels through which they express themselves, communicating to others their identities, values, status, and ranks in society (Cantoni et al., 2020).

Fashion and tourism articulate space and geography differently: the former hosts the human body, fashioning its appearances and boundaries, while the later hosts human mobility and negotiates its destinations. There are many links between fashion and tourism, and even more ways and approaches to analyze and understand them. This chapter provides a classification of the connections between the two, starting from people themselves, their bodies, and relationship with fashion, their movements in space as tourists, and how these activities are interconnected. The approach is interpretive in nature: it employs secondary data materials and descriptive scenarios.

Today, when one thinks of fashion, the reference is mostly to clothes and apparel. However, fashion can cover a much larger set of objects and experiences, such as makeup, cosmetics, eyewear, and accessories. This chapter presents several layers of fashion in their broad sense and their degrees of distance from the human body. It gets more in-depth regarding the links between fashion and tourism. To do this, the layers of fashion proximity to the body described in the first section will be utilized to explore how they are being translated into activities and practices performed by a person when she is a tourist. Related communication practices that unite fashion and tourism are further discussed.

Both fashion and tourism are currently undergoing a profound digital transformation, which further highlights their similarities and close connections. The example of the selfie, a self-portrait photograph taken with a digital camera or a smartphone, as an emblematic (digital) communication object typically and extensively used in both domains is presented at the end of this chapter. Its iconic, indexical, and symbolic functions are discussed, while providing further opportunities to reflect on common traits connecting fashion and tourism within the digital communication realm.

RELATIONSHIP OF FASHION AND TOURISM

All human beings are born unclad. People cover themselves, mainly for three reasons: (1) modesty, to cover at least genitals; (2) functional needs, to protect the body; and (3) self-expression and communication. Considering the last reason, one could say that people dress to visually disclose an entire world of meaning, which otherwise would remain almost completely inaccessible. While dressing up, one shares values, style, rank in society, and explicitly disclose tastes. In other words, people cover the body to unveil the soul.

The word "fashion" is rooted in the ancient Latin language, from the verb *facio*, meaning "to do." In French, the word *façon* indicates how something is done. Then the word entered Middle English with a normative twist, becoming: "the right way to do things." While the French language has mediated the

English term "fashion," nowadays widely adopted across many languages, the French equivalent "mode" (Italian: "moda") comes from a different Latin word: *modus*, which indicates the right way, as in the famous proverb "est modus in rebus" (there is a proper measure in all things). For instance, "Á la mode de Paris" indicates the way people in Paris dress, which is the best way, *bien sûr* (Kurkdjian, 2021). *Modus* has also generated "models": both designs used to produce and replicate specific items (as in paper patterns), as well as people who represent a (ideal) person who is wearing clothes on the catwalks and is being featured on images and videos by fashion brands.

Today, when one thinks of fashion, reference is first made to clothes and apparel. However, as mentioned earlier, it can cover a much larger set of objects and experiences related to them, including makeup, cosmetics, eyewear, and accessories. Fashion could be mapped onto four layers, which could be organized depending on the degree of distance of such an object from a body (Table 3.1).

In the first layer (I) the outer border of the figure can be considered: skin, nails, hair, and its shape. Such inner layer encompasses body shapes, including diets, fitness and sport, and all the activities that help the person to stay and look healthy and fit. It also includes plastic surgery, tattoos, and

Table 3.1. Exemplified Layers of Fashion and Degree of Distance From a Body.

		Layers	*Proximity to the body*	*Facio/Façon/Modus Fashion*
Kosmeo		I	The outer border of our figure	*Our body and its outer borders* encompass skin and hair, and body shapes. It includes diets, fitness and sports activities, as well as tattoos, piercings, perfumes, cosmetics, and hairstyles.
Habeo	*Abito/ garment*	II	Around my body (in contact)	All *clothing items, shoes, and accessories*, which are put around our bodies.
	Abitare/ inhabit	III	Around me (less close)	The environment of a person, especially those items made of fabric or leather. It is the world of *furniture, décor of interiors, and of transportation vehicles.*
	Habit	IV	Around me (wide)	Specific cultural traditions, social practices, and individual styles (habits), which collectively could be referred to as *lifestyles.*

piercings that help human beings to make their bodies better or different. Hairstyles, perfumes, and cosmetics belong to this layer as well. The term "cosmetics" comes from ancient Greek and refers to the verb *kosméo,* meaning "to order," like in "kosmos": an ordered universe. In its original meaning, thus, *cosmesis* indicates the act of highlighting human beauty and its harmony, much more than a simple makeup intended to dissimulate limits covering them with a fabricated beauty. From here on, another Latin word can guide the discussion – the verb *habeo* (to have) in its frequentative form of *habito.* It means to have something on a routine, on a regular basis.

The second layer (II) represents garments (*abito* in Italian), meaning all clothing items, shoes, and accessories, which a person puts around his or her body regularly. The person is doing this to cover the body from the nudity, to protect it in harsh weather conditions, and also to express herself. The third layer (III) refers to the house that is inhabited by someone ("inhabit," *abitare* in Italian). It can relate to the familiar environment in which the person lives, especially to those items that are made of fabric or leather. Here the world of décor of interiors and of transportation vehicles comes into discussion. All those items belonging to the three layers are connected, adopted, adapted, and enacted according to specific cultural traditions, social practices, and individual styles (*habits*), and to the way a person lives, their virtues or vices (*abitudini*, in Italian). They could be referred to, collectively, as lifestyles. Their *habits*, indeed. They would belong to the fourth layer (IV) that is proposed in this chapter.

Four Layers of Fashion and Tourism

Tourism indicates that someone visits a place and returns home. It is exactly such a turning movement that defines it, as expressed by its etymology from Latin *tornare* – "to turn." While moving from one place to another, tourists might be dressed in the same way as they were at home or might decide to "localize" themselves while dressing differently to fit the new context better and to express their travel purpose(s) (Table 3.2).

Our Body and its Outer Borders. The first layer (I) is the one that takes care of the body, its skin, hair, and body types. This is done mostly while at home, but increasingly also while traveling. The role of cosmetics and wellness is especially relevant at this stage. The role of sun protection creams in "Sea, Sun, and Sand" tourism or during the holidays in mountain resorts can be examined here. On the other hand, particular types of tourism: health or spa and thermal tourism, or different types of wellness retreats (yoga or pilates), whose goals might be to adjust or change the appearance of the body and its shape are of relevance in this layer of the analysis. Moreover, different clothing styles might expose larger parts of skin, requiring further cosmetic/fitness practices or creating possible health-related impacts. Plastic surgery

Table 3.2. Four Layers of Fashion and Tourism Activities and Practices.

		Layers	*Facio/Façon/Modus* Fashion	*Torno* Examples of tourism-related items, activities and practices
Kosmeo		I	*Our body and its outer borders* encompass skin and hair, and body shapes. It includes diets, fitness activities, as well as tattoos, piercings, perfumes, cosmetics, and hairstyles.	Sun protection creams Wellness retreats (e.g., yoga or pilates) Spa and thermal tourism Medical tourism and plastic surgery
Habeo	*Abito/ garment*	II	All *clothing items, shoes, and accessories*, which are put around our bodies.	Eyewear and sunglasses Proper clothing to visit religious attractions Sports clothing and equipment Luggage as a fashion item Ad-hoc cruise collections, by fashion brands Deseasonalizing fashion items and destination-wear Shopping tourism and souvenirs Tourism destinations as fashion capitals Fashion museums and exhibitions Textile and fashion practices as Intangible Cultural Heritage enlisted by UNESCO
	Abitare/ inhabit	III	The environment of a person, especially those items made of fabric or leather – it is the world of *furniture, décor of*	Fabrics and leather created by fashion brands as furniture and other décor elements of tourism

Table 3.2. *(Continued)*

		interiors, and of transportation vehicles.	enterprises (e.g., hotels) Transportation-related companies that own fashion brands Fashion brands that own hotels and restaurants
Habit	IV	Specific cultural traditions, social practices, and individual styles (habits), which collectively could be referred to as *lifestyles.*	Lifestyle umbrella by newspapers and magazines Lifestyle tourism destinations created by fashion actors Lifestyle trends that cross both sectors (e.g., sustainability, ecology, fitness, mindfulness, etc.)

can also be mentioned here, which might be done abroad during the so-called medical tourism (Connell, 2013).

Clothing Items and Accessories. The second layer (II) presents all clothing items, shoes and accessories which are worn while traveling to and within a destination. "When in Rome, do as the Romans do" is a famous proverb attributed to Saint Ambrose from Milan (Italy). Those who can afford to go on vacation have always seen such experiences as an opportunity to explore new clothing practices and expand their wardrobe and accessories. For instance, eyewear has been closely connected to sport and winter tourism, while sunglasses accompany most vacations. Stereotypical colonial attire can characterize safaris and "big five" tours and expeditions. While traveling, people might have to or be willing to change their clothing accordingly. In fact, in some cases, this might be compulsory. There are specific clothing requirements to enter religious buildings, tourist areas, or even the country (Temerak, 2019). In other cases, very different climatic environments might require proper clothing: Visit Iceland, for instance, offers a dedicated section, "Pack Warm Stay Happy" within its online Iceland Academy. Many sports request dedicated equipment, which might be mostly (if not exclusively) connected to tourism by some people. Skiing, hiking and climbing, sailing, and skippering do require a specific attire that tourists should wear. This attire can be brought from home or bought directly at the destination.

Packing luggage has always been an essential practice (nearly a ritual) of any tourism experience. It might mean leaving almost everything at home, if one is preparing for a pilgrimage or walking the Camino de Santiago (Spain), or adding sophisticated garments and accessories, well thought out before the trip. In a sense, packing means deciding which parts of home to leave behind and what to bring along. The luggage itself is a fashion item: among luxury brands particularly focused on bags and other travel items, one can mention Dior, Gucci, Hermès, Louis Vuitton, and Prada. Globe-Trotter, for instance, an England-based company established in 1897, presents itself as "Accompanying the well-travelled for 123 years and counting." On the other hand, the diffusion of sneakers and backpacks well beyond sportswear and travel equipment has added a touristic turn to everyday attire, becoming even a sign of contemporary (digital) nomads.

Fashion brands have always considered touring people, and recently launched ad hoc cruise collections (Pinchera & Rinallo, 2019) that cater for their willingness to be adequately dressed in tourism-related circumstances. Moreover, international tourism has offered major opportunities for deseasonalizing fashion items. For instance, beach- and swim-wear, which used to be sold in the Northern hemisphere mostly in summertime, have recently become an all-year-round sold item, due to the appearance of low-cost airlines and the possibility of reaching exotic destinations also in wintertime (Macalister-Smith, 2015). That has also led to the emergence of a new category within fashion: "destination wear." The swimwear category expanded beyond swimsuits and espadrilles and gave birth to a new genre of holiday destination wear that works as well in the city as on the sand and includes items like "crochet shorts, palazzo pants, cotton kaftans, embroidered cover-ups, beach hats, canvas bags, bohemian sandals and fringed tunics" (Macalister-Smith, 2015).

While shopping might be one of the main drivers of tourism (Correia et al., 2019), clothing and accessories are among the most important souvenirs (Litirell et al., 1994; Park, Reisinger, & Noh, 2009). A fashion item, bought at the destination, becomes something that reminds you of a trip, belongs to the destination. Its materials, colors, styles, and craft practices become yours at the point that it is worn. Some things one can easily pack in the bag or buy last minute at the airport, which are not likely to be damaged while being handled. Later, by wearing them when one is back home, they help the person to go back to memories of the trip and to become an unofficial ambassador of the destination.

Fashion might be itself a destination, or a major part of what makes a place attractive. In their tourism promotion, some cities present themselves as fashion capitals or destinations, focusing on their fashion legacy and tradition. This happens especially to those cities that host major fashion weeks, as they can leverage them as attractive tourism events, and extend that fashionable *aura* to cover all year round (Kalbaska et al., 2018; Rocamora, 2009). Travel guides do their part as well, including sections and tours that showcase fashion attractiveness (Biondo, 2021). International music festivals have also become major fashion events, further strengthening the relationship between music and fashion. Coachella, for instance, has been attracting models and designers in an opportunity to showcase their products and launch new trends (Noris & Cantoni, 2022).

For a long time, fashion items have been marginalized by the museum and cultural heritage communities: for instance, garments and accessories have usually been given only very limited space within museum collections (Noris & Cantoni, 2022). However, in recent years, museums dedicated to fashion, brands, and individual designers have been booming (Permatasari & Kalbaska, 2022). Fashion exhibitions also in nonspecialized museums have become a major attraction for locals and tourists. Up to the point that the most visited ever exhibition at the Metropolitan Museum of Art (MET) has been "Heavenly Bodies: Fashion and the Catholic Imagination," with more than 1.5 million visitors from May 10 to October 8, 2018 (Metropolitan Museum of Art, 2018; Noris & Cantoni, 2022). In addition, cultural tourism is becoming increasingly intrigued by fashion, thanks to the inscription of textile and fashion practices as Intangible Cultural Heritage by The United Nations Educational, Scientific and Cultural Organization (UNESCO), as in the case of Indonesian Batik (Permatasari & Cantoni, 2019).

Décor of Interiors and of Transportation. The third layer (III) presents the environment of a person when she is traveling, especially those items made of fabric or leather. It is the world of décor of interiors, for instance, of hotels and transportation means. Fashion companies have been involved for a long time in using fabrics and leather for garments and furniture and other home and interior décor. Fabrics and leather surround people – while in bed, or sitting on a sofa, or being veiled by curtains, or walking on a carpet. This is the case when one stays at home, or when on the road. The same can be said when travel is by car, yacht, or any other vehicle. Furbishing them, especially for high-end luxury travel, has always been a matter of distinction. In recent years, the partnerships between fashion and tourism have been celebrated through the establishment of hotels owned by fashion brands (Dallabona, 2015), and have also extended to include restoration. Gucci, the famous Italian fashion brand, recently launched Gucci Osteria, with restaurants in Florence, Beverly Hills, and Tokyo. Such openings are adding up to the tourism offer and eventual attractiveness of the destinations.

Transportation-related companies are launching their own fashion brands, selling bags or tourism-related items. They design the travelers' environment so as to fully embed them into a (luxury) vacation experience. It is the case of Orient Express and its "Grand Suites," of cruise companies, airlines, and car companies, such as Ferrari, Porsche, Fiat, and Piaggio. Even during the global pandemic crisis of COVID-19, Ferrari has launched a menswear collection with a fashion show that took place on June 13, 2021, in Maranello (Italy), home to the luxury car company.

> There is such heritage and mystique around the Ferrari name. It conveys a sexy feeling of ultimate luxury. Pivoting his attention to the creation of new non-automotive products, Nicola Boari, Ferrari Chief Brand Diversification officer, seems to have his finger on the pulse when it comes to being attentive to social and cultural developments. The strategy to develop the collection seemingly merges man and machine within one brand culture. (DeAcetis, 2021)

Lifestyles. The fourth layer (IV), the one of "lifestyle," features the way people live, their habits, beliefs, and social practices. A well-known example can be brought here of Talita Getty and Getty Jr, which were photographed in Marrakech (Morocco) at the beginning of 1970s and featured by Vogue. This photo shoot and its global popularity, contributed to the creation of Marrakech as a lifestyle destination. Sports tourism is clearly connected with dedicated equipment as well as with certain lifestyles and rituals, in turn connected with given dress codes. Golf, tennis, and equitation are the most prominent examples. It is not by chance that both domains of fashion and tourism are frequently associated under the "lifestyle" umbrella by newspapers and magazines. The same can be said about publishers. For instance, Condé Nast publishes *Condé Nast Traveler* as well as *Vogue*, along with many other magazines guiding their audiences within both the travel world and the fashion one, including home décor. Hearst, Meredith, and other publishing companies offer similar cases. Lifestyle trends do cross both sectors, with major interconnected and highly topical issues around the globe, such as sustainability, ecology, fitness, mindfulness, local production, and consumption.

Fashion and Tourism Are (also) Communication

The way one dresses and where and how travels is a major channel through which people express themselves, and communicate their identity, values, status, and ranks in society to others. One could say that "we cover ourselves in order to unveil that we are much more than our body; the materiality of clothes displays the immaterial/spiritual side of us" (Noris & Cantoni, 2022, p. 8). While modesty and functionality should never be forgotten when thinking of fashion and its various layers, its expressive and communicative functions will be further explored in the following lines. The way people dress can say a lot about them. Clothes show social status and help share values. This might happen involuntarily (as in the case of a beggar, whose clothes suggest that he is poor and is unable to choose and buy different items) or voluntarily (as in the case of a person who can take decisions about how to dress). Clothes could then act as a type of code, where items and their combinations can acquire specific meanings. Eco (1971) and Barthes (1973), among others, have particularly stressed this language-like structure of fashion, even if – as objected by Svendsen (2006) – apart from specific domains, like in the case of military uniforms, it is impossible to provide a consistent and comprehensive grammar of such language.

The communication side of fashion is constantly intertwined with images and texts, both written and oral. In this regard, example include texts printed on fabrics (as in T-shirts or in African Kanga), logos and labels being used by fashion brands; images and written text printed in the packaging and fabric care instructions, up to catalogs, posters, fashion books, and magazines. Oral communications are also used in discourses about fashion: what is fashionable and what is not, emerging or fading away, proper or not. These are all ways used by individuals and communities to negotiate fashion. This is done constantly through comments, praises, or critics, during the conversations in the shops and elsewhere. "How was she/he dressed?" "Whose attire was the best one?" are among main conversation starters.

Seen from the perspective of communication, changes in fashion can be interpreted as changes in language, where "some elements might change at a swift pace (like for denim and sneakers), while others do remain unchallenged/unchanged for several decades if not centuries. In language, for instance, while new words are constantly created (and others become obsolete), morphology remains very stable over time. In fashion, colors, materials, models, and shapes do change quite frequently, while other dimensions remain stable. Consider, for example, the fate of trousers in Europe and in Western societies: they are (almost) the only shape allowed for men to dress their lower body" (Noris & Cantoni, 2022, p. 59). The same communication point of view suggests that one can interpret fashion in tourism as learning (or not) a second language. When traveling people might just speak their own language (= dress the same way at home), or adapt, somehow, to the different context and communication environment (= fashion practices), embarking on a complex translation or localization process. Such a process could end up with a quasi-native fashion-related behavior, or with significant differences from local practices, being perceived as "foreigners." Such differences could be due to limited knowledge of such practices, too little familiarity with them, or – vice versa – to an explicit and voluntary decision not to adopt them. In current practices, all nuances or shades between such polarities take places. Here, the acculturation theory applied to language learning might help to further understand the dynamics. According to it

> . . .social factors and affective factors tied to language could be major variables influencing L2 acquisition. From this perspective, the more positively identified with and the more psychologically integrated into the target language group, the more likely the learner is able to succeed in L2 acquisition. Learners should acquire the target language to the

> degree they acculturate to the target language group, therefore the essence of successful L2 acquisition is to identify with, and get involved in, the target culture socially and effectively. (Jiang et al., 2009, p. 482)

A similar process might be working for fashion: the more people want to become – and be perceived – as integrated within the tourism destination cosmetics and clothing practices, as well as within its décor and lifestyles, the more they will change accordingly.

Zooming-Out Selfies

After providing a map of the overlapping dimensions and close links between fashion and tourism, one can approach their digital transformations. The goal here is not to provide an extensive overview of the different areas in which fashion and tourism interact with information and communication technologies, both undergoing a deep digital transformation. This has been done elsewhere for tourism (Buhalis & Law, 2008; Cantoni, 2020; De Ascaniis & Cantoni, 2022; Inversini et al., 2015), and more recently for fashion (Kalbaska et al., 2018, 2019; Noris, Nobile, Kalbaska, & Cantoni, 2021; Nobile et al., 2021; Sádaba et al., 2021). Instead, the focus is on a selfie, a self-portrait photograph taken with a digital camera or a smartphone. The selfie represents an emblematic communication object, where all the elements that were tackled by this chapter – tourism, fashion, digital, and communication – are interconnected. While visuals play a major role in fashion, and its digital representations, the same can be said about tourism. According to a Google study, images and videos are among essential triggers when a person starts dreaming about a destination, and eventually planning to visit it (Google, 2014). Moreover, the role of places within movies has been highlighted by the so-called screen tourism, as recently examined in a report by UNWTO – the UN World Tourism Organization and Netflix (UNWTO & Netflix, 2021).

In current practices of digital photography, selfies are emerging as a major trend also in academic research in both fashion and tourism (Deeb-Swihart et al., 2017; Dinhopl & Gretzel, 2016; Kedzior et al., 2016; Kim et al., 2017; Paris & Pietschnig, 2015). In recent years, digital photography has offered endless opportunities for tourism and fashion to showcase their destinations and products, at the same time offering, through social media, the opportunity also to nonprofessional photography to be shared and displayed. User-generated content and digital word-of-mouth are extensively cocreating the image of brands and destinations (De Ascaniis & Gretzel, 2013; Gretzel & Yoo, 2008), and are contributing to their (online) reputation (Marchiori & Cantoni, 2011). Such importance has brought about the emergence of influencers and influencers' marketing practices: people who are considered leaders by their followers (SanMiguel, 2020).

The popularity of selfies in both domains comes from the increased use of smartphones, connected to the internet, and equipped with front-facing cameras, and from the dramatic growth of social media platforms that support and promote the sharing of visual content. Indeed, social media apps, such as Instagram or Snapchat, allow the possibility to use features such as filters or geolocations; while linking the image to the place where it was taken. Furthermore, images placed on social media sites can be accompanied by text, such as written descriptions and hashtags (Karamalak et al., 2021), which give the possibility to the user to describe their location or a destination, for example, "#Switzerland" or "#Milan." This allows users to indicate the place even if it is not clearly recognizable based on the image itself. However, under specific circumstances, it might play a major role also in fashion-related selfies, for instance, while taking selfies in "instagrammable" locations, while showing restaurants, hotels, private jets, etc.

Some recent technological developments, such as selfie sticks or drones, which are used to take photographs or videos by positioning a digital camera device beyond the normal range of the arm, allowed shots to be taken at angles and distances that would not have been possible with the human arm itself. This endorsed more panoramic image capture and better featuring of other objects being present in a picture. Now, the cloth, accessories, and shoes have higher visibility, along with a potential tourism destination or its attractions. It should be noted that, especially in the tourism domain, not only faces are featured on selfies. For instance, the "foot selfie," a photograph taken of one's feet while sunbathing at exotic locations, has become popular (Jenson, 2013). Selfies are often casual in nature or are made to appear casual. The popularity of selfies comes from how easy they are to be taken and shared and from the control they give people over how they look like and present themselves digitally. In fact, in the fashion domain, selfies are seen as a powerful tool to help promote different beauty standards and are particularly influential among those users who are typically not featured in mainstream media (Bennett, 2014).

To better understand the notion of a selfie, one should distinguish between the iconic, indexical, and symbolic functions of photography and images in general (Mazzali-Lurati & Cantoni, 2006). The iconic dimension refers to the similarity between what is pictured and the picture itself: it provides a trustable representation of reality as it could be seen. Both in fashion and tourism, selfies want to represent the photographers themselves, how they look like, with specific stress on their appearance, their dress, their feeling relaxed and comfortable because of the vacation environment or the way they are dressed or made-up (Figure 3.1). In tourism, such iconic representation extends to include the background landscape or specific monuments.

The indexical dimension refers to the fact that a picture demonstrates a physical proximity between the photographer and what is photographed. In selfies the distance is the one allowed by the photographer's arm, a

Figure 3.1. A Selfie Taken in Porto, Portugal.

selfie-stick, or a mirror, or – more recently and less frequently – a drone operated by the same person. The indexical value in fashion selfies stays in the message: "it's me, dressed that way," or "the dress that adheres to my body is my dress." The further environment is less relevant, be it one's home, a fitting room or elsewhere. In tourism, on the contrary, the indexical function operates on the context in which the picture is taken: "it's me who is in that place" (Bell & Lyall, 2005, p. 151). Indeed, "the desire to show that a person 'was there' as proof in tourism photography appears to be the reason for many tourist photos in front of 'mandatory sites'" (Dinhopl & Gretzel, 2016, p. 133). However, in selfies the person is always at the center of the communication, hence highlighting the way she is dressed, her skin, makeup, and hairstyle.

The symbolic or conventional dimension refers to elements that depend on codes or conventions. In both realms, fashion and tourism, one can find memes, or trends, which are understood by addressees as long as they share the same background knowledge. For instance, a selfie taken with the Eifel Tower in the background presents an iconic spot of Paris, at the same time emphasizing the outfit of the depicted person, who is in a fashion capital. The same could be said about iconic fashion streets or similar shopping related places. While taking selfies and often sharing them on social media, users show their ability to travel to certain places and be dressed in a certain way, representing their lifestyle.

What selfies communicate is multifacet, and confirms the connection between *habeo* and *cosmeo*, and all four are connecting layers between fashion and tourism that were discussed above:

Layer 1: "This is me/my face/my skin/my body"
Layer 2: "dressed in this way"
Layer 3: "enjoying this attraction/destination, which is around me"
Layer 4: and here there is a piece of evidence that "this is my lifestyle"

In sum, the selfie represents an emblematic communication object, where all four elements covered in this chapter – tourism, fashion, digital, and communication – are interconnected.

CONCLUSION

This chapter has presented four layers of fashion and their degree of distance from the body. The first layer includes the body and its outer borders, which encompasses skin and hair, and body shapes. In the fashion-related domains it includes diets, fitness, and sport activities, as well as tattoos, piercings, perfumes, cosmetics, and hairstyles. The second layer includes all clothing items, shoes, and accessories, which are put around bodies. The environment of a person, especially those items made of fabric or leather – it is the world of the décor of interiors and of transportation – belong to the third layer. While specific cultural traditions, social practices, and individual styles (habits), which collectively could be referred to as lifestyles, create the fourth and last layer.

The second part of this chapter presented the links that connect fashion and tourism, by using above-mentioned layers. It introduced and discussed various tourism-related items, activities, and practices, such as wellness and medical tourism; proper clothing to travel in different climatic environments or visit religious attractions; textiles used in the décor elements of tourism enterprises (like hotels), and specific cultural traditions, social practices, and individual styles (habits), which collectively could be referred to as lifestyles. Finally, it argued that a selfie, as a symbolic (digital) communication object and a complex phenomenon facilitated by changing technological affordances, social practices, and societal functions can be an excellent case of exemplifying the complex relationships between the two domains: fashion and tourism.

Chapter 4

TOURISM AND FASHION INFLUENCERS
Comparison of Visual Practices

Ulrike Gretzel
University of Southern Calffornia, USA

Abstract: Social media influencers increasingly determine what is fashionable. By creating and sharing visual contents, predominantly on Instagram, they shape what social media users see and aspire to. Their contents reflect Instagram esthetics and their own personal brands. This chapter argues that their visuals also represent emerging visual practices and styles that are typical of influencers and transcend fashion and tourism contexts. Using a netnographic approach, this chapter examines Instagram posts of 20 tourism and fashion mega-influencers. It finds common practices but also identifies differential ways in which fashion and tourism visuals are constructed. This chapter highlights how the subjects have intertwined, especially when it comes to influencers. **Keywords**: Social media influencer; visual practice; netnography; Instagram esthetics; social media gaze; esthetic labor

INTRODUCTION

People's desires to consume and their esthetic sensitivities are increasingly shaped by what is encountered on social media, especially on visual platforms like Instagram (Leaver, Highfield, & Abidin, 2020). Social media influencers and their skilled "mise-en-scène" of objects, people, and places in their attention-capturing and shareworthy posts increasingly fill these social media feeds and play an ever-greater role in affecting what is considered fashionable (Lewis, Kerr, & Burgess, 2019). Social media influencers are content creators that strategically amass and engage with targeted audiences

Fashion and Tourism: Parallel Stories
Tourism Social Science Series, Volume 26, 47–58

ISSN: 1571-5043/doi:10.1108/S1571-504320230000026004

and often collaborate with fashion and tourism brands to provide their followers with enticing contents or promotional deals (Gretzel, 2018). Social media influencers engage in elaborate self-branding activities (Duffy & Hund, 2015; Liu & Suh, 2017) and adopt esthetics that make them attractive to followers and brands (Hund, 2017). They are skilled visual communicators whose images entertain, instill trust, and persuade (Jin & Ryu, 2020).

The visual practices of social media influencers mimic general social media conventions, such as carefully crafted selfies (Dinhopl & Gretzel, 2016), but often innovate, sensationalize, and at the same time professionalize the ways in which fashion items and/or destinations are featured in their posts. In the influencer world, much more so than in traditional advertising, fashion and tourism go together, with outfits requiring suitable backdrops and selfies taken at destinations inevitably communicating fashion statements. Both are central to the identity work of influencers and to audience engagement (Abidin, 2018). Because of their influential nature, these visual influencer practices then become adopted by other social media users and have the potential to change general consumer expectations and behaviors.

By examining the specific visual practices of top fashion and tourism influencers on Instagram, this chapter explores this interplay of fashion and destinations in social media posts and the resulting new conventions in tourism and fashion photography. Using a netnographic approach to deriving cultural insights from social media contents (Kozinets, 2020), the research investigates what is pictured and how on Instagram to derive a typology of visual influencer practices that relate to fashion and tourism.

VISUAL PRACTICES OF SOCIAL MEDIA INFLUENCERS

Social media influencers are social media platform users who are able to attract and engage other users and who are of interest to tourism and fashion marketers because of the distinct, authentic, consistent, and persuasive content they produce. They can impact the behavior of consumers because they are successful in creating aspirational personal brands that others want to emulate and associate with. Their contents are informational and entertaining, but also represent an esthetic quality and unique perspective that information-saturated social media audiences seek out and appreciate (Gretzel, 2022). They usually entertain parasocial relationships with their followers and provide guidance in terms of personal style and lifestyle. They become role models for consumers and can turn into idols through celebrification processes (Brooks, Drenten, & Piskorski, 2021).

Social media influencers have become an integral part of the communication space that underlines the tourism system. Not only do they produce a vast amount of high-quality tourism content, but they have also become important stakeholders for the tourism industry (Femenia-Serra, Gretzel, &

Alzua-Sorzabal, 2022). Guerreiro, Viegas, and Guerreiro (2019) find that Instagram plays a significant role in finding inspiration and information regarding destinations and that those who follow influencers on the platform do consider them as credible information sources and tend to visit the places they promote in their posts. In the fashion context, Pedroni (2022) highlights the increasing power of fashion influencers as cultural intermediaries. Fashion influencers are important tastemakers who have established themselves as an integral part of the fashion system through their ability to curate audiences (McQuarrie, Miller, & Phillips, 2013). Chetioui, Benlafqih, and Lebdaoui (2020) empirically confirm their positive influence on the attitudes of fashion consumers. SanMiguel, Guercini, and Sádaba (2018) describe them as important sources of inspiration, as role models and as trend setters.

Social media influencers perform a type of emotional labor that has been coined as "aesthetic labor" (McFarlane & Samsioe, 2020). It involves the ongoing visual construction of their selves, of their work, and of their living environments on social media (Brydges & Sjöholm, 2019). De Perthuis and Findlay (2019) explain that fashion imagery depicts the fashionable ideal and influencers embody it in their social media contents. Wissinger (2015) refers to their efforts as "glamor labor" because they need to stress the extraordinary to garner attention and engagement from their followers. Thus, their visual practices are central to their existence as influencers.

Tourism and Fashion Visual Practices

Photography has a long tradition in both tourism and fashion contexts. In the tourism context, photography portrays destinations as available for possession and consumption (Smith, 2018). In fashion photography, photos convey fashion or a "fashionable" lifestyle (Hall-Duncan, 2022), and the world is usually used as décor or background (Barthes, 2020). Both serve commercial endeavors as well as self-representation and impression management purposes (Titton, 2015).

Social media have democratized the production but especially the distribution of tourism and fashion photography. In addition, social media, in conjunction with emerging technologies, such as image filters, digital cameras, and drones, change photographic practices and visual esthetics (Dinhopl & Gretzel, 2015). In relation to tourism, the self becomes a lot more important, and the destination becomes a stage for the self (Dinhopl & Gretzel, 2016). Not only are different perspectives possible, but there are also new possibilities and expectations for editing. Once an image is posted, it is immediately subject to reactions and public scrutinizing. Images to be posted on social media are therefore produced with this social media gaze in mind (Urry & Larsen, 2011).

Images shared on social media also do not appear in isolation but are typically part of larger curations, so-called profiles, or feeds. They therefore become a means of personal branding for social media users through which a consistent and unique style is portrayed. Especially in the tourism context, the social media-based photo is no longer just a memento or proof but, rather, a complex communication device that can be used to convey messages to other social media users and manage impressions (Schwarz, 2021; Siegel, Tussyadiah, & Scarles, 2022). In the context of fashion blogs, Rocamora (2013) describes social media as privileged spaces of self-construction but also notes how the social media gaze continues to objectify women.

Social media influencers not only engage in regular visual practices but also must find a unique style and professionalize their visuals to support their personal branding efforts and to capture the attention of actual and potential followers. Not only their fashion and tourism styles but also their visual styles are admired and subsequently copied by their followers. Consequently, they are shaped by but also actively shape visual practices in tourism and fashion. It is the aim of this chapter to explore which specific visual styles fashion and influencers use to promote themselves, engage their audiences, and successfully partner with brands.

Study Methodology

Netnography is a qualitative research methodology that is specifically suitable for deriving understandings from social media data, because it offers techniques for identifying rich data sites, for recognizing and appreciating the context of particular platforms, and for dealing with the ethical questions that arise from gathering data online (Kozinets, 2019). While it adopts foundational principles from ethnography, it adapts ethnography's aim of deriving deep, cultural, and contextual understanding through participant observation and a cocktail of other methods to the specific affordances of social media. Further, in contrast to the "anything goes as long as it is ethical" spirit of ethnography, netnography does require adherence to basic principles in terms of data collection steps, documentation, reporting, and ethics (Kozinets & Gretzel, 2022).

Netnography has been applied extensively in the context of tourism (Kozinets, 2020) to understand a diverse range of phenomena, from Chinese RV travelers (Wu & Pearce, 2014) to Muslim women's experience of virtual destinations (Tavakoli & Mura, 2015), mothers making family tourism decisions (Bae & Yeu, 2021), and tourists experiencing shopping tours guided by locals (Atsız & Seyitoğlu, 2022). It has also been applied in recent research on anime tourists' experiences (Liu, Liu, & Rahman, 2022), tourists' interactions with feral rabbits (Usui, 2021), destination advocacy in virtual communities (Lever, Elliot, & Joppe, 2021), destination residents' discussions of social justice issues

(Rastegar, Zarezadeh, & Gretzel, 2021), destination boycotts (Yousaf, Razzaq, & Fan,7 2021), the online activism of Airbnb hosts (Hardy, Dolnicar, & Vorobjovas-Pinta, 2021), genealogy tourists' use of mobile apps (Kennedy-Eden & Gretzel, 2021), and many others.

In the fashion literature, Loureiro, Serra, and Guerreiro (2019) have used netnography to illuminate how brands communicate on social media. Choi and Kim (2019)'s research on consumers who love sneakers investigated how these 'sneakerheads' share information and interact in an online brand community. Reid and Duffy (2018) explored how netnography can deliver in-depth understanding of product launch events and the social media conversations that accompany them.

Netnography has been specifically used to examine the practices and impacts of social media influencers (Patterson & Ashman, 2020). In tourism, netnographies have examined how influencers and their visual practices frame destination images, how they work with different stakeholders in tourism, and how they establish themselves as credible, authentic, and relatable information sources for tourists (Deng, Benckendorff, & Wang, 2022; Femenia-Serra et al., 2022; Gholamhosseinzadeh, Chapuis, & Lehu, 2021; Motahar, Tavakoli, & Mura, 2021; Shao & Gretzel, 2011). In relation to fashion influencers, netnographic research has investigated how influencer contents are consumed, how they present themselves on social media, how their esthetic labor shapes perceptions, and how their activities lead to market transformation (Kretz, 2012; Logan, 2015; McFarlane & Samsioe, 2020; Scaraboto & Fischer, 2013). It has also looked at fashion influencers and their relationship with fashion brands (Casais & Gomes, 2022).

Data Collection and Sample. Netnography builds on three distinct but interconnected data collection movements: immersion, investigation, and interaction. All netnographies must have an immersion component, while the other two movements are optional (Kozinets & Gretzel, 2022). The research presented in this chapter combined immersion and investigation. The immersion phase was rather brief as the researcher is very familiar with netnography and had years of experience as a social media user following fashion and tourism influencers online. It mostly involved engaging with influencer content to understand post frequency and potential differences across post types. However, immersion was critical to be able to interpret specific posts within the context of larger feeds and in relation to what a regular social media user would post. The investigation phase was focused on collecting data from tourism and fashion influencers that could inform similarities and differences in the visual practices of these communicators.

As part of the data scouting phase (Kozinets, 2019), Instagram was selected as the platform on which to conduct the research. Not only is Instagram widely used among consumers across many verticals, but also specifically for tourism and fashion (Guerreiro et al., 2019; McFarlane & Samsioe, 2020). It also constitutes the top platform for influencers and influencer marketing (Campbell, 2022). As a predominantly visual platform (Leaver et al., 2020) with an emphasis on esthetics (Kusumasondjaja, 2020), Instagram is a particularly rich source of data for analyzing visual practices.

The research examined the Instagram feeds of the top tourism and fashion influencers for 2021 as listed by the digital marketing agency A&E (https://www.amraandelma.com/). The agency curates and updates these lists annually for its influencer marketing services clients. Assignments to the broad categories of fashion and tourism reflect the influencer profile, contents, and past brand collaborations. Using a predefined categorization by experts adds external validity and conforms with practice in previous research studies (Ramos-Serrano & Martínez-García, 2016).

To make the sample more comparable across fashion and tourism, female influencers were selected. Only the public posts in the Instagram feed were considered. For each influencer, a full year of posts was examined to account for possible seasonal variations. The first 10 female tourism influencers and 10 female fashion influencers were selected from the published lists, resulting in a total of 20 influencers considered for the analysis. Tables 4.1 and 4.2 list the influencer name, their Instagram handles, the number of followers at the time of data collection, and the number of total posts available on the account. All influencers have either over or close to 1 million followers and, thus, fall into the so-called mega-influencer category.

Data Analysis. Screenshots were captured from the Instagram feed for the year 2021 and saved in an Excel spreadsheet. Only the images were considered for analysis. The analysis followed the principles of thematic analysis

Table 4.1. Sample of Fashion Influencers.

Influencer Name	Instagram Handle	Number of Followers	Total Number of Posts
Chiara Ferragni	chiaraferragni	26.7m	15,700
Camila Coelho	camilacoelho	9.6m	11,649
Lauren Conrad	laurenconrad	5.8m	1,696
Aimee Song	aimeesong	6.3m	10,099
Negin Mirsalehi	negin_mirsalehi	7m	7,569
Julie Sariñana	sincerelyjules	6.5m	7,656
Olivia Palermo	oliviapalermo	7m	1,865
Alexa Chung	alexachung	5m	6,754
Karen Wazen Bakhazi	karenwazen	7.3m	4,408
Caroline Daur	carodaur	3.5m	5,552

Table 4.2. Sample of Tourism Influencers.

Influencer Name	Instagram Handle	Number of Followers	Total Number of Posts
Jennifer Tuffen	izkiz	2.8m	1,284
Lauren Bullen	gypsea_lust	2m	1,638
Blair Eadie	blaireadiebee	1.8m	4,073
Janni Olsson Delér	jannid	1.3m	4,375
Tara Whiteman	taramilktea	1.3m	2,250
Emilie Ristevski	helloemilie	1.3m	1,521
Angelica Blick	angelicablick	1.1m	5,845
Chelsea Yamase	chelseakauai	952k	1,233
Carin Olsson	parisinfourmonths	874k	5,069
Aggie Lal	aggie	822k	1,678

(Braun & Clarke, 2012). The visuals were coded manually and separately for the fashion and for the tourism samples. The coding focused on three elements: the influencer, the outfit, and the image background. The resulting themes were then compared across the two groups. The data was not anonymized because these influencers are major public figures, and their contents are openly visible on the Instagram platform.

Study Findings

Not surprisingly given their status, the influencers from both categories have mastered Instagram esthetics (Masdari & Hosseini Sarvari, 2021). This means their feeds are highly curated, their posts are meticulously framed and constructed, and their contents are very well tailored to viewers who want to be inspired, entertained, and visually stunned, instead of informed, shocked, or challenged. Whether it is tourism or fashion, whatever does not fit this Instagram esthetic was edited out of the visuals. For instance, other people do not appear or appear only as tiny figures in the backgrounds of these pictures (even in the case of busy urban destinations), permitting the focus of the viewer to be on the influencer. The influencer bodies all conform to the beauty standards one generally associates with those who are "instafamous" and to what Gillespie (2019) identified as the face of the ideal influencer. Additionally, the lifestyles depicted in the posts are elaborate, luxurious, adventurous, and admirable, or what Hall-Duncan (2022) calls “fashionable.” In this sense, they all fall into the category of fashion photography.

For both contexts, the photographs are not intimate, spontaneous selfies but clearly taken by another person and staged to attract viewer attention and engagement. Interestingly, while it is technically possible to take a picture of fashion items (especially accessories) without a model and of tourism without a tourist, almost all photos across both categories feature the influencer as consuming the aspirational lifestyle. The influencers first and foremost communicate their personal brand. Moreover, the places depicted in the visuals are not just backdrops, but the influencers engage with them (for example, the fashion influencers are enjoying their Parisian balconies and their Spanish pools while the tourism influencers walk through Saudi Arabian deserts or stroll down picturesque Italian streets). The Instagram posts represent snapshots of their activities.

The results further illustrate the blurring of fashion and tourism in influencer posts and highlight specific strategies used to amplify one by including the other. The popular influencers clearly carefully select their outfits to match their personal style/brand as well as the esthetics of the destination backgrounds. The outfits are far from practical or casual, the influencers look like models, and their poses are as constructed as those of the fashion influencers. The fashion influencers often pose in front of major tourism attractions, in hotels or besides infinity pools to communicate cosmopolitanism and glamour. In addition, the fashion influencers frequently depict themselves traveling (with suitcases, on trains, in airplanes).

Thus, the classification offered by the advertising agency that formed the basis of the sampling for this research seemed very arbitrary at times as all tourism influencers appear in beautiful outfits in their posts and all fashion influencers pose in front of backgrounds outside of their home locations. Slight differences occur in terms of the types of destinations included. While fashion influencer posts are very coherent in terms of the destinations they feature (Milan, Paris, New York, Venice, London) and influencers often seem to be in the same place at the same time for fashion events, tourism influencer content is more diverse and exotic in terms of the kinds of destinations it represents. Fashion influencers seem to distinguish between travel for work and travel for pleasure, with the latter posts clearly aimed at underlining their authenticity and at fostering intimacy with the social media audience. Interestingly, fashion influencers tend to have more posts from their home cities, making them important ambassadors for their respective home destinations.

However, there are indeed some distinctions in the visual practices and styles of the influencer categories. These pertain to the framing of the image in terms of the body of the influencer, the background, and the gaze of the influencer and are explained in greater detail below. It is important to note that the style is tied to the image rather than the influencer, meaning they can both appear in the same influencer feed. For example, Karen Wazen Bakhazi's Instagram feed contains images conforming to the fashion visual style that show her standing up, facing the camera, with her body filling much of the image and the place only being visible as a distant landscape in the background. However, her Instagram feed also contains images that reflect the tourism visual style with the image being a wide angle shot showing her sitting down at a pool, looking into the distance. Fashion influencers tend to favor the fashion visual style while tourism influencers generally adopt the tourism visual style but sometimes post content that follows the fashion visual style. Influencers like Aggie Lal, Angelica Blick, and Blair Eadie are very versed in both visual styles and frequently switch between them in their feeds.

Fashion Visual Style. The fashion visual style is more centered on the model than the tourism style. The influencers' bodies fill up most of the picture frame and they typically face the camera and look straight at the viewer or only slightly to the side. The images are full-body shots, and the influencers tend to stand in the pictures. These findings largely correspond with earlier findings of Ramos-Serrano and Martínez-García (2016) based on a visual semiotic analysis of the types of shots and camera angles used in the Instagram images of personal style bloggers.

However, these styled influencer bodies are mostly situated in places rather than presented in front of abstract backdrops. As further explained in Table 4.3, the places in the fashion visuals generally fall into one of five categories: everyday place, non-place, in-between place, identifiable place, and iconic place. The everyday place category of posts situates the influencer wearing their outfit in an everyday living situation, like during a walk in the local park. Nonplaces refer to places that could be anywhere and most resemble the backgrounds used in traditional fashion shoots. In-between

Table 4.3. Depiction of Place in Fashion Visuals on Instagram.

Type of Place	Example
Everyday place	Park, coffee shop, home, garden
Nonplace	Staircase, wall, doorway, elevator, swimming pool
In-between place	Airplane/private jet, train, limo, boat/yacht
Identifiable place	Hotel room or lobby, restaurant, street, bridge, lake
Iconic place	Eiffel tower, New York skyline, Galleria Vittorio Emanuele II in Milan, Venice bridge

places refer to situations that show the influencer "on the move" from one place to another. While there are some "regular" transportation backgrounds, the in-between places are usually as luxurious as the outfits. The identifiable places refer to locations that are either identifiable through a location or business tag in the post or within the context of a feed, or the name of the destination or business (hotel, restaurant) is visible in the background. Last, but not least, fashion images often include iconic tourism attractions that would be recognized by many followers.

Tourism Visual Style. In a typical travel visual, the influencer is visible but is often looking away or is portrayed from behind. Their bodies are portrayed in full, but in comparison with fashion imagery, they are much smaller in relation to the destination. In tourism images, the influencer more often sits or lies down in comparison to fashion visuals. The influencer bodies in a tourism visual are embedded in "scapes" that unfold behind the influencer. These scapes can be very generic landscapes (streetscapes, beachscapes, mountainscapes, cityscapes, desertscapes, junglescapes, poolscapes, seascapes) or touristic scapes like the Sydney harbor, the island of Santorini, or the pink sandstone cliffs of Petra in Jordan.

Figure 4.1 compares and contrasts tourism and fashion visuals and illustrates how influencers from both categories might use the varying styles. The visual representation further emphasizes the importance of the influencer herself in these photographs and the blurring of tourism and fashion in relation to outfits and destinations. What is astonishing is the general applicability of these styles despite the unique self-branding efforts of each influencer. The visuals in Figure 4.1 (source: author based on data collected from Instagram) also underline how different these pictures are from consumer-generated contents in terms of their perspective, professional quality, and editing.

CONCLUSION

Instagram tourism mega-influencers appear in stylish outfits in pictures (Figure 4.1) and immersed in empty destination-scapes. Their fashion counterparts pose eloquently in places that often become destinations for their followers and they also portray themselves as active tourists. The findings further illustrate that particular styles exist for tourism and fashion visuals involving influencers, but that influencers mix and match these styles in their Instagram feeds. Both styles are Instagram-mediated and are designed for the gaze of a loyal audience of followers who consume tourism and fashion in conjunction with the personal brands of the influencers they admire. While both types of visuals allow intimate glimpses into the exceptional lives of these influencers and seem spontaneous, they are as carefully

Figure 4.1. Tourism and Fashion Visual Styles.

staged as professional photographs and are aligned with the influencer brand and Instagram esthetics.

This chapter provides insights into a phenomenon that has important ramifications for traditional advertising and consumer behavior in both fashion and tourism contexts. From a theoretical perspective, this chapter contributes to the growing literature on technology-mediated visual practices as well as on influencers. It also highlights the fashion-tourism nexus in contemporary consumer culture. Methodologically, it underlines the importance of netnography as a way to study the practices of influencers who are social media "natives" and difficult to study otherwise. From a practical point of view, it emphasizes that tourism and fashion brands can consider working with the same categories of influencers and could even do so in collaboration with brands from the other category, as their contents and styles blend easily. However, it also suggests that fashion and tourism marketers should be aware of the particularities of the two influencer categories in terms of the more distinct elements of their visual practices and esthetics.

One of the limitations of the research is that it only looked at mega-influencers. It is likely that smaller influencers are not only less polished but also more diverse in their styles and more spontaneous in their visual practices. The study also did not consider how consumers might interpret the visuals differently depending on whether their interests lie in tourism or fashion, or whether their interests blend as much as the contents posted by these influencers. Another avenue for future research could be an investigation of industry practices in terms of how tourism and fashion influencers are categorized and promoted and how brands interact with them.

PART II
FASHION(ABLE) DESTINATIONS

Chapter 5

FASHION AND TOURISM
Between Promotion and Integration

Gianluigi Di Giangirolamo
Paris 1 Panthéon-Sorbonne University, France

Abstract: This chapter explores the evolution of public and private intervention in the fashion sector in France from the end of World War II to the mid-1960s, highlighting the first connections in the relationship with tourism, a link between the two that is increasingly consolidated today and in which the mutual influence between them is becoming more relevant. For this reason, a historiographical reconstruction of the initiatives undertaken in Paris for the promotion and organization of the fashion sector is proposed. The chapter discusses the main aspects at work which shape the interconnection between fashion and tourism. **Keywords**: Fashion history; tourism history; Parisian couture; contemporary history; French fashion system; made in France

INTRODUCTION

This chapter investigates the evolution of public and private intervention in the fashion sector in France from the end of the World War II to the mid-1960s, highlighting the first connections in the relationship with the tourism industry.

Today, the link between fashion and tourism is increasingly consolidated, and the mutual influence is more relevant due to various two-way interactions. The fashion system, with its creators, fashion houses, events, communication networks, and consumers, continues to contribute to the creation and definition of places, spaces, and cities (of fashion). In this sense, fashion's link with the territory in which it develops is well-defined and relevant (Breward, 2004) and generates value in tourism practices, hence broadening the offer in the tourism industry. The tourism industry, in its

Fashion and Tourism. Parallel Stories
Tourism Social Science Series, Volume 26, 61–74

ISSN: 1571-5043/doi:10.1108/S1571-504320230000026005

turn, is a relevant element in the fashion field. Through its tools, such as itineraries, guides, and specialized magazines, fashion has contributed to the creation of fashion places and capitals since the end of the 19th century (Gilbert, 2006).

Furthermore, reference is made to the definition of "creative tourism" (Richards & Wilson, 2007) as postcultural tourism in which, on the one hand, tourists' tastes and roles vary and, on the other hand, cultural demand and the concept of culture itself expand (Friel & Peres, 2018). In that case, the practices of fashion and the cultural and creative activities are even more influential as attractors and in defining new and renewed forms of tourism (Di Giangirolamo & Mariotti, 2021).

The institutional ventures launched in France after the war led to the defense of French *haute couture* traditions. They formed the backbone of the country's fashion system – meaning the coordination of all participants, from designers to business, consumers, and local actors (Di Giangirolamo, 2020), also defining the characteristics of a sector of considerable interest and emerging relationships with the tourism industry. The coverage sheds light on organizational, institutional, and political initiatives in a historical perspective, focusing specifically on intervention strategies which, following a change in prerogatives during the years of reconstruction and economic recovery (Paladini, 2017), reflected transforming cooperation between the public and private, as well as a very first relationship between fashion and tourism in France.

Fashion ventures form a unique phenomenon which emerges from the analysis proposed in this chapter. This is from the point of view of various actions undertaken to administrate and organize the sector. Fashion's many institutions were set up with the scope of communicating business demands, coordinating those activities overarching the presentation and promotion of collections, and thus developing a management policy for the entire sector. Analyzing the French experiences after the World War II, one finds that efforts emerged after liberation from Nazi occupation in the context of the sector's unstable rebirth (Milleret, 2015). At the outset of the 1950s, Paris witnessed a vacillating recovery of the *haute couture* sector and the launch of a system of public subsidies.

In France, unified management of the fashion sector at a central level happened under the auspices of Paris's Chambre Syndicale de la Couture (Couture Trade Association) (Grumbach, 2008). This is remarkable compared, for example, to Italy, where by 1951, there were at least 13 organizations dedicated to fashion, from Venice to Palermo (Pinchera & Rinallo, 2017, p. 15).

In exploring the institutional processes of fashion and tourism, this chapter draws upon the following archival documentation: the funds kept at the *Centre des Archives Économique et Financiers* of the French Ministry for the Economy and Finance related to the public funding of Paris debates, stored at the *Bibliothèque de l'Hôtel de Ville*. From a historiographical point of view, there is a limitation. An initial investigation could not uncover the historical archives of the Chambre Syndicale in Paris, kept at the Fédération de la Haute Couture et de la Mode, which remain inaccessible.

FORMALIZATION OF FASHION AND TOURISM

The foundations of the French fashion system were laid in the second half of the 19th century (Grumbach, 2008; Milleret, 2015), with the birth of *haute couture* and establishment of the *Chambre Syndicale pour la Couture et la Confection* (Couture and Garment-Making Trade Association). This was the very first name of the trade association founded in Paris in 1868, with M. Despaigne serving as its first president. *Haute couture* was born in France in 1858, when English tailor Charles Frederick Worth set up his atelier in Rue de la Paix in Paris (Giusti, 2009). At this point, Parisian *maisons* governed the fashion system under the guidance of luminaries of women's *haute couture* who dictated the canons of elegance. Worth defined the new figure of a couturier as something more than a simple handicraftsman who relied upon technical skills alone (Belfanti, 2008). In doing so, he upset the relationship between the tailor and the client. The desires of the clientele gave way to the tailor's creativity. A creative verve developed within the *maisons*, which in Paris became real institutions (Barrère & Santagata, 2005).

On the other hand, tourism associations appeared in France in the last third of the 19th century. The most relevant in terms of numbers and means of initiative is the Touring-Club de France, created in 1890. It aimed to encourage and develop all forms of tourism unlike the Club Alpin Français, founded in 1874, or the Automobile-Club de France, created in 1895, whose actions were sectoral and whose fields of action were less extensive, the former being limited to mountain tourism, the latter to automobile tourism (Larique, 2007).

State intervention in the tourism industry dates to the beginning of the 20th century when, aware of the importance of tourism activity for national wealth, the State created the Office National du Tourisme in April 1910. It assigned two main missions to the office: first, to centralize and make available to the public information of all kinds concerning tourism in all its forms and second, to seek all the appropriate means to develop promotion (Jégouzo, 2019). The office was founded as an autonomous administrative body in charge of developing tourism in France, and it marks an important step. It symbolizes the first official intervention of the public administration in the promotion and enhancement of tourism. Nevertheless, it can be considered a resolutely innovative experiment albeit unsuccessful in the end. In fact, its life was quite short since it was abolished in 1935 (Larique, 2007).

French State Interventions in Fashion

Significant marketing efforts were needed to overcome France's isolation during the war and German occupation and redirect the attention of the international press to the accomplishments of Parisian couture and French textiles. The arrival of the Germans in Paris in summer 1940 radically changed the situation in France, toppling the Third Republic and installing the Vichy regime in its place (Veillon, 2002). However, the German occupation did not end couturiers' creative activities, which adapted to circumstances and continued producing. Even so, the number of models, quantity of fabrics, quality of materials, and even the shape of dresses themselves were modified to satisfy German restrictions (Veillon, 2002).

The Nazis aspired to destroy France's hegemony over fashion. German officials visited the headquarters of the Chambre Syndicale de la Couture Parisienne at the end of July 1940 to gather information and decipher the industry's current circumstances. The Reich revealed its intentions during a meeting the ensuing month with the chamber's president, Lucien Lelong, to transfer the chief couturiers to a designated German institution in Berlin or Vienna (Veillon, 2002). Lelong had to meet with Nazi officials many times in the ensuing years; sometimes, he needed to travel to Berlin. The Nazis' dream of transferring couture's creative center to their own capital was never accomplished, and they were forced to leave the fashion sector in Paris (Steele, 2017). "For four years we fought to preserve the place *haute couture* has always occupied in the world," Lelong declared at the end of the war (Veillon, 2002).

Following the liberation in 1945, Parisian fashion immediately returned to the international stage, thanks to the spirit of its creators and the initiative of its corporate body. The Chambre Syndicale organized an event at Paris's Museum of Decorative Arts from 28 March to April 29, 1945, which achieved such public success that it was extended until December. It was not a runway show or the presentation of models to a restricted clientele but a display of 180 dolls – between 70 and 80 cm tall – made of metal wire (Grumbach, 2008). Arranged in 14 different scenes created by renowned set designers and French theater professionals like Jean Cocteau (Veillon, 1990), the dolls were outfitted in dresses, hats, bags, and accessories designed by famed Parisian couturiers, including Fath, Lelong, and Lanvin. Organized under the artistic direction of Christian Bérard and Boris Kochno, the exhibition was entitled "Théâtre de la Mode." Its success was such that the exhibition was presented in numerous cities across the globe, from London to Copenhagen and from Rio de Janeiro to New York. The creations sparked admiration and helped Paris to demonstrate that the war had not compromised the talent of its couturiers. Lelong said of the venture, "this is Paris and nothing but Paris: this theatre of fashion! Its smile, its courage, its spirit, its allure" (Veillon, 2002).

The French government sought to regulate the couture sector by classifying those enterprises active in *couture-création* (Di Giangirolamo, 2018). This approach was adopted during the war for the distribution of raw materials (Grumbach, 2008) and later formalized in the decrees 45–147 of January 29, 1945, and June 30, 1947 (JORF July 18, 1947). These defined a series of precise, rigorous rules for *maisons* to abide by, subject to inspection by an ad hoc *couture-création* classification commission. The commission's recognition was crucial to enabling a company to carry out its work. Indeed, only those who had earned the classification could employ the terms *couturier, haute couture, so* or *couture-création* (Milleret, 2015).

To earn this classification, fashion houses had to present original models for garments, internally conceived and created, at least twice a year in Paris. They had to produce a new collection for the spring–summer and autumn–winter seasons. Fashion shows were to be scheduled in the timeframe established by the Chambre Syndicale (FEPTHCP [1950–1952 A]). The garments needed to be produced by the company itself according to buyer specifications. For this reason, the creative process had to include one or more fittings on the client or mannequin. Models could then be reproduced and sold directly or indirectly to French and foreign businesses (FEPTHCP [1950–1952 A]).

Haute couture flourished in the postwar period. Parisian couturiers reconquered such international renown with their models that one can speak of as a golden age (Steele, 2017) of Parisian *haute couture*. Christian Dior, who leapt to the international stage in 1947 with the New Look, is a classic example. Dior's sales soared from 1.2 million francs in 1947 to 12.2 million in 1949 (Milleret, 2015). French *haute couture*'s success rested on fragile foundations, however. Fourteen *maisons* were forced to close between 1947 and 1951.

Paris Couture, Defense of a Tradition

The need for both political and economic action on the part of the government soon became clear in France. The Council of Paris expressed this urgency in March 1948 (BMO, April 8, 1948). Both communist and *Rensemblent du Peuple Francais* councilmen requested that the prefect of the department of Seine-et-Oise sponsor official measures to promote *haute couture* in French trade deals and support efforts to expand Parisian fashion in foreign markets (BMO, April 8, 1948). From the national government's point of view, weak *haute couture* exports at once reflected the costliness of *maisons* creations and the nature of this type of enterprise, which was incapable of generating large quantities of sales in the form of exports. Nonetheless, the Ministry of Industry and Commerce set to work researching solutions to aid Parisian couturiers, supported by national and international organizations engaged in the fight against design theft, with the ultimate aim of regulating relations between design creators and reproducers through sales contracts (BMO, June 26, 1948).

Despite the international fame of names like Dior, Balenciaga, and Givenchy, rebuilding the French luxury fashion industry at the outset of the 1950s was a struggle. Professional representatives were forced to request financial assistance from the government (FEPTHCP [1950–1952 B]). A Chambre Syndicale analysis revealed that no matter how efficient their management, most couture *maisons* were unable to amortize the high costs of their collections while lowering the sales price of their models, as markets demanded. They estimated that the average design cost 100,000–120,000 francs (€3,120–3,750) to produce, for an overall cost to all *maisons* of 960 million francs (€30 million). Each year, the Parisian fashion houses presented about 8,000 models for the spring and winter collections, in addition to the midseason summer and autumn collections. Such production costs could only be sustained by an estimated 9.5 billion francs (€300 million) in sales, yet the industry's revenue amounted to only 4.5 billion (€140 million) at the time (FEPTHCP (1950–1952 C)).

One potential solution – lowering the quality or number of garments created – was rejected as endangering the reputation and tradition of French design. To avoid this, about 500 million francs (€15,600,000) in funding were needed (FEPTHCP (1950–1952 C)). Chambre Syndicale decided to request a system of subsidies amounting to an estimated 450–500 million francs (€15–14 million) from the national government. In February 1950, it drafted a proposal for a project entitled *Projet d'action à mener pour assurer la* "survie" *des industries de mode parisienne* (Action plan to ensure the "survival" of the Parisian fashion industries) (FEPTHCP [1950–1952 B]). The proposal argued that the research and creativity behind *haute couture* and fashion design could drive the development of the consumer goods sector at large. The Chambre Syndicale judged it crucial to not only maintain but preferably increase the quality of output among Parisian fashion houses (FEPTHCP [1950–1952 C]). Indeed, *haute couture* represented a laboratory of innovation, experimentation, and creativity, able to inspire the production of mass-produced fashion targeted at an expanding market (Riello, 2012). All of this, in the chamber's point of view, would incentivize the development of the rest of the consumer goods sector.

On August 1, 1951, Chambre Syndicale president Raymond Barbas submitted his request for subsidization of the *couture-création* sector to the government (FEPTHCP [1950–1952 C]). He proposed using the 1945 *couture-création* classification system to select among those enterprises that wished to access public funds. In addition to earning the *couture-création* classification, *maisons* participating in the subsidy program had to purchase at least 90% of their fabrics from French producers and could not receive other public subsidies.

The criteria for splitting public aid centered on the number of created and registered models, from a minimum of 60 to a maximum of 125 per season, and on total consumption of French fabrics. Grant money was allocated according to *création* points, each worth 1,350 francs (€42). Fifteen points were awarded for each presented design, and five for each tranche of fabrics employed amounting to 20,000 francs (€625). Finally, each fashion house had to keep its registers up-to-date to certify its right to access *création* points (FEPTHCP [1950–1952 C]).

The French textile sector participated directly in the plan proposed to the government.

Management of financial funds was entrusted to the *Union des Industries Textiles* (Textile Manufacturers Union), which was to ensure their distribution adhered to the guidelines laid out by the *couture-création* classification commission (FEPTHCP [1950–1952 C]). A January 11, 1952, letter from UIT president Philippe Roy to the Minister of Finance testified to how vital government financing was for industry representatives. Roy affirmed that public aid was indispensable to safeguarding *haute couture*, itself of fundamental importance to shaping the French textile's unique character. This was an emergency: without financial support, the creation of collections could no longer honor the traditions of Parisian couture. Another key aspect for Roy was promotion. In the letter, he proposed supplementing the plan with an additional 100 million francs (€2,400,000) from the Textile Manufacturers Union and 100 million (€2,400,000) from the "Fund for Textile Production" to be invested in advertising campaigns in France and abroad. He affirmed,

> There again, marketing efforts are needed to create in the customer the desire and need to dress the right way, as her circumstances permit, and to remedy a crisis in consumption that has already led to the most deleterious effects for the textile industry and manpower (FEPTHCP 1950–1952, D).

Roy's arguments underlined not only the irrefutable interest of professional industry associations in nurturing demand for French textiles but the will to safeguard the creativity and originality of Parisian *haute couture*. France's cultural heritage and *savoir faire* were endangered by the transformation of consumption habits and markets.

As the analysis of the sources reveals, the Chambre Syndicale's ultimate aim was to preserve the tangible and intangible heritage of Parisian couture, especially the practices and *savoir faire* endangered by the evolution of markets and industry. It provided financial assistance to those companies that enacted, within their own ateliers, practices that characterized and shaped French *haute couture*, defined as an "immense laboratory of creation [...] irreplaceable organism of promotion for national creations" (FEPTHCP [1950–1952 B]), in essence, an inheritance that is central even today to producing creativity. In this sense, the heritage of the past plays almost as essential a role in the organization and performance of the fashion system as in its development (Barrère & Santagata, 2005).

Funding Program

The act formalizing the aid program was signed on July 24, 1952 by the Minister of Industry and Commerce, Minister of Finance, president of the Textile Manufacturers Union, and president of the Chambre Syndicale (FEPTHCP [1950–1952 E]). The stipulated agreement was born of *haute couture*'s strategic importance for the textile sector and French economy, in general; a grant of 300 million francs (€7,200,000) was provided through a "special fund to encourage textile production." Financing provided to the Union of Textile Manufacturers could be used to pay for the execution of Parisian *maisons* collections and publicity and administrative expenses.

The state subsidy program was open only to couture businesses headquartered in and around the city of Paris, classified as *maisons couture-création*, that had presented a collection of at least 60 original models for three consecutive seasons. The official act evidenced the public and private sphere's interest in defending and developing *haute couture*.

The French government's subsidization of Parisian *haute couture maisons* began in 1952. The Chambre Syndicale and Textile Manufacturers Union collaborated for almost 10 years to ensure its renewal until 1960. A subsidy program was launched to help a scenario that in the early 1950s saw the disappearance of *maisons,* such as Lucien Lelong, Molyneux, Robert Piguet, and Marcelle Dormoy, each with 150–400 employees. Despite this attempt, in many cases, the subsidies only served to prolong the agony of companies already in financial difficulty.

Over the program's first three years, some of the most important Parisian *maisons*, famed across the globe, disappeared. Marcelle Chaumont closed in 1952; Agnès Drecoll, Jeanne Lafaurie, Callot Soeurs, and Marcel Rochas in 1953. The Schiaparelli house shut down its couture activities the following year. Numerous other companies joined the great *maisons* in being unable to carry forth their work. The Chambre Syndicale saw 362 companies close in three years, destroying 1,200 jobs in *haute couture* (FEPTHCP [1953–1954 A]). From 1953 to 1959, 19 *maisons* failed despite receiving state assistance (FEPTHCP [1959–1961 A]). On the other hand, the sources testify to a restructuring of the Chambre Syndicale's services, with the institution of offices dedicated to propaganda and national- and international-level protective measures. In 1959, the chamber set up an internal office dedicated to publicity, promotion, and the protection of French couture design.

Another important element of the Chambre Syndicale's new strategy was the opening of a representative office in New York to publicize French fashion in the American market. The Chambre Syndicale's board voted to commission an in-depth survey of the American market from New York's Gottlieb firm on September 13, 1957. The result was a four-volume report. This work, together with the Gottlieb agency's own inclusions, led the Chambre Syndicale to open an office in New York. The new branch had the task of defending Parisian couture's American interests and taking all necessary steps to drive up sales of French models in the American market (FEPTHCP [1958–1959]).

In order to establish the personal contacts that would be indispensable for carrying out promotional activities in the United States, Jacques Heim, a prominent fashion entrepreneur and president of the Chambre Syndicale, together with two associates, organized a trip to New York in September 1958. They met with numerous retail store managers, representatives from the most important clothing companies, journalists, and notable figures like Gotshal, a legal expert in intellectual property rights and commercial advisor to the French embassy. A series of marketing initiatives was born out of these meetings, including, for example, seasonal vacation packages to introduce American buyers to Parisian couture.

On the commercial side, a "passeport-couture" was designed for buyers, intended to strengthen commercial ties between couture and its American clients, or at least facilitate relations between buyers and couturiers. Chambre president Heim may certainly be considered a leading actor in the ideation of stateside marketing activities. In fact, he presented a proposal for numerous Parisian couture events in the key cities of the American market for the year 1960. He envisaged presenting 50 models from the autumn–winter collection to major American cities over the course of September. His objective was to bring French couture products directly to the American public and strengthen France's reputation as an international fashion leader.

Christened "Manifestations Parisienne en Amérique," the events were organized with the support of the Gottlieb agency. The firm was responsible for selecting a group of high-ranking individuals and involving them in the organization of social events such as charity balls during Parisian fashion events. The agency partnered with French governmental representatives to establish contacts with each city's foremost fashion figures. To ensure the events' success, local players – from owners of the most famous boutiques to the media – had to be engaged in the effort. The Chambre Syndicale in Paris was tasked with selecting the best designs and models to present. The fashion show presenter had to be chosen with care: someone well-known in the fashion world and able to speak on behalf of Parisian couture during press interviews. Events were immediately scheduled for four cities: Chicago, Philadelphia, Boston, and Cincinnati. The Gottlieb agency also planned to organize future events in New York, Houston, and San Francisco (FEPTHCP [1959–1961 B]).

New Forms of Promotions

Beyond the industry's close link with textile production, *haute couture* had a vital impact on different sectors of the national economy and in creating the image of Paris we are still familiar with today. *Haute couture*'s commercial activity consisted in selling the right to reproduce its models to tailors, shops, and dressmakers, both in France and abroad; beyond this, *maisons* produced exclusive custom-made garments in their ateliers for French and – to an even greater extent – foreign customers. Indeed, two very distinct types of buyers acquired *couture-création*.

The direct purchase of "made-to-measure" women's clothing by private clientele formed the basis of *maisons*' traditional activity. Foreign customers maintained the habit of traveling to Paris for the specific purpose of having dresses made into the 1950s and 1960s, although this type of demand was in decline (FEPTHCP (1959–1961) C).

Professional buyers were the second type of customer. They traveled to Paris to purchase numerous reproductions for resale in boutiques and department stores until the end of the 1930s. Then, thanks to the development of the clothing industry, the purchasing system began to evolve. Though buyers attended presentations and fashion shows, in most cases, they were interested in buying the rights to models to be mass-produced elsewhere (FEPTHCP [1954–1955]). This marketing system meant that each season, Parisian couture collections attracted buyers from 35 countries around the world in the early 1950s: the directors and managers of international companies in the clothing sector and department stores which wanted to see the new collections and trends firsthand (FEPTHCP [1953–1954 B]). This flow of buyers clearly benefited different sectors of French industry, among them surely those of services and tourism.

Buyers who went to Paris to see the couture collections were also consumers of other categories of production, such as textiles, lace, trimming, hats, and women's accessories. Department stores representatives, in particular, bought various types of products uncorrelated with the couture industry. The *haute couture* presentations also boosted consumption in the service sector. The increase in demand for transportation, hotels, entertainment, and other local services by thousands of foreign tourists cannot be overlooked. It was estimated in 1958 that spillovers from couture generated 10 billion francs (€195 millions) per year in profits for the tourism industry. Further, the increase in spending during seasonal presentations yielded higher tax revenue for the French government (FEPTHCP [1959–1961 C]).

Fashion Promoting Tourism

As it is true for the fashion industry from 1950s onward, the economy in France became an essential driving force for innovation: product innovation, which was at once technical, economic, and sociocultural; organizational innovation through the new forms of public–private linkage that were implemented; and marketing innovation through the perpetual construction of the consumer's desire for spaces of distinction. This recognition of the economic, social, and spatial importance of tourism, and even its institutionalization, contributed to the originality of the French development model (Bouneau, 2007). For this reason, at the end of the 1950s, a formal establishment by the government for the tourism industry was needed. Preceded by the creation in July 1959 of an Interministerial Committee for Tourism, the official recognition of the tourism industry was consecrated in 1962 by the establishment of a Commissariat for Tourism, under the direct authority of the Prime Minister (Bouneau, 2007). In this context, what emerges from the analysis of the sources is the awareness of a strong relationship between tourism and fashion and the need of pursuing a common action of promotion.

Thanks to the appeal it held to the international press, Parisian couture was an undoubtedly effective promotional channel for Paris and France. A study by the Chambre Syndicale found that the most prominent women's magazines worldwide dedicated several pages, if not entire special issues, to Parisian couture twice a year. All major newspapers, weeklies, and monthlies devoted significant space to Parisian fashion. For this reason, numerous foreign journalists, photographers, correspondents, and fashion experts traveled to the French capital in February and August for the runway collections. In 1953, reporters from 245 accredited newspapers and 296 correspondents (FEPTHCP [1953–1954 B]) attended from all over the world, figures which doubled in 1958 to more than a 1000 foreign press officers and journalists from 448 newspapers and magazines, together with radio and television network employees (FEPTHCP [1959–1961 C]). The events ultimately represented a massive marketing campaign for France and its capital. Each year, references in the world press to Parisian couture numbered in the millions (FEPTHCP [1953–1954 B]). It was first among all French entrepreneurial activities in influence and renown.

For Jacques Heim, joint industry, tourism, and promotional action were needed. He envisioned a tourism marketing campaign unlike any yet conceived in France, coordinated by a designated governmental body. Heim's primary objective was to attract an elite clientele to Paris, which would, in turn, encourage the development of mass tourism (FEPTHCP [1959–1961 C]).

Parisian institutions followed the example of several foreign countries in partnering with industry organizations to plan events welcoming buyers and press officers to the city. The city council organized a reception in their honor in 1953. The following year, the Chambre Syndicale established a special buyer service with the objective of fostering relationships that could translate into expanded trade (FEPTHCP [1959–1961 C]). The service grew over time, receiving a dedicated area of the Bois de Boulogne in 1958 and the Hippodrome de Vincennes in 1959, which hosted over 1,200 participants. A mean of 16.9% of the state subsidies, or 259 million francs in total, was dedicated to promotional activities during this period (FEPTHCP [1959–1961 A]). A large share of this was used by the Chambre Syndicale to set up marketing and press offices. Since 1952, 100 million francs (€195,000) had been allocated to buyer receptions and gala evenings in cities, such as Cannes, Nice, and St. Moritz, as well as to print publications, radio, and television.

It is evident from promotional plans that French designs were presented in numerous cities and countries. Examples include tours in South America and Scandinavia, French Weeks in London and Dallas, and international events like the Brussels World's Fair. Most of the funding was used to cover transportation and lodging costs for organizers and models and to finance *haute couture* events like a debutante ball held at the Versailles Orangerie in 1959 (FEPTHCP [1959–1961 A]).

The Chambre Syndicale's marketing service was carefully structured and placed under the direction of an executive committee known as the *Bureau Executif de Propagande* (FEPTHCP [1959–1961 A]). A larger promotional department coordinated the marketing, press, and intellectual property offices. This department, internal to the Chambre, determined the seasonal schedule and corresponding budget. It was responsible for cultivating relationships with the New York office, embassies, French commercial advisors abroad, the Permanent Committee of International Trade Fairs and Events, as well as institutional relations with the various ministries. The press office performed several tasks involving interaction with press officers and public relations. Each season, it drew up lists of all French and foreign newspapers and radio and television stations with Chambre Syndicale accreditation granted by sending a special form, translated into five languages.

Admission to haute couture events for press officers was regulated by a pass system. A "carte presse-couture" was created for journalists. Independent photographers and journalists were granted a special permit provided they were Paris residents registered in the commercial or professional register or representing a magazine or news agency specialized in fashion. The promotional department's press office established the schedule of spring–summer and fall–winter runway shows and then disseminated it to the press, buyers, textile organizations, and French commercial advisors abroad. The Chambre Syndicale press service's other responsibility was public relations. It ran an information office dedicated to authorized personnel, which received 2,000–3,000 visits yearly (FEPTHCP [1959–1961 A]).

The Chambre Syndicale's intellectual property and economic studies office had the mission of protecting designs and safeguarding *maison* interests. *Haute couture* creators and entrepreneurs were central to the effort to protect designs and logos and supervise buyers and contracts. One of the office's most important activities was the fight against counterfeiting; to this end, it set up couture model depositories in France and Bern, where *the Bureaux Internationaux Réunis pour la Protection de la Propriété Intellectuelle* was founded in 1893 following the Convention for the Protection of Literary and Artistic Works (Ricketson, 2017).

The Bureaux Internationaux Réunis pour la Protection de la Propriété Intellectuelle provided a surveillance service that conducted investigations and reported persons to be monitored or refused entrance to runway shows; it also dealt with complaints and cooperated in police and customs investigations. The protection of brand names and logos entailed monitoring abusive brands and acting abroad to defend the use of designations such as "Champs-Elysées-Paris" or against the use of symbols like the Eiffel Tower, which could create ambiguity regarding an item's origin and endanger the reputation of Parisian fashion (FEPTHCP [1959–1961 A]). In such a context, this confirms the link between the symbolic spaces of the city and the fashion product itself.

CONCLUSION

The coverage of this chapter spans the period from 1945 to the mid-1960s which concluded in the end of public subsidization of *haute couture* and the launch of new forms of promotion in France. During these two decades, it is possible to identify several touchstones in public and private initiatives related to the fashion industry, linked to a first involvement of tourism that emerges from the analysis of the sources.

In particular, the study of the Parisian case reveals the peculiarities of the French experience, based on centralized interventions, able to recover from the halt imposed by war to once more dominate the international scene. This has been the case, for example, in the development and study of relations with the American market, from which initiatives have emerged that have a strong link with tourism, such as seasonal vacation packages to introduce American buyers to Parisian couture at the end of the 1950s. At the same time, what emerges from the sources is the involvement of local authorities in the awareness of the relevant role of fashion presentations, particularly in the tourism industry, and contributing to the definition of Paris as a world-class tourism destination. This is an initial reconstruction of the links between fashion and tourism and is intended to allow a broadening of the historical and scientific debate on the definition and relationship of these two empowered industries.

Note for the conversion in euros: The conversion in euros is based on the purchasing power of a sum en France francs of a given year into an equivalent sum in euros in 2022, adjusted for the inflation observed between the two years. In addition to inflation, the converter takes into account the change from old francs to new francs in 1960 and the change from francs to euros in 2002 (1 € = 6.55957 FF). *Source:* https://www.insee.fr/fr/information/2417794.

ARCHIVE SOURCES

Journal Officiel de la République Française (*Official Journal of the French Republic*)

- JORF July 18, 1947 *Décision du ministère de l'industrie et du commerce* V.I.A. 29.

Bulletin Municipal Officiel de la Ville de Paris (*Official Municipal Bulletin of the City of Paris*)

- BMO, April 8, 1948, Council of Paris, meeting of March 25, 1948.
- BMO, June 26, 1948, Council of Paris, meeting of June 15, 1948.

Centre des Archives Économique et Financiers (*Centre of Economic and Financial Archives*)

FEPTHCP: Fonds d'encouragement à la production textile à la Haute Couture Parisienne (*Fund to Encourage Textile Production for Parisian Haute Couture*)

- FEPTHCP (1950–1952) A, *Classification Couture Creation.*
- FEPTHCP (1950–1952) B, *Project d'action à mener pour assurer la "survie" des industries de mode parisienne.*
- FEPTHCP (1950–1952) C, *Demande de subvention de la couture-création.*
- FEPTHCP (1950–1952) D, *Lettre de Philippe Roy Président de l'UIT à M. Labry Secrétaire d'Etat aux Finances et aux Affaires Economiques, January 11, 1952.*
- FEPTHCP (1950–1952) E, *Aide à la création-couture parisienne. Convention.*
- FEPTHCP (1953–1954) A, *Note concernant la situation de la couture parisienne, March 24, 1954.*
- FEPTHCP (1953–1954) B, *Influence Internationale de la couture parisienne.*
- FEPTHCP (1954–1955), Sans titre.
- FEPTHCP (1958–1959), *Rapport sur les activités aux Etas Unis.*
- FEPTHCP (1959–1961) A, *Note sur les subventions à la haute couture parisienne.*
- FEPTHCP (1959–1961) B, *Projet de "Manifestations de la couture parisienne" dans les ville-clefs du marché américain.*
- FEPTHCP (1959–1961) C, *Note sur le Plan d'Aide, May 30, 1960.*

Chapter 6

FASHION HERITAGE DESTINATIONS
The Twist of Tradition in Modernity

Puspita Ayu Permatasari
Breda University of applied sciences, Netherlands

Faruq Ibnul Haqi
University of South Australia, Australia

Fitri Utami Ningrum
University of Indonesia, Indonesia

Triana Rosalina Dewi
Trisakti Institute of Tourism Jakarta, Indonesia

Abstract: From Batik cities to woven textile regions, Indonesia possesses several fashion destinations with remarkable textile heritage. The rise of fashion heritage destinations is characterized by avid textile lovers and fashion followers that promote the regions. Several diversifications of tourism alternatives are analyzed, such as rural tourism with experiential textile-making workshops, urban destinations connected to contemporary fashion heritage, architectural works inspired from/to textile heritage, as well as fashion week cities that spark the interests of global fashion designers to visit the country. This chapter evaluates the current

Fashion and Tourism: Parallel Stories
Tourism Social Science Series, Volume 26, 75–92

Published under exclusive licence by Emerald Publishing Limited
ISSN: 1571-5043/doi:10.1108/S1571-504320230000026006

state, its rising challenges, and to what extent it may be promoted through digital technologies, based on local practitioners and the governmental perspectives. **Keywords**: Intangible cultural heritage; destination branding; textile heritage; fashion heritage destination; musealization; textile cultural routes

INTRODUCTION

United Nations Educational, Scientific, and Cultural Organization (UNESCO) recognizes intangible cultural heritage as a living tradition whose cultural practices are acknowledged and preserved by the community(ies) and transmitted from generation to generation (UNESCO, 2019). Fashion is a domain where the tangible and intangible elements of textile are manifested. The two dimensions are seen both from the cultural meanings contained in its symbols affect or affected by the society (pattern, design wearing rules), as well as the cultural practices and the knowledge within its production (Kalbaska, Sádaba, & Cantoni, 2018b; Permatasari & Kalbaska, 2022; Sikarskie, 2016). The word "fashion" comes from the Latin word *facere* and *façon* in the Old French, which means "to make, the way to do" (Barnard, 1996 cited in Kawamura, 2018). Since the 15th century, "fashion" is adopted as an English word, addressing the usages of dress (Kawamura, 2018), prevailing custom, the process of making, and a mode of life. This concept widens the notion of fashion heritage as a way to describe the integration of traditional textiles into contemporary fashion.

Known for its ethnic diversity, Indonesia possesses a rich intangible cultural heritage in form of textile that is strongly valorized in all its 34 regions. Indonesian textile is classified into three types, "batik as" wax-resist dyeing textile (UNESCO, 2009), "tenun" woven textile and Papuan "noken" woven textile (UNESCO, 2012). Traditional textile is seen as an intergenerational vehicle of cultural values, which are maintained by the community through practice and strong adherence to its wearing rules in various social contexts. As an element of the cultural landscape, textile heritage possesses devoted meanings in all levels of Indonesian society, for which its diversity brings color to the fashion characteristic of each region (Permatasari & Cantoni, 2019a). The presence of textile-making tradition in each region improves the development of local creative industries, especially fashion, while at the same time, enriching tourism offers that add value to the cultural attractions of rural areas (Hengky, 2015).

The historical connection between places and textile production creates opportunities to develop cultural tourism offers that go beyond the place of origin of fashion products (Bellini & Pasquinelli, 2016). Cultural experience, such as the way textile heritage is produced, becomes one of the essential elements from a tourism perspective. The question lies in how to interpret the urban ecosystem of the cultural destination where the textile producers and tourism stakeholders synergize into a creative nucleus. Cultural villages and cultural activities, such as textile-making attract tourists to live, engage in the traditional activities like locals, as well as to participate in the cause that brings benefit to the local communities (Jonathan & Tarigan, 2016). Leveraging on the textile heritage, a region may develop tourism offers that strongly depend on its creative industry, such as textile craftsmanship and fashion, in order to deliver authentic meaningful experiences for the tourists (Bellini & Pasquinelli, 2016). The relationship established between fashion heritage, region, and the city contributes to boosting innovative value creation and the experiential level of a cultural destination (Permatasari & Kalbaska, 2022; Pasquinelli, 2013).

In light of promoting textile heritage safeguarding and tourism valorization, iWareBatik digital technology was launched in 2020 as a result of an international collaboration between the Indonesian government and USI UNESCO Chair in Switzerland. Presented in a form of a website and artificial intelligence (AI)-powered mobile application, iWareBatik serves as a main online source of Indonesia's textile culture for domestic and international audiences (Figure 6.1). It illustrates the richness of textile culture, its singularities, and its origin along with other tourism destinations in 34 Indonesian regions (Garuda, 2020). This public initiative increased the participation of local stakeholders, especially the young generations, to actively engage in iWareBatik online campaigns on the socialization of textile culture preservation at local destinations, conducted through Instagram social media. Several educational workshops, participated by 997 students from 33 Indonesian universities, in the period from August to October 2021 have led to the attention of Indonesian education stakeholders nationwide in order to raise people's awareness of local identity and to support sustainable

Figure 6.1. The Interface of www.iwarebatik.org and iWareBatik Mobile App (iWareBatik, 2020a, b, c; Permatasari, 2022).

valorization of regions' creative sector and rural tourism (iwarebatik, 2021; Permatasari, Ningrum, Uriawan, & Cantoni, 2023).

The emergence of fashion heritage destinations in Indonesia can be analyzed through the actor-network theory (Elbanna, 2009). This theoretical framework defines a phenomenon by which a large scale of the network, comprising multilevels of stakeholders, depicts heterogeneous connections and involves collaborations between human and nonhuman actors. The mobilization of each actor toward the short- and common long-term objectives is influential to transcending an urban space along with its subsisting values (Wang, 2019). This chapter examines the local actors and the interplay among fashion, heritage, and tourism, as those elements lead to the rise of fashion heritage destinations. Wang (2019) identified multifaceted networks contributing to the preservation of batik's intangible cultural heritage through education in the creative city of Pekalongan. The study also outlines an overview of the emergence of fashion heritage destinations in Indonesia from the perspective of the local government, which serves as a preliminary study of the Indonesian context.

From batik cities to woven textile regions, this study highlights several case studies on tourism offers emerging through the promotion of fashion heritage destinations based on literature, interviews, and online content analysis of fashion heritage-related events. Several cases of diversification of tourism offers are analyzed, such as rural tourism with experiential workshops of batik and woven textile-making, and festival cities as urban destinations (Gravari-Barbas, 2009). They are connected to fashion heritage, architectural works inspired from/to textile heritage, as well as fashion week cities (Kalbaska, Ramírez, & Cantoni, 2018) that spark the interests of global fashion designers to visit the country. Most of the existing research outlines cultural destinations and creative industries in Indonesia. This chapter investigates the rise of fashion heritage destinations explained from the local perspectives, such as practitioners, existing heritage, communities and the government support, both seen from literature and its publication outlet.

FASHION HERITAGE AND TOURISM

Fashion heritage refers to the valorization of cultural heritage in forms of traditional textile in fashion (Permatasari & Kalbaska, 2022). It is elaborated into the notion that fashion involves any fabrics embodying sociocultural values related to the intangible cultural heritage, which is recognized and practiced by the community as a way to preserve their cultural tradition. Besides its reputation as one of the top 10 global clothing exporters (Lu, 2019), Indonesia leverages in supporting and promoting its millennial textile tradition through tourism and fashion activities (Permatasari & Cantoni, 2019b). Considering the importance of the fashion industry in the landscape of the national creative economy, the valorization of textile heritage has become one of the priorities and is supported by the national government (MTEC, 2021b).

Pike (2011) asserts that a complex network of associations of sites, people, and cultural institutions composing products and services constitute "reputational assets" of the city. Brand origin can be classified on a smaller scale, such as the "region of origin" or "city of origin." The word "origin" is not only a geographical term that signifies where the product comes from (Pasquinelli, 2017). As the batik producers reside and regroup in different places in the region, local brands developed by small and medium enterprises (SMEs) and textile artisans from the region amplify the reputation of the place or city as a fashion destination. Pasquinelli (2014) asserts that the city and its associated local fashion brands merge as collective brands. This collectivity forms a complex network, composed of products, spaces, organizations, and involved stakeholders. Referring to Thakor and Kohli (1996), a cultural destination can be known as a brand origin where it is perceived to belong. Taking the example of batik and tenun woven textile as fashion heritage, its unique representation (motifs, pattern, etc.) that are varied from region to region, might be of influence to boost the tourism branding of a destination. The singularities within textile heritage production make this form of cultural heritage become an effective medium to promote the regions as cultural destinations. Indeed, the interplay of cultural assets and tourism branding further impacts public diplomacy (Anholt, 2005). This led to the implementation of the Indonesian national policy, which is established to achieve global leverage on tourism, heritage preservation, and creative industry.

As traveling activities imply different meanings to different social groups, tourists' objectives are mostly connected to personal needs for self-expression, self-image, and personality (Arnoud & Thompson, 2005; Branch, 2011). The brand-new life experience, affecting self-images and personal growth obtained from tourism experience in contemporary society, supports the formation of a symbolic economy or an economy of signs (Lash & Urry, 1993). Cultural cities provide memorable tourism experiences through products and services. While exploring the cultural richness of the creative cities, tourists tend to seek products with high symbolic and memorable meanings as a piece of memory to take back home. Commercial exchange is one of the mediums where they obtain a passive cultural experience during their stay at the destination (Richards, 2014). City and its creative expression play an important role as a "place of affect," which is incorporated within the product experience (Thrift, 2004). In this regard, sustainable destination branding emphasizes on the functional, experiential, and symbolic dimensions of the place.

The original values and meanings, as manifested through existing cultural, social, natural, and economic dimensions of local communities, shall be addressed at the first place to maintain authenticity of the destination (Gnoth, 2007). The symbolic relationships between fashion workshops and cities build a value ecosystem that nurtures mutual associations of the place of origin (city), products, fashion firms/workshops, and people (Pasquinelli, 2013). Furthermore, some cultural cities, with a strong presence of fashion heritage, attempt to boost their regional tourism attraction and rebuild their branding through ephemeral fashion weeks and textile museums (Kalbaska, Ramírez, & Cantoni, 2018a).

Cultural Expression in Textile Heritage and Creative Cities

The interplay of heritage and creativity creates a hybrid cultural industry, which serves as a strategy that operates at all levels of the fashion supply chain, from design creation and production to communication. The living components of fashion as cultural heritage are incorporated within the synergy of the traditional ateliers, the know-how or le *savoir-faire*, archival inventories, community producers, and imaginaries, both in terms of narration and sartorial presentation (Pistilly, 2018). In this way, the valorization of textile heritage starts from drawing inspirations from local identity and the story behind the textile to *la mise en scène* (staging) of these qualities in visual and written communication. The interplay of heritage and creativity can be seen from elaborating immaterial elements of tradition as symbolical and cultural manifestations. With creativity as a new agent, the fusion sets a linkage, connecting its social significance in the past with its current usage values in the present and the future.

While fashion and its valorization activities enter the tourism domain, this multi-sectoral symbiosis leads to the development of creative cities. Through the exhibition and cultural events, creative cities offer experiential learning activities by discovering city history and its linkage between the past and present time. Creative tourism provides opportunities for individuals to boost and enrich creative minds in an array of cultural activities (Richards, 2014). Thanks to the presence of textile heritage villages and galleries, Indonesian creative cities widen their tourism offer spectrums and shift as emerging shopping destinations (Chan, Alexandri, & Tresna, 2019).

The creative collaboration of local actors to capitalize on their traditional public events serves as a key factor in new urban space development (Gravari-Barbas, 2009). The frequent events of rituals, parades, harvest festivals, and contemporary urban activities bring on enormous tangible and intangible investments that further shape and progress the city. From public to private entities, these urban events embrace all levels of society, triggering new thinking, and building a new paradigm to produce innovative concepts of contemporary cities with sustainable tourism objectives (Cazes, 1997). Many Indonesian destinations shift to be festival and creative cities, thanks to the active cultural initiatives and fashion heritage celebrations events. Those ephemeral events and the spectacular nature of organizations contribute to improving the negative reputation and image of a destination, from a marginal societal space into a thriving economic society (Gravari-Barbas, 2009).

Experiential Hub of Fashion and Tourism

Fashion destination signifies places where the relationship between geographical location and fashion as a creative industry spurs the connectivity of designers and the shopping places (Breward & Gilbert, 2006). Textile heritage business chains might serve parallel roles, one as the supply of the fashion industry and the other as an experiential hub for value creation integrated within urban tourism. Since the very beginning, fashion heritage and places of origin continuously shape symbolic associations of the local community, artifacts, and the way of living. This symbolic association is continuously carried within the evolution and development of a region into an urban space (Pasquinelli, 2017). The new insight obtained along the ancient routes associated with the textile heritage form a novel narration and the interpretation of the textile culture.

Textile heritage meets the objectives of tourism and fashion purposes through its intrinsic and extrinsic usage values (Permatasari & Kalbaska, 2022). The spatial aspects of fashion products lie in the process of shaping geographical associations within the production, circulation, consumption, and management (Pasquinelli, 2017; Pike, 2011). The production of textile heritage entails certain spatial circuits of meanings and values that are circulated inside the region. The stipulation of the "one village one product" movement in Indonesia since 2008 encourages further the diversification of local products (Saroso & Fauzi, 2013). This practice is an Indonesian public policy that encourages stakeholders engaged in creative sectors at rural level to produce textile motifs based on the local characteristics. This policy was launched with the aim of promoting local products and developing regional economics through collective collaboration among government, business entities, and local artisans. Traditional textiles created within each region possess distinguished characteristics and local wisdom, making them deserving to obtain national recognition (MOI, 2020). The typical nature of textile heritage meets the key criteria for the "one village one product" nomination in terms of "cultural uniqueness and authenticity." In an attempt to integrate the local excellence into tourism offers, the spatial circuits of batik and other textile heritage production are identified and woven into cultural routes. These intercity or interregional connections allow the involving regions associated with textile traditions to become the hub of creative business and cultural destinations.

Pasquinelli (2013) proposes that fashion heritage destinations shall meet three elements: the contribution of fashion brands (or textile heritage products) as part of the city's heritage; the incorporation of architecture and/or artworks in venues related to fashion; and the establishment of cultural institutions of the city dedicated to textile art, such as musealization creating an experiential connection between fashion product and the city. Additional categories may complement the above-stated principles, such as frequent public events related to fashion and textile, like parades, carnivals, fashion weeks (Gravari-Barbas, 2009; Kalbaska et al., 2018b), and cultural routes in relation to textile heritage production incorporating workshop centers such as batik/tenun village, textile community center, and more (Permatasari, 2016; Santoso, 2019; Wang, 2019).

Case Studies

Reflecting on the importance of fashion and tourism within the atmosphere of textile heritage safeguarding and valorization, the way a tourism site meets the criteria of a fashion heritage destination is discussed in this session. According to Pasquinelli (2013), fashion destination is an emerging cultural destination, whose developments are mostly contributed by frequent promotional collaboration between fashion firms and local tourism. In order to better understand the current development carried out within the fashion heritage destinations, this study collected primary information based on a literature review (Tseëlon, 2015) in combination with qualitative and quantitative methodology.

Several case studies were obtained from the series of ethnographic field research, respectively conducted in Madura Island of East Java province in 2016 and Central Java province (Lasem and Solo city) in 2018. In September 2020, virtual interviews were conducted with a number of Indonesian heritage and tourism stakeholders, including a tour guide, batik artisans, batik gallery owners, a batik curator, cultural tourism activists, a consultant working in the Ministry of Tourism, and representatives of rural art centers. From April to June 2020, the study quantitatively analyzed each official Destination Management Organization's websites of 34 Indonesian provinces in order to investigate the online contents with regard to the promotional activities of fashion heritage–related events. The online content analysis aimed at mapping the cultural events dedicated to highlighting the local textile heritage that is officially published and promoted online by the local government.

Fashion heritage destination elements introduced by Gravari-Barbas (2009), Pasquielli (2013), Permatasari (2016), Wang (2019), and Kalbaska et al. (2018b) were considered: one, textile heritage brands associated with cities; two, textile heritage in connection with local architecture, which describes architectural works inspired from/to textile heritage as a tangible integration of the two masterpieces; three, cultural activities conducted by museums or cultural institutions offering experiential tourism of fashion heritage; four, the emergence of creative cities and regular public events dedicated to fashion and textile heritage promotion; and, five, musealization and cultural routes connecting the historical places and textile heritage craftsmanship. The collected data were analyzed based on the triangulation of those five elements adapted to the context of Indonesian fashion heritage destinations, connecting tourism offers engendered by diverse institutions with a meaningful exploration of the communities and local wisdom behind the textile tradition.

Textile Heritage Brands Associated With Local Architecture

Textile heritage fashion businesses serve as catalyzers of the socioeconomic development of a region or a city (Santoso, 2019). As social and business entities, those brands further grow and weave sociocultural fiber of the society, building a strong associative image of the brand with the city. This notion is presented in several regions, such as Jakarta, Central Java, and West Java. Since 2006, the success of Iwan Tirta's private collection, a high-end fashion heritage brand, has promoted Jakarta as an *haute couture* fashion heritage destination (MTEC, 2016; Tirta, 2022). In Central Java, several textile heritage brands actively collaborate with the local government to promote the city as cultural tourism in fashion, such as Anne Avantie in Semarang city (Avantie, 2022), Dian Pelangi in Pekalongan city (Martawardaja, 2019), and Danar Hadi Heritage in Solo city (Hadi, 2022).

Indonesian cultural destinations mostly possess local wisdom reflected in their architecture and textile tradition. In the case of Indonesian destination management branding, local architecture plays an important role in enhancing cultural tourism experiences. All 34 regions have their own typical local architecture, whose wooden carving and intricate motif influence are inspired by textile motifs produced by local communities. In addition, local architecture adds value to the shopping experiences (Bellaïche, Kluz, Mei-Pochtler, & Wiederin, 2012). The shopping destination plays a key role as an instrumental occasion for a destination to leverage its creative products. Rintamäki, Kuusela, and Mitronen (2007) asserted that the shopping experience becomes the main and end objective of the tourists. As part of the cultural experience, urban architecture along with the cultural landscape and associated local meanings provides a "mood-setting" physical environment of the destination (Pasquinelli, 2017; Rahman & Cherrier, 2010).

The relationship between architecture and textiles has a vast history of providing protective benefits in building envelopes derived from hand-sewn animal skins (Wigglesworth, 2010). Architecture discipline retains the way how physical woven construction and the use of membranes in the lightweight tent structure are used as a human habitation (Goerner, 1986). The possible connections between architecture and textiles are not only seen in the way an architectural building is constructed but also within the substantial meaning of the building and its interior. The significance between the two allows and carries complex imprints of geographical, social, cultural, and personal influences.

Textiles are a vigorous medium, rich with esthetic significance and symbolic meaning (Hann, 2013). As a medium that has an essential role in architecture, textiles should become cutting-edge architecture at this time (Nayak & Mishra, 2016). Nevertheless, textiles in architecture have become somewhat neglected and are only limited to the interior aspect. This raises various questions, and one of them is about the extent to which the practicality of textiles can continue to be used for weather and visual protection purposes in building architecture. In some Indonesian regions, one may observe traditional textile materials and structures still used for lightweight roof coverings with membrane structures.

The remarkable pattern diversity of Indonesian textile heritage represents rich local wisdom that influences the design evolution of fashion and architectural ornaments. There is much evidence to suggest that textiles share an everlasting relation with architecture, dress, and the "fabric of society." Boehlke (2008) identifies the adoption of the batik motif manifested in the flooring ceramic tile as the interior ornament of *Keraton* (Javanese royal palace) in Yogyakarta. The same motif inspires the creation of batik motifs for modest contemporary fashion in the same region (Figure 6.2).

Other than textiles, woods are a common medium of local artisans to showcase the tribal visual codes, such as motifs and patterns. Indonesian

Figure 6.2. Keraton Tile Motif (Left) and Batik Motif in Muslim Apparel.
Source: Paradise fashion brand of Yogyakarta.

Figure 6.3. Rangkiang, West Sumatra Songket Woven Textile Motif.
Source: iWareBatik (2020d).

textile heritage patterns (not limited to batik, woven and embroidery textiles) can be found on the wood carving on ceilings and the wooden pillars of traditional houses and religious buildings. These examples can be seen in the traditional houses located in the historical villages in Aceh, North Sumatra, West Sumatra, East Kalimantan, Bali, and Central Java (Kusumaningrum, 2018; Sianipar, Gunardi, & Rustiyanti, 2015; Soedigdo, Harysakti, & Usop, 2014). Many architectural interiors are also inspired by textile heritage motifs. Alimin (2016) identifies the strong influence of the local textile motif on the wooden interior wall of Padang Grand Mosque of West Sumatra, which resembles a typical West Sumatra Songket woven textile motif called Rangkiang (Figure 6.3). These examples present the linkage and influence of textile heritage into local architecture, while showcasing fascinating blends of textile heritage's usage values in today's society.

Experiential Tourism on Fashion Heritage by Museums

Since 2016, the national tourism organization launched cultural tourism that highlights textile heritage destinations. This experiential tourism connects textile museums in several cities in Indonesia while offering tourists to

Figure 6.4. The Actual Batik Textile Workshop.
Source: P.A Permatasari own documentation, taken during field trip in Cirebon and Pekalongan in April 2017.

discover cultural routes in relation to the history of textile heritage and its production regions. A number of batik museums exist in several cities on Java Island, such as Pekalongan, Cirebon, Yogyakarta, Jakarta, Tangerang, and Surabaya.

Figure 6.4 presents an outlook of the Batik Museum in Cirebon (West Java) and Pekalongan as Batik's creative city. The interview conducted with a representative of Larangan Batik art center in Tangerang confirms the inclusion of textile cultural routes in regional tourism promotion to connect tourists with locals and support textile practitioners in continuing the tradition. In addition, an extensive social media campaign had been conducted by local tourism players and the government to promote Larangan village as the living museum of batik textile heritage (Aulia & Alfansyah, 2019).

Besides discovering textile heritage galleries in the village, the tourists are invited to produce their own batik creation with the help of local producers and take it as souvenirs from the art center. Specific museums for woven textile are present in other regions, such as the Cual Woven Textile Museum in Pangkal Pinang City of Bangka Island and the Sikka Woven Textile Museum in Ende city of East Nusa Tenggara. Besides governmental initiatives, fashion heritage destination branding is supported by the presence of fashion brand heritage existing in the region. According to Pasquinelli (2017), fashion brands as cultural institutions adopt the musealization strategy that connects the product as an integrated brand experience with the urban experience. For example, the Danar Hadi Museum in Solo city of Central Java is one of the batik museums related to fashion brand heritage (Hadi, 2022).

Creative Cities and Public Events for Promotion

Charles Landry first raised the origin of the creative city's idea in 1991 in his research entitled "The Creative City and Its Cultural Economy" (2008). He mentioned that the notion of a creative city is how the government is able to observe how society thinks, plans, and acts creatively in the city. UNESCO, since 2004, has developed the Creative Cities Network program, which intends to identify those regarded as "creative cities" and build networks among them. This program requires synergy between government, academics, industry, community, and media, often referred to as Penta Helix (Sumarto, Sumartono, Muluk, & Nuh, 2020). The collaboration and synergy among these variables will create new ideas and more high-value innovative products (Cerisola, 2018).

Indonesia has designated a total of 63 creative cities, classified in many different fields such as art performance, handicrafts, fashion, film, applications and games, culinary, and fine arts (MTEC, 2020). Seventeen creative cities located in six Indonesian big islands were identified based on their eminent textile arts and fashion (Figure 6.5). Among them, Pekalongan and Bandung city are renowned as UNESCO creative cities. Recognized as such respectively in 2014 and 2015, both cities are famous as home to a number of well-known artists and designers working on traditional and contemporary fashion. In addition, Pekalongan city also gained its position to win the UNESCO label of Good Safeguarding Practices in 2009 through education and training programs for Indonesian batik intangible cultural heritage.

The inauguration of the two cities as Creative Cities in Indonesia is considered relevant to Government Act No. 32 of 2004 concerning local government or more popularly, regional autonomy. This achievement proves national commitment to spur city management based on its potential (Haqi & Pandangwati, 2020). This notion is mentioned by a tour guide who works in the education area in Pekalongan city interviewed in September 2020. He asserted that there is an increasing demand in terms of educational tourism by domestic tourists in discovering the history of textile culture, textile

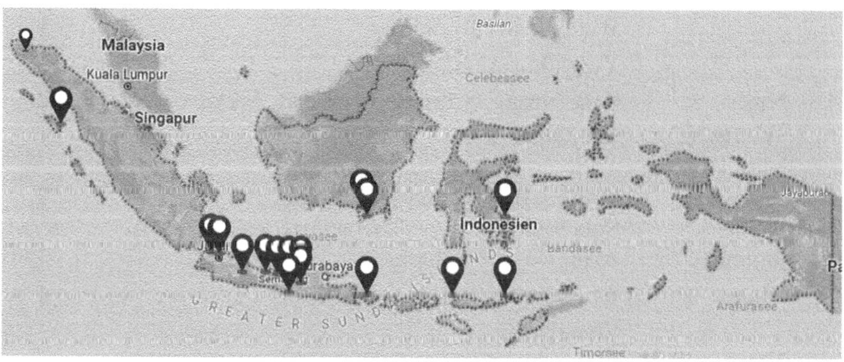

Figure 6.5. The Map of Indonesian Creative Cities.
Source: Authors illustration from Google Maps.

villages, and the cultural heritage sites existing in Pekalongan. He affirmed the importance of improving the destination branding by focusing on the educational aspects of textile culture, philosophical meanings of the textile motif, and its relation to the creative sector, instead of narrowing the tourism promotion of the city as a mere shopping destination.

Another example of a UNESCO creative city is Bandung city. Inaugurated as an Indonesian creative city in fashion in 2007, the city has received international support that led to a broader recognition as a creative city in Asia in 2011. Since November 2015, UNESCO has designated Bandung City as a Creative City in the field of design. Table 6.1 outlines 17 creative cities, whose strength lies in their interdisciplinary cooperation and initiatives for textile heritage valorization through fashion events. The multiethnicity and cultural diversity, in combination with modern innovations in developing regional potential, led to the success of the cities as a national creative city. Such interregional collaborations are needed to bring a greater impact, not only from the sustainable tourism point of view, but also in terms of community development.

Table 6.1. Indonesian Creative Cities of Textile Arts and Fashion.

No	Name of Island	Name of Region	Creative Cities of Textile Arts and Fashion	Number of Cities
1	Bali Island	Bali	Denpasar	1
2	Kalimantan Island	South Kalimantan	Banjarmasin, Banjar Baru	2
3	Java Island	Banten	Cilegon, Tangerang Selatan	2
		Central Java	Pemalang, Pekalongan, Rembang, Batang, Semarang	5
		West Java	Bandung	1
		Yogyakarta	Bantul	1
4	Nusa Tenggara Islands	East Nusa Tenggara	Manggarai Barat, Sikka	2
5	Sulawesi Island	Southeast Sulawesi	Konawe Selatan	1
6	Sumatra Island	Aceh	Sabang	1
		North Sumatra	Gunung Sitoli	1
	Total			17

In order to capture the landscape of fashion heritage destinations, it is important to analyze the presence of fashion heritage destinations emerging thanks to the organization of fashion-related events in connection to the textile heritage. With 633 ethnicities spread across 34 regions, Indonesia's cultural diversity serves as the main driver of the national cultural and creative industry (Statistic, 2015). The ministry of tourism and creative economy established a public policy that encourages each region to leverage its resources and cultural potential through festivals and cultural events (MTEC, 2021a). A consultant working in the Ministry of Tourism participated in the interview. He confirmed the extensive fashion heritage events that were conducted in support of regional creative sectors while promoting textile villages as a cultural destination to the public. A total of 1,467 cultural events in 34 regions are identified from 34 official regional government websites.

From the total samples, there are 136 (9%) cultural events associated with fashion and textile heritage valorization, such as fashion carnivals, fashion heritage exhibitions, and fashion weeks, in which the organizers promote the diverse types of traditional attires for men and women. Table 6.2 shows the number of fashion heritage events per region within the period of 2019–2020. Among all regions, Jakarta, Gorontalo, Lampung, East Kalimantan, and Riau are the most active regions in organizing fashion heritage–related events. The collaborations among local stakeholders, mainly among governmental actors with artisans and tourism actors, show a high degree of local enthusiasm toward the preservation of textile heritage through fashion events.

Musealization and Cultural Routes

The uniqueness of batik textile is not only related to its philosophy, but also to the varied methods that differ from region to region. Today, some ancient routes connected to the textile-making tradition are still preserved and manifested into cultural routes. One of the most famous cultural routes is Batik Tiga Negeri Lasem or Lasem Batik of the "Three Kingdoms." The ancient route of Batik Tiga Negeri is linked to the places where the three coloration processes of this rare type of batik textile take place in three cities in Central Java (Malagina, 2018).

A piece of Batik Tiga Negeri contains at least three colors, by which the blue color is done in Pekalongan city, the rustic dark brown color or slogan is done in Solo city, and the red *finissage* (finishing) as the last process takes place in Lasem city. Another batik route was created in Madura island (Permatasari, 2016) as it connects four different cities of Bangkalan, Sampang, Pamekasan, Sumenep city in Madura island, East Java (Figure 6.6).

Table 6.2. Fashion Heritage Events in Indonesia in 2019–2020.

No	Name of Regions	National Cultural Events	Fashion Heritage Events
1	Jakarta	200	13
2	Gorontalo	86	11
3	Lampung	43	11
4	East Kalimantan	27	7
5	Riau	114	7
6	South Kalimantan	82	6
7	Aceh	65	5
8	Bangka Belitung	54	5
9	West Sumatra	45	5
10	Yogyakarta	70	5
11	Riau Islands	153	5
12	South Sumatra	42	5
13	South Sulawesi	69	5
14	Central Java	12	5
15	West Java	50	5
16	East Java	113	4
17	North Sumatra	18	4
18	West Nusa Tenggara	15	4
19	Banten	15	4
20	Maluku	31	3
21	Bengkulu	15	2
22	North Maluku	45	2
23	Central Kalimantan	3	2
24	Bali	10	1
25	West Kalimantan	4	1
26	West Papua	2	1
27	West Sulawesi	16	1
28	Southeast Sulawesi	21	1
29	North Sulawesi	5	1
30	Central Sulawesi	20	1
31	Jambi	11	1
32	East Nusa Tenggara	7	1
33	North Kalimantan	2	1
34	Papua	2	1
	Total	1,467	136

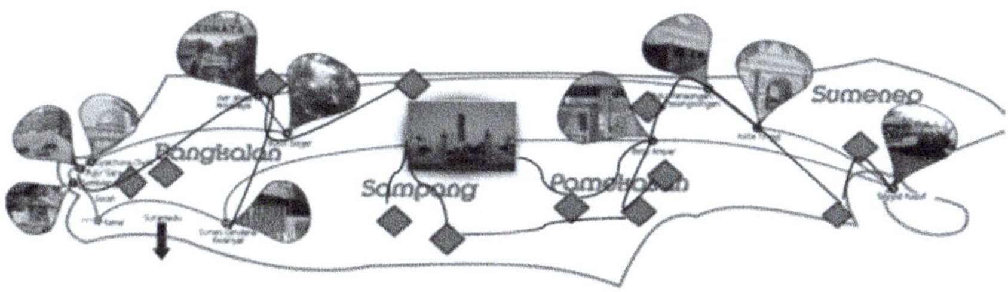

Figure 6.6. Madura Batik Cultural Routes in Four Cities (Permatasari, 2016).

The cultural route guides tourists to discover the variety of batik in Madura, from the agrarian and royal types to coastal batik.

CONCLUSION

The valorization of Indonesian textile heritage in multidimensional ways has led the country to grow as an eminent fashion heritage destination. The usage values, incorporated within the sociocultural context of textile heritage, are embraced within all levels of Indonesian society. From traditional to contemporary contexts, the country leverages the cultural capital – especially in textile tradition – with the intention to develop an experiential hub of fashion and tourism in the regions. Through several case studies, there is a strong correlation among tourism branding, reputation, and destinations as "places of affect" with the omnipresence of textile heritage in each region. Such illustrations are explained through the map of fashion heritage events including carnival and fashion weeks, cultural expression in textile traditions and creative cities, architectural works inspired from/to the textile, cultural routes, and musealizations.

Some examples indicate that the emergence of fashion heritage destinations is supported by an array of public engagement initiatives, either top-down or bottom-up approaches. The government's role as the enabler supports the local initiatives, which spurs the interplay of heritage and creativity at the regional level. The landscape of fashion heritage destinations is highlighted by 15 creative cities on fashion and textile heritage, as well as its cultural routes. Indeed, both national and UNESCO labels in supporting the existing creative cities do help local communities to leverage its potentials and future expansions. The enactment of the "one village one product" policy, as well as other policies in relation to creative cities and fashion as a creative industry, are well-attuned with the local initiatives in favor of heritage preservation and tourism valorization.

The case studies presented in this chapter meets many factors of fashion heritage destination elements, such as textile heritage brand associated with cities, textile heritage in connection with local architecture, cultural activities conducted by museums, or cultural institutions connecting the experience of textile heritage, fashion, and tourism offers, regular public events dedicated to fashion and textile heritage promotion, and cultural routes connecting the places with strong history and relationships of textile heritage craftsmanship. These categories might also be used to classify and measure to which extent certain tourism destinations are developed into fashion heritage destinations.

As the primary introduction to Indonesian fashion heritage destinations, the scope of this study was limited to the general identification of Indonesian fashion heritage destinations through common practices, governmental support, and the existing evidence related to textile traditions. The research does not address the impacts and any potential changes related to the emergence of fashion heritage destinations. Future studies could be directed to address the (de)generative influences identified from the transformation of these type of destinations, including the effects resulted from the creative process and cultural exchanges occurring over time. This research can be expanded in terms of the online benchmarking studies, as well as qualitative and quantitative analysis of specific fashion heritage destinations. It is also important to observe and examine the way each destination builds its online reputation and digital initiatives in support of its core competencies. Textile tradition is a form of cultural heritage, whose preservation also needs to be sustainably maintained and taken care of by all stakeholders who benefit from its usage values.

Indonesian fashion destinations are to pay attention to the needs of local producers and prioritize the capacity building of the local communities involved within the heritage, fashion, and tourism sectors. The continuous development of human resources may contribute to an ever-growing creative innovation, improve the product and service quality, and boost the regional economic growth. It is crucial to equip the promotional aspects of fashion heritage destinations, both online and offline publication, with engaging narratives that focus not only on the usage values, but also on the awareness of textile heritage preservation. As part of the global tourism and fashion landscape, Indonesian fashion heritage destinations and its multisectoral engagements may set a positive example of the interplay between traditional and modern concepts in valorizing textile heritage in its due contexts.

Chapter 7

WHEN TOURISM AND FASHION COCREATE
Narratives From Greece

Eirini Vlassi
Neapolis University Pafos, Cyprus

Georgios A. Deirmentzoglou
Neapolis University Pafos, Cyprus

Konstantina K. Agoraki
University of Piraeus, Greece

Andreas Papatheodorou
University of the Aegean, Greece

Abstract: Fashion is linked to destination branding as it constitutes an important aspect of cultural heritage. Fashion events and exhibitions enhance destination brand awareness and increase tourism demand. This chapter attempts to highlight the interdependence between fashion and destination branding focusing on how attributes are portrayed by inflight and fashion magazines. A comparative qualitative analysis of *Blue* (Aegean Airlines inflight magazine) and *Vogue Greece* is undertaken. This chapter provides insights to inform destination and fashion partners in Greece regarding their future campaigns and extend their collaboration at various levels. **Keywords**: Destination branding; place branding; brand cocreation; inflight magazine; fashion magazine; fashion and tourism

Fashion and Tourism: Parallel Stories
Tourism Social Science Series, Volume 26, 93–106

Published under exclusive licence by Emerald Publishing Limited
ISSN: 1571-5043/doi:10.1108/S1571-504320230000026007

INTRODUCTION

In the past decades, tourism has become one of the most important, dynamic, and fast-growing industries of the global economy. Tourism and hospitality are the main locomotive for job creation and economic development of local, regional, and national economies as well as behind the promotion of cultural exchange and products marketing. Today's industry is being shaped on the basis of new organizational and management principles and remains one of the most important drivers of economic development and social well-being (Brida, Gómez, & Segarra, 2020; Hall, 2019; Katemeliadis & Papatheodorou, 2021). According to the World Travel and Tourism Council (WTTC, 2021), tourism revenues account for 20.3% of GDP and 21.1% of total employment in Greece. The total number of incoming tourists in Greece approached 31 million approximately, accounting for €20.3 billion in 2019 (UNWTO, 2020).

On the other hand, fashion is a global phenomenon playing a significant role in the international economic development (Demirovic & Pivac, 2010) with a major impact on the Western world (Bada, 2013). The global apparel and footwear accounted for $1.8 trillion in 2018 and is expected to rise to $2 trillion in 2023 (Euromonitor International, 2021). According to the British Council (2021), fashion contributed £35.5 billion and 890,000 jobs to the UK economy. In Greece, the total consumer spending on clothing and footwear accounts for $5.5 billion in 2019 and it is expected to increase in the future (Statista, 2021). During the years of austerity, the fashion industry suffered, and revenues declined by 50% (Vogue Business, 2019).

In the academic literature, there are many fashion definitions; they are usually categorized into three main groups related to behavior, imitation, and differentiation, and being appropriate for a specific occasion (Lewis, Kerr, & Burgess, 2013). Fashion can be described as the way that individuals or groups of people behave regarding the processing and transmission of social meanings that occur in a particular period and location (Pritchard & Morgan, 2005; Sullivan, Gallarza, Fayos, & Calderon, 2015). It has an important role in arts and sciences, and it is also related to music, media, sports, clothing, and accessories (Barnes, 2013; Sullivan et al., 2015). In this chapter, the term "fashion" is related to the production of textiles and garments. The consumer purchases specific garments for their features, such as the design, quality, and style, but also for their symbolic value included in the designer's brand. Through fashion, individuals express themselves, communicate, and connect with others (Barnes, 2013).

As both industries, tourism and fashion, have direct effects on the global and the national economic development, their interrelation needs to be analyzed. When *Vogue Greece* was relaunched in 2019, after a period of pause caused by the downturn of the Greek economy, Vogue Business, the online fashion industry publication, announced the recovery of the fashion industry in the country (Vogue Business, 2019). The article pointed to the relation that exists between the two industries, as the highest percentage of the revenues of the luxury fashion brands and boutiques in the capital and in the famous island destinations derives from tourists. Additionally, it is evident that a branded city (Skivko, 2016) attracts more tourists, but at the same time the local brands benefit from the incremental tourism demand creating a win-win situation (Capone & Lazzeretti, 2016; Kalbaska, Ramírez, & Cantoni, 2018).

The cooperation between the interrelated industries became a matter of vital importance to the Greek economy during the years of the severe economic crisis, which cultivated the ground for public–private partnerships (Vlassi & Papatheodorou, 2021). In this vein, the Athens Tourism Partnership was created, which consists of the Athens International Airport, Aegean Airlines, and the Athens Development and Destination Management Agency. The partnership is a long-term marketing agreement launched in December 2016 to enhance Athens' brand awareness and to promote it as a city-break destination under the guidance of Bloomberg Associates (Athens Partnership, 2021). As the pandemic crisis of Covid-19 has made the situation even harder for both tourism and fashion, it is important to provide insights that may help destination and fashion partners in Greece (and elsewhere) to inform their future campaigns and extend their collaboration at various levels (Euromonitor International, 2021).

DESTINATION BRANDING AND THE ROLE OF FASHION

Given the changing and challenging global tourism industry, the role of destination marketing and branding is of considerable importance, while destinations are multidimensional compared to consumer goods and other types of services (Pike, 2005). The concept of place branding is considered as an effort to deliver and construct the image and is an integral part of the place's marketing. It includes, but is not limited to, the creation of a new logo, the inspiration for a new slogan, and the planning and implementation of the destination's advertising campaign. Place branding aims to increase attractiveness and to detect and highlight the factors that differentiate the place and enhance its competitiveness (Morgan, Pritchard, & Pride, 2011). Destination branding differs from place branding as it is limited to the tourism development of the city or region (Briciu, 2013). It is evident that while destination marketing and branding is of major importance to the development of tourism, it incorporates several complicated and sometimes conflicting parameters (Qu, Kim, & Im, 2011).

First, a destination brand incorporates both tangible and intangible aspects, the combination of which constitutes the value proposition of the destination (Cai, 2002; Kapferer, 2011). For example, in the case of Paris, the tangible aspect of salient products, such as haute couture and the designers' luxury brands and the intangible aspect of communications, such as the promotion of haute couture catwalks, are integral parts of the destination's brand (Kapferer, 2011). The destination brand and all future marketing promotions express the true identity based on the product that the destination has to offer (Gartner, 1993; Govers, Go, & Kumar, 2007; Richards, 2019).

Fashion is regarded as an important component of the destination brand that enhances the attractiveness of the place (Capone & Lazzeretti, 2016; Skivko, 2016). Fashion shapes the identity of an area, as it carries and expresses cultural elements with a symbolic content (Capone & Lazzeretti, 2016; Skivko, 2013). Capone and Lazzeretti (2016) examined the role of fashion in the branding of Florence and the research indicated its importance in the formation of the destination image and the perceptions held by incoming tourists. Moreover, the results revealed that local brands, such as Prada and Gucci, enhance the city's attractiveness.

Fashion brands located in a destination can cultivate a positive image in the actual and potential tourists' mind; while at the same time, these brands receive value in return (Capone & Lazzeretti, 2016; Skivko, 2016). Skivko (2016) used the metaphor of "branded cities" to describe urban places where fashion brands are located, making them to be perceived as fashion destinations with a specific character for tourists. Paris was used as an example of a destination where tourists can find a variety of fashion boutiques, offering products for fashionable glamorous women. In the same vein, Gravari-Barbas (2019) mentioned boutique windows among the other elements that make Paris look like Paris and states that those windows were used in the case of the Paris Las Vegas Hotel/Casino to create a themed environment that would be in line with the Paris imaginaries.

Imaginaries are defined as "a set of representations, images, beliefs, sense and meanings created and recreated by a society." (Horlent & Salemme, 2015, p. 184). Tourism imaginaries are linked with geographical spaces and touristic practices and actors. "Tourist imaginaries are imaginaries of individuals or social groups concerning other places other than their primary residence where certain types of leisure activities could take place." (Gravari-Barbas & Graburn, 2012, p. 1). These imaginaries can be related with family experiences in early age or with what has been taught in school about places and people. They are associated with tangible images (posters, postcards, films) and intangible images such as legends, tales, memories (Gravari-Barbas & Graburn, 2012).

Furthermore, fashion events can enhance the image that tourists have of a destination (Kalbaska, Ramírez, et al., 2018). Events constitute opportunities to promote a place while they enable tourists to interact with the local community (Butler, 2014; Kalbaska, Ramírez, et al., 2018). Fashion weeks are events that aim to create a buzz concerning the upcoming season and during which designers present their latest work (Demirovic & Pivac, 2010; Swanson & Everett, 2013). As they are disseminated through the media and they attract celebrities, international suppliers, and tourists, they achieve to increase the destination's awareness (Swanson & Everett, 2013). Fashion weeks spread through fashion networks strengthen the destination's brand. According to Swanson and Everett (2013), in some cases, fashion weeks help capitals to enhance their brand and to promote themselves as fashion leaders.

Fashion events and shows can be used by the of smaller cities as central building blocks of a meaningful destination brand strategy and as tools to confront seasonality (Lewis et al., 2013). Butler (2014) mentioned that fashion shows, among other events and actions, can supplement the destination's existing offering or even change it. They can be used by the Destination Management Organizations as strategic tools in their effort to capture a higher share of an existing market or to attract a new market. An example can be Bendigo, a regional city in Australia, which incorporated Bendigo Art Gallery in the tourism strategy of the city, and which achieved to increase the number of day trips, extend its target market, and enhance its awareness as a short break destination (Laing & Frost, 2013). According to the Gallery's Director, in comparison with other forms of culture, fashion has the power to grab the attention of the press and to attract more people, giving them a reason to travel (Laing & Frost, 2013).

Fashion Brands to Enhance Brand Performance

Fashion brands use destinations to enhance their brand performance by organizing their shows in places with strong image, using destination as a background for their products and linking their products with it through the "made-in" concept that carries a symbolic value (Jung Jung, Lee, Kim, & Yang, 2014). The "made-in" attachment is related with the value of the brand's "country-of-origin" image and constitutes an important factor that formulates its value and equity (Yasin, Noor, & Mohamed, 2007). As already mentioned, destinations may strive to organize events and fashion shows to increase tourism demand and sometimes to control seasonality. On the other hand, famous fashion brands organize shows in locations around the world, in archeological sites, that have a strong brand and carry a cultural meaning to market their collection, cultivate positive impressions of their brand, and indicate their source of inspiration (Calinao, 2020). For instance, Karl Lagerfeld, in 2007, had a fashion show in the Great Wall of China; Chanel, in 2016, turned Paseo del Prado in Havana into a runway; Dolce and Gabbana, in 2019, organized a fashion show in Sicily's Valley of the Temples; and Christian Dior, in 2020, showed their new collection at an event in El Badi Palace in Marrakesh (Zhang, 2020).

Fashion brands seem to strengthen their brand performance by promoting their products through images related to the context within which they will be used. According to Jung and Childs (2018), Michael Kors uses New York's images in his advertisements to promote a specific fast-paced city lifestyle. Their study examined the importance of including a destination as a background in product advertisements. The results revealed that when consumers see a product within a favorable destination, they have an increased desire for purchase. By successfully placing the product in a destination context, the consumer can envision its end-use and their perception concerning the brand as well as the overall experience of the product can be enhanced. Consequently, the product's placement within a destination seems to be linked with a greater brand equity and intention to buy than when the advertisement is not related to a destination.

Study Method

This chapter analyzes and contrasts content that combine fashion with places to demonstrate the relationship between fashion and destination branding. The study reveals how a fashion magazine and an in-flight magazine combine fashion and place attributes. For the purpose of this research, the content from two publicly available sources was collected, analyzed, and compared. The 2019 and 2020 issues of the *Blue* inflight magazine, nine in total (six issued in 2019 and three in 2020), and of *Vogue Greece*, 12 in total (out of 18), were downloaded and imported to MAXQDA. *Blue* is the inflight magazine of Aegean Airlines which is the largest Greek airline operating in 151 destinations, 31 domestic and 120 international ones (Aegean Airlines, 2021). *Vogue Greece* is the Greek edition of the fashion and lifestyle magazine "Vogue."

To select an issue and include it in the sample of this study, it needed to contain at least one page with an article, advert, or cover page that combines both attributes of a Greek destination and fashion at any level and degree. Each page under analysis will be mentioned as "unit." The selected units were cover pages or parts of adverts, articles, and photo tributes. To include a cover page, an advert, an article, and a photo tribute in the sample, a clear reference to a Greek destination or to features of Greece as a destination should have been present (such as the name of the destination, a landmark, the unique architecture or cityscape) while at the same time a fashion product should be included and displayed in it.

The total number of the collected pages were 414 (247 from *Vogue Greece* and 167 from *Blue*) as shown in Table 7.1. It is interesting that from the 247 units that derive from *Vogue Greece*, 150 were included in the issues of 2019 and 97 in the issues of 2020. In the same vein, from the 167 units that derive from *Blue*, 150 were part of the issues of 2019 while only 18 were included in

Table 7.1. Types of Analyzed Content.

Types of Content	Blue	Vogue Greece	Total
Cover	7	7	14
Article that includes a photo tribute	15	4	19
Photo tributes	0	16	16
Whole page advert	15	20	35
Images in tributes and articles	137	209	346
Total units (pages)	167	247	414

the issues of 2020. The decreased number of units that were detected in the issues of 2020 might be explained by the fact that both fashion and tourism faced a shock due to the severe consequences of the pandemic crisis. Scheduled flights and fashion shows had been canceled due to the pandemic outbreak causing negative financial impact and changing the marketing goals of businesses in both fashion and tourism industries. At the end of the process, a total number of 346 images were collected and analyzed. From the total number of images, 312 (90%) were full-page images.

A conceptual content analysis followed and about 65 concepts were detected. Both a bottom-up and a top-down coding were used, as some codes derived from the literature review while others emerged from the data. Concerning the top-down coding, data were scanned to detect destination attributes which have been derived through previous research (Vlassi & Papatheodorou, 2021). The list of attributes included cultural heritage (religion, museums, landmarks, music, folklore, crafts, philosophy), everyday life (rural and urban life, local people), architecture, natural environment (sky, sea, sun, flora, wildlife), events and festivals, gastronomy (local cuisine), and activities (dining) (Vlassi & Papatheodorou, 2021).

Other concepts revealed from the literature review in the field of fashion, such as fashion designers, made-in product, fashion editors, and fashion shops. A critical analysis of the images took place in order to detect whether fashion or destination features appear in the background or in the foreground or if both features are in balance. At last, in an attempt to further interpret data, such concept as promoting, promoting fashion, and promoting the destination were produced. To address bias, a second auditor was asked to code a sample of data and the results obtained as well as their interpretation were discussed, while no significant differences appeared (Glaser, 1978).

Data Analysis

Concerning the issues of 2019 about 10% of the total pages of each issue of *Blue* contains content in which destination features and fashion coexist. This does not happen in the issues of 2020 in which the presence of fashion is limited. Three types of content were collected during the inflight magazine scanning. There were adverts found in the inflight magazine that meet the criteria. Two jewelry brand adverts were featured in the magazine, and they aimed to link their products' characteristics with specific destination aspects, stating in that way their designers' source of inspiration. Full-page images were used for that purpose to blend the destination features with the products.

In nine issues, seven were dedicated to a specific Greek destination (Thessaloniki, Athens, Mykonos, Lemnos, Milos, Corfu, Epirus) where the airline operates. Seven covers were inspired by the specific destination and all of them contain a fashion statement as well. All the issues included short articles mentioning an attribute of the specific destination, followed by an extensive photo tribute. While the length of the text was limited to two short paragraphs (covering half of the page), the pages that were covered by photos accompanying the text ranged from 7 to 22. The images in combination with the short text attempted to explain why the depicted area is attractive and should be visited. It is important to mention that full page images were used in most of the cases (118 out of 136). While all the issues contained extensive guiding articles for several places in Greece, only in one issue, that of Corfu, the extensive guiding article included fashion. Finally, two cases of articles provided information (technical and emotional) concerning a fashion show.

The *destination attributes* that were detected in the collected material are noted in Table 7.2. Cultural heritage is mentioned more than the other attributes, as it was detected 66 times. The features through which cultural heritage appeared include traditional ceremonies/events, folklore clothes and dances, crafts, traditional music, religion, philosophy, and history. On the other hand, the concepts related to fashion that appeared in the data are fashion designers, editors, events, and shops.

Efforts were made to measure and interpret the degree of importance of the destination and the fashion attributes in the collected articles and photo tributes. An observation of the images revealed the emphasis that was placed on these features. Two-axis codes were created, "destination in the foreground" and "destination in the background," to measure the attention that is given by the inflight magazine to them. In the same vein, the codes "fashion in the foreground" and "fashion in the background" were also set to measure the attention given by the inflight magazine to fashion. The research indicated that the number of incidents is equal, and that the most important aspect seems to be the harmony and balance between the fashion and the destination features. If the aspects are "in line," then a more impressive and attractive outcome seems to be created and it might lead to increased levels of value for both the destination and the fashion designer/shop (Figure 7.1; *Blue,* 2019).

Table 7.2. Destination Attributes in the Inflight Magazine *Blue*.

Code	Number of Incidences
Cultural heritage	66
Sea	24
Locals life	20
Rural life	14
Architecture fashion shops	12
Natural environment	16
Fashion shops	12
Crafts	8
Ancient times	7
Flora	6
Traditional cuisine	6
Traditions/events	5
Activities (Dining)	5
Folklore	4
Music	4
Local products	5
Fashion events	2
Nightlife	2

Figure 7.1. Fashion in Line With Destination Attributes ("Credits to Mara Desipris (Photographer))".

Source: Blue (2019).

To further analyze the collected images, an investigation of their scope and aim was conducted. The images under scrutiny meet the needs of three different audiences: the fashion designers/fashion shops, the destination, and the tourist. The concept of "promoting" had two dimensions: "promoting fashion" and "promoting the destination." The former is used when images aim to increase the readers' awareness of and intention to buy a fashion product while the latter is about guiding the tourist or increasing the intention of the potential tourist to visit the destination by providing information about it. In 122 (out of 136) cases, the images promote both the destination and the fashion products, in 14 cases, the promotion of destination is the only aim, with only two cases in which the promotion of the fashion product outweighs the promotion of the destination. The interpretation of the aim of an image containing a fashion product depends on the context. For example, the concern of the same image may be perceived to be the promotion of a fashion product when it is published in a fashion magazine, or to create a status for the (potential) tourist when it is part of a travel magazine dedicated to a specific destination.

An important consideration that emerged from 63% (76 out of 122) of the images that included both destination and fashion features was that they aimed to describe and influence the status of the reader. Although they promote the companies that have designed the clothes or the shops that sell them, this might not be their main concern. It is more like the images intended for an average onboard passenger flying to the destination. It could be interpreted as a reflection of the carrier's marketing strategy and a channel to talk directly to its audience. The problem is that sometimes this marketing technique may not be so successful, as the persona depicted in the images may differ from the actual passenger onboard, and especially so when noticing that almost all images include women, except one case in which a man appears. These conditions need to be further investigated.

In the case of *Vogue Greece*, of the 18 issues of 2019 and 2020 that were collected and analyzed, content that combines the destination features with fashion was found in 12. Surprisingly, the combination of destination features, and fashion was used in 7 of the 12 cover pages of the magazine. The related content was comprised of adverts and photo tributes accompanied by shopping information created by the magazine's editorial team. The articles provided styling ideas, informing the audience about the current fashion trends. Destination features were used in 75% (157 out of 209) of the photos included in the tributes. The editorial team used them either as a point with which to align or to contrast. Figure 7.2 (Vogue Greece, 2019c) displays an image taken in Kythera, where the colors of the model's dress matched the colors of the shipwreck of Kythera.

In the 209 images that were collected from the 12 Issues of *Vogue Greece*, there were 141 incidences in which destination features matched fashion and created a balanced outcome and only 11 cases in which the destination

Figure 7.2. Fashion Aligns With the Destination Attributes ("Credits to Mr Richard Phibbs (Photographer) and Laurijn Bijnen (Model))".
Source: Vogue Greece (2019c).

features were in contrast with fashion. The word "destination," not "place," was used as the majority (13 out of 16) of the tribute titles contained such keywords as summer, sea, mare nostrum, Mediterranean Sea, or road trip and popular Greek summer destination names such as Mykonos, Tinos, Kythera, Mani, and Santorini. Even the tribute that used the city of Athens as a case presented the city as a summer destination and beachwear was presented in the cityscape. The detected destination attributes were urban life, rural life, architecture, scenery, cultural heritage (museums, sculptures, landmarks, religion, traditions, folklore clothes) and such aspects of the natural environment as the sea, the blue sky, and the sun.

In fashion magazines, such as *Vogue*, the emphasis is on fashion and not on the destination, with the destination mainly used as a background theme. There were images in which the destination features were found "in the foreground" (15 out of 209) or "in complete balance" (47 out of 209) with fashion. Most images promoted the designer/shop, but there were many where the presence of the destination features was strong (even when appearing in the background; 69 out of 209), perhaps with the intent of promoting the destination. An interpretation can be that most of the photos

Figure 7.3. Tourists Versus Locals ("Credits to Mr Thanassis Krikis (Photographer))".

Source: Vogue Greece (2019b).

attempted to create value for the designer/shop, but there were pictures in the fashion magazine that added value for the destination. Fashion magazine attempted to capture the persona of the (potential) tourist of the destination (28 out of 209). In other cases, locals were rarely featured in the photos (22 out of 206). For example, Figure 7.3 (Vogue Greece, 2019b) attempts to create a persona for the tourist going to Greek islands. Finally, the concept of "made in" emerged from the data only once and that was in an advert.

CONCLUSION

This chapter examines the interrelation between fashion and tourism destination branding in order to detect possible areas of cooperation that can lead the stakeholders into a win-win situation. To gain an understanding of the common interests that link the two, review of the literature helped revealing how tourism destinations use fashion to increase their tourism demand and to strengthen their brand. The literature also indicated the ways that fashion brands use destinations to improve their performance.

Issues of the inflight magazine *Blue* and the fashion magazine *Vogue Greece* were collected and analyzed. In the sample, 7 out of 18 cover pages of the latter and 7 out of 9 cover pages of the inflight magazine blended destination features with fashion. All the tributes to the destinations that appeared in the inflight magazine contained fashion products. The same trend was detected in many image tributes of the fashion magazine, in which Greek destinations or their features were used to support the fashion statements. It is also evident that both magazines made references to popular Greek island destinations and almost the same destination features were presented. As a result, the work of the fashion editors of both magazines seems to support the notion that by placing fashion products within favorable destinations consumers' desire to buy increases and in that way the literature has been confirmed (Jung & Child, 2018). In this vein, a case of a luxury fashion designer was detected who chose the famous island destination of Mykonos to take the photos of their new campaign.

Consequently, both Aegean airlines and *Vogue Greece* recognize the interrelation which exists between the fashion and tourism industries, something which has been reported in academic journals and industries' magazines (Butler, 2014; Capone & Lazzeretti, 2016; Kalbaska, Ramírez, et al., 2018; Skivko, 2013). Fashion brand advertisers place garments in scenarios that mirror everyday reality to convince consumers to adopt a positive attitude toward them. The fact that Greece is a popular tourism destination and that tourists constitute an important market share for fashion designers and boutiques is depicted in the fashion magazine's images which use famous Greek destinations or destination attributes in the foreground or in the background. If tourists are perceived as fashion's target market, then it is obvious that fashion magazines will attempt to promote the everyday reality of a potential tourist in the context of a destination. On the other hand, most of the collected images from both magazines used locals as a destination feature and a point of inspiration but not as a potential market. There were a few cases in which fashion editors attempted to depict everyday life and to place fashion in the real city setting so that the locals could identify themselves within the illustrations.

Furthermore, although the "made-in" concept derived from the literature as an important aspect of the product's branding, only a few incidences were found in the collected data. As a result, there is room for improvement and cooperation between fashion and inflight magazines and the national tourism organization or Destination Management Organizations. Such cooperation could create value for all the parties. Additionally, while the importance of fashion events has been highlighted by the literature, only one case of such an event was detected in the issues collected. That was the case of a famous Greek fashion designer who presented her collection in the Temple of Poseidon in Athens. The designer used the cultural heritage site due to its cultural and historical meaning and its international recognition (Calinao, 2020).

While there is literature that supports the notion of fashion having geography, with Paris, London, New York, and Milan constituting the fashion capitals and competing with each other (Gilbert, 2019; Webster,

2013), it seems that there is room for new cities to develop in the field (Webster, 2013). The fashion industry constitutes a powerful tool for the development of tourism destinations at an international level, as it influences the potential tourists' destination selection process and their behavior (Lewis et al., 2013). With tourism being a pivotal industry for the prosperity of the Greek economy and multiple stakeholders being important (Carlisle, Kunc, Jones, & Tiffin, 2013), further research into the field is needed to gain a deeper understanding of the existing interrelationship and its potential. A qualitative research is suggested through interviews with four different audiences: fashion magazine editors, inflight magazine editors, fashion magazine readers, and airline passengers.

Chapter 8

FROM IMAGINARIES TO SYNERGIES
Christian Dior Cruise Collections

Sandra Krim
Panthéon Sorbonne University, France

Abstract: By celebrating tourism destinations through cruise collections, luxury brands open to new influences. They may develop deeper connections with certain geographical areas, but may also challenge the quintessentially national dimension of luxury brand culture. The best example of synergies between a luxury fashion brand and tourism destinations are the Christian Dior cruise collections with Maria Grazia Chiuri at the helm. This chapter is to understand how cruise collections may enhance luxury fashion houses' brand culture through the connections they develop with tourism destinations. Further, the chapter assesses the extent to which destinations can benefit from the exposure provided by luxury fashion brands' cruise collections. **Keywords**: Cruise collections; tourism destinations; cultural appropriation; cultural appreciation; brand culture; affective transfer theory

INTRODUCTION

Cruise collections, also known as resort or prespring holiday collections, were originally created a century ago, in the early 1920s. Gabrielle Chanel, perhaps not the originator, was certainly an early pioneer of lightweight and easy-to-wear pieces aimed at wealthy clienteles who would spend their winters aboard yachts in the Mediterranean (Saillard, 2019).

Top couturiers' cruise collections have long been small capsule collections for elite customers. However, their popularity began to wane over the decades until the early 2000s, when they made a triumphant comeback in the

Fashion and Tourism: Parallel Stories
Tourism Social Science Series, Volume 26, 107–132

Published under exclusive licence by Emerald Publishing Limited
ISSN: 1571-5043/doi:10.1108/S1571-504320230000026008

industry, spearheaded by Karl Lagerfeld. Chanel was the first to stage a fully fledged show for its 2007 cruise collection, and was soon followed by other leading luxury fashion houses, such as Christian Dior, Louis Vuitton, and Prada.

Cruise collections are a key area of competition between luxury fashion brands, as acknowledged in "The Business of Cruise: Go Big or Go Home" (*The Business of Fashion*, 2017). They are seen as a twofold opportunity to inject fresh desirability with a mid-season collection. First, by taking place outside the fashion week schedules and locations, cruise collections give luxury brands far more freedom in terms of communications through their esthetics, inspirations and locations. Second, cruise collections are also highly profitable as they allow luxury fashion brands "to appeal to a broader and more diverse audience, who deal with a diversity of climates" according to Sass Brown, Founding Dean of the Dubai Institute of Design and Innovation (cited by *UAE News*, 2018). In addition, they stay longer in stores (typically from November to March) and are not generally included in sales.

By celebrating broader themes with their cruise collections, in addition to tourism destinations, luxury fashion brands' ethics and esthetics are exposed to new influences. In some cases, luxury fashion houses may develop deeper connections with certain geographical areas. The clearest example of synergies between a luxury fashion brand and destinations is to be found in Christian Dior's cruise collections with Maria Grazia Chiuri at the helm. Since her appointment as Artistic Director of the French luxury fashion house in July 2016, Christian Dior cruise collections have been going far beyond merely seeking inspiration and locations for their fashion shows (unlike the vast majority of their competitors); they have been increasingly cementing relationships and forging collaborations between the brand and local artisan and arts scenes, with each informing the other's image and intrinsic value.

From a luxury fashion brand management standpoint, it is worth stressing that what creates the luxury status of purchases from a consumer perspective is not the product itself, but rather the symbolic value of the brand. This symbolic capital is, therefore, a particularly sensitive issue for luxury brands. It needs to be maintained and nurtured through communication. A growing facet of the symbolic power of luxury fashion brands is their cultural dimension.

Luxury fashion houses' brand culture has many different sources, including their founding myth and heritage, but the geographical origin of a brand is of the utmost importance. By celebrating a destination through a cruise collection, a luxury fashion house nurtures its own brand culture by communicating around that destination and its culture. This practice challenges the intrinsically national dimension of luxury brand culture (Heine & Atwal, 2022) and underscores the need for a clearer understanding of the role of nondomestic elements in the enhancement of the brand culture of a luxury house. This issue, despite its importance, is not addressed in this discourse. The purpose of this chapter is to understand how cruise collections dedicated to tourism destinations can enhance luxury fashion houses' brand culture through the connections they develop with their geographic location. This chapter further assesses the extent to which such destinations can benefit from the exposure provided by luxury fashion brands' cruise collections.

By analyzing and showing how Christian Dior has been developing real synergies between its own creative savoir faire and non-French cultures, this chapter identifies the criteria for, and the benefits of, a successful cruise collection in terms of brand culture, as well as issuing a strong caveat regarding the risk of controversy around cultural appropriation and addressing the means to avoid this. It also raises the possibility for destinations, as well as their arts and crafts, of benefitting from exposure to cruise collections.

THE CASE OF CHRISTIAN DIOR CRUISE COLLECTIONS

This chapter explores the levers and methods through which cruise collections dedicated to tourism destinations can enrich luxury fashion houses' brand culture and thus favor a more transcultural approach, by collaborating with and showcasing the local artisan and art landscape.

Luxury Fashion Brand Identity and Culture

A company's brand has both an economic and a symbolic function (Aaker, 1991; Marti, 2019). The symbolic aspect is especially important for luxury brands and luxury fashion brands because of the social symbolism associated with their consumption (Kapferer, 2012; Roux, 1991). Consumers buy not just products, but also the brand image (Kapferer & Laurent, 1992). Consumers identify with the personality and values of luxury fashion brands (Aaker, 1997), which are an aspect of their cultural dimension (Dubois & Duquesne, 1993). Some scholars even consider brands to be cultural forms, "a way of interpreting and organizing the world" (Cayla & Arnould, 2008, p. 101).

The issue of luxury fashion brand identity is crucial insofar as brands aim for uniqueness and play a part in building the identity of their consumers (Kapferer, 2012; Shimul & Phau, 2022). Although history, heritage, and visual aspects are integral components of a luxury fashion brand's identity, one needs to take a dynamic approach to understanding that identity (Michel, 2022). Brand identification (which implies a reiteration of its codes) differs from the identity itself. Although the concept of identity imposes a temporal dimension of permanence and continuity, expressing one's own identity implies not only permanence but also self-belief (an obligation on the part of the brand to be consistent) while incorporating a semblance of alterity (Heilbrunn, 2018).

Brand culture as one aspect of brand identity is "a system of values, source of inspiration of the brand" (Kapferer, 2007, p. 239). More precisely, it can be viewed as the "cultural codes of brands – history, images, myths, art, and theater – that influence brand meaning and value in the marketplace" (Schroeder et al., 2016; cited by Heine & Atwal, 2022, p. 534). As it is part of the brand identity, which treads a fine line between permanence and remaining current, brand culture must be generative (Bô, Guével & Lellouche, 2019; Fournier & Alvarez, 2019).

Postmodern capitalism allowed luxury product consumption to become more emotional and experiential (Lipovetsky & Roux, 2003), both hedonistic and symbolic (Lipovetsky & Serroy, 2013). In this context, the cultural dimension of luxury fashion brands is significant because they must satisfy consumers' desire for meaning and experience. They must act as true cultural producers, while still balancing the dynamics of the permanence of the luxury brand and the requirement to stay current.

Imaginary Territories of Luxury Brands

Most fashion brands offer precollections in addition to their Spring/Summer and Fall/Winter biannual collections, but only the most prestigious houses have cruise collections. It is their preserve, according to Frédéric Godart (2010). These collections, often intended for "exotic places" (Pinchera & Rinallo, 2020, p. 1), allow brands to diversify their offer, showcase brand-new communications, and, in the case of their artistic directors, draw on a source of inspiration less closely aligned with the house identity.

Luxury brands, including luxury fashion brands, are usually deeply rooted in their home territory and consider their nationality to be a strong component of their cultural DNA, along with their history and heritage. For example, French luxury fashion brands are all members of institutions such as the Fédération de la Haute Couture et de la Mode, which organizes Paris Fashion Weeks, or the Comité Colbert (an association of luxury brands representing a quintessentially French *art de vivre* and know-how) which promotes the influence of French luxury fashion abroad. Therefore, the national dimension of luxury fashion brands plays an important part in their identity and their brand culture. Consumers' awareness of the Country of Origin of luxury fashion brands relies essentially on the recognition, promotion, and renown of domestic workmanship and know-how (Godey et al., 2010; Heine & Atwal, 2022). This national dimension is a guarantee of authenticity throughout the luxury goods market, and offers the possibility of traceability.

This geographical territoriality of the Country of Origin fuses with the imaginary territory of the brand in consumers' minds, as it relates to their mental representations of the brand (Lacoeuilhe, 2000; Paivio, 1971). Just as imaginary territories of brands exist, so too do tourism imaginaries, since "tourism involves the human capacity to imagine or to enter into the imagining of others," a form of "mythologized and exoticized imaginaries of Otherness" (Salazar & Graburn, 2014, p. 1). These tourism imaginaries may be defined as individuals' or social groups' mental representations of places other than their primary residence. For example, in a leisure context, this includes the places and tourism practices associated with specific spaces, as well as their local communities (Gravari-Barbas & Graburn, 2012). By referring to a local culture, which differs from the national culture of the luxury fashion brand via a fashion show introducing this place, cruise collections add a tourism imaginary to the imaginary of the brand, and to its brand culture. This tourism imaginary adds greater exclusivity to the event (Ferrero-Regis & Lindquist, 2020).

Fashion Shows as a Powerful Communications Tool

According to Didier Grumbach, Honorary President of the Fédération de la Haute Couture et de la Mode (and former President of the Federation for 16 years), "To maintain visibility, there is nothing like a fashion show [. . .]. It is a way to broadcast ideas. It is a medium" (Tungate, 2012, p. 120). In a digital world, social media further enhances the power of fashion shows as a communications tool.

Fashion shows are one of the elements of the marketing mix of a luxury fashion brand, and more specifically its promotional mix. They have multiple functions: they reassert the brand status, reinforce the identity, uniqueness, and positioning of the brand, communicate brand values, ensure strong media coverage, and provide content for other elements of the promotional mix.

To differentiate themselves from competitors and to maximize the impact of their most effective communications tool, luxury fashion brands invest substantial amounts and add an artistic dimension (Skov, Skjold, Moeran, Larsen, & Csaba, 2009). This dimension allows them to enhance their emotional relationship with consumers (Christopher, Payne, & Ballantyne, 2013; Fournier & Alvarez, 2012; Varey & Ballantyne, 2006), and the emotional connection between the consumer and the brand personality (Aaker, 1997; Valette-Florence & Valette Florence, 2020) creates a congruency effect which reinforces the link with the brand (Shetty & Fitzsimmons, 2022).

Digital technology generates an exponential increase in consumers' commitment to fashion shows: consumers are receivers, as well as stakeholders and social media commentators. As consumers can "attend" the show via a live stream, they belong to the brand community. As a sociological phenomenon, fashion helps them to forge their identity and plays a role in social construction. Consumers feel more committed to the brand and simultaneously send out a message about their own social status, thus achieving "the highest levels of Maslow's hierarchy, which are esteem and self-actualization" (Stark, 2018, p. 92).

It is commonly agreed that a fashion brand is a cultural form (Cayla & Arnould, 2008) that can achieve an iconic dimension (Holt, 2003), but cultural recognition of fashion shows features very little in the literature, and then essentially in the communication science, cultural studies, and fashion studies fields. It is, therefore, pertinent to have a deeper understanding of the extension of the scientific concept of iconicity to elements other than brands themselves. Iconicity arises in the context of symbolism: "Icons are valued because, through them, people get to experience powerful myths" (Holt, 2003, p. 1). Holt considers that consumers perceive the myth created by the brand as embodied in the product or service which is offered. By buying the product or the service, they intend to consume the myth and forge a relationship with the brand itself, a process known as "ritual action" in anthropology. Because fashion shows materialize fashion (Entwistle & Rocamora, 2006), they can be construed as "marketplace elements," which may also become "iconic, and sustain their iconicity, through frequent mentions in diverse media and creative adaptations in multiple spheres of social life" (Gopaldas, 2016, p. 264).

Fashion shows by luxury brands have the ability to give social significance to consumers, but need to remain culturally relevant in order to maintain their iconicity in an oversaturated media landscape. Staging a fashion show in an evocative tourism destination is a way of nurturing this iconicity. As part of contemporary visual culture, luxury fashion brand's cruise collection shows intersect with tourism and can efficiently promote tourism destinations (Crouch & Lübbren, 2003). In this respect, cruise shows may be seen as place-based cultural tourism promotion (Smith, 2015).

Luxury Fashion Brands and Cultural Appropriation

Cultural appropriation is a complex phenomenon, drawing together threads from history, law and regulations, ethics, and ethnography. It originates in the concept of cultural heritage and is defined in its most basic form as "the act of taking or using things from a culture that is not your own, especially without showing that you understand or respect this culture" (*Cambridge Dictionary*, 2021). In the fashion industry, cultural appropriation issues have emerged and charges have been leveled at several luxury fashion brands. In a digital world, such controversies can provoke a reputational crisis and be highly detrimental to a fashion brand's image (Sábada, LaFata, & Torres, 2020).

Literature traces the initial phase of modern cultural heritage appropriation back to the 18th and 19th centuries, when European monarchies expanded their colonies across the world. According to Shand, "All manner of tangible cultural heritage of indigenous peoples [. . .] became available for appropriation into the cultural language of the very colonizers who had initially dislocated them" (Shand, 2002, p. 52). This historical origin concurs with the definition of cultural appropriation given by Vézina, which in turn refers to the definition of "traditional cultural expressions " or "expressions of folklore" provided by the World Intellectual Property Organization (WIPO) in 2000. According to Vézina, cultural appropriation is "the act of a dominant culture on taking a TCE whose holders belong to a minority culture and repurposing it in a different context, without the authorization, acknowledgement and/or compensation of the TCE holders" (Vézina, 2019, p. 6).

As far as creativity is concerned – in art or in fashion – it may sometimes be hard to distinguish between mere inspiration or appreciation and actual cultural appropriation. Inspiration is part of the creative process, and it is useful to unpack the scientific concept behind it. Inspiration has been theorized as having three core characteristics. "Evocation" is a response to a stimulating influence, while "transcendence" refers to an epistemic change, and "approach motivation" brings an idea to fruition (Thrash & Elliot, 2003). In terms of its components, "being inspired by" differs from "being inspired to" (Thrash & Elliot, 2004). Recent literature summarizes the relationships between the characteristics and components of inspiration: "*Being inspired by* gives rise to the characteristics of evocation and transcendence; *being inspired to* corresponds to approach motivation" (Cui, Thrash, Shkeyrov, & Varga, 2020, p. 9). One can also construe these components as the source and the expression of creative ideas. If it can be scientifically proven that creativity does include external influences in its process, the use (or misuse) of such influences will determine whether they are mere inspiration or actual appropriation.

From a historical perspective, European fashion has been influenced by other cultures since the opening of the Silk Road, and the Orient has been a cyclical source of inspiration. During the first half of the 20th century, French couturier Paul Poiret became famous for reinterpreting Orientalism in fashion. Taking inspiration from other cultures and reworking it is, in fact, a basic element of the creative process in fashion. This is why a distinction should be made between cases where inspiration can be construed as creative reinterpretation (such as Gucci Cruise 2017's gothic ode to British iconic symbols and eccentricity) and cases in which cultural appropriation may be offensive and harmful to ethnic groups (as part of the Sikh community felt after Gucci Fall 2018 show, where models wore religious Sikh-style turbans) or might lead to an undesirable commodification of cultural symbols through their decontextualization (like Carolina Herrera's 2020 Resort Collection, which included typical Mexican pieces that were claimed by Alejandra Fausto, the cultural minister of Mexico) (Pozzo, Filippetti, Paolucci, & Virgili, 2020).

Cultural symbols, such as material culture or performance, may also be altered in their cultural function or significance by tourism, which transforms cultural assets into tourism commodities (Rodzi, Zaki, & Subli, 2013). Like fashion – and despite the fact that cultural appropriation is not a uniform practice (Arya, 2021) – tourism leads to a form of commodification of local artifacts and ideas (Berliner, 2020; Chambers, 2009).

Study Methods

This chapter has two objectives: one, to understand how cruise collections dedicated to tourism destinations can enhance luxury fashion houses' brand culture through the connections they develop with these tourism destinations and two, to assess to what extent tourism destinations can benefit from the exposure afforded by luxury fashion brands' cruise collections. A two-step methodology was adopted. First, all luxury fashion brands that staged cruise shows from 2011 to 2021 (cruise collections 2012–2022) or that had planned to stage such shows but were forced to present online during the COVID-19 pandemic were identified through secondary data available on brands' websites and social media profiles, in online magazines, on the *Vogue Runway* application, as well as on the Institut Français de la Mode's online library. The different types of connection those brands had with tourism destinations through their cruise shows and cruise collections were also identified. This phase highlighted the unique specificities of Christian Dior cruise collections under the tenure of Maria Grazia Chiuri.

Second, based on the literature review, a theoretical grid positing the main issues raised by the influence of cruise collections on Christian Dior's brand culture and on destinations was constructed. This theoretical grid is divided into four main categories viewed from the perspective of the luxury fashion brand and from the associated perspective of the tourism destination: culture, imaginaries, communication, and cultural appropriation (Table 8.1).

Table 8.1. Theoretical Grid.

	Culture	Imaginaries	Communication	Cultural Appropriation
Luxury fashion brand				
Tourism destination				

Regarding the case study of Christian Dior cruise collections with Maria Grazia Chiuri at the helm (cruise collections 2018–2022), the analysis employs secondary data based on interviews and articles from newspapers, magazines, and trade journals, in English and French, all dealing with Christian Dior cruise collections since the appointment of Maria Grazia Chiuri, as well as information available on Dior's website. The data collected were analyzed using the theoretical grid constructed from the literature review.

Study Findings

Since her appointment as Artistic Director for women's fashion and accessories at Christian Dior Couture, Maria Grazia Chiuri has led a "Dio(r) evolution," according to the neologism printed on some of the t-shirts from her first collection for the prestigious Paris fashion house. She has reinvigorated the brand image and brand culture with her feminist and inclusive vision, as exemplified by the famous protest "We should all be feminists" t-shirts that went down the runway for her first show in 2016, as well as her collaborations with feminist artists, either on collections (Vicky Noble for 2018 Cruise Collection) or for the sets of the runway shows (Judy Chicago for Spring 2020 Haute Couture show). She also inspired Dior female mentoring scheme (Women@Dior).

Furthermore, while Maria Grazia Chiuri has developed Dior's brand culture in terms of societal values and feminist positioning, she has also opened up the culture of the French fashion house to nondomestic influences, incorporating know-how from other cultures through collaborations with local crafts persons. She introduced various new practices through her cruise collections, which gives them a unique synergy, as was apparent from the study of all the cruise shows staged from 2011 to 2021.

In order to identify the luxury fashion brands that actually stage cruise shows and to gain a better understanding of the links that such shows create between brand imaginary territories and tourism imaginaries, Table 8.2 provides an overview of cruise shows staged over a period of 10 years from 2011 to 2021 (cruise collections 2012–2022) or initially intended to be staged during the COVID-19 pandemic period. It also provides indications of the types of linkage between brands and destinations (merely staging a show in or drawing inspiration from a destination and/or collaborating with the local crafts and cultural scene). The table "Cruise shows by luxury fashion brands from cruise 2012 to cruise 2022 collections" highlights the various types of relationship that luxury fashion brands' cruise collections can create with tourism and destinations.

As Table 8.2, there are five types of cruise collection, which can be categorized from the lightest to the strongest link with tourism and destinations:

Table 8.2. Cruise Shows by Luxury Fashion Brands From 2012 to 2022.

Cruise Collection	Brand Name	Fashion Week Membership	Artistic Director	Show Staged in a Destination	Collection Inspired Destination	Collaboration With a Tourism Destination
2012	Chanel	Paris, France	Karl Lagerfeld	Antibes, France	•	
	Christian Dior	Paris, France	Bill Gaytten			
	Gucci	Milan, Italy	Frida Giannini	New York, USA		
	Louis Vuitton	Paris, France	Marc Jacobs	London, UK		
	Prada	Milan, Italy	Miuccia Prada			
2013	Chanel	Paris, France	Karl Lagerfeld	Versailles, France		
	Christian Dior	Paris, France	Bill Gaytten			
	Gucci	Milan, Italy	Frida Giannini			
	Louis Vuitton	Paris, France	Marc Jacobs			
	Prada	Milan, Italy	Miuccia Prada	New York, USA		
	Saint Laurent	Paris, France	Stefano Pilati	New York, USA		

2014	Chanel	Paris, France	Karl Lagerfeld	Singapore, Singapore	
	Christian Dior	Paris, France	Raf Simons	Monaco, Principality of Monaco	
	Gucci	Milan, Italy	Frida Giannini		
	Louis Vuitton	Paris, France	Marc Jacobs		
2015	Balenciaga	Paris, France	Alexander Wang		
	Chanel	Paris, France	Karl Lagerfeld	Dubai, UAE	•
	Christian Dior	Paris, France	Raf Simons		
	Gucci	Milan, Italy	Frida Giannini	United States of America	
	Louis Vuitton	Paris, France	Nicolas Ghesquière	Monaco, Principality of Monaco	•
2016	Chanel	Paris, France	Karl Lagerfeld	Seoul, Korea	•
	Christian Dior	Paris, France	Raf Simons	French Riviera, France	
	Gucci	Milan, Italy	Alessandro Michele	New York, USA	
	Louis Vuitton	Paris, France	Nicolas Ghesquière	Palm Springs, USA	

Table 8.2. *(Continued)*

Cruise Collection	Brand Name	Fashion Week Membership	Artistic Director	Show Staged in a Destination	Collection Inspired Destination	Collaboration With a Tourism Destination
2017	Balenciaga	Paris, France	Demna Gvasalia		North Africa	
	Chanel	Paris, France	Karl Lagerfeld	Havana, Cuba	•	
	Christian Dior	Paris, France	Studio	Oxfordshire, UK		
	Gucci	Milan, Italy	Alessandro Michele	London, United Kingdom	•	
	Louis Vuitton	Paris, France	Nicolas Ghesquière	Rio de Janeiro, Brazil		
2018	Balenciaga	Paris, France	Demna Gvasalia		Airport souvenir shop	
	Chanel	Paris, France	Karl Lagerfeld		Greece	
	Christian Dior	Paris, France	Maria Grazia Chiuri	California, USA	•	•
	Gucci	Milan, Italy	Alessandro Michele	Florence, Italy	Athens	
	Louis Vuitton	Paris, France	Nicolas Ghesquière	Kyoto, Japan		
	Prada	Milan, Italy	Miuccia Prada	New York, USA		
	Valentino	Paris, France	Pierpaolo Piccioli	New York, USA	•	

2019	Chanel	Paris, France	Karl Lagerfeld			
	Christian Dior	Paris, France	Maria Grazia Chiuri	Chantilly, France	Mexico	•
	Gucci	Milan, Italy	Alessandro Michele	Arles, France	•	
	Louis Vuitton	Paris, France	Nicolas Ghesquière	Saint-Paul de Vence, France		
	Prada	Milan, Italy	Miuccia Prada	New York, USA		
2020	Chanel	Paris, France	Virginie Viard			
	Christian Dior	Paris, France	Maria Grazia Chiuri	Marrakesh, Morocco	•	•
	Gucci	Milan, Italy	Alessandro Michele	Rome, Italy		
	Louis Vuitton	Paris, France	Nicolas Ghesquière	New York, USA	•	
	Prada	Milan, Italy	Miuccia Prada	New York, USA		
	Saint-Laurent	Paris, France	Anthony Vaccarello	Malibu, USA	Morocco	

Table 8.2. *(Continued)*

Cruise Collection	Brand Name	Fashion Week Membership	Artistic Director	Show Staged in a Destination	Collection Inspired Destination	Collaboration With a Tourism Destination
2021 (COVID-19)	Chanel	Paris, France	Virginie Viard		Capri	
	Christian Dior	Paris, France	Maria Grazia Chiuri	Puglia, Italy	•	•
	Gucci	Milan, Italy	Alessandro Michele	Rome, Italy		
	Louis Vuitton	Paris, France	Nicolas Ghesquière			
2022	Balenciaga	Paris, France	Demna Gvasalia			
	Chanel	Paris, France	Virginie Viard	Les Baux-de-Provence, France	• •	•
	Christian Dior	Paris, France	Maria Grazia Chiuri	Athens, Greece		
	Louis Vuitton	Paris, France	Nicolas Ghesquière			

Cruise collections by luxury fashion brands may merely be inspired by a destination but staged in the usual fashion week city of which the brand is a member. For example, the Chanel Resort 2018 Collection inspired by ancient Greece was staged at the Grand Palais in Paris, like all Chanel Fashion Week shows (Leitch, 2017; Yotka, 2017).

Cruise collections may also be staged in a destination without it inspiring the collection, as was the case with Louis Vuitton Cruise 2012 Collection, staged at the Four Seasons Hotel pool in New York. But this was inspired by a "Parisienne" theme (Vogue Runway, 2011), or the Christian Dior Cruise 2016 Collection, which was staged in the famous Palais Bulles in Cannes (*Blanks*, 2015). More rarely, cruise collections may be staged in one destination but be inspired by a different one, like the Saint Laurent Cruise 2020 Collection which was inspired by Morocco but staged in Malibu or the Gucci Cruise 2020 Collection which was inspired by ancient Athens but staged in Florence (Phelps, 2017).

Most commonly, cruise collections are both inspired by a destination and actually staged in it. The first major destination show influenced by local culture was Singapore, for the Chanel Cruise 2014 Collection; this set the bar for competitors. One of the most talked about cruise shows, also by Chanel, was staged on the Paseo del Prado in Havana for the 2017 cruise collection. As was identified by *i-D Magazine*, "criticisms have percolated," despite the fact that "there is no doubt that the show was a wholehearted celebration of local culture" and that "millions of people will see these images (and) they will encourage tourism" (Syfret, 2016). Among the issues raised was the fact that staging a luxury fashion extravaganza in a communist country could raise ethical problems.

Most of the time, cruise shows are positively received despite growing concerns around climate change and the environmental impact of these shows (Binkley, 2019). In certain cases, cruise collections may also have deeper connections with a destination when they are staged there and are the result of a collaboration between the luxury brand and a local crafts and/or cultural scene, as is the case with Christian Dior cruise collections since Maria Grazia Chiuri joined the luxury house (Phelps, 2020; Singer, 2018).

While the territorial and national dimension is one of the essential elements of brand culture for luxury fashion brands, the inclusive and collaborative practices with regard to cultures from other geographical origins of the Christian Dior cruise collections designed by Maria Grazia Chiuri makes their study particularly interesting, as the French fashion house stands out as the only brand to go beyond the inspiration of getaway imaginaries to create real synergies with destinations. Over her five cruise collections for Christian Dior, Maria Grazia Chiuri appears to have established a new tradition within the Paris fashion house (Table 8.3).

After forging cultural connections with California and Mexico for her first cruise shows, the artistic director went on to establish actual collaborations

Table 8.3. Christian Dior Cruise Shows and Collections.

Cruise Collection	Show Destination	Show Date	Connections to Destination
2018	California Calabasas Desert	May 12, 2017	• Collaboration with Vicki Noble, a Californian artist and feminist author on the *Motherpeace Tarot* prints
2019	Chantilly Château stables	May 25, 2018	• *Charreada* showpersonship by a Mexican *Escamurazas* Rayeni team, wearing Dior custom-made traditional *Adelita* dresses
2020	Marrakesh El Badi Palace	April 29, 2019	• Opening look designed by Moroccan women artisans from the Sumano organization, who also made the cushions featured on the set • Wax prints designed and made by Uniwax, an Ivory Coast-based factory which uses traditional techniques • Collaboration with Ivorian designer Pathé'O, and African-American artist Mickalene Thomas • Use of Ivorian and Moroccan fabrics
2021	Puglia Lecce	July 22, 2020	• Woven fabrics made by local craft organizations: Tessitura Calabrese and Le Constantine Fondazione • Traditional *tombolo* embroideries made by local craftswomen • Prints designed by the Italian contemporary artist Pietro Ruffo • Giant traditional Puglia light installations, called *luminarie*, designed by Italian contemporary artist Marinella Senatore • *Luminarie* prints designed by Italian contemporary artist Marinella Senatore • Music played by the local Orchestra Popolare
2022	Athens Panathenaic Stadium	June 17, 2021	• Live concert by the National Orchestra of Athens and the Greek singer Ioanna Gika

Table 8.3. *(Continued)*

Cruise Collection	Show Destination	Show Date	Connections to Destination
			• Greek President Katerina Sakellaropoulou among the attendees • Prints designed by Greek artist Christiana Soulou • Dior iconic Bar jackets and Book Totes embroidered with traditional Greek detailing by local artisans (Aristeidis Tzonevrakis) • Woven fabrics made by the Greek artisanal factory Silk Line, based in the ancestral silk hub of Soufli in Greek Macedonia • Traditional Greek fishermen's caps made by the Athenian workshop Tsalavoutas

with the local arts and crafts landscape beyond the show, for the design and the production of collections dedicated to Africa, Puglia, and Greece. For this reason, Christian Dior has been chosen as a case study for this chapter.

The case study data analysis highlights four main findings: One, Dior cruise collections by Maria Grazia Chiuri have fostered a more inclusive brand culture at the house since she joined and go further than any other luxury fashion houses to stage cruise shows; two, that developed real synergies between the brand and the local art scene and craftspersonship; three, as well as allowing destinations to benefit from the exposure afforded by Cruise shows; and four, Maria Grazia Chiuri has established a new approach to cruise collections going beyond mere inspiration by a destination or even cultural appreciation, and developing respectful collaborations with local artisans and craftspeople.

Although identity and brand culture form the basis of a brand's uniqueness, and therefore its symbolic value in the eyes of the consumer (Holt & Cameron, 2010), the literature suggests the dynamic character of identity and brand culture (Heilbrunn, 2018). This is even more important for luxury brands, whose uniqueness and rarity are enhanced by their culture (Kapferer, 2012). Luxury fashion brands can renew themselves through innovation and creativity, and even through a form of activism (Holt, 2016), while enhancing and revitalizing their heritage which, therefore, has a generative aspect.

The literature review illustrates this identity and the cultural generativity of a luxury fashion brand. For Maria Grazia Chiuri, "It's important to look to the heritage, but it's important to see it with the eye of the now, otherwise you are doing vintage or a museum piece" (Iredale, 2017). Even for cruise collections where links to the culture of luxury fashion brands are generally more tenuous, the designer's approach is to draw in detail on the archives and history of the fashion house, so that the creative process remains authentic and rooted in the heritage of the fashion house. For example, for her first cruise collection inspired by the American Wild West and shown in California, "She obliged house heritage by finding a concrete California connection to Monsieur Dior, who visited San Francisco in 1947" (Iredale, 2017).

At the same time, the artistic director is very aware of current societal trends and the social role that luxury brands must now play to remain relevant to consumers, especially the younger demographic who feel the need to identify with the brand's values and culture. According to Maria Grazia Chiuri,

> With the development of new media, fashion customers, especially the younger ones, are becoming more and more familiar with the industry. When they buy a brand's collection, they also want to buy into the message and influences. It is no longer just a question of aesthetics; clothes must express values but also adapt to changes in fashion. (Chahine, 2017)

In Le Figaro, Maria Grazia Chiuri justifies the societal dimension of Dior's brand values: "Today's pressing issues such as inclusion, cultural appropriation and feminism were barely mentioned five years ago. Fashion has more moral, environmental and societal obligations" (Faure, 2020).

In another interview with Le Figaro, Maria Grazia Chiuri sets out her vision of a more inclusive luxury fashion, which embraces cultural diversity:

> Fashion is quintessentially made of these blends, it is simply necessary to explain them, to put them in their context. We must constantly project the house into the future, open ourselves to the world. Things change quickly, and I try to understand the times in which I live. (Faure, 2019)

This type of inclusive luxury is both sustainable and necessary in order to adapt to the evolving luxury market.

From Fusion of Imaginary to Creation of Actual Synergies

"Like Mexico and Italy, the countries celebrated by Maria Grazia Chiuri with her previous cruise collections for the house of Dior, Greece has a strong evocative power" (Deeny, 2021).

For Dior's Artistic Director, "The Cruise Collection emerged from a dream and an idea of location, like a movie" (*Abriat*, 2018). Referring to her Dior Cruise Collection 2018, she confided to that she

> ...let the location, the desert landscape and natural California elements, inspire the collection, which was flush with handcrafted details, artisanal touches — fur, shearling, feathers, fringe — and rich desert colors. (Iredale, 2017)

Luxury fashion houses showing cruise collections also define locations according to other criteria, which are superimposed on the creative dimension. The location must correspond to regional development needs and evoke a tourism imaginary that consumers can only dream of. "Dior is not the first fashion house to capitalize on Los Angeles' rising cultural capital. In 2015, Louis Vuitton showed in nearby Palm Springs, while Burberry staged a show at the Griffith Observatory" (Sherman, 2017).

Referring to the Dior Cruise Collection 2019 show, Maria Grazia Chiuri believed the Mexican rodeo riders

> ...were a big inspiration for this collection. In this way, a narrative between past and present was developed, bringing together the spirit of equestrian sport and the know-how of the countries of the southern hemisphere. All defined by the French tradition of the House of Dior. (Dupuis, 2018)

Although the designer stresses the fusion between the imaginary territories of the house and Mexico, her approach is much more profound and rooted in a desire for openness, sharing, and solidarity. Based on the observation that,

> Craftspersonship continues to be undervalued, this is the case in Italy but also in Mexico and India. Everywhere in fact." In this field, she considers that, "France is an exception. The French are interested in arts and crafts, they respect them, they incorporate them within their culture and the historic fashion houses are keen to pass them on. (Faure, 2020)

In an interview, Grâce Wales Bonner (a British designer of African origin, who won the LVMH Prize in 2016 and whose graduation collection was called "Africa") comments on the Dior Cruise Collection 2020, on which she collaborated and agrees with the approach taken by Dior's Artistic Director. "I find Dior's approach and all this work on wax really interesting ... It seems to me that in this day and age, collaboration is the key." For this collection, she explains that Maria Grazia Chiuri entrusted the teams of a local wax print manufacturing brand with the long-standing brand codes of the fashion house (notably Toile de Jouy fabrics and tarot cards) and "she asked the Uniwax teams to reinterpret them with their own eyes and sensibility" (Dolivo, 2019). In Dior's approach, we can, therefore, identify a real collaboration with local crafts and cultures as well as an avoidance of decontextualization. Such a celebration of globalization and inclusivity corresponds to a current trend in luxury fashion brands, but apparently no other fashion house has taken its brand statement this far.

Moving beyond occasional synergies, which benefit the regeneration of the brand, the designer's motivation is also to help local artisans to regenerate their own production and thus enable them to survive and even develop. Her aspirations for the artisans following their collaboration with Dior and her hope that "It can help them also to translate that, to use it in a different way for the future, without losing the essence of that tradition" (Diderich, 2020).

From Ultimate Communications Tools to Mutual Soft Power Benefits

According to Sidney Toledano, CEO of the LVMH Fashion Group, "The cruise collections are exclusive collections, shown to VIP clients and the international press in exceptional settings around the world. These places always resonate with the history of the fashion house and illustrate the inspiration for the collection." The source notes that "this type of ultra-selective event was actually created as a reaction to the democratization of the fashion industry as a whole" (Michault, 2017).

For some time, the most prestigious fashion brands (such as Dior, Louis Vuitton, and Chanel) have been investing millions of Euros in shows staged in tourism destinations (recalling the original spirit of travel). This allows them to inject novelty (Zocchetti, 2019), to generate dedicated media coverage with a guaranteed and far-reaching impact compared to a Fashion Week show where brands share a very busy schedule (Denis & Reali, 2017), to engage top-spending clients with unique getaway experiences (The Business of Fashion, 2017), to stimulate sales of accessories in stores through "media coverage" (Denis & Reali, 2017), and to activate regional markets around the chosen destination (The Business of Fashion, 2017).

"Today's consumers are overloaded with information and overwhelmed with choice, they constantly need to be motivated by fashion houses, in the form of experiences (the context) and visual and interactive media (the content)" (Abriat, 2018). There is no doubt that a spectacular show in a getaway dream location, such as "a lavish spectacle complete with Dior-branded hot air balloons held in the Santa Monica mountains just outside Los Angeles" (The Business of Fashion, 2017), gives the collection local color and atmosphere, while allowing the brand to showcase itself exclusively and dominate the news cycle on social media for a longer period.

These are "major image vectors," according to Madame Figaro (Zocchetti, 2019); it would even appear that "If, in the past, haute couture enjoyed an unmixed supremacy [...], today it is the more commercial cruise collections that set the pace" (Michault, 2017). The power of the media coverage generated by these shows allows brands to assert not only their financial and creative capabilities, but also their power and standing. As Michael Burke, former CEO of Louis Vuitton, points out, cruise shows, which are true identity manifestos, make it possible to "offer a fashion house portfolio." This is also the conclusion drawn by the magazine, for which "The Cruise is not a fashion show. It is the most formidable weapon of soft power" (Denis & Reali, 2017).

This manifestation of "soft power" remains the prerogative of a few of the most prestigious luxury fashion brands. Their formats, like the locations, always read like an identity statement. For example, Sidney Toledano, former CEO of Christian Dior Couture, explained that "The choice of a location is a convergence of factors: the inspiration of the designer meets the history of the fashion house and the economic reality" (Denis & Reali, 2017).

Often the most spectacular fashion show of the year for any fashion house, the presentation of the cruise collection (as well as the lavish festivities that surround it) allows the brand to capitalize on delocalization by choosing fairy-tale settings, which it associates with its image. The intense and very positive media coverage of these locations also benefits the destination. These events are "also an opportunity to discover a city" and to promote this tourism destination (Dedet & Simon, 2019). This illustrates the idea "that tourism is a mediated activity" (Chambers, 1997), that is not circumscribed to relationships between "hosts" and "guests" (Smith, 1977); other actors or institutions can promote and influence tourism, especially in a postpandemic era, which notes that "the Dior show comes at a crucial time for the country, as it seeks to rev up tourism after a lost year." According to Pietro Beccari, former CEO of Christian Dior, "I was told that there was a very emotional press conference today with Maria Grazia and the Greek press. People were crying." "I'm very happy if we can contribute modestly to the image of Greece with this event, which will be seen by millions of people" (Diderich, 2021).

This show was indeed of the utmost importance for Greek tourism and was even attended by Greek President Katerina Sakellaropoulou. Greek Travel Pages reported that the show was broadcast live worldwide and communicated that "the French fashion house also pays tribute to Greece with a week of events [...] promoting works made in Greece by Greek creators with Greek textiles and materials" (Paravantes, 2021).

Even before the pandemic, in 2018, local online tourism media considered that the staging of the Gucci cruise show in the Alyscamps necropolis in Arles was actually good for local business and turned a welcome spotlight on the city from a tourism perspective (Garrabos, 2018; Hernandez, 2018). Arles-info.com reported that this event had "a positive impact in terms of image: for a few days, the name of Arles is being spread on blogs, in worldwide general and trade magazines, and is associated with this luxury universe." Furthermore, it links "the aura of the Alyscamps [to] the aura of Gucci" (Garrabos, 2018). This was reiterated in an article entitled "Why You Need To Add Arles To Your Travel Bucket List" (Thawley, 2018). Turning to Louis Vuitton, the fashion house's cruise shows for which the artistic director chooses "a modern architectural masterpiece for each venue" are pitched as "a cultured world tour" that can promote cultural tourism (Cartner-Morley, 2018).

Dior's Cruise 2020 extravaganza in Marrakesh received even more positive comments from Moroccan websites (Owen-Jones, 2019; Visit Morocco, 2019). *The Africa Report* states: "the Office national Marocain du Tourisme, with its modest budget of DH 750m ($78m), could not have afforded better advertising" (as is the case for most other places where luxury fashion brand destination shows are staged), adding that "Marrakesh is banking on viral marketing to attract more of this upmarket clientele" (Iraqi, 2020). It is true that few tourism offices can compete with the communications budget of luxury groups and achieve the same viral impact. For instance, "the live on social media channels recorded 11 million views" while "5.5 million saw it on demand, with a strong following in the Asian continent" to the "great satisfaction of the mayor of Lecce" (Natale, 2020).

In addition to the tourism destination itself, local crafts and know-how can also be showcased. This is the approach taken by Maria Grazia Chiuri and Dior, which is currently unique among luxury fashion houses showing cruise collections. "[S]ince she joined Dior, as Artistic Director, Maria Grazia Chiuri has celebrated craftspersonship and traditions of other countries or localities" (Numéro, 2021), and that "since her debut at Dior in 2017, Maria Grazia Chiuri has made a point of highlighting craftspersonship more than ever" (Jorif, 2020). Thus, the artistic director revealed to Le Figaro that for the 2021 cruise collection, "I wanted to present another extraordinary, lesser-known destination in Italy. Another side to the coin. Above all, to celebrate the crafts and traditions of Puglia. [. . .] The traditions of this region are being forgotten" (Faure, 2020). "[T]he locals were absolutely the story here" (Phelps, 2020), while "an ode to Puglia" and considers that "Dior's Cruise show celebrates Italian craftspersonship" (Rishika, 2020).

In parallel with tourism, Maria Grazia Chiuri and Dior prove that luxury fashion brands can highlight local arts and crafts; "Maria Grazia Chiuri has collaborated with several Greek workshops that perpetuate with virtuosity of invaluable techniques, combining tailoring and embroidery, but also jacquards and passementerie" (Crash Magazine, 2021), which is confirmed by Greek Travel Pages (Paravantes, 2021). Using fabrics and embroideries from traditional local crafts and communicating on these collaborations also casts "a welcome spotlight on techniques that otherwise risk dying out, including wax, which is under threat from cheaper digital copies" (Diderich, 2019) and shows, according to Dior's Artistic Director, "how much value there is in craftspersonship (in Puglia) and how important it is, for the future generations, don't lose it, but reinvest in all of this" (Natale, 2020).

From Cultural Appreciation to Respectful Collaboration

In the digital era, and as societal concerns about discrimination in all its forms are growing, a relevant question on the occasion of the Dior Cruise 2020 show staged in Marrakesh was:

> Can you draw inspiration from the African Continent when you are a major Western luxury fashion house? At a time when people are protesting against cultural appropriation of their heritage by fashion, the issue is particularly sensitive. (Brunel & Porret, 2019)

For this cruise collection, the Dior Artistic Director collaborated closely with a host of guest designers from the African continent and made sure local women artisans were involved at many levels in the organization of the event. These artisans "also designed the opening look, a cream-colored opera coat with henna-painted geometric motifs at the hem, and made the hand-painted plates that graced the tables at the welcome dinner" (Diderich, 2020). The idea behind Maria Grazia Chiuri's approach was "to develop a more equitable dialogue" between the luxury fashion brand and local crafts (Brunel & Porret, 2019). In an interview, Pietro Beccari, CEO of Christian Dior Couture, explained "This is our first show in Africa. It is also the first time that a luxury brand has been *made in Africa*. This message is very powerful" (Faure, 2019). Chiuri added that "Inviting people means working together on a project. It means building something together" (Diderich, 2019).

From the very start of the project, Maria Grazia Chiuri wanted to make sure that this could not be misconstrued as cultural appropriation. Reportedly she confessed,

> I had a very interesting conversation with Grace Wales Bonner on cultural appropriation, a matter which is extremely important to her. The fashion industry has been very harshly criticized in this debate. But I am convinced that creation has no boundaries. [...] In this dialogue, we found ourselves with a mutual passion for fabrics, especially wax, which fascinates me. [...] For me, this collection in Marrakesh was a way to generate other collaborations, to put them in the spotlight. To interact with local craftspeople, with different local traditions. I think it helps us to know each other better. These points of contact are good for fashion. I like that we are helping each other. This develops our knowledge about our mutual passion. (Jorif, 2020)

She, therefore, collaborated "with a host of guest designers from the African continent and beyond in a shared tribute to craftspersonship"

(Diderich, 2019). All prints and embroideries were designed and manufactured in Africa and the garments were then assembled in the fashion house's Paris workshops (Diderich, 2019; Dolivo, 2019; Faure, 2019).

To assist Maria Grazia Chiuri in her approach, the designer called on the expertise of Anne Grosfilley, an anthropologist specializing in African cultures and fabrics. According to the anthropologist, the artistic director "didn't take any traditional codes from elsewhere and make them her own. On the contrary, she arrived with the long-standing Dior brand codes and invited African women to revisit them. It was completely new." Rejecting any accusations of cultural appropriation, the academic concludes: "This Dior collection reflects all these encounters. It is not intended to be African; it wants to be humanist" (Dolivo, 2019).

Evidently, "For each Dior collection, hundreds of craftspersons join forces, cultures interact under the banner of preservation, sharing and open-mindedness" (*Crash Magazine*, 2021). This reflects the comments made by Maria Grazia Chiuri when she stated that

> . . .if there are no brands that have a huge platform and huge visibility to promote certain products, the risk is that they will be lost, but I think it's our responsibility. That's part of what it means to be a couture brand: to maintain this kind of tradition. (Diderich, 2019)

With their unprecedented vision of cruise collections, Maria Grazia Chiuri and Dior aim to celebrate cultural appreciation and collaboration in a shared tribute to craftspersonship. While obviously beneficial to local designers and artisans, such a vision also benefits Dior by enriching its own culture and savoir faire.

CONCLUSION

The Christian Dior Cruise Collections case study provides important insights for both scholars and practitioners around developing a holistic understanding of how the brand culture of luxury fashion houses should evolve and open up to a more transcultural approach in order to retain its relevance in the context of contemporary consumer culture.

The Christian Dior case study confirms and illustrates the literature review regarding the generativity of the concepts of identity and brand culture (Heilbrunn, 2018). In respect to cruise collections, the case study highlights that the media power of cruise shows outstrips traditional Fashion Week shows and also benefits the tourism destinations concerned. In addition, the brand's imaginary territory can be associated with nondomestic tourism locations and not just with the concept of Country of Origin. Furthermore, it demonstrates, in the case of Christian Dior's cruise collections under the artistic direction of Maria Grazia Chiuri, that the reputational risk of cultural appropriation is lower when references to nondomestic cultures are motivated by a genuine contextualized cultural appreciation and accompanied by real collaborations with local stakeholders.

But lessons can also be learned about the enhancement of luxury fashion brands' culture through cruise collections, both from research and management perspectives. From a research perspective, the Dior Cruise Collections case study highlighted two main points. First, this chapter highlights that cruise collections are a powerful marketing tool to inject both a new desirability and a new dimension to the concept of virtual rarity (Kapferer, 2012), which is now central to luxury identity. With the democratization and globalization of mega-luxury brands, these brands face the loss of objective (physical) rarity and have had to develop virtual rarity, to maintain the aura of luxury and sustain their high price policy. To create this impression of rarity, luxury fashion brands rely mainly on communications and limited editions. The artification of luxury fashion brands feeds into this phenomenon (Massi & Turrini, 2020), as do cruise collections. Cruise collections are indeed all about offer and communication.

Second, this chapter shows how luxury fashion brands and tourism destinations can mutually benefit from partnering on cruise collections and cruise shows. The cornerstone of these mutual influences and of how they are perceived by consumers is the emotional dimension (Lipovetsky & Roux, 2003) of luxury fashion consumption and tourism consumption (Frochot & Batat, 2013). This resonates with the concept of affective transfer discussed by McCracken (1989): luxury fashion brands, like tourism destinations, often have feelings or emotions associated with them. This is expressed with reference to the city of Marrakesh by Pietro Beccari, CEO of Christian Dior Couture: "The choice of this destination was an obvious one. Designers are inspired by Marrakesh, the French and our international clients feel good here. Everyone loves this city" (Faure, 2019).

The affective transfer theory implies that luxury brands can benefit from the positive feelings and emotions linked to destinations with which they are associated. By the same token, tourism benefit from the positive feelings and emotions toward a prestigious luxury fashion brand in the context of a cruise collection dedicated to a destination and staged there.

This case study highlights two key management considerations. One, this chapter suggests that real synergies between a luxury fashion brand like Christian Dior and a tourism destination – through respectful collaborations – can provide welcome exposure for local arts and crafts as well as increasing or restoring authenticity in the eyes of consumers, which is crucial for luxury brand management. Consumer perceptions of authenticity (Bruhn, Schoenmüller, Schäfer, & Heinrich, 2012) are key to the image of luxury fashion brands, whose storytelling and brand discourse must align with their practices.

Two, this chapter demonstrates that luxury fashion brands must be more inclusive in their cultural approach to remain relevant to their customers. Approaching cruise collections or inspiration from foreign material culture through actual and fair collaboration would, furthermore, comply with the requirement to protect local arts and crafts. In this respect, the approach developed by Christian Dior is fully aligned with certain governments' calls for fashion brands to collaborate with local communities. Mexico, for instance, works with the United Nations and UNESCO to enhance and protect local creative communities. According to Mexico's Culture Secretary, Alejandra Frausto Guerrero, "behind a garment, there is a cultural community" and that "you invite people you pay tribute to when you make a tribute" (Diderich, 2021). Another challenge for luxury fashion brands is to find the right balance between the symbolic power conferred by their national identities and the need to adopt a more transcultural approach.

Dior sets an example through its cruise collections of strong synergies between a luxury fashion brand and nondomestic cultures, benefiting both brand culture and these tourism destinations. It may, therefore, inspire other luxury fashion houses to build what Maria Grazia Chiuri considers a "fairer and more authentic future" (Roche, 2020), while enhancing their own brand cultures and symbolic equity in the eyes of consumers. In a postpandemic world, the promotion of tourism destinations, including their local cultural scene and crafts, by luxury fashion brands may also serve as a reminder of their attractiveness and contribute to the sustainability of their local cultures.

PART III
FASHION, TOURISM, AND THE CITY

Chapter 9

PARISIAN DEPARTMENT STORES AND FASHION TOURISM

Sophie Kurkdjian
American University of Paris, France

Abstract: This chapter explores how department stores came at the end of the 19th century to be at the origin of what is now called "fashion tourism." Contributing to a new "geography of commerce," it highlights the role of the space of the department store both as a place of conspicuous fashion consumption and tourism. Further, it demonstrates how Parisian department stores helped consolidate Paris's place as the capital of fashion and luxury. Far from being only places to buy the latest in fashion, the latter became indeed a symbol as quintessentially Parisian as the Eiffel Tower and as necessary to visit for the "Paris experience." **Keywords**: Department stores; fashion tourism; fashion consumption; shopping tourism; Paris; Parisian fashion

INTRODUCTION

Fashion has substantially contributed to the development of tourism in Paris and vice versa. Parisian brands, Paris fashion week, and fashion exhibitions attract tourists from all over the world, while the rise of tourism encourages the purchase of "fashion souvenirs" – a striped sweater, a luxury bag, or a fancy pair of sunglasses – from a fashionable shop on the avenue de Montaigne or the Champs-Élysées. The City of Paris is active in promoting Paris as a fashion capital. In 2015, with the "Paris loves fashion" campaign, the Town Hall not only wanted to encourage tourists to come to Paris for its cultural institutions but also for its fashion creations (Guilbaut, 2016; Isaad, 2018).

Fashion tourism developed significantly at the beginning of the 21st century when the City of Paris and the Presidency of the Republic stepped up

Fashion and Tourism: Parallel Stories
Tourism Social Science Series, Volume 26, 135–153

Published under exclusive licence by Emerald Publishing Limited
ISSN: 1571-5043/doi:10.1108/S1571-504320230000026009

initiatives to attract customers and tourists to Paris during Fashion Week (Craik, 2013). Tourists are eager, at least for once in their lives, to step into one of these luxury boutiques to see for themselves the marvels they have heard so much about: the monogrammed Speedy from Louis Vuitton, the Lady Dior by Dior, Birkin and Kelly bags from Hermès, the 2:55, and the little "timeless" tweed jacket from Chanel.

To enter one of these fashion palaces, to be welcomed in the richly decorated setting and to see the array of wonderful things to buy, this is the "luxury of experience" that, according to the philosopher Yves Michaud, has replaced the earlier luxury of expensive objects (Michaud, 2013). While they could likely get the same items in department stores near home, or even online, many tourists are keen to buy their Saint Laurent or Dior bag in Paris, because, according to Vanessa Friedman, editor-in-chief of the *New York Times'* fashion department, it gives them the feeling of acquiring a part of France they can take home with them (Friedman, 2015).

In addition to the timeless traditions of window shopping and the "shopping trip" (Vallée, 2013), the contemporary close alliance between fashion and tourism explains why people speak today of "fashion tourism," which has created around itself a whole range of opportunities to see, to fantasize, and to buy: Fashion Weeks, European Heritage Days, the LVMH Journées Particulières, created in 2011, the tailor-made offers proposed to clients and tourists, consisting of masterclasses that claim to make tourists "a true Parisian in ten lessons," visits to fashion exhibitions, guided tours of the Paris of historical fashion, and even personal meetings with designers. The initiatives are private and carried out by young start-ups. Airbnb offers, for example, a fashion offer: makeovers, style coaching, neighborhoods tours, and more. These events can be found all over the world, such as the Fashion's Night Out in New York, the Dubai Shopping Festival, the Hong Kong Summer Spectacular. The link between tourism and fashion is explicitly laid out on the official website of the Parisian Tourist Information Center. Here fashion tourists can find a "Paris Shopping" section, where a 40 *Art de Vivre Paris* (the art of Living Paris) press kit is available, translated into English, German, Portuguese, Chinese, and Korean – a sign of the direct implication of Paris in its fashion offer and a proof of the sector's dynamism.

The marriage of tourism and fashion is recent but not new. Foreigners have been coming to Paris to shop since the middle of the 18th century. Fashion tourism really took off at the end of the 19th century, thanks to the rise of department stores, at a time when, according to Benjamin (1935), Paris imposed itself as the capital of the 19th century. If shopping was an old practice among tourists who came to Paris to get hold of items from the latest collections, the department store – that is, a space full of exciting possibilities intimated by way of advertisements, almanacs, postcards, and much more – gave a new structure to the old practice of "fashion tourism." Indeed, as the department store developed, it became something more than a commercial space. It became rather a sort of historical and cultural monument that tourists came to admire and from which they returned home with a fashionable Paris "souvenir."

In this manner, the department store developed at the end of the 19th century as a touristic venue *par excellence*, paving the way to "fashion tourism" in the same way the beaches of Deauville promoted seaside tourism and, somewhat later, Chamonix created winter-sports tourism. The department store helped consolidate Paris's place as the capital of fashion and luxury (Spode, 2010). Between the end of the 19th century and the middle of the 20th century, the department store gave rise to tourism linked to fashion and conspicuous consumption. It also became something more – not simply an ideal place to buy the latest in fashion, but a symbol as quintessentially Parisian as the Eiffel Tower; and as necessary to visit for the "Paris experience." The merger of "tourism spot" and "shopping spot," according to Picon-Lefebvre (2013), has made department stores "manufacturers of an imaginary Paris"; that is a sort of "hyper Paris," attracting numbers of tourists longing to acquire a veneer of Parisian *je-ne-sais-quoi* (I don't know what).

This chapter considers the department store both as a *lieu* (the place) of consumption, where customers buy clothes, accessories, and furniture, and as an object of consumption in itself; that is, as a tourism spot where people come to stroll, to buy, or to spend a few hours in the reading room or on the rooftop. In other words, the department store has become an *experience*. The aim of this chapter is to explore how department stores, standing at the crossroads of the cultural, social, and business history of fashion, where consumers find the latest creations of the fashion industry, came to be at the origin of what is now called "fashion tourism" at the end of the 19th century (Blaszczyk, 2008; Belfanti, 2014; Rocamora, 2009). It intends to contribute to a new "geography of commerce," which emerged in the 2000s out of the older subdiscipline of economic and social geography, following the work of Louise Crewe, Christopher Breward, and Gilbert Davies. As a method, the *New Geography of Retailing* highlights the role of the unique space of the department store – a place, at once free, available to all (in particular, to the middle class), and without an obligation to buy anything (Breward, 2014; Crewe, 2000, 2017; Goss, 1993). It thereby illuminates their transformation to fashionable consumption and makes it possible to understand the new links between department stores and tourism that were forged at the end of the 19th century (Lemarchand, 2011).

This study is based on numerous secondary sources and especially on the monographs and primary studies of Parisian department stores (Andia, 2006; Miller, 1987). It has also benefitted from an assortment of ephemera produced by department stores (postcards, almanacs, diaries, posters, and the like), collected to show how they appeared early on with the objective of shaping the minds and fostering the loyalty of the customers – the better to empty their purses – through advertisements, brochures, and lithographs.

SYMBIOTIC RELATIONSHIP BETWEEN FASHION AND TOURISM

Department stores flourished between 1880 and 1914, a period in which the economic and technical conditions combined to make the existence of the department store possible (Pasdermadjian, 1949). Specifically, their development was linked to the growth of the urban population and to the revolution in public transport – the omnibus, the tram, and the underground railways (metro) which enabled stores to attract more customers.

The Bon Marché was created by Aristide Boucicaut in 1852 (Miller, 1987). It was born with the Second Empire and designed in harmony with the urban renewal policy of Napoleon III. Architecturally imposing, it was seen as a symbol of the modernity of the Parisian capital – unmissable from the outside, unforgettable from the inside. The marketing revolution it embodied rested on four innovations: the sale of products at low margins; in large volumes and renewed frequently; the sale of products at a fixed price; and free entry with no obligation to purchase (Pasdermadjian, 1949).

A second *grand magasin* Printemps was founded in 1865 by Jalluzot, followed by La Samaritaine in 1860, and Galeries Lafayette in 1893, under the direction of Théophile Bader and Alphonse Kahn (Andia & Leveau, 2006; Avenel, 1894; Caracalla, 1989; Chatriot & Chessel, 2006; Verheyde, 1993). All were distinguished by their distribution model: the sale of varied and frequently renewed products in a same space "with a reduced brand rate merchandise of current quality." In other words, the major characteristic of department stores was the juxtaposition of different types of products in one place under a single management.

Department stores also distinguished themselves from other stores then in vogue with respect to their architecture. Hrant Pasdermadjian considers that Printemps marked a decisive step toward the birth of an architecture specific of department stores that aimed at reconciling an efficient general use of the vast space formed by the building and an intelligent distribution of products on different floors – "the harmony of the whole depending on the balance of the proportions of each department" (Pasdermadjian, 1949, p. 28).

Paris, Capital of the 19th Century and the Figure of the Parisian

Paris became the "capital of the 19th century" precisely because it combined commercial know-how with the genius for style and luxury that had fostered and protected its status as the center of fashion for 200 years (Kurkdjian, 2020) Even in the early period, fashion had become a tool of soft power, thanks principally to Louis XIV (1638–1715) and his minister Jean-Baptiste Colbert (1619–1683), who recognized the commercial potential of French craftsmanship and decided to support artisans financially and materially (Kurkdjian, 2021). Building on centuries-old high-quality craft traditions,

Colbert put French fashion to work polishing the brand in international markets and supporting his mercantilist economic system.

In the 18th century, the emergence of the figure of the "marchande de mode" (fashion merchant), replaced in the middle of the 19th century by the "grand couturier" (fashion designer), as well as the development of the fashion press, enhanced the prestige of Paris as the capital of fashion and luxury (Kurkdjian, 2019; Sapori, 2010; Trubert-Tollu, Tetart-Vittu, Hattemberg, & Olivieri, 2017). In the economic, social, and urban planning strategy put in place to consolidate the reputation of Paris, the development of the department store played a leading role. Undeniably, the symbiosis between Parisian department stores and the city's status as the international capital of fashion depended on the fact that the former were not only places of commerce but also tourism sites.

Having become must-see stops on any tour of Paris, indeed the place where "fashion tourism" was born, the department stores were not only commercial additions to the geography of Parisian fashion, but themselves icons of that fashion. As a showcase for French know-how and innovation, the department store was seen from its inception as more than a simple place of commerce. It was a soft power tool used by France to promote its international profile. As an advertising brochure published by the Grands Magasins du Louvre in 1936 explained, "Finally, on account of its commercial relations through the creation of offices and agencies in overseas countries [the Grands Magasins du Louvre] widely disseminated the idea and French culture abroad." The idea of forging the taste of future customers, of educating them, is visible in all the advertising documents published by the department stores, which declared that the distribution of their commercial catalogs "powerfully helped the evolution of taste at the end of the 19th century, both in the clothing and in the furnishings" (Grands Magasins du Louvre, 1936).

Taking part in several Universal Exhibitions, even to the point of building their own pavilions, the department stores demonstrated the status they had assumed since their inception: that of showcase and ambassador of French taste to the world. Beyond being a place to buy things, especially exquisite things, the *grands magasins* intended to play a cultural and diplomatic role by embodying French taste and creativity. The presentation of their pavilions marked a further step in stamping the idea of "Frenchness" in the imaginations of present and future customers. This can be observed in the Universal Exhibition of 1900, the International Exhibition of Modern Industrial and Decorative Arts in 1925, and the International Exhibition of Arts and Techniques in Modern Life in 1937, for which the leading department stores – Bon Marché, Galeries Lafayette, Printemps, and Grands Magasins du Louver – erected their own buildings, an additional way of making themselves visible and desirable to people, including many tourists.

In 1900, Printemps built an Art Nouveau pavilion, designed by architect Charles-Auguste Risler and poster artist Jules Chéret, at the very heart of the Universal Exhibition, while Bon Marché commissioned its own structure (423 square meters), designed by Risler and inspired by the small Trianon of Versailles (Les Magasins du Bon Marché, 1900). It also published a special brochure for the occasion, as well as lithograph advertisements. According to historian Michael Miller, this participation demonstrated Boucicaut's (the founder of Le Bon Marché) desire to conceive the department store as a "symbol of Paris and France – for sightseeing, like the Louver or the Eiffel Tower" (Miller, 1987, p. 173). Twenty-five years later postcards from the International Exhibition of Modern Industrial and Decorative Arts showed the crowd thronging in front of the Bon Marché building, the "Pomone" pavilion, named after the Atelier d'Art Moderne du Bon Marché, created in 1922 to promote the creation of furniture and interior decorations for the department store.

In 1925, the Atelier Pomone, whose participation in the Salon des Artistes Décorateurs and the Salon d'Automne had already expressed its ambition to influence the development and democratization of decorative art, put up a pavilion designed by the architect Louis-Hippolyte Boileau and Paul Follot. At the same 1925 Exhibition, the Galeries Lafayette offered its own pavilion, created by La Maîtrise, advertising their Applied Arts Workshops, opened in 1922 to make all works of art available (furniture, fabrics, rugs, ceramics) and directed by Maurice Dufresne (Galeries Lafayette, 1925). Printemps, not to be outdone, gave the public "Primavera," its art workshop created in 1912 (Sentac, 1925). For its part, the Magasins du Louvre asked Albert Laprade to build the Studium Louvre (Studium-Louvre, 1925). All the great department stores thus played a role in promoting the France of luxury, good taste, and excellent shopping.

Besides the international universal exhibitions, the Parisian department stores were often mobilized during the commemorations of national events or the official visits of foreign heads of state, evidence of their role as embodiments of national power and prestige. From April 22 to 25, 1914, for example, the Louvre Hotel and Department Stores displayed dozens of French and English flags on their façades in honor of the visit of the English sovereigns. Department stores took the opportunity to have a postcard printed in memory of this event, and the mass of people gathered in front of the Hôtel du Louvre attested to the symbolic dimension of the place (Grands Magasins du Louvre, 1914).

In 1919, the Grands Magasins du Louvre, whose facade was entirely covered with the French flag and those of the allies, the national rooster, and the French Republic crest, celebrated the Souvenir des Fêtes de la Victoire and published a postcard attesting to the significance of the event (Grands Magasins du Louvre, 1919). In 1938, the Grands Magasins du Louvre celebrated Great Britain with 10 figures of bobbies affixed to the facade and surrounded by the British flag on the occasion of the visit of the new George VI and Queen Elizabeth in July 1938 (Grands Magasins du Louvre, 1938).

The Making of Department Store a Tourism Spot

Department stores were not founded as "tourism spots" but primarily as places of commerce and consumption; that is, as places to make money. However, very early on the stores mobilized certain tools to add services and advantages likely to attract potential French and foreign customers even beyond the possibility of buying new products, thereby acquiring a "tourism dimension." From the beginning, the *grands magasins* began to target two different audiences: one, local and middle class, interested in the department store as a convenience store; the other, international, attracted by the unique format that combined commerce, leisure, and culture. By the end of the 19th century, traditional consumers of Parisian fashion, coming from the four corners of the world, were already flocking to the department stores, which had made themselves beacons of Parisian taste. These elite consumers were already familiar with Parisian fashion, thanks to the French press which circulated in Europe and the Americas, but also thanks to distance selling.

The reach of Paris fashion extended further when well-known couturiers opened branches of their stores in foreign cities, enabling customers to acquire Parisian products without the expense and bother of traveling to France. For those who did come to Paris, however, the growing sector of department stores, making good use of advertising and the tourism media, established themselves as a third option, between the fashion houses themselves and their boutiques in New York, Buenos Aires, and other cities (Coëffé & Morice, 2019).

How did these shopping spaces go about turning themselves into "tourism sites"? It began with the commercial imagination of the founders, who believed they could make their stores more than simple places to find all the latest novelties and reconceived them as places for "recreation," providing for the "controlled release of the constraints on the emotions" (Elias & Dunning, 1994, p. 1). Several elements contributed to this impression of recreation, of breaking away from everyday life: reading rooms, restaurants, tea rooms, galleries of art, photographic studios, shop windows to admire, rooftop vistas, and toilets. These included all the services shoppers could find at the Bon Marché or Samaritaine. Vincent Coëffé and Jean-René Morice use the word *heterotopia*, coined by Michel Foucault in 1967 in his conference on "Other spaces," to describe these material utopias (Coëffé & Morice, 2020).

According to Coëffe and Morice, the space of heterotopia, perfectly embodied in the *grands magasins*, allowed individuals to break away from the places and routines of their daily life (Andriotis, 2010). This strategy is easy enough to see in the typical department store window, a place encoded as an elsewhere, associated with a certain exoticism. The internal layout of the department store also helped to reinforce and amplify such imagination, as shown by the Bon Marché which created a full experience with a sense of wonder through the aestheticization of the physical sales space in a theatrical context" (Coëffé & Morice, 2020, p. 1). At once monumental, theatrical, and fantastic, the department store, and in particular the Bon Marché whose owner, Boucicaut, saw his department store as one of the monuments of Paris, developed into a must-see attraction (Miller, 1987, p. 169).

Department Stores Featured in Tourist Guides

Guides for tourists played an essential role in promoting tourism in department stores (Moret, 1992; Hancok, 2003). Even before the creation of the Bon Marché, tourist guides promoted what they called the "bazaars" to be found in many Parisian passages. In 1852, for example, the Chaix *New Guide for Foreigners in Paris*, included for the first time the "Travel Bazaar" at 14 boulevard Poissonnière. This was the first appearance of a business in a tourist guide, reflecting, according to Joanne Vajda, and marked the emergence of tourism that was not exclusively cultural (Vajda, 2006). Commercial advertising and shopping tips were gradually incorporated into travel guides as leisure and shopping infiltrated the tourist arena.

According to Vajda, the guides provided store addresses, offered to transform the tourist into an elegant Parisian, and thereby helped "to make Paris the capital of the luxury industries" (Aubusson et Kugelmann, 1843; Vajda, 2006). One of the examples cited by Vajda, the *General Guide in Paris for 1855 followed by a visit to the Exhibition*, is particularly interesting. Addressing tourists who "wanted to buy profitably," it intended to lead them past the "windows of Parisian houses which best represented the high perfection of the Parisian article" (Guide général dans Paris, 1855, p. 121).

In 1863, Henri Conty, in his practical guide to foreigners, provided the addresses of bazaars – notably the European bazaar, the Bonne-Nouvelle bazaar, and the Montmartre bazaar – as spots to be visited so as to "take some souvenir from Paris" (Conty, 1863, p. 185). The passages, sometimes known as "glass galleries," were among the other places recommended by the Conty guide, which described in particular the passages of Panoramas: Jouffroy and Verdeau on the Boulevard Montmartre, Vivienne and Colbert on the Rue Vivienne, Vero-Dodat on the Rue de Rivoli, and the passage Choiseul on Rue de Choiseul (Conty, 1863, p. 185). Another guide, published at the time of the Universal Exhibition of 1867, mentioned the shops in the galleries of the Palais-Royal, where "fashion had set its mobile empire," and where the tourist can find anything that "can tempt, and luxury and fashion, to flatter the senses, charm the eyes and seduce minds and hearts" (Parville & Montémont, 1867, p. 151).

Department stores soon found their way into tourist guides. As Frédéric Moret explains, "Contrary to what was still the case in 1889, the department store won out over the traditional stores; that is to say that travelers were sent as a priority to department stores, sometimes even to make a visit merely out of curiosity" (Moret, 1992, pp. 83–84). In 1867, the *Almanac of the foreigner* integrated the Magasins du Louvre (1855) in its recommendations for buying corsets, lingerie, fabrics, and novelty items (Almanach de l'étranger, 1867). In 1890, the "large and luxurious" Printemps stores and the "luxury Bon Marché stores" appeared as places to see in the ninth and seventh arrondissements of Paris in the guide *The Stages of a Tourist in France: Paris, Promenade in the 20 Arrondissements* (Martin, 1890). The Grands Magasins du Louvre in the first arrondissement was also mentioned. Happy rivals of the Bon Marché and the Printemps, "they were open to all curiosities and meet all desires."

In 1874, the *Guide for Foreigners in Paris and its Surroundings,* distributed by the Hôtel du Louvre, recommended the Grands Magasins du Louvre and the Belle Jardinière (Guide de l'étranger dans Paris et ses environs, 1874). Similarly, the Bon Marché in 1900 published *The Illustrated Guide to Bon Marché* (illustrated with 175 engravings and 9 color maps), which contained guides for that year's Universal Exhibition (Les Magasins du Bon Marché, 1900a). Guides contributed to the notoriety of department stores, since not all the Parisian places appeared in those guides but only a selection passed the test and were presented as "must see." Guides were meant to trigger the desire to visit. They constituted the act of information that preceded the act of mobility and purchase.

Language of Fashion and Art

From the beginning, according to Shoshana-Rose Marzel, art was always part of the department store model, and the stores had always tried to advertise this fact by way of their general architecture and interior decoration, as well as through their posters, catalogs, and diaries often produced by recognized designers and artists. Most of all, however, they established their cultural credentials through their displays, designed, in effect, as art exhibition programs within their buildings (Marzel, 2017). These cultural signals had two objectives: to educate people by shaping their tastes (Perrot, 1981), while at the same time attracting them with an original experience that went beyond mere shopping by offering customers the opportunity to discover artists and works of art and, beyond that, parts of history and art history.

Art works were also conceived by store managers with a view to adding glamor to the clothes sold by the store. Museums – in particular fashion museums, like the Palais Galliera and the Musée des Arts Décoratifs – and department stores developed at the same time at the end of the 19th century, pursuing similar esthetic, educational, and commercial objectives (Slowinska, 2014), even if the commercial space of the *grands magasins* exceeded what contemporary museums could dedicate to their collections, In 1975, Andy Warhol said "all department stores will become museums, and all museums will become department stores." (Warhol, 1975). During the first half of the 20th century, museums, long reserved for a small number of visitors, who alone had the time, money, and knowledge of the existence of cultural institutions to appreciate them, opened their doors wider. There was an "almost complementary relationship between the action of major museums and the mission of department stores" (Capart, 1932, p. 127).

The Grands Magasins du Louvre was the store that exploited this idea to the fullest extent, even borrowing the world-famous name of the great museum (Giffard, 1882). Many of its advertisements undoubtedly played on the confusion produced in the mind of customers. Beyond postcards and posters focusing on this muddle of names, the Grands Magasins du Louvre went so far as to put its name on a catalog of *Masterpieces from the Louvre Museum*, where it retraced the history of the Louvre and that of its collection of paintings which was "the oldest, the most varied, and perhaps the richest in the world."

The first 14 pages cleverly interweaved the history of the Louvre's department stores, written in red on the left pages, and that of the Louvre Museum, written in black on the right pages. In its history of the Louvre, the catalog explained that Napoleon III fulfilled the dream of François Ier, making the Louvre "the richest temple of art" in the world. In fact, the completion of the Louvre did not take place until 1855, when the store catalog took the opportunity to link the history of the store to the history of the museum "Commerce and democracy," according to the catalog, "have found the ground ready to receive this Hôtel du Louvre and these Magasins du Louvre," which were also symbols of a great thing, "the blossoming of the industrial power of France ... We can therefore say that the opening of the Louvre Stores is a memorable date in the history of the 19th century" (Les Grands Magasins du Louvre, 1900, p. 5). Managers of department stores had every interest in working with museums to curate "the tastes of a discerning clientele" or to "improve the taste of buyers" – in other words, to inspire customers to turn their homes into little museums and then to satisfy that desire (Capart, 1932, p. 125).

Ernest Cognac-Jay opened Samaritaine in 1870 near the Pont-Neuf. In 1872, he married Marie-Louise Jaÿ, the first saleswoman in the clothing department at Bon Marché. Samaritaine acquired four new buildings between 1905 and 1910 on the Rue de Rivoli. At the same time, Ernest and Marie-Louise brought together a collection of 18th century works of art to be exhibited in Samaritaine de Luxe, which they opened in 1917. *Le Monde*

Illustré described the store as a temple where commerce and that of taste stood side by side, "attesting by their presence" the fruitful union of business and art" (Conlin, 2000, p. 193). Cognac-Jay exhibited his art collection there in November 1925, then twice in 1926 and one last time in October 1927 (Dirion, 1926). Among the works exhibited were paintings from Boucher, Quentin La Tour, Renoir, Pissaro, and Monet (Le Monde Illustré, 1929, p. 196). The exhibition commingled the store's commercial space with its artistic space since the paintings were displayed side-by-side with the objects for sale.

In 1928, after the death of Ernest Cognac-Jay, the collection became the Cognac-Jay museum and fell under the aegis of the City of Paris. The gathering of these works of art did not reflect a specific interest in beautiful objects or any desire to profit from buying and selling them. Rather, Cognac-Jay's art collection was part of his strategy for promoting his store by making it a "national cultural institution," where visitors could exercise their "good taste" (Conlin, 2000, pp. 195,199). Department stores allowed people who were intimidated by museums, or simply had no interest in beauty for its own sake, to discover the latest fashions and works of art. Perhaps this amounted, in a peculiar way, to the democratization of art.

If the art works exhibited at the Bon Marché comprised only those pieces had not been accepted at the official Salon of the Académie des Beaux-arts (Miller, 1987, p. 168), they nonetheless formed a different species of "museum rooms," spread over different locations (reading room, shopping arcade, clothing showroom) in the department store. In fact, the Bon Marché published a pamphlet in 1910 ("Modes de Paris since Louis XVI according to the documents of the National Library of France for the period from 1775 to 1860 and according to the models and Creations of the Bon Marché for the period from 1860 to 1910," Au Bon Marché, 1910) that explicitly urged customers to read the sections of the store as they would the rooms in a museum. Thus, it described the Furniture and Carpet Gallery:

> It is a luxuriously and conveniently installed store; the vast gallery, at mezzanine level, which runs along the Rue de Babylone, is a living room resplendent with all the wonders of ancient art and modern' artifacts; all the splendors of the past and of the future make this salon a veritable museum, near which can be found the old tapestries, old silks and embroidery so sought after by amateurs. (Les Magasins du Bon Marché, 1910)

The pamphlet went on to depict the different rooms of this Gallery as forming a "Permanent Exhibition" that enabled visitors to project themselves into their future homes. Some of the items on display and for sale were copies of older works of art; others were included only as inspiration. The pamphlet further testified to the department store's desire to establish itself in the cultural and scientific sphere by offering a history of fashion developed with that most emblematic institution of culture and French knowledge: the National Library of France.

The Bon Marché reading and painting rooms, put together, measured 20 meters long and 8 meters high and were explicitly designed in the style of a gallery in the Louvre (Miller, p. 168). The reading room, on the first floor, allowed customers to read the press and do their correspondence while contemplating paintings and sculptures that had been assembled for the high-brow atmosphere they created – but that could also be purchased – a place "where trade has put on artistic modern finery" (Les Magasins du Bon Marché, 1910, p. 67). From 1872, store customers could take guided tours of the reading room, given by an "inspector-interpreter," except on exhibition days.

The practice of turning commercial spaces into mini-museums spread across the world of *grands magasins* at the end of the 19th century. Georges Dufayel (1855–1916) brought together statues, paintings, columns, bronzes, and earthenware in the Dufayel Department Store (Williams, 1982). The process was facilitated by the fact that many department store owners were also collectors. This was also the case of Jules Jalluzot (1834–1916), co-founder of Printemps, of Théophile Bader (1864–1942), at the head of Galeries Lafayette (Boime, 1979), and of Ernest Cognac-Jay, at Samaritaine.

Other store owners and directors were generous patrons of the arts. This was the case of Alfred Chauchard (1821–1909), director of the Galeries du Louvre, and of Marguerite Boucicaut (1816–1887), director of the Bon Marché, who later bequeathed its collection to the Louvre Museum. Department stores further blurred the lines separating art and commerce by publishing postcards featuring paintings by the great masters, which they distributed to their customers free of charge. Whether it was a reproduction of "L'Accordée du Village" by Jean-Baptiste Greuze, exhibited at the Louvre Museum and distributed at the store by Samaritaine, or "Les Glaneuses" by Jean-François Millet, presented by the Louvre and circulated by the department store À Réaumur, these artifacts helped link department stores to France's cultural patrimony and reinforce its reputation for artistic flair.

Department Stores as Monument

"Monument," "palace," "exhibition gallery," "establishment unique in the world," and "one of the most remarkable curiosities in Paris" are among terms used to describe fin-de-siècle department stores, borrowed shamelessly from the lexicon of tourism. And they sent tourists the unmistakable message that the *grands magasins* were as much a part of the "Paris experience" as the Eiffel Tower, the Garnier Opera House, or the cathedral of Notre Dame. The very location of department stores, near train stations and hotels, only reinforced their touristic appeal (Picon-Lefebvre, 2013). According to Virginie Picon-Lefebvre, who recalls that Henry James installed his American hero next to the Saint-Lazare station, the department store district was typically occupied by foreigners with hotels and apartments for rent (James, 2016). Moreover, once the department stores fully grasped their potential as tourism destinations, they began to produce maps and *agendas* that highlighted their store's location alongside other standard sites of Tourist Paris.

The department store agenda (a small notebook customers could use to record their daily tasks, their shopping lists, and their accounts, etc.) could also serve as a durable advertisement, a material memory of a tourist visit to Paris. The agendas could also contain more explicit sorts of advertising for hotels, restaurants, and museums. Capart called the agenda sponsored by the Bon Marché, "an indispensable book" that enabled him to speak directly to an "innumerable clientele" and to tell them, for example, that "among the most important things to achieve during the year 1931 was a visit to the Royal Museums of Art and History, to the Parc du Cinquantenaire, in Brussels." Capart believed that the documents appearing in the department store agendas helped to "improve the taste of buyers" and send "new customers" – the term was chosen on purpose – to cultural venues. He explained further that there was "an almost complementary relationship between the action of large museums and the mission of department stores." "What is a museum," he asked rhetorically? "It is a great depository where no item is for sale. And what is a department store? It is a big museum where everything is for sale" (Capart, 1932, p. 127).

Beyond *agendas* and tourist maps of the capital, department stores expanded their scope, publishing *plans* of "monuments in the surrounding region." For example, the Bon Marché collaborated with the Commission of the Historic buildings to create a map of the Ile-de-France with pictures showing the nearby castles, churches, abbeys, and towns across the Greater Paris area. At the center of this plan, Paris, represented in the form of a circle, had only one monument indicated. Not surprisingly it was the Bon Marché. In 1931, on the occasion of the Colonial Exhibition, department stores published maps of the Exhibition, which they offered to their customers. Galeries Lafayette was an interesting case. Since the store was in the center of Paris, and not near the Porte dorée, where the exposition was being held, it does not appear on the Galeries Lafayette map of the exposition. On the other hand, the map does show the Galeries Lafayette stand *within* the exposition. This suggests that, while the map in this instance did not aim to highlight the store's role in the greater tourism ecosystem, it nonetheless wanted to remind everyone that Galeries Lafayette remained a central player in Parisian cultural life.

In the end, at least three elements came together to allow the big department stores to present themselves plausibly as tourism spots. These elements promoted relentlessly in their promotional materials were the architectural uniqueness of the stores themselves; the ability to serve customers in languages other than French; and, the panoramic view offered from the roof of the store.

Architectural Revolution of Department Stores

Even before they developed advertising policies to attract tourists at the turn of the century, the *grands magasins* had begun to emphasize the architectural distinction of their buildings to stimulate the interest of potential visitors. Picon-Lefebvre points out how the stores established their *bona fides* as tourism sites through the "architectural devices of monumental staircases, cupolas, and sumptuous entrances [which staged] fashion, luxury, and Paris in an increasingly theatrical way" (Picon-Lefebvre, 2013, p. 131). The department stores stood out, both on the Parisian skyline and in the minds of people, for their imposing exteriors, which made them exemplary symbols of the more general archetype that Baron Haussmann had developed in the 1850s and 1860s, as he reinvented the urban landscape in the capital.

The monumental dimension, which was embodied in the domes of Galeries Lafayette and the Bon Marché, is easily discernible in postcards and photographs of the era. The novelist Emile Zola made his own contribution to the iconography of department stores in his fictional description of the Bon Marché:

> The iron staircases, with a double revolution, developed bold curves, multiplied the landings; the iron bridges, thrown over the void, ran straight, very high and all this iron put there, under the white light of the windows, a light architecture, a complicated lacework in which the day passed, the modern realization of a dream palace, of a Babel. (Zola, 2009)

The initial construction and successive redevelopment of the *grands magasins* had been inspired through the years by other examples of grand public architecture. They include the 19th century grand hotel, the 1930s ocean liner, the 1950s mall, and the airline terminal of the 1990s. They all had been preeminently sites of tourism (Picon-Lefebvre, 2013, p. 131). Glazed rotundas and galleries made of steel beams and reinforced concrete, inspired by the Exhibition of 1867, were their major features. The store buildings engaged famous architects – including Gustave Eiffel, engineer of the eponymous tower, He took part in the construction of the Bon Marché, which succeeded in establishing itself as "a permanent fair, an institution, a fantasy world, a spectacle of extraordinary proportions, so that going to the store became an event and an adventure." The monumental exterior of the building gave people the feeling of entering a theater, an opera hall, or even a temple, while the lavish interior arrangement and decoration brought to mind a museum – visual impressions that contributed to making the Bon Marché a unique and attractive place (Miller, 1987, p. 167).

Frantz Jourdain was the chief architect of the Bon Marché. He also designed one of the new Samaritaine buildings constructed between 1905 and 1910, in addition to the even more luxurious art-nouveau *Samaritaine de Luxe*, on the Boulevard de Capucines, that became home for the Cognac-Jay collection. First put up in 1865, Printemps was rebuilt by Paul Sédille in 1881, following a fire. A great traveler, Sédille was a defender of what was called polychromatic monumental style; that is, the practice of decorating architectural elements in a variety of colors. He reconstituted the department store on a perimeter of 2,950 m^2 extending from the Boulevard Haussmann to the Rue du Havre, the Rue de Provence, and the Rue de Caumartin. Using iron as a visible decorative element on stairs and walkways, Sédille organized the store around a central nave, surrounded by galleries connected by a central bridge and accessible by a large staircase. The building was equipped with an electric lighting system in 1883. In 1906, Printemps was again modernized by René Binet who endowed it with a large hall adorned with a 42m-high dome lighting the store and a central staircase of Art Nouveau inspiration.

As monumentalism goes, Galeries Lafayette stands out for its 86m frontage built by architect Georges Chedanne. Chedanne, having started his career building or renovating hotels – such as the Hôtel Watel-Dehaynin (1900) and the Hôtel Mercédès (1903) in the 16th arrondissement, the Elysée Palace Hôtel (1898), and the Grand Hôtel Château Perrache in Lyon (1905) – wanted to use the same principles he applied to the construction of hotels to department stores (to build in length and with an imposing perspective). Yet it was the Galeries du Louvre that pushed this architectural conflation between hotel and department store to the greatest extent. Beyond borrowing its name from the museum, the store also shared it with the Grand Hôtel du Louvre, created by Emperor Napoleon III in 1855, on the occasion of the Universal Exhibition.

With 700 rooms, the hotel was groundbreaking, offering an unprecedented set of services to its clients: omnibus transfers between train stations and the hotel, guides, interpreters, and local information, as well as more than 40 shops on its ground floor. The hotel called these shops the "Galeries du Louvre." In 1857, it rechristened them the *Grands Magasins du Louvre*. By 1888, having sprawled so much, they took over the entire hotel and in effect became a full-fledged department store: the Grands Magasins du Louvre. The hotel, was moved to the other side of the Place du Palais-Royal, to give full latitude to the department store. As the advertisement noted, "The entire Louvre hotel converted into a store" (Machado, 2008). A promotional brochure, published by the Grands Magasins du Louvre in 1936, aptly summed up the desire of the owners to link the store to the hotel to the museum in the minds of customers. The brochure, pompously titled "Les

Grands Magasins du Louvre." Their role in national, social, and economic life from 1855 to 1936 (Les Grands Magasins du Louvre, 1936) featured a reproduction of the Louvre Hotel and Department Stores on the cover and, on the back cover, an illustration of the Louvre Museum in 1888 and 1936.

As Coëffé and Morice analyze the workings of the semiotic system of the department store, the visitor was "engaged" by the structure and the scenography of the store window, which served as an essential interface between the exterior and the interior, this setting functioned as a screen suggesting the architectural, decorative, and commercial potentialities within (Coëffé & Morice, 2019; Conchoy, 2011). Taking the department store as a showcase for French fashion and luxury, its windows featured an elegant illustration of Parisian taste. But they were as opaque as they were transparent – a suggestion and a tease, as well as a straightforward presentation – arousing visitors' curiosity and inviting them inside to explore the promise implied by the display. In fact, the window displays soon became a cultural phenomenon, in their own right.

At Christmas time, for example, elaborate presentations invited clients to exotic wintry travels. The Bon Marché inaugurated its Christmas exhibition in 1909 with a reconstruction of the North Pole, followed by the Galeries Lafayette, then by Printemps in 1920. Shoppers and passers-by crowded in front of the windows to admire the extraordinary performance. On the inside, free entry, and the "intoxicating" sense of being in both an "oriental bazaar" and an "exhibition gallery," made the department stores perfect venues for wandering as well as buying, in the manner of Zola's character Mme. Guibal in his novel *Au bonheur des dames* (the Ladies's Delight): "strolling through the store for an hour, enjoying the spectacle of accumulated wealth without buying even a yard of calico" (Zola, 2009, p. 164). In this respect, the department stores made themselves heirs to the *passages* of the 18th century, bringing together various shops and stalls, becoming preeminent places of promenade and sociability, where unexpected meetings and discussions could occur. A staple of 19th-century tourist guides of Paris, these passages had provided the perfect setting for the figure of the flâneur the rambler through interesting public scenes.

As the 20th century dawned, flâneurs increasingly took their perambulations to the department stores, where they could meander stylishly without having to buy anything. In a more practical sense, however, the store interiors were imagined as commercial spaces and aimed above all at "intoxicating" customers, with a view to having them purchase things (Berdet, 2013). Galleries, serving to transport customers from one space to another, directed their gaze, and the entire scenography was orchestrated in such a way as to turn visitors' attention to the incomparable array of commodities to desire and to buy. The different sections of the store, according to Barbara Henderson-Smith, were laid out in a coherent and logical way, offering patrons a palette of both useful and frivolous products, from underwear to clothes to accessories, in much the same way that museums served as educational spaces – but museums educated the public on behalf of civil society, department stores stoked their public's desire to consume (Henderson-Smith, 2003).

Support for the Visitor-Customer and Rooftop View

To complement their beguiling architecture, department stores also set up services aimed at welcoming foreign customers and facilitating their shopping. Their postcards and advertising brochures translated into English and Spanish, left no doubt about the international character of their customers (Sorrieu, 19th century). The Bon Marché, for instance, published numerous advertising documents in both French and English to explain the system, of quality and fair prices on which the sale of their products was based. With a cover illustration depicting the store, these brochures functioned like business cards.

At the Bon Marché, Aristide Boucicaut, the founder and owner, set up delivery systems abroad, recruited multilingual correspondents to facilitate purchases by foreigners, and hired "interpreters in all languages". He arranged tours and demonstrations within the store itself, delivered in French but also available in English (Idenstadt, 2016). The visitor who followed this tour was led from department to department, in the process discovering not only clothes but also works of art such as paintings and sculptures. An archetypical postcard of the Bon Marché at the beginning of the 20th century features a Reading Room with several paintings arranged in a row one on top of the other, in a way that mimicked an exhibition hall. Visitors stopped here, not to buy new products but to read the press and admire the works of art. In this way, writes Deborah Andrews, the department store imposed itself as a kind of "public museum" (Idenstadt, 2016, p. 19).

Like the Eiffel Tower, Montmartre, or the Arc de Triomphe, each department store had a viewpoint, a terrace from which to observe Paris. Customers could enjoy the grand view of Paris with no obligations. Postcards produced by department stores highlighted this privilege. The Galeries Lafayette touted their "Panorama of Montmartre taken from their Terrace," featuring two women leaning on a railing and admiring the Sacre-Coeur Basilica on the hill (Aux Galeries Lafayette, 1910a). In summer, the store also offered a tearoom on its "monumental terrace" provided with around 70 parasols, making it look like a restaurant.

The terrace, which offered "afternoon tea and concert in front of the magnificent Panorama of Paris" (open from 3p.m. to 6p.m.) was no gimmick but rather an integral part of the experience proposed by the store, an illustration of its overall good taste. Similarly, a brochure entitled "Aux Galeries Lafayette: Parfumed Home," declared that "The Department Store at Galeries Lafayette with its monumental terrace is one of the main curiosities" of the city (Aux Galeries Lafayette, 1910b). Other publicity referred to the terrace as one of its "the greatest attractions" and invited visitors to come up and take a "tour of Paris" (Aux Galeries Lafayette, 1931). The terrace remained engraved in collective memory as the place where the famous aviator, Jules Védrine, the first man to fly faster than 100 miles per hour, landed his Caudron C3 on its 28m by 12m surface in January 1919 (Aux Galeries Lafayette, 1919). Not long thereafter, Védrine was killed when his plane crashed near Lyon. But customers continued to visit the monument erected on the roof of the store to "commemorate the most daring of exploits."

Propelled by commercial strategies that elicited an enthusiastic response among clients and visitors and taking advantage of opportunities inherent in the expanding advertising media of the 19th century (articles in the daily press, almanacs, posters, postcards, lithograph brochures), Paris department stores reimagined themselves as museums, as much as markets, and thereby put themselves, quite literally, on the map of the city's tourist sites (Chaney, 1983). In effect, they sold products that allowed visitors to return home with a piece of Paris.

CONCLUSION

Today, the process by which museums become more like stores, and stores become more like museums, continues. More and more museums have turned themselves into brands that export their collections internationally. There is even a Louvre in Abu Dhabi, which aims to reproduce the exhibition rooms, the restaurants, the library, and even the stores to be found in the original *pavillons*. At the same time, museums and department stores have moved closer together. Thus, in Paris tourists can visit the Louvre Museum, and then stroll right next door, to the Printemps store located in the adjacent space of the Carousel du Louvre. Meanwhile, within the *grands magasins,* designers and marketing experts have only expanded their relations with the art world. The Galeries Lafayette, for example, created in 2013 a foundation dedicated to creativity and contemporary art, the *Lafayette Anticipation*, and it currently houses its own art gallery on the Boulevard Haussmann, the *Galerie des Galeries*.

The *rapprochement* between fashion and museums over the last 15 years has been especially dramatic. Such luxury brands as Lanvin and Chanel have instituted their own archival projects to promote their history and stimulate interest in their products. They have partnered with museums, lending their exquisite and valuable clothes and accessories for public viewing, and sometimes curated their own exhibits of fashion history. Some houses, such as Yves Saint Laurent and Dior, have gone so far as to open their own museums – not so much blurring the line between commerce and art as eliminating it altogether. In yet another attempt to link their brands to great art, in 2017 Louis Vuitton organized a dinner at the Louvre Museum, in the very room where the *Mona Lisa* sits. The occasion was to launch a new line of luxury handbags – the "Masters for Louis Vuitton"–designed by the visual artist Jeff Koons reproducing famous paintings by Rembrandt, Van Gogh, and Rubens. More recently, fast fashion brands, following the luxury sector, have decided to collaborate with cultural and touristic places. In 2021, Le Louvre signed a partnership with the fast fashion brand, Uniqlo, to sell tee-shirts featuring some of its best-known masterpieces.

Since the 1990s, the intermingling of fashion and art has given birth to the "concept-store," described by Donatien Grau and Emanuele Coccia in *Le Musée transitoire* (The Transitory Museum, 2018) as a hybrid space where the esthetic experience of fashion and its consumption as a commodity are reconciled. Compared to "transitional museums," concept stores deal in objects that can be both observed *and* bought. This way, they function more like art galleries, where paintings and such are displayed not just for admiration but for sale (unlike museums). Objects on display are staged in an artistic way to allow potential buyers to discover new designers and artists, as well as to stoke their desire to own. This is all part of a contemporary trend, "curation," which is itself a perpetuation of the historical tendency examined in this chapter, wherein the methods of culture and merchandizing come together in the service of both art and profit (Marchetti, 2016; Stoppard, 2020).

Chapter 10

ON A GRAND SHOPPING SPREE

Erina Cavalli
Independent Researcher, Switzerland

Abstract: This chapter seeks to elucidate specific behavioral patterns that occur when people travel and consume luxury items using concepts drawn from sociocultural and economic theories. These concepts are Walter Benjamin's "aura," Karl Marx's "commodity fetishism," and Arnold Van Gennep's "liminality." These concepts are deployed within the spheres of tourism and luxury in order to analyze how tourists on a shopping spree search for forms of authenticity, how this type of travel is similar in many respects to a religious quest, and, finally, how the design of luxury outlets in European capitals convey religious overtones. **Keywords**: Aura; commodity; fetishism; authenticity; ritual; flagship store

INTRODUCTION

One of the most striking yet commonplace images one might encounter as a resident of Paris is the long line of Asian tourists waiting outside Louis Vuitton's flagship store at Avenue des Champs-Élysées. These affluent Chinese, Japanese, and South Korean tourists are waiting their turn to enter the brand's "temple" to purchase a handbag. The main reasons Chinese visitors, for instance, choose to shop abroad include better product selection, lower prices due to China's high taxes on luxury items, and greater "show-off" value (Fung, MacAusland, & Chang Mazza, 2012). The first two arguments follow reason. Quite obviously, Paris offers a wider selection of items than the Chinese capital. China's import tax for luxury items, added to value-added tax, results in a price tag about a third higher than for a luxury handbag purchased in Paris. The third reason, "show-off" value, is a slightly vague, magical dimension concealed within the luxury item and in the

Fashion and Tourism: Parallel Stories
Tourism Social Science Series, Volume 26, 155–173

Published under exclusive licence by Emerald Publishing Limited
ISSN: 1571-5043/doi:10.1108/S1571-504320230000026010

experience of shopping abroad. This chapter is an attempt to elucidate this third dimension.

The argument of this chapter builds upon three foundational concepts in the fields of cultural theory, economic theory, and anthropology, borrowed from classical and contemporary texts. The first concept is Walter Benjamin's "aura," which unravels object agency. The second is Karl Marx's "commodity fetishism," which untangles subject agency. The two concepts are deeply connected. The third concept is Arnold Van Gennep's "liminality." This chapter does not aim to bring new understanding to concepts that maintain solid ground in contemporary theory. It is rather to deploy them to elucidate specific behavioral patterns of people who purchase luxury items when traveling. "Aura" has three dimensions which, seen from the perspective of tourism and luxury, are authenticity, authority, and access. The former in particular connects to recent tourism theory. "Commodity fetishism" points to an uncanny force that objects acquire as soon as they enter the sphere of exchange. Since Marx disdained the sphere of luxury, his concept has been applied to luxury studies by later theoreticians working within a Marxist framework. "Liminality" describes the central moment in a rite of passage in which the subject (in this case, the tourist on a shopping spree) is in a state of suspension from normative social relations and is, therefore, particularly receptive.

This chapter expands on these three concepts to attempt to demonstrate that the auratic effect produced by luxury items and their display captures the tourist's desire for authenticity. This desire is comparable to the quest for a religious experience. The form of this text does not follow conventional, linear argumentation but is constructed as a set of analogically connected paragraphs. It is more a map representing a space of ideas than a logical progression from one idea to the next. This structure was inspired by the figure of the *flâneur* which fascinated Walter Benjamin. *Flânerie* actually crystallizes an increasingly rarefied form of contemporary tourism, one in which "aimless wanderings can reveal things hidden to those intent on purposive goals" (Savage, 1995, p. 40), and whose meanderings become a metaphor for a form of loosely interwoven writing.

The Aura of Objects

Some of the deepest insights into the agency of objects and their relationship to subjects are found in German cultural critic Walter Benjamin's analyses of the nature of "aura." Aura comes from the Greek "breeze, soft wind" and later the Latin "breeze, breath of air." The word was used in spiritualist circles by the end of the 19th century to describe a supposed subtle emanation from an object or a body, what is now called its electromagnetic radiation. The concept of aura appears in a number of Benjamin's writings. Crucially, his concept comes very close to the Marxian definition of commodity fetishism, a point which is developed later. Arendt has, though, a word of caution: "The trouble with everything Benjamin wrote was that it always turned out to be *sui generis*" (Arendt, 1968, p. 3) and thus "incomparable." Following the dual signification of this word, what Arendt meant is that Benjamin's texts are both "matchless" and "radically different" to antagonistic texts within the academic canon. Benjamin never actually isolated aura as a concept, which leaves it open to reinterpretations.

Benjamin's earliest known formulation of aura, arguably the most wonderful, appears in his 1931 essay, *Little History of Photography*. Benjamin writes,

> What is aura, actually? A strange weave of space and time: the unique appearance or semblance of distance, no matter how close it may be. While at rest on a summer's noon, to trace a range of mountains on the horizon, or a branch that throws its shadow on the observer, until the moment or the hour become part of their appearance – this is what it means to breathe the aura of those mountains, that branch. (Benjamin, 1931, pp. 518–519)

The distance intended here, which Benjamin will clarify in later texts, is to be understood as remoteness, an unapproachability. It is an auratic aloofness that comes from the grounding of an object in a tradition. Aura draws us toward the mystery and the distance of the world as we perceive it. Benjamin already hints at the loss of aura in the reproduction of an original object to produce a copy, an idea he will develop in his 1935 formulation.

> The peeling away of the object's shell, the destruction of the aura, is the signature of a perception whose sense for the sameness of things has grown to the point where even the singular, the unique, is divested of its uniqueness – by means of its reproduction. (Benjamin, 1931, p. 519)

Owing as much to mysticism as he did to Karl Marx, Benjamin was attracted to the "supernatural." Like many other intellectuals of his generation, he was fascinated by how drugs altered perception, resulting in the entanglement of time and space and in the liquefaction of the subject–object relationship. Between 1927 and 1934, he experimented with hashish, opium, and mescaline with friends in Marseille, Ibiza and Berlin. He called his records of these events "Protocols of Drug Experiments" and dreamed of a book to collect them. His records were posthumously published in *On Hashish*, by Howard Eiland, who translated the original German book by Tillman Rexroth (1972). Benjamin starts attacking the "conventional and banal ideas of the theosophists," to then provide his formulation of the nature of aura.

> First, genuine aura appears in all things, not just in certain kinds of things, as people imagine. Second, the aura undergoes changes, which can be quite fundamental, with every movement the aura-wreathed object makes. Third, genuine aura can in no sense be thought of as a spruced-up version of the magic rays beloved of spiritualists and described and illustrated in vulgar works of mysticism. On the contrary, the characteristic feature of genuine aura is ornament, an ornamental halo [*Umzirkung*], in which the object or being is enclosed as in a case. (Eiland, 2006, p. 58)

In defining these three properties, Benjamin reveals the breadth and complexity of his concept and its resistance to flattening or reduction.

Benjamin witnessed the advent of photography and the possibilities it offered as a mechanized medium freed from the action of the human hand. Aura, for him, was "the historical presence or authenticity of the object outside the reproducible signs of its existence" (Eiland, 2006, p. 2). He was, therefore, torn by the idea of the loss of aura produced by mechanized reproduction. On the other hand, he understood that the decay of the aura, of authenticity, was actually an emancipatory dynamic. Photography and cinema, through their automated mechanical processes, had the potential to destroy the auratic aspects of art and thus liberate people from the oppression of ritual and tradition so as to unveil a new world stripped of myth.

In his seminal essay (Benjamin, 1935), *The Work of Art in the Age of Mechanical Reproduction* (now titled *The Work of Art in the Age of Its Technological Reproducibility*), he expands his investigation of aura started four years before. This text contains its most developed formulation. While his previous analysis concentrated on the aura as an invisible property of objects, an elusive spatial and temporal property that is inherent in them and is felt by the subject, he now focuses his attention on artworks and the context of their presentation. This context is the domain of tradition, which is tightly interwoven with the idea of ritual. Benjamin states that the uniqueness of an artwork is precisely its aura, and that its authenticity as functional value is found in ritual.

> The uniqueness of a work of art is inseparable from its being imbedded in the fabric of tradition. This tradition itself is thoroughly alive and extremely changeable. An ancient statue of Venus, for example, stood in a different traditional context with the Greeks, who made it an object of veneration, than with the clerics of the Middle Ages, who viewed it as an ominous idol. Both of them, however, were equally confronted with its uniqueness, that is, its aura. Originally the contextual integration of art in tradition found its expression in the cult. We know that the earliest art works originated in the service of a ritual – first the magical, then the religious. It is significant that the existence of

> the work of art with reference to its aura is never entirely separated from its ritual function. In other words, the unique value of the "authentic" work of art has its basis in ritual, the location of its original use value. (Benjamin, 1935, pp. 223–224)

The value Benjamin refers to is clearly Marx's concept of use-value: an object's utility in satisfying a need or want, in this case a spiritual need. Importantly, in this text, Benjamin expands his discourse to nonartworks:

> One might subsume the eliminated element in the term "aura" and go on to say: that which withers in the age of mechanical reproduction is the aura of the work of art. This is a symptomatic process whose significance points beyond the realm of art. One might generalize by saying: the technique of reproduction detaches the reproduced object from the domain of tradition. By making many reproductions it substitutes a plurality of copies for a unique existence. (Benjamin, 1935, p. 4)

The third mention of aura in Benjamin's writings appears in 1939 in *On Some Motifs in Baudelaire*. The essay elucidates a particular quality of aura, that of a gaze in reverse. Aura, this "strange tissue of space and time: the unique appearance of a distance, however near it may be," generates the sense in the viewer that his or her gaze is returned, despite this distance. In a key passage, Benjamin writes:

> Inherent in the gaze, however, is the expectation that it will be returned by that on which it is bestowed. Where this expectation is met (which, in the case of thought processes, can apply equally to an intentional gaze of awareness and to a glance pure and simple) there is an experience [*Erfahrung*] of the aura in all its fullness. [...] Experience of the aura thus arises from the fact that a response characteristic of human relationships is transposed to the relationship between humans and inanimate or natural objects. The person we look at, or who feels he is being looked at, looks at us in turn. To experience the aura of an object we look at means to invest it with the ability to look back at us. (Benjamin, 1939, p. 338)

This passage states with crystalline clarity a connection between aura and the gaze, aura and the face, and, by extension, the body. It also implies a transference: the interaction of human agencies shifts to a response between human and nonhuman agencies, and in reverse. It is now possible to draw a connection between the experience of aura when facing an object and Marx's abundance of the "metaphysical subtleties and theological niceties" (Marx, 1867, p. 163) that an object generates as it is absorbed into the sphere of exchange. In his introduction to Benjamin's essays on Charles Baudelaire,

Editor Michael Jennings notes that the lyric poetry of the French *flâneur* was "marked by the disintegration of the aura" (Jennings, 2006, p. 23), in other words, by the collapse of "distance," a new condition produced by modernity. In *On Some Motifs in Baudelaire*, Benjamin quotes Georg Simmel, who had observed that,

> Interpersonal relationships in big cities are distinguished by a marked preponderance of visual activity over aural activity. The main reason for this is the public means of transportation. Before the development of buses, railroads, and trams in the nineteenth century, people had never been in situations where they had to look at one another for long minutes or even hours without speaking to one another. (Eiland, 2006, p. 341; Simmel, 1908)

The fact that aura involves "the unique apparition of a distance" implies that under the condition of the disintegration of the latter, an object can no longer return the gaze of the viewer. The loss of aura implies, as its ultimate effect, that the scopic response dehumanizes the viewing subject.

Commodity Fetishism

Benjamin's interest in the surface of culture, its appearance, is clear in his critique of the cultural superstructure of 19th century France. One finds multiple references in his 1935 exposé, *Paris, the Capital of the Nineteenth Century,* in his *Passagen-Werk* to what Marx had called the fetish dimension of commodities, which pointed for Benjamin to the phantasmagorical "luster with which the commodity-producing society surrounds itself" (Eiland & McLaughlin, 2002, p. 938). Two passages in this text (2002, p. 18) clearly point to Marx's commodity fetishism: "The enthronement of the commodity, with its glitter of distractions [...]" and "Fashion prescribes the ritual according to which the commodity fetish demands to be worshipped." Like many intellectuals of his generation, Benjamin owed his understanding of Marxist theory, especially the fetish dimension of the commodity, to the chapter on reification in Georg Lukács' *History and Class Consciousness*. Benjamin shows in other passages in his writings some misinterpretations of Marxist theory. It is, therefore, necessary to turn to Marx.

Marx's critique dissected the economic regime of 19th century British industrial capitalist society. He briefly engaged the concept of luxury means of consumption in *Volume II* of *Capital*. Marx does not, however, address the rapidly expanding sphere of fashion. He, therefore, leaves one without a specific framework to examine this sphere today. Moreover, the distribution of fashion products through flagship stores and boutiques is thoroughly different from Marx's "market" in industrialized England. These outlets appear more and more as "temples" where commodities exert a magic force over subjectified consumers. Yet, the Marxist analysis of the dual and fetishistic nature of commodities remains valid to this day and can be deployed within this specific market.

Marx had read *A Discourse of Trade* by the British financial speculator Nicholas Barbon, who is credited as one of the first advocates of the free market. Barbon believed that fashion, which relied on the production of difference to sustain itself, had an effect on economy by stimulating consumption:

> Fashion or the alteration of Dress, is a great Promoter of *Trade*, because it occasions the Expence of Cloaths, before the Old ones are worn out: It is the Spirit and Life of *Trade*; It makes a Circulation, and gives a Value by Turns, to all sorts of Commodities; keeps the great Body of *Trade* in Motion. (Barbon, 1690, p. 33)

Marx quotes Barbon in a note without comment in *Volume I* of *Capital*, which means he tacitly agrees with him: "Desire implies want; it is the appetite of the mind, and as natural as hunger to the body... The greatest number (of things) have their value from supplying the wants of the mind" (Marx, 1867, p. 125, n. 2). Marx, fundamentally a moralist, was radically critical of fashion. For him, fashion belonged to the sphere of "Articles of Luxury," as opposed to the "Necessities of Life." The canonical quote reads, "Luxury goods are absolutely necessary for a mode of production which creates wealth for the non-producer and which therefore must provide that wealth in forms which permit its acquisition only by those who enjoy" (Marx, 1867, p. 1046), thus barring poor producers, including working children dressed in rags, from them. Luxury products did not provide the objective material elements of "expanded reproduction," or excess supply enabling economic growth, therefore generating wealth for all social classes.

> *Luxury* means of consumption [...] enter the consumption only of the capitalist class, i.e. can be exchanged only for the expenditure of surplus-value, which does not accrue to the workers. (Marx, 1885, p. 479)

Moreover, because of its unregulated mode of production, "the sudden placing of large orders that have to be executed in the shortest possible time" placed extraordinary pressure on the already strained poor producers. Marx summarized his view of fashion with this phrase "the murderous, meaningless caprices of fashion" (Marx, 1867, pp. 608–609). Marx based his critique of capitalist production in the analysis of the commodity, that is, the tradeable object. The nature of the commodity is different than that of an object. Martin Heidegger clarified this in *The Thing*, an essay written in 1949. A thing becomes an object when it serves a common function. An object becomes a commodity when it is socially encoded and is exchanged in a market. The same works in reverse. A commodity becomes an object when it loses its social encoding. An object becomes a thing when it can no longer serve a common function. In his discussion of commodity fetishism, one of the most often read sections of *Capital*, Marx borrows from anthropology to engage the supernatural sphere. As much as Benjamin was intrigued by the supernatural, Marx was fascinated by the presence of an animistic undercurrent within capitalist production and commodity exchange.

Philosopher Böhme writes that "Animism means that all things and living beings, as well as the world as a whole, are filled with invisible forces." These forces have no connection to physical causality and, therefore, cannot disrupt it, yet, "In the widest sense, this magical dynamism determines what is alive in this world" (Böhme, 2014, p. 184). Contrary to reason, Marx had realized that commodities acquired spectral qualities as soon as they circulated in the market. Marx characterized the belief in the force of commodities as similar to the belief in fetishes, objects worn close to the body or as symbolic substitutes for it, which are assumed to have an occult power over people. He, therefore, deployed the word "fetish" to engage this uncanny force, making brilliant use of its many semantic folds. Feitiço for "magic spell" in Portuguese has a phonetic proximity both to the German word *faktisch* for "factual" and to the Latin word *factitius* for "manufactured, artificial." Marx writes that

> ...A commodity appears at first sight an extremely obvious, trivial thing. But its analysis brings out that it is a very strange thing, abounding in metaphysical subtleties and theological niceties. (Marx, 1867, p. 163)

Marx alludes here to the dual nature of a commodity: its use-value, which is concrete and visible and its exchange-value which is socially encoded and invisible. As soon as an object enters the sphere of exchange to become a commodity valued by money in the form of exchange-value, it seems to assume a magical quality. The concept of "magic" is to be understood in its commutational meaning, that is, as "the practice of making things that are absent present and things that are present absent" (Gumbrecht, 2004, p. 82). As the human labor congealed in the commodity disappears during its production and distribution process, the commodity assumes a supernatural agency as a mediator among humans, resulting in their reduction to carriers of its value. The commodity becomes a medium of "material [*dinglich*] relations between persons and social relations between things" (Marx, 1867, p. 166). Böhme writes that

> As something transformed in this way, as commodity value, it [the commodity] must also take a spectral journey through another world, in order to be able to complete the physical movement from person to person, from place to place. This spaceless journey through

metamorphoses and medial mediation is the process from which fetishism is born. (Böhme, 2014, p. 255)

He merges these two worlds with an interesting image: "Things are the batteries and stabilisers of the power of a person's validity, insofar as they radiate an added value of the meaning that their owner has invested in them" (Böhme, 2014, pp. 80–81). In other words, goods – especially clothing goods – act as switches between the objectal and the spectral spheres as they mediate the performance of the self in society. Following anthropologist Viveiros de Castro, it is not far-fetched to write that commodities act like "certain perspectival 'commutators', like shamans" (Viveiros de Castro, 2014, p. 66, n. 25). When the artwork discussed by Benjamin turns out to be a luxury commodity, and much more so an iconic one, an analogy can clearly be drawn between the "strange tissue of space and time: the unique appearance of a distance, however near it may be" that this tissue radiates and the magical force that Marx's fetish exerts on a subject.

This text may now turn to German sociologist Sombart, a friend and colleague of Max Weber, for an analysis of important aspects of capitalism that Marx did not care to explore, namely the sphere of luxury. Sombart unreservedly admired Marx as a theorist of capitalism. He felt, however, the need to complete Marx's economic determinism and dialectic materialism. He did so by introducing a psychological and cultural dimension to the analysis of the emergence of capitalism and of its nature. Recognizing that luxury had a real influence on capitalism's growth, Sombart analyzed the precise relation between luxury and capitalism, which was left underdeveloped in *Capital*. Sombart's classic account in *Luxury and Capitalism* states that the principal cause of the expansion of trade, industry, and finance capital between 14th and 19th centuries was the demand for luxury goods, especially by the nouveaux riches, the courts, and the aristocracy (Sombart, 1912).

An intensification of the demand for luxuries, often sexual in origin, made fashion a driving force of social elites. Their desires could only be satiated by ever-increasing quantities and ever-differentiated qualities of consumer articles. It is generally accepted, after Weber, that the spirit of Protestantism gave rise to that of capitalism. Against Weber, Sombart gave historical precedence to Judaism in this narrative. Jewish people, he argued, turned their attention to economics because of their transnationalism resulting from diaspora, and their exclusion from full citizen rights. This, in turn, gave rise to strong stereotypes against them and more alienation from society as a whole. The acquisition of wealth by Jews made banking and lending possible, which created the securities and credit networks necessary to introduce the cooly calculating spirit of capitalism into England through Antwerp and Amsterdam.

Political theorist Berry describes another shift, that of the notion of desire. Desire moves from a transgressive compulsion in premodern times to an aspirational force in modern times (Berry, 2006). During this transition, the desire for luxury was not seen anymore as a vice but as a virtue and a search for happiness. This change, which he terms the "demoralization" of luxury, occurred in Europe between the 17th and 18th centuries as consumption expanded due to a shift from agrarian to metropolitan capitalism and as marketing structures became more complex. Berg and Eger state that "luxury gradually lost its former associations with corruption and vice, and came to include production, trade and the civilizing impact of superfluous commodities" (Berg & Eger, 2003, p. 7). Sombart recognized desire as a positive force, stimulating consumption and therefore growth, particularly in the sphere of luxury. Armitage and Roberts (2016) credit him for coining the term "Spirit of Luxury." They claim that "there is an intrinsic link between Sombart's notion of the spirit of capitalism and his work concerning what we call the spirit of luxury" (Armitage & Roberts, 2016, p. 10). In *Luxury and Capitalism*, Sombart writes that

> All personal luxury springs from purely sensuous pleasure. Anything that charms the eye, the ear, the nose, the palate, or the touch, tends to find an ever more perfect expression in objects of daily use. And it is precisely the outlay for such objects that constitutes luxury. (Sombart, 1912, p. 61)

Sombart is even more precise, contending that personal luxury is based on the erotic impulse: "In the last analysis, it is our sexual life that lies at the root of the desire to refine and multiply the means of stimulating our senses, for sensuous pleasure and erotic pleasure are essentially the same." He established a relation between women's sexuality, vanity, and the consumption of luxury goods. The last sentence of *Luxury and Capitalism* has the scent of electral love: "Luxury, then, itself a legitimate child of illicit love – as we have seen – gave birth to capitalism" (Sombart, 1912, p. 171). The original German phrase is even more luscious: *So zeugte der Luxus, der selbst, wie wir sahen, ein legitimes Kind der illegitimen Liebe war, den Kapitalismus.*

Tourism's Search for Authenticity

The word "tourism" comes from the old Anglo-Saxon term *torn*, from the French word *tour*. This term derives from the Latin *tornus*, meaning "to turn," deriving from Ancient Greek *tornos* describing a lathe. The word "tourism," then, contains the idea of a circle. Etymologically, a tourist is then someone who walks a circle. Tourism, therefore, denotes circular travel: moving away from a place but with an intention to return. The reference to the lathe also suggests a productive dimension, because this tool produces a concrete form. In the regime of tourism, this form is abstract. It is the experience and spiritual elevation gained while on travel. From a historical perspective, some scholars claim that tourism refers to the leisure trips taken by English peasants during the 12th century (Fuster, 1967), but there is no overall consensus on this. Tourism, as it is understood today, is born much later with illuminism and the "The Grand Tour" of the European aristocracies.

There is no widely recognized modern concept of what a tourist is. This essay takes its cue from anthropologist Valene Smith's well-known definition of a tourist as a "temporarily leisured person who voluntarily visits a place away from home for the purpose of experiencing change" (Smith, 1977, p. 2). This delineation has the double advantage of implying the idea of a return to the point of departure and of setting a timeline. Differentiating a tourist from a traveler remains, however, problematic. Travel is generally considered as an "orbital" professional trip, and tourism as a "centrifugal," leisure-oriented journey focused on the exotic and reflecting anthropological legacies (The Grand Tour). Early tourism theory actually incorporated the two figures, but with a simplistic taxonomy. The traveler, *Tornacense rara*, would be the "species" that stays away from the pack. The tourist, *Tornacense vulgaris*, would be the "species" found in "herds, droves, swarms and flocks" (Löfgren, 1999, p. 264). The extremes of this dichotomy would be the "brooder," the melancholic flâneur à la Benjamin, who "dwells on fragments, clouded by a tormented sense of occluded significance dwelling in insignificant things" (Leslie, 1999, p. 117), and the "dreambuster" (Inglis, 2000) who will "point out the horrors and the boredom of actually existing tightly packaged trips, the mutual exploitation of tourist and native [...]" (Inglis, 2000, p. 5).

Recent tourism theory has moved from these crude dichotomies and produced more nuanced perspectives on the phenomenon of tourism. This chapter proposes to view tourism in a positive light as a modern form of the search for authenticity which is arguably, in many aspects, similar to a religious quest. The contemporary moment has seen a massive increase of the industry of tourism. Concomitantly, the tourist has now been elevated from the stereotypical fringe figure analyzed in early studies to a paradigmatic, maybe even normative one. As mentioned before, the first analyses of tourists were typological. Marketing research and consulting executive Stanley Plog was possibly the first to produce a model of the tourist through typological differentiation (Plog, 1974). He claimed that tourists could be located on a continuum from the psychocentric to the allocentric. Psychocentric tourists were risk-averse and would seek familiar environments. Allocentric tourists were risk-prone and would instead seek new places and cultures. His model was published in 1974, but its core ideas, which draw in part on psychological behaviorism, originated in 1967 as part of a consulting project assigned to his market research company.

From the 1970s on, social scientists, such as Erik Cohen, Dean MacCannell, and Valene Smith, produced finer conceptualizations of this figure.

Sociologist Cohen led the typological study of tourism with his classification into four types: organized mass tourists and individual mass tourists (institutionalized types) and drifters and explorers (noninstitutionalized types). Additionally, Cohen outlined the range of touristic experiences along a continuum of five phenomenal modes: recreational, diversionary, experiential, experimental, and existential (Cohen, 1979). In the wake of Cohen's work, Valene Smith established seven tourist taxa: explorers, elite, off-beat, unusual, incipient mass, mass, and charter (1977). These typological models are interesting in that they call attention to the fact that tourism is not a monolithic but a broadly diverse phenomenon. Yet these taxonomies are overly deterministic as models of human behavior and provide limited insights into agency and motivation. Cohen's and Smith's work is perhaps more suited to strategists of tourism marketing than to researchers. One must turn to more recent studies for analyses which are subtler and informed by cultural theory.

An important point from early studies which is relevant to this essay is Cohen's conflation of the figures of the tourist and the pilgrim. He made brilliant use of Bellman–Zadeh's fuzzy set theory, which was exposed in a 1970 research report commissioned by the National Aeronautics and Space Administration. In this chapter, mathematicians Richard Bellman and Lofti Zadeh claim that much decision-making in the real world takes place within a fuzzy environment, that is, "an environment in which the goals, the constraints and the consequences of possible actions are not known precisely" (Bellman & Zadeh, 1970, p. 1). The two mathematicians contend that there is a need to differentiate "randomness and fuzziness, with the latter being a major source of imprecision in many decision processes." "Randomness has to do with uncertainty concerning membership or non-membership of an object in a non-fuzzy set. Fuzziness, on the other hand, has to do with classes in which there may be grades of membership intermediate between full membership and non-membership" (1970, pp. 1–2).

Cohen remarked that in the conceptual space of travel, the figures of the tourist, the pilgrim, and the explorer often coalesce, forming at least two new subject positions, that of the tourist-pilgrim and the tourist-explorer, therefore suggesting a continuum of phenomena without clear boundaries. As Edith and Victor Turner later pointed out, "A tourist is half a pilgrim, if a pilgrim is half a tourist. Even when people bury themselves in anonymous crowds on beaches, they are seeking an almost sacred, often symbolic, mode of communitas, generally unavailable to them in the structured life of the office, the shop floor, or the mine. Even when intellectuals, Thoreau-like, seek the wilderness in personal solitude, they are seeking the material multiplicity of nature, a life source" (Turner & Turner, 1978, p. 20).

Sociologist MacCannell, with his essay *Staged Authenticity* (1973) and his seminal book *The Tourist: A New Theory of the Leisure Class three years later* (1976), was possibly the first to break from typological analyses and to introduce complex theory into the study of tourism. As a result of his groundbreaking research, he provided the bedrock for the emerging field of tourism studies and was influential to the foundation of the journal *The Annals of Tourism Research*, established in 1973. First, MacCannell discovered that the tourists he was studying were in fact instrumental for the sociological study of modernity. Working within the framework of modernism, he argued that modern individuals perceive their everyday lives as inauthentic, and that "authentic experiences are believed to be available only to those moderns who try to break the bonds of their everyday experiences and begin to 'live'" (1976, p. 159). Second, he introduced Walter Benjamin's concepts of aura and authenticity into tourism theory. This is remarkable and relevant to this text. MacCannell understood that Benjamin's insights into the experiential connection between authenticity, ritual, and subject through an engagement with aura could be applied to analyzing the "authenticity" of the touristic experience.

Tourists searched authentic experiences to escape their perceived and real alienation in modern lived conditions, but then encountering forms of "staged authenticity" where simulacra of the autochthonous were performed instead, often in tacky ways. In the end, however, tourists would accept staged authenticity as a protective substitute against the trauma of the original, which could manifest itself as a radical Otherness. MacCannell invoked Erving Goffman's (1959) distinction between front and back regions to describe sites in which authenticity was staged. Front regions are spatial assemblages in which hosts and tourists perform socially encoded roles. Back regions are sites where hosts act nonperformatively because their audience has withdrawn. Front regions actually fit into Michel Foucault's definition of heterotopias. The sixth principle that Foucault enunciates in Of Other Spaces (1967) reads "another space, another real space, as perfect, as meticulous, as well arranged as ours is disorderly, ill construed and sketchy. This would be the heterotopia not of illusion, but of compensation" (Foucault, 1967, p. 21). Increasingly though, back regions are shown to tourists as a token of authenticity, therefore becoming, in turn, staged spaces.

Turning back to aura, Jillian Rickly-Boyd, a geographer and researcher in tourism theory, argues that the authenticity of a site is "a result of its embodiment in a tradition of which tourism is a ritual," and that "the authenticity of the experience is a part of an engagement with aura" (Rickly-Boyd, 2012, p. 271). This illuminates the concept of "emergent authenticity," which describes the fact that an inauthentic site may become authentic over time. If tourists are engaging with both a site and its aura, that experience is somehow different to that of interacting with an object. It is the experience of a particular weave of time: not temporalized space but spatialized time. Benjamin had attempted to supplant "the narrative encoding of history through a textual practice that disrupted the historiographic chain in which moments were clipped together like magnets" (Gregory, 1994, p. 234).

A site, considered as an extended "spatial object," can act in a similar way, as a juxtaposition of concretions of loosely connected historical threads that collide with each other. The relationship among tourists, sites, and aura is rendered more complex by Benjamin's well-known distinction between states of distraction and concentration. In *The Work of Art in the Age of Its Technological Reproducibility*, he states

> Distraction and concentration form polar opposites which may be stated as follows: A man who concentrates before a work of art is absorbed by it. He enters into this work [...]. In contrast, the distracted mass absorbs the work of art. This is most obvious with regard to buildings. Architecture has always represented the prototype of a work of art the reception of which is consummated by a collectivity in a state of distraction. (Benjamin, 1935, p. 18)

Benjamin's words – "absorbed," "enters" – are quite strong. Following him, then the attentive tourist truly "enters" a site, engaging and experiencing its aura, whereas the distracted tourist is absorbed into the staged, safe spaces of contemporary sites (cities, generally speaking) characteristic of late capitalist modernity, with their normalized, cosmeticized "eversame" structures (airports, hotels, food, and fashion chains) and staged "urban authenticity," which are all designed to avoid the "shock experience which Benjamin had detected in the modern city" (Savage, 1995, p. 49). Benjamin's polar opposition between two qualities of attention could in fact be reformulated in temporal terms, therefore connecting to aura's quality as a "strange weave of time." One character in Thomas Pynchon's novel *Gravity's Rainbow*, Mondaugen, formulates an interesting law: "Personal density [...] is directly proportional to temporal bandwidth." "Temporal bandwidth" is the width of your present, your now. [...] "The more you dwell in the past and in the future, the thicker your bandwidth, the more solid your persona. But the narrower your sense of now, the more tenuous you are" (Pynchon, 1973, p. 509). The attentive tourist might thus be more connected to history, thus ritual, than the distracted one.

The practice of tourism connects to ritual in specific ways. Dean MacCannell and anthropologist Nelson Graburn are not far away from each other with their respective claims that tourism is a "modern ritual" (MacCannell, 1976) and a "secular ritual" (Graburn, 2001) and thus a liminal experience, from *limen* for "threshold" in Latin. Graburn grounded his analysis in *The Rites of Passage*, the major work of ethnographer Arnold Van Gennep, written in 1909. This book possibly provides the most appropriate framework for analyzing the phenomenon of ritual. Van Gennep, building on the work of Henri Hubert and Marcel Mauss, carried out fieldwork in Algeria and throughout France, examining rites of passage in terms of their pattern and substance. He defined these practices as "rites which accompany every change of place, state, social position and age" (cited by Turner, 1977, p. 36). Van Gennep determined that rites could be sequenced in three phases: preliminal rites (rites of separation), liminal rites (rites of transition), and postliminal rites (rites of reincorporation). Graburn recontextualized Van Gennep's work to secular cultures, claiming that tourism is the modernist equivalent to rites of passage, such as pilgrimages found in religious cultures. He reconfigured Van Gennep's trichotomic division by stating that the performative dimension of tourism includes three phases: a mundane state, a liminal state, and a return to a mundane state. Simply put, in a secular culture, the liminal state that exists away from the workplace is leisure.

Cultural anthropologist Victor Turner further analyzed Van Gennep's concept of liminality, the apartness that defines the central phase of a ritual. "Liminality" distinguishes sacred time from the profane time of everyday life in religious cultures (Turner, 1969). Turner proposed the analog term "liminoid" to distinguish leisure time from the everyday in secular cultures (Turner, 1977). In both cases, in this phase, social relations are characterized as anti-structure, by reference to the determinative oppositions of class, rank, or status in "normal," segmentarily structured life. He called this absence of structure "communitas" and described it as a state of apartness in which social relations are no longer normative, hierarchical, and distant but close and egalitarian. It is also a state of ambiguity or disorientation for participants in that their preliminal status dissolved and a postliminal status did not take form yet. The receptiveness of the shopper on travel to hosts or strangers is in fact a liminoid state without structure other than that defined by the opening hours of shops and facilities.

The Aura of Luxury

"Distance" remains the crucial word in Benjamin's wonderfully eerie yet specific description of aura, "a strange tissue of space and time: the unique appearance of a distance, however near it may be." This allows for an articulation of the contextual or site-specific dimension of aura. Benjamin's "distance" floats between the work and the viewer. It is, paradoxically, most often a temporal distance. This is because a work of art is inscribed in a tradition, whereas the viewer is temporally located in a present tense. In other words, the presence of the work in time and space is the result of a historical process to which it was subject during its existence. "Even the most perfect reproduction of a work of art is lacking in one element: its presence in time and space, its unique existence at the place where it happens to be," and further "the presence of the original is the prerequisite to the concept of authenticity." He then writes, as quoted earlier in this text, that "the unique value of the 'authentic' work of art always has its basis in ritual" (Benjamin, 1935, pp. 3, 6).

Kovesi, a historian, investigates discourses surrounding luxury and consumption in early modern Italy, calls into use Benjamin's aura in her attempt to establish a relationship between the religious veneration of sacred objects such as relics (as the skeletal foot of Catherine of Siena in a church in Venice) and the contemporary awe toward objects from luxury brands. Kovesi points out in her essay that three dimensions are necessary to produce and maintain the aura of any object. She writes that

> ...the brand is no longer enough to contain the aura of the good. It is the location of the brand that is decisive. In an age of mechanical reproductions of mechanical reproductions, the aura depends on a meshing of three factors: the original object, the brand, and its location. (Kovesi, 2016, p. 116)

These three factors, or rather dimensions, are re-elaborated here as authenticity, authority, and access. Authenticity indicates a quality of a natural or manufactured object, it being an original. Authority refers to Benjamin's embeddedness in "ritual," which points to the institutions that held the object in custody throughout its history. Access points to the permission granted to a person to be in the object's presence, which is generally a temporary condition. Translated into the sphere of luxury, these three dimensions would read as follows: authenticity is the fact that a luxury commodity is an original, authority is the exclusivity bestowed on it by a luxury brand, and access is the brand's strategy that establishes a rite of passage into a store and a right of access to a product. The rite of passage is an unspoken rule internalized by the customer as an expectation about his or her appearance and demeanor. The right of access can be more discriminating. It is possibly best exemplified by the rules set by Hermès to grant "entrée" to their iconic Birkin handbag, one of the most sought-after items in the history of fashion. Hermès limits production and strictly controls distribution of these entirely handmade bags, enforcing a waiting list that can stretch up to six years and setting record high prices. Borrowing from a financial metric, these handbags have limited reverse liquidity. In other words, the path to convert cash into the coveted object is arduous.

In April 2016, *The Daily Mail*, United Kingdom's highest-circulated daily newspaper, published the result of an interesting experiment titled "The Bag You are not Allowed to Buy" (Brennan, 2016). The newspaper sent three "regular" women to purchase a Birkin handbag in various stores: Hermès London at Sloane Street, the brand's concession at Selfridges London, the new boutique at Bond Street, and the Hermès boutique at House of Fraser in Manchester's city center. The three customers were told inconsistent arguments about why their money could not buy this handbag. One line was that store directors do not keep stock nor know when and even if they will receive one from Paris. Another line was that the production of the Birkin is limited because it is entirely dependent on a small number of craftsmen who are trained three to four years before they can produce a single exemplary. A third, unspoken line is that one needs access. That is, one needs to be a celebrity or have a record of extensive purchase history. One of the women described her experience, when being allowed briefly to reach out and touch a similar bag, as being in a museum. The aura of exclusivity and glam that surrounds the Birkin handbag is a carefully designed and very successful marketing strategy. Contrary to other designer brands that adopted tacky strategies of market saturation, Hermès opted for limited supply and tight control, to the point where their handbags are badges of wealth even for A-listed people, who must register in the waiting list, too.

Examining further the parallel between religious veneration of relics and contemporary awe for luxury items, Kovesi writes that "The Church authorities' strategies of acquisition, of display, and of restricted access are all designed to elicit from their faithful flock a heightened sense of the numinous, the ineffable presence of the divine." Correspondingly, "The luxury flagship store, with bodyguards carefully regulating access to the coveted objects, tries to ensure that the 'aura' of the brand is kept intact. Where that object is made, its true value and worth, become less important than the mythic story woven around its origin, the brand stamped upon it, and the quasi-sacral space given to its display" (Kovesi, 2016, pp. 113, 120). This implies that the construction of aura can be attempted regardless of the intrinsic quality of the object on display. Kovesi draws on "the halo effect" to discuss the power that a brand has on conferring aura to its products. This effect was discovered in 1920 by American psychologist Edward Thorndike, a pioneer in behaviorism. It is a cognitive bias by which a first impression of someone, formed from the perception of a single trait, influences the overall judgment of unrelated traits of this person. Thorndike found out that American servicemen who were taller and more attractive were also rated as more intelligent and better soldiers (Thorndike, 1920). The halo effect can quite obviously be extended to nonhuman entities, namely objects. Specifically, a positive bias over a specific aspect of a brand can influence the judgment of all of its products.

This is fundamental in that a luxury brand can never be certain which of their products might take iconic value and be a market success. As noted earlier, aura also works in reverse. The fact that an object is embedded in "ritual" bestows aura on the custodial institution. In the case of the Birkin bag, this is the result of exquisite craftsmanship. Conversely, its iconic status spills light on the store that carries it. It follows that the strategies through which luxury brands manifest the auratic dimensions of authority and access should be examined. A preamble on the Grand Tour is useful here. The practice of integrating shopping to travel has, of course, its historical precedent in the Grand Tour, the 17th and 18th century trip through southern Europe undertaken by young men of the British aristocracy and later by young European gentlemen of sufficient means and rank. The voyage was a way to complete a young man's education by exposing him to the legacy of antiquity and the Renaissance. The Grand Tour could last from several months to many years. Gents from polite societies would return home with crates filled with books, paintings, sculptures, and other cultural or scientific artifacts. Two centuries after the Grand Tour, which would provide to the European elites the opportunity to buy artifacts unavailable in one's country, the global circulation of commodities and luxury products has made them available to a larger metropolitan public.

The legacy of this form of travel and consumption can be seen in what could be called the Grand Tour Express, a fast-shopping spree through flagship stores or luxury boutiques of Paris, Milan, or Rome while on travel. This spree is a kind of pilgrimage which rests in aura, the invisible effect produced by luxury items and the context of their presentation. The trip through the city's wonders (cafés, restaurants and clubs) acts as a transformative journey, a preliminal rite of passage that primes the tourist for its liminal event inside the site of luxury: the absorption of an item's totemic force through its purchase. The journey is over as the tourist completes his or her elevation to a higher "spiritual" level. As argued earlier, the skin and the body of contemporary flagship stores and boutiques conjure up aspects of a temple, in which luxury items are displayed as religious relics or treasures.

Luxury brands make use of specific signatures to build visual identity, which originate in their history and culture. Some of these signatures have a religious encoding. Bulgari intersects early Christianity with the use of the Colosseum motif. Dolce and Gabbana visually belong to the baroque current within the catholic tradition. Alexander McQueen is rather gothic, with catholic components. Jil Sander's minimalism has a clear protestant substrate. These signatures are obviously manifest in the design of the brand's stores. This is exemplified, on the Catholic end of the spectrum, by Bulgari's flagship store in New York designed by Peter Marino. On the minimalist side, more attuned to the Protestant end of the spectrum, one finds Jil Sander's flagship store in Avenue Montaigne in Paris designed by British architect John Pawson. Strikingly, Pawson's office also built monastic buildings such as the Cistercian community of Sept-Fons in Burgundy. The image of sparsely displayed clothes on hangers at Sander's Avenue Montaigne boutique unmistakably resembles the orderly alignment of the robes of monks hanging from a wall at Sept-Fons. A somewhat ironical signature is Prada Marfa's project by the Danish-Norwegian artist duo Michael Elmgreen and Ingar Dragset, a "pop architectural land art" in their own words, which is more attuned to the origins of Christianity. A pure display with no access inside, lost in the desert along US Highway 90 northwest of Valentine in Texas, the store invokes the devotion of the Desert Fathers, the early

Christian mystics. It acts as a biting critique of the quasi-religious voyage that the search for iconic fashion objects has become.

CONCLUSION

Drawing from three solid concepts of cultural critique, economic theory, and anthropology – "aura," "commodity fetishism," and "liminality," respectively – this chapter attempted to elucidate and substantiate how the auratic effect produced by luxury items and their display captures the tourist's desire for authenticity. The tourist chooses to temporarily dwell outside of normative social relations and is, therefore, particularly receptive to persuasion. This state is, arguably, similar to that of the pilgrim undertaking a religious voyage.

Acknowledgments – Precious advice of visual artist Marco Poloni in preparing this chapter and of visual artist Chelsea Knight in proofreading the text is acknowledged.

Chapter 11

AFFLUENT TOURISTS
Luxury Consumption in Milan

Mario Paris
DISA – Università degli Studi di Begamo, Italy

Abstract: Luxury fashion brands have started differentiating their investment strategies and enlarging their sectors of activity, for instance, entering tourism. The overlay between traditional behaviors and innovative strategies has left a mark on the cities and neighborhoods. This chapter explores the spatial distribution of luxury tourism infrastructure in Milan. This transition does not affect only preeminent locations, such as monumental squares and high streets, but also places traditionally excluded from the "luxury circuits." The location of 5-star hotels and premium tourism facilities in Milan (Michelin restaurants and spas) differ from the general tourism infrastructure. The study identifies polarization in the touristic offer and a parallel influence in the real estate market. **Keywords**: Urban planning; Milan; real estate; identity; luxury hotels; tourism

INTRODUCTION

Traditionally, luxury brands developed through the work of single entrepreneurs – designers/artists/producers, managers, and coordinators – or families. This process produced small companies, even those that achieved market recognition. When business understanding supported creativity and knowledge, those companies became players at a global scale and increased in size, adding sectoral competencies and expertise, consolidating the corporate structure, and reinforcing their role in the market. Over the last decade, and thanks to the general growth of luxury, the sector evolved even more and affected many different fields, including tourism.

Fashion and Tourism: Parallel Stories
Tourism Social Science Series, Volume 26, 175–192

ISSN: 1571-5043/doi:10.1108/S1571-504320230000026011

Due to the crisis of certain business models, generational replacement, or market strategies, a few players (often supported by hedge funds) started acquiring individual brands to form "strategic groups" (Hunt, 1972; Meilich, 2019; Porter, 1980). These firms consolidate a portfolio of *maisons* (LVMH, Estée Lauder, Compagnie Financière Richemont SA, and more). Therefore, while customers maintain a perception of the market as composed of independent brands and competitors, in fact only a small number of autonomous players have all the control over their identity and choices. In this light, while the luxury sector grows in terms of business, workforce, and revenues, the variety of the players is maintained only in appearance, and the number of actors involved in the decision-making process is decreasing. This dynamic generates agglomeration economies, risk-reduction strategies, and the reinforcement of those few groups who dominate the market. At the same time, it provokes a reductive simplification in the interaction among single brands that often belong to the same owner and must follow team-based strategies in their business development.

The expansion of luxury groups through the brand takeover is a consolidated reality, which differs from the industrial agglomeration strategies because the benefits go beyond simple cost-reduction. According to Ijaouane and Kapferer (2012), these processes affect value creation at the corporate level and produce vertical relationships between the corporate center and the businesses and the horizontal relationships among the businesses (Knoll, 2008). Without entering into the financial, marketing, and management implications of a group's creation, it is recognized that through them, firms increase their global diffusion and multiply their presence by adding locations in new cities and different countries. The success of these operations, linked to the global expansion of the luxury market, which implies a boost in revenues, imposes a diversification in the business strategies of luxury groups, which need to expand their domains of investment to include new sectors. According to recent studies (Paris, 2020), over the last 10 years players took a more integrated approach, developing activities in parallel with their core business, based on selling goods and often services and, finally, by becoming multi-business firms.

This chapter reflects on the manifestation of this transformation in the tourism market, from an urban planning perspective. Therefore, the study focuses on the spatial implication of these transformations that customers perceive at global and local scales, in the settlement strategies of luxury groups and *maisons* and in the spatial distribution of their venues over the cities and within continents. The coevolution of a luxury demand in the tourism market and a provision of premium leisure infrastructure is currently triggering a series of transformations in global cities.

Luxury market dynamics in the field of tourism are explored, including the potential effects of the evolving premium offer at a local scale. In the case of Milan, Italy, the role of luxury in the enlargement of tourism circuits is discussed, as are its impacts in terms of local economy and livability. Based on a quantitative analysis of provincial and municipal tourism data for Milan in 2008–2019, an increasing demand for hotels and luxury services was identified. The information about hotels and premium facilities (Michelin star restaurants, luxury spas) in 2021–2022 was mapped. The reflective cartography thus generated became a useful benchmark for exploring the spatial distribution of touristic demand. The maps also facilitate reflections on the impact of this market on the urban space, particularly considering real estate market data provided by the *Agenzia delle Entrate* (Italian national revenue agency). Luxury tourism has polarized certain neighborhoods and public/shared spaces. This will have a significant influence on the transformation of the built environment and its vocations in the medium–long term.

This chapter first outlines the general context of luxury tourism and its recent transformations, including how the consolidated demand for premium venues evolved in response to experience tourism demand. Contemporary literature notes that luxury tourists show a variety-seeking behavior (Alananzeh, Jawabreh, Al Mahmoud, & Hamada, 2018; Jawabreh, Jahmani, Khaleefah, Alshatnawi, & Abdelrazaqe, 2020; Lue, Crompton, & Stewart, 1996; Ngwira & Kankhuni, 2018; Weidenfeld, Butler, & Williams, 2011) based on the ability of operators to satisfy consumers' experiential expectations. Tourists are now looking for an increasingly integrated set of services and experiences (Broughton & Beggs, 2007; Buchanan, 1983; Schroeder, Cornicelli, Fulton, & Merchant, 2019; Schuett, 1993; Tinsley & Tinsley, 1986), shifting from traditional 5-stars hotels to urban facilities, services integrated with the urban pattern. With increasing curiosity, they are asking for place-based forms of consumption. This added value depends on the quality and the identity of the space in which customers enjoy their purchases, in a contemporary version of "here and now" that increases the added value and the scarcity of experiences that are unique, unrepeatable but highly sharable through social media, and, consequently, luxurious and appealing. According to Benur and Bramwell (2015), the *new* luxury hotel offer, which is more integrated to the city and the facilities of the context, attracts tourists because it does satisfy their needs better than the traditional one.

Subsequently, the chapter reflects on the role that the peculiar identity of a city, a neighborhood, or a specific corner can assume in becoming part of the luxury tourism consumption, thus increasing attractiveness for this specific target. The urban identity reinforces the uniqueness and, therefore, the exclusiveness and prestige of this offer. Marketing plays a key role in promoting the relationship between a global image of certain cities or urban areas and the proposed item, even when it is a part of the touristic infrastructure, such as a hotel. This discussion is followed by a concrete example, the case study of Milanese luxury tourism infrastructure. The spatial description is the basis for reflecting on the impact of this kind of offer on the overall infrastructure and on the city. The conclusions focus on the growing importance of luxury in the everyday sociocultural and economic lives of cities (Roberts & Armitage, 2020), pointing out critical aspects and emerging questions.

EXPERIENCE URBAN LUXURY AND THE CITY

Today's stakeholders in the luxury market are changing their location strategies and, with them, their impacts in cities and territories. The consolidated settlement strategies of luxury operators have focused on the productive and business functions that affect urban and preeminent locations – such as monumental squares and high streets – in order to take advantage of their symbolic and physical characteristics. Merchants and service providers have taken advantage of the presence of affluent inhabitants and, with the evolution of tourism and globalization, of city users and tourists.

Luxury, as an economic sector (Berg, 2005), represents a significant contribution to the local economies of certain cities, which benefit from it directly (employment, taxes, and more) and indirectly (skills and talent attraction, innovation, and image promotion). This has been demonstrated in both academic studies (Amatulli, De Angelis, Pino, & Guido, 2020; Dion & Arnould, 2011; Halwani, 2021) and industry annual reports (Bain & Company, 2021; Boston Consulting Group, 2021) produced to underline the role of those groups in the everyday life of a city and its inhabitants, even if they are not luxury customers. This chapter focuses on luxury as a catalyst for spatial transformation, and its role in promoting the attractiveness of certain urban spaces for specific targets, even if they are not traditionally luxurious at all.

Alongside occupying some of the most prominent locations in the cities – maintaining visibility in historical centers and monumental squares – luxury operators have also developed other location needs, connected to their evolution as global players. They need offices, large headquarters, or campuses to host the complex apparatus behind their functioning. They have also enriched their sectors of activity and, consequently, must buy or build containers to host these new functions. Finally, they have incorporated investment differentiation strategies. The overlay of traditional behaviors and innovative strategies marks where cities are active and which neighborhoods are excluded from "luxury circuits." Over the years, these spaces have come to host a specific tourism market, which affects specific locations and presences, and produces flows that innervate the space of the city. Indeed, up until the crisis of the tourism sector due to the COVID-19 pandemic, luxury tourism had been experiencing an explosion, and polarized the offer of hotels and facilities in cities. Locations where luxury operators develop their activities attract a market of rich customers in search of a specific kind of experience, which does not consist only in the purchase of clothes or goods but, more generally, in the consumption of a "luxury experience," based on the connection between real values and their narrative. In this light, the chapter aims to explore the geography in this network of locations, in which luxury boutiques, restaurants, and hotels become hubs for flows of affluent tourists who want to explore and consume culture (museums, art galleries and spaces for temporary exhibitions, and events), experiences (clubs, open spaces, and show rooms), and services (based on the work of distinguished professionals, artisans, and experts).

Urban Luxury Tourism

Luxury customers represent an important category within a growing and evolving tourism industry who expect premium experiences, encompassing accommodation and transport (Kadam & Deshmukh, 2019). Since 1800, and especially after World War II, ubiquitous mobility and progressive acceptance of consumption beyond necessity, the use of free time (away from wage labor) and holiday entitlement (Urry, 1990) have also influenced tourism as a mass-phenomenon. In this global process, luxury tourists have produced key economic impacts in their vacation destinations of choice and due to the attention dedicated by the investors to this segment.

Nowadays, practitioners, including scholars in the field of sociology, cultural studies, and marketing, debate the exact definition of a "true luxury tourist" and the parameters for defining a taxonomy for this segment, which encompasses the subcategories of premium, aspirational, and supreme. Less attention has been dedicated to analyzing the role of these tourists in the cities they temporarily colonize, how they influence the evolution of the local supply of goods and services, and the impacts of their lifestyles and behaviors on the everyday lives of local inhabitants. In response, this chapter simplifies this "definitional anxiety" (Bauer, 2005) by taking advantage of accepted explanations to move to the analysis of less explored themes. In their recent report, Kadam, Ambegaonkar, and Deshmukh (2021) consider luxury tourists to be anyone looking for indulgent experiences marked by a certain level of exclusivity, high-standard services, controlled privacy, and security. Boston Consulting Group (BCG) (2021), in a survey developed for Altagamma, translated this qualitative vision into a set of parameters connected to consumption/expenditure habits that define the profile of a true luxury tourist. People belonging to this category travel at least 12 times per year, including two long stays (more than a week) and 10 weekends, investing at least €20k per person every year in accommodations and spending more than €15k on shopping during their stays. The study also pointed out the drivers for selecting a destination. Location (in terms of general attractiveness, visibility, and recognizability) remains the key factor for most interviewees. The other two factors in the selection of a specific destination are the provision of luxury hotels/accommodations and tourism convenience (such as easy accessibility and provision of transport alternatives). Among the destination typologies, luxury tourists prefer the sea (both, as seaside and boat options), megacities (like New York, Paris, and London), and art cities (Florence, Venice, Prague, and others).

Focusing on urban destinations, the frameworks discussed in the literature propose a scenario where tourists visit a city and spend their time living in and around premium hotels, consuming goods, services, and experiences. According to recent studies (Bain & Company, 2021), luxury hotels in Italy represent less than 1% of the existing global total. They attract more than 15% of the overall tourist spending in reception facilities (reservation, transport, stay, and food and beverage), and this segment generates 25% of the overall tourist spending in Italy (visits, shopping, travel, and the like).

In 2019, Bain calculated that luxury tourists spent 10 times more than average tourists, and the fare for their hotel accommodation is normally a third of their overall expenditures. They invest €1,300 to €1,700 per day and per person for accommodation (over six times the spending of an average tourist), €170–230 for transport, and €380–420 for food and beverage inside and outside their hotel. In addition, each luxury tourist normally spends €2,400–3,400 on shopping and/or other needs per day. This market segment represents €6–7 billion of direct spending, which produces induced spending for almost €25 billion. Moreover, as pointed out before and shown in Table 11.1, scholars and practitioners have identified several features for this type of urban tourism, which requires the provision of quality accommodation along with other comfort factors.

Table 11.1 further offers a summary of what practitioners state that luxury tourists expect not only opulent, comfortable, and fully serviced accommodations buy also want a set of services, amenities, and goods that belong to

Table 11.1. Definition of Luxury Travel From Practitioners.

Interviewee	Company	Kind of Good/Service/Experience Expected
George Morgan-Grenville	Red Savannah	Access to the people, places, and experiences that represent all that is authentic about a destination.
Andrew Carr	Kennedy & Carr Ireland Travel	Local insight, independence, and flexibility because tourists want to get under the skin of local society in a way that is personally meaningful.

Table 11.1. *(Continued)*

Interviewee	Company	Kind of Good/Service/Experience Expected
Becx Whitefield	TripAfrica	Exceeding exclusivity and having the experience to yourself, feeling pioneering, exploratory, and included.
Steve Allen	WEXAS Tailor-made Travel	Seamless and personal service helping clients enjoy authentic, quality experiences in relative comfort that will be long remembered.
Gareth Harding	The Cruise Line Ltd.	Undertaking a new experience and immersing oneself in a new destination while indulging in the best levels of personal and attentive service, lavish and sumptuous accommodation, exquisite and unrivalled levels of gastronomy, and informative and educational guides.
Selina Jackson	ReadyClickAndGo Ltd.	Experience created for your own personal preferences that combines enrichment, enjoyment, and education, with the time to appreciate your surroundings at a price that represents value for money.
Lorne Blyth	Flavours of Italy Ltd.	Time to enjoy the landscape, an opportunity to luxuriate in culture, to stretch out, observe, and lose yourself in the place you are visiting.
Engi Bally	SilverDoor	Authentic, simple, and genuine experiences that incorporate elements of environmental awareness and social responsibility.
Rory Pilkington	Bailey Robinson	Luxury travel means you can sit back, relax, and enjoy the experience safe in the knowledge that every aspect will surpass expectation.

Source: M. Paris's elaboration based on Johnson, 2013.

the city in which they are immersed. These compose and give quality to their experience. Indeed, when they visit a global city for leisure, they would like to feel the vibrant urbanity "extremely dense and intense" (Sassen, 1991) connected to public spaces and high streets. Normally, luxury tourists look for the complexity of vibrant spots in the city, the overlays of influences of diverse cultures, and, at the same time, enjoy certain nuances related to the deep identity of the urban space. In this light, the hotel space is important in supporting these needs, but it is not enough. A new kind of expectation has emerged among affluent customers that involve spaces, facilities, and services in the city, where they can have contact – even if "mediated" or even "fake" – with the real population and identity of the destination. Indeed, current trends in luxury tourism show that tourists want something other than the exclusivity of traditional luxury, where guests stay in lavish enclaves. They now prefer a more itinerant, strolling kind of experience, where they have contact with the city, its true nature, and all the places and facilities that contribute to its identity. In this mediated image and for certain cities, such as New York or Paris, fashion and shopping are critical factors that influence the overall experience and impact the attractiveness of the image of the city.

The aforementioned survey developed by BCG and Altagamma (2021) shows that tourists of many cultural backgrounds enrich their touristic experience by shopping, visiting museums and art collections, eating out, and accessing exclusive services. The quality and the availability of all these facilities and services characterize their ways of living and moving in the cities they visit. Therefore, the analysis of luxury tourism cannot disregard the relationships and interactions that the flows of tourists create between their hotels and these other urban spaces, such as museums, shops and boutiques, restaurants, and spas. Access to these spaces and the continuous movement among them during a stay create a sort of circuit that, when mapped and viewed from above, defines a new, alternative geography of the city, based on a hierarchical order generated by tourists' habits. This in turn influences the everyday life of the inhabitants. These facilities and amenities become an interface space between the two, the host and guest populations. At the same time, their spatial distribution influences the real estate market and the evolution of the local contexts in which they are immersed.

Milan as a Luxury Destination

In luxury studies, at both the national and international level, Milan represents an important case due to its longstanding eminence in the fields of fashion and design, and due to the variety of transformations that have marked the city and its metropolitan area over the last decade. According to the *Camera di commercio* (Chamber of commerce in Milan), in 2021, Milan was home to 13,000 companies in the fashion industry. This cluster employed more than 91,000 workers and produces more than €20 million annually, 20% of the overall national revenue in this sector. Milan is not only an agglomerated cluster for fashion in terms of design, production, and management but is also an important market for both inhabitants and tourists.

Milan houses the headquarters of several Italian fashion and luxury brands, and many international groups also have their national offices in this cosmopolitan city. Over the last year, the consolidated urban core and its close periphery have become a testing ground for luxury firms proposing original retail formats, newly integrated offers, and a range of spaces and venues. A set of facilities and functions (museums, cultural foundations, and exhibition centers) sponsored or owned by companies involved in this sector have influenced the cultural and leisure offerings of the city and its attractiveness for local and international tourists. In the planning field, Milan and the environs represent an interesting case (like Armani Sylos, Fondazione Prada, Gucci Hub, or Oasi Zegna). This metropolitan core is a plural and polycentric space (Balducci, Fedeli, & Curci, 2017; Paris & Balducci, 2019) in which the central city and other consolidated small and medium settlements configure an articulated system (Armondi & Di Vita, 2018). Interactions and mutual influences among these different elements mark this system. Moreover, the greater metropolitan area of Milan is the only Italian urban region that has been affected by a mature process of metropolitization since the end of World War II. Due to the complexity and interactions of these factors, unpacking the territorial nature of the city represents a challenge as well as an opportunity for planners and scholars involved in luxury studies.

After the Expo 2015, tourism increased in Milan, and the flows of luxury tourists stimulated the market. Investors responded with a set of new hotels and venues, and the spatial distribution of the same, together with all the other activities that compose the experiences of premium tourists, form circuits that shape a new geography in the city.

Reinforcement of the Luxury Hotel Market

Over the last two decades, Milan has experienced an evolution in its attractiveness to tourists, especially the luxury segment. Especially after the Expo in 2015, the city saw an increase in tourists, from 11.74 in 2008 to 12.94 million of tourists in 2019, followed by the dramatic drop-off in 2020 (only 3.5 million registered) due to the pandemic (Table 11.2).

The explosion of tourism pressures on the city affected the accommodation market in many ways. According to municipal data, in 2021, Milan had 5,537 accommodations for tourists, divided according to formats which the Italian law classifies as either "hotel accommodations" and "nonhotel accommodations." The first includes "hotels of all categories" and "hotel apartments" and counts 471 units. The second encompasses all other formats (such as guesthouses, holiday homes and apartments, bed and breakfasts, hostels, and camping), as well as apartments rented through the home

Table 11.2. Tourists in Milan (2008–2020) by Accommodation.

Year	Guests in Hotels (Units)	Guests in Other Accommodations (Units)	Year Variation (%)
2008	6,973,124	288,519	
2009	7,377,047	328,455	5.8%
2010	8,056,134	364,296	9.2%
2011	8,579,396	440,572	6.5%
2012	8,651,618	512,113	0.8%
2013	8,808,787	1,125,626	1.8%
2014	9,034,341	1,198,055	2.6%
2015	10,308,180	1,433,194	14.1%
2016	9,457,130	1,519,354	−8.3%
2017	10,088,702	1,663,131	6.7%
2019[a]	10,063,696	2,882,369	−0.2%
2020	2,263,774	1,259,171	−77.5%

Source: Comune di Milano (2021).

[a]Data from 2018 not available.

sharing platforms. Due to the considerable success of this offer in the last years, the second category includes 5,066 structures, more than the 90% of the total. In 2017–2019, short-term accommodations in apartments almost doubled and today supplies 25% of the overall demand, up from 1.6 million tourists in 2017 to 2.9 million in 2019.

The recent stop due to the global reduction of mobility produced a delay in this process of transformation, and future enhancement on the perspective will be beneficial, a topic which is beyond the scope of this chapter. What can be observed is that, despite the large number of these apartments, the overall number of rooms and beds for structures that belong to the "nonhotel accommodation" is still limited in comparison to those of "hotel accommodations." Indeed, within these structures, there are 14,317 rooms and 32,543 beds, meanwhile hotels and hotels apartments offer 28,066 rooms and 52,038 beds. Thus, despite the relevance of the nonhotel accommodation in the city and the success of home-sharing formats, the hotel accommodation is still the larger offer in Milan, representing roughly two thirds of the market, particularly for customers focused on premium opportunities.

Between 2002 and 2021, Milan experienced an increase in the number of hotels, from 411 structures in 2002 to 471 in 2021, a growth rate of 14.4% as shown in Table 11.3. Despite this general increase in the offer, the data show a different trend by category. The number of 1-star hotels decreased (−36 units, −35%).

Table 11.3. Hotel Accommodation in Milan (2002–2021) by Typology.

Hotel	2002	2005	2010	2015	2021	Evolution 2002/2021	
						Units	%
Hotel 1-star	103	96	74	69	67	−36	−35.0%
Hotel 2-star	51	57	64	64	63	12	23.5%
Hotel 3-star	117	122	118	130	131	14	12.0%
Hotel 4-star	80	84	119	134	144	64	80.0%
Hotel 5-star	11	14	14	21	22	11	100.0%
Hotel apartments	49	54	47	48	43	−6	−12.2%
Other hotels	0	0	0	0	1	1	
	411	**427**	**436**	**466**	**471**	**60**	**14.4%**

Source: Comune di Milano (2021).

"Hotel apartments" also declined (−12.2%). This trend is due to a form of rationalization and modernization of the network, with a decrease in lower quality structures. In parallel, the affirmation of the role of short-term accommodation produced a substitution in the market, and the structures that were least attractive to tourists have lost their role in the market.

In parallel, all the other typologies increased, with 4-star hotels increasing from 80 to 144 (+64 units, +80.0%) and 5-star hotels doubling, from 11 to 22. Other data provided by the municipality of Milan (only available until 2018) show the evolution in terms of rooms and beds in hotel accommodation by typology. Table 11.4 shows that the luxury hotel offers increased from 2,294 rooms in 2002 (corresponding to 4,945 beds) to 3,056 (6,177 beds), a rate of increase that was double that of the overall total (+33.2% for luxury rooms, versus +17.4% overall), and represented 11.2% of the overall offer of rooms, compared to an initial value of 9.8% in 2002.

The data reflect the affirmation of Milan as a tourism destination over the last 20 years, supported also by the Expo 2015, in which luxury hotels acquired a prominent role in the accommodation market. If 5-star hotels provide all the services and support that luxury customers need, this chapter views them as a network of hubs for premium clients who temporarily inhabit the municipality. In this light, a set of questions arise connected to the spatial distribution of these hotels.

Spatial Distribution of Luxury Facilities

As recognized by Park, Reisinger, and Noh (2009), the luxury goods market has evolved over time, and the result of this progressive evolution is a larger spectrum of categories that customers consider to be "luxuries." The current market includes products, services, and experiences that play with the sense of self-indulgence of customers, fostering the process of acceptance of premium items "from a morally dubious sociocultural construction and activity to a fully economic commodity" (Roberts & Armitage, 2018, p. 23). Therefore, over the last 15 years, the concept of luxury tourism products has moved away from the traditional luxury approach, where tourists concentrated their purchases in the accommodation, to a wide variety of exclusive and unique experiences (Bakker, 2005). Tourists want to experience the city through a set of fashionable and custom-designed events, which take place in distinct locations, often outside the consolidated spaces of the luxury hotels and exclusive enclaves recognized as "luxury spaces" in the city. This process has occurred over the last 20 years in Milan, defining a new spatial distribution of luxury facilities that does not always coincide with the geography of premium hotels.

A process of spatialization of different kinds of information related to the research field resulted in a new "luxury geography." This includes the spatial distribution of luxury hotels, restaurants, and spas. In addition, the luxury infrastructure was also mapped using the locations of the premises of companies in the top three luxury groups in Milan (Paris, 2020). This is only a sample (based on the locations of producers/arts and craft, shops and flagship stores, cafes, bars, and restaurants that belong to luxury groups) of the complex network of luxury facilities and services spread around the city, but it offers a useful benchmark to evaluate the mutual influences in terms of location and real estate market between hotels and other functions.

The 5-star luxury hotels (the top category, with 11 elements) are located in the area between the Stazione Centrale and Piazza Duomo. Two clusters polarize the area: one connected with the railway space, which is also the best connected to the airports (by train and bus), and the other located in proximity (but not completely embedded) in the *quadrilatero della moda* (Fashion district), the traditional and iconic space of globally renown where luxury *maisons* use to have their flagship stores (Via Montenapoleone, Via della Spiga, elsewhere).

The first cluster contains the largest and most recognized structures, which according to the Milan Municipal Authority (Comune di Milano, 2022) are Principe di Savoia (305 rooms, 607 beds), Excelsior Hotel Gallia (235 rooms, 476 beds), Westin Palace (227 rooms, 464 beds), and Me Milan – Il Duca (132 rooms, 298 beds). All of them, except for the Excelsior Hotel Gallia, are in Piazza della Repubblica, a threshold between the old city, the mobility node, and the new business district of Porta Nuova (Figure 11.1).

Smaller structures belonging to international companies (Mandarin, Four seasons) or luxury groups (Bulgari Hotel and Armani Hotel) form the second cluster, within the historical neighborhood of Brera. Those hotels occupy consolidated buildings and refurbish private palaces and have to contend with the qualities and the limitations of the existing urban fabric, where it is not easy to provide all amenities and facilities within the space of the hotel.

Table 11.4. Rooms and Beds in Hotels in Milan (2002–2018) by Typology.

Hotel	2002		2015		2018		Evolution 2002/2018			
							Rooms		Beds	
	Rooms	Beds	Rooms	Beds	Rooms	Beds	Units	%	Units	%
Hotel 1-star	1,425	2,415	943	1,575	945	1,573	−480	−33.7%	−842	−34.87%
Hotel 2-star	1,151	1,892	985	1,680	939	1,600	−212	−18.4%	−292	−15.43%
Hotel 3-star	5,517	9,085	6,062	10,258	5,792	9,904	275	5.0%	819	9.01%
Hotel 4-star	10,159	18,040	14,964	28,045	14,769	27,646	4,610	45.4%	9,606	53.25%
Hotel 5-star	2,294	4,945	2,292	4,711	3,056	6,177	762	33.2%	1,232	24.91%
Hotel apartments	2,758	5,885	2,077	3,823	1,860	3,394	−898	−32.6%	−2,491	−42.33%
	23,304	**42,262**	**27,323**	**50,092**	**27,361**	**50,294**	**4,057**	**17.4%**	**8,032**	**19.01%**

Source: Comune di Milano (2018).

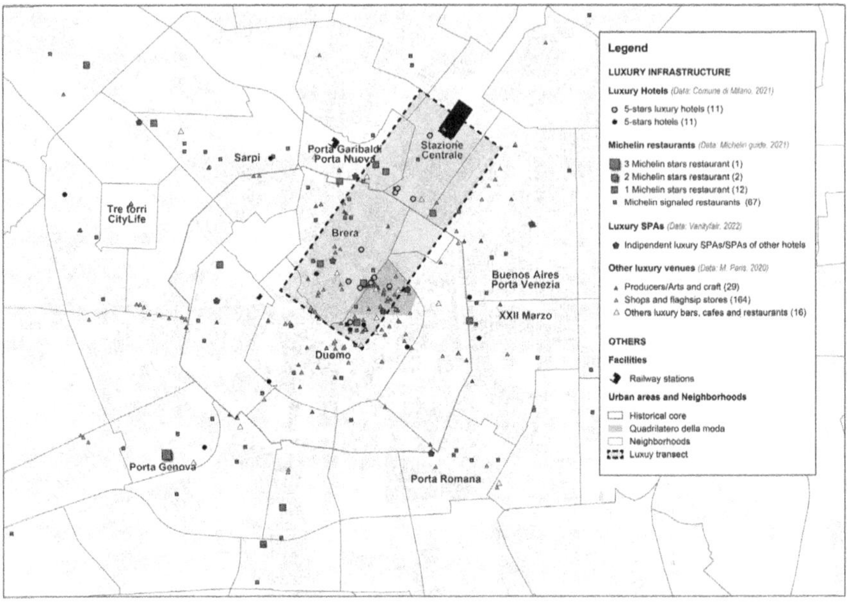

Figure 11.1. Spatial Distribution of Luxury Facilities in Milan (Elaboration of M. Paris From Comune di Milano [2021], Michelin Guide [2021], and Vanityfair [2022]).

These are multifunctional venues, and the offer provided often includes conference and exhibition spaces for events, restaurants and café-bars open to external clients, gyms and fitness areas, and, in many cases, spas and private pools.

Eleven additional 5-star hotels complete the offer. The map depicts an aggregation around the second cluster (on the southern side, still in the central area but further away from the central station). Other stand-alone structures have various locations, connected to specific functions, such as the Tre Torri/CityLife area (former venues of the *Fiera*), the Stazione Cadorna, and the Navigli, other iconic or touristic neighborhoods in the city.

Facilities Location

As already pointed out, hotels are not the only facilities and venues where luxury tourists consume goods, services, and experiences. According to the current approaches in tourism studies, a satisfactory stay includes a welcome in the hotel for residential services and those scattered throughout the city. This is even more relevant for luxury tourists, who can often enjoy exclusive formulas without any budget limits. They ask for prestigious offers that can also embody the identity and real taste of the city.

There are very few existing examples of this kind of analysis, and the current approaches only allude to methodologies for identifying these processes and studying their spatial impacts. The present study focused on luxury restaurants and spas because they are key services that luxury hotels provide to customers. To define this geography, the activities included in the Michelin guide 2021 were mapped, with special attention to the distinct categories identified. The Michelin Guide rates the restaurants in four categories: the most exclusive have 1, 2, or 3 stars, while other attractive structures are mentioned in the annual edition. The spas mentioned in luxury travel guides (Pregnolato, 2017) were also taken into consideration.

According to Michelin Guide, 3-star restaurants are worth a dedicated journey, and their locations are independent of touristic circuits. Nevertheless, in Milan, the only 3-star restaurant is Enrico Bartolini al Mudec, a commodity of the Museo delle Culture, a cultural venue far from the consolidated city center. It is located at the end of Via Tortona, an axis marked by the presence of a set of luxury and fashion headquarters (Armani, Fendi, Stella McCartney, Herno, Moncler).

The locations of the 2 Michelin star restaurants are different. Seta by Antonio Guida is a facility connected to the Mandarin Oriental Milano, one of the 5-star luxury hotels that compose the cluster linked to the quadrilatero della moda. The second, Il luogo di Aimo e Nadia, is not depicted on the map. It is in the western periphery at the back of the Jewish quarter and has maintained its historical location for the last 60 years.

The 12 restaurants awarded 1 Michelin star are independent activities, not connected with the hotels, although their spatial distribution is connected. There is an interesting accumulation along the area formed by the 5-star luxury hotels, but there is also an offer distributed in the city, and connected to recognizable spaces (Arco della pace, Corso Sempione) and neighborhoods that are trying to consolidate a precise identity (NaPa neighborhood, along the Naviglio Pavese). The 67 restaurants listed in 2021 have an even more dispersed distribution, where agglomerations can not only be found in the Duomo and Brera neighborhoods but also Paolo Sarpi, Porta Romana, and along the Viale XXII Marzo. Together with these facilities, the study also identified several luxury spas within the city.

The relationship between the general luxury infrastructure and the venues dedicated to luxury tourism produces a twofold figure. On one hand, these commodities occupy the most established central spaces. This process reinforces the existing areas with this vocation. Therefore, the Quadrilatero della moda remains the prominent luxury area of the city, with incremental enlargement and integration due to the diffusion of luxury functions in the surroundings. On the other hand, one recognizes the development of a new aggregation close to the Duomo square, in the Galleria Vittorio Emanuele space, around the Piazza della Scala, and in the new spaces of Porta Nuova, a neighborhood that also attracts investments in luxury housing (such as the *Bosco verticale*, and other new luxury compounds) will continue to attract more in future.

The spatial distribution of the tourism facilities and hotels provides a proxy for the detection of all the areas affected by pressure. The research points out a transversal diffusion on the central area of the city, and the correspondence between their presence and the increases of real estate values in those neighborhoods (Figure 11.2). Therefore, the location of luxury infrastructure depends on a neighborhood's identity, the quality of the built environment, and the locational opportunities of the property market. Together, these three drivers sometimes take advantage of existing tourist flows, and sometimes introduce new ones, generating interest among tourists in little-known neighborhoods, thanks to the power of fashion brands. This double condition generates new flows within the city, and new relationships between urban spaces, functions, as well as temporary and local populations in these districts, even though they are not usually involved in the "mental map" (Lynch, 1960) of luxury enthusiasts.

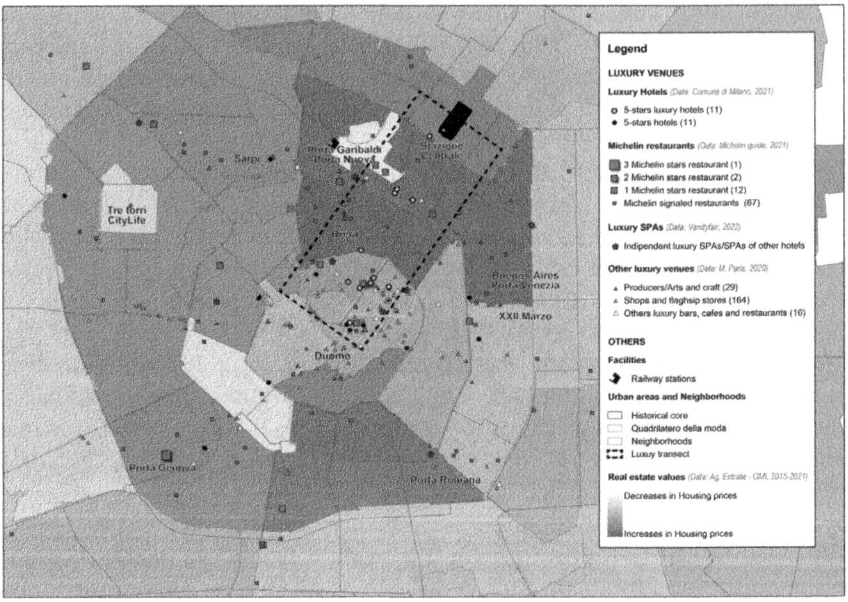

Figure 11.2. Luxury Facilities and Real Estate Values in Milan (Elaboration of M. Paris From Comune di Milano [2021], Michelin Guide [2021], Vanityfair [2022], and Agenzia delle Entrate – OMI [2015–2021]).

CONCLUSION

This chapter dealt with urban luxury tourism to provide an overview of the ongoing dynamics for the case study of Milan. The exploration of the spatial distribution of luxury hotels and facilities reveals that the stays of luxury tourists have evolved over the last years. Nowadays, they prefer to spend their time fully experiencing the city, not relegating themselves to premium hotels, but moving outside these venues, strolling, and using existing facilities that are also open to inhabitants and city users. They consume the city and its identity in a contemporary version of the "grand tour" that includes an overview of monuments and museums, selective events, and the enjoyment of some "typical" and prestigious (even commercial, or nontraditional) activities.

This increasing demand has influenced the multiplication of the services and functions oriented to affluent tourists, and the parallel reinforcement of those that already existed within the city. The result is a new pattern of exclusive facilities and locations, which involves the consolidated spaces of luxury (in Milan, the study recognized an area that it defined "a transect") and has also expanded, now affecting other neighborhoods as well. Therefore, the presence of these functions and facilities generates a new set of relationships within the city, based on interactions among tourists and local users/clients in spaces that may be physically distant or unattractive for a specific category of users/temporary inhabitants. The inclusion of new urban spaces and activities in the luxury circuits affects peripheral/semi-central neighborhoods and raises several open questions about the potential effects of these dynamics in terms of livability and affordability for local inhabitants. Very few studies focus on critically observing the spatial evolution of those areas within the city. But the impacts are deep, and they affect socioeconomic, functional, and cultural dimensions that are still unexplored.

The study reported in this chapter is limited by the selection of functions and venues that represent the "luxury infrastructure." The sample selected is sufficient to define the main spaces of luxury in Milan, but this simplification erases several nuances. Italian and, especially, Milanese luxury groups, such as Armani, Dolce & Gabbana, or Prada (originally from Tuscany), are smaller than the international groups analyzed within this discussion and have different settlement logics that are not always represented by the current focus. Further developments of this research should consider those differences and involve a more precise geography of these functions. In addition, how the identities of the city and within the city change under the pressures of affluent customers and temporary inhabitants should also be considered. It is already difficult to frame this phenomenon, but as urban planners – intended as practitioners involved in a policy community and within decision-making processes – attempts should be made to critically analyze them to provide input for territorial governance. The progressive spread of luxury circuits in the city depends on the will of investors, the opportunities they take, and the attractiveness of the urban space that they colonize. It is not easy to define governance for the first two dimensions, but municipalities and local stakeholders must deal with the third. Such examination generates new opportunities for the local dimension and/or foster new fragmentations, the appearance of new borders, and forms of exclusion in the city.

Acknowledgments – The author is extremely grateful to Angela Rigliaco and Elena Paris for their patience and support during the elaboration of this chapter. They work in the luxury field, and thanks to the discussions over the last months, a clearer perspective about this sector emerged. This chapter would not have been possible without their help.

Chapter 12

THE CITY WEARS PRADA
Urban Transformation and Cultural Tourism

Sandra Biondo
Université Paris 1 Panthéon-Sorbonne (EIREST), France

Abstract: In contemporary cities, private actors, such as luxury fashion houses, increasingly participate in projects, affirming themselves as relevant players in urban transformation. Based on the case of "SouPra" district (Milan, Italy), this chapter focuses on the effects of the opening of a fashionable artistic venue on the tourism development. It explores the promotional actions implemented by tourism entrepreneurs after the opening of the Prada Foundation. The analysis leads to two main results: actors in tourism exploit the urban brand conveyed by Prada, which becomes an integral part of the city branding. Fashion houses also act as marketing devices, producing new urban narratives that influence both the tourist and the real estate market. **Keywords**: City branding; short-term rentals; fashion destination; urban representation; tourism marketing; pradization

INTRODUCTION

Since 1993, Milan's luxury brand Prada has diversified its portfolio by investing in tertiary activities not directly related to fashion. They include the creation of the Foundation Prada, a private entity dedicated to the promotion of contemporary art. Since its inception, the Foundation (which is financially detached from the brand but is closely linked to the brand's identity and name) has benefited from a strong international media presence. From a geographical point of view, the Foundation has various locations in

Fashion and Tourism: Parallel Stories
Tourism Social Science Series, Volume 26, 193–213

ISSN: 1571-5043/doi:10.1108/S1571-504320230000026012

Italy. After the launch of a first permanent site in Venice (called Ca' Corner della Regina) in 2011, Prada opened new majestic headquarters in 2015 in Milan, within a district located on the edges of the city (Scalo di Porta Romana). The urban operation, resulting from a long negotiation with the local authorities, carried out within a neighborhood that until then had been considered unattractive and dangerous, has been involved in a process of urban transformation, with important spatial and socioeconomic effects. In just a few years, the entire district, nicknamed "SouPra," became a proper tourism destination.

This chapter analyzes the influence of the launch of the Foundation both on the spatial patterns and on the estate market. The analysis is based on two main hypotheses. One, tourism entrepreneurs, specifically short-term rentals investors, own and convey an urban esthetic and an image of the city aligned with the Prada brand to enhance the tourist value of the territory. They intentionally submit to tourists a specific vision of the district linked to a luxurious urban representation. Two, the creation of a Corporate Foundation, together with private tourism-oriented initiatives, has significant impacts on the territory (and can produce trickle-down effects on the neighborhood), such as estheticization of the urban landscape, touristification, or even the gentrification of the area.

This chapter places emphasis on the spatial practices and representations that contribute to the emergence, transformation, and touristification of certain districts. More generally, this chapter focuses on the dialectic between the socio-spatial dimension and the discursive dimension within the urban framework. Studies on tourist imaginaries and urban narratives associated with city realities are complex, as they attempt to analyze the urban space from a "metaphorical" perspective: within this context, the city risks becoming a "place of hypersemiotization" (Nancy, 2002, original edition 1999).

The purpose of this chapter is to explore a specific aspect of the global phenomenon (treated by M. Paris in this book), namely, the impact of the settlement of luxury infrastructures on peripheral/semi-central neighborhoods. This chapter and Chapter 11 in this volume analyze two different facets of the same phenomenon through the study of distinct stakeholders. The latter focuses on luxury industries and on the spatial distribution of luxury tourism infrastructure in Milan: it highlights how the multiplication of tourist-oriented services has created a new pattern of exclusive facilities and locations. This involves a consolidated set of "luxury spaces" within the city. This chapter focuses on tourism entrepreneurs, specifically short-term rentals investors, and discusses the articulation between the local financial touring initiatives carried out by the latter and the "luxury spaces" (mentioned earlier). Based on the case of SouPra (meaning South of Prada) district in Milan (Italy), the present contribution underlines how the establishment of a fashion venue (such as a Corporate Foundation) can ultimately affect the real estate market of a district.

This chapter is divided into three main parts. The first part outlines the general framework and explores the state of the art, insisting on the reciprocal links between fashion and the city. The second part contextualizes the case study by exploring the geographical and morphological specificities of the SouPra district and, more generally, of the southern part of Milan. The third part introduces the notion of "pradization," a term coined here to define the phenomenon of creating a destination based on the assets of the Prada brand. Tourism entrepreneurs reinvent the district identity according to tourists' desires (Cocola-Gant, 2018), capitalizing on the fashionable and luxurious urban image conveyed by the Foundation itself. This chapter ends with a question: whether the Prada Foundation can be considered a catalyst for (tourism) gentrification.

OBSERVING THE PRADIZATION PHENOMENON

Due to the diversity of meanings attributed to the notion of "fashion," the lack of precise scientific data (Caves, 2000), the multitude of actors involved in the "fashion system," but also the deficit of scientific legitimacy that has long affected this domain (Crane & Bovone, 2006; Lipovetsky, 1987, 1991; Monneyron, 2017), fashion remained a real "terra incognita" for geographers until the 1990s (Zelinsky, 2004).

In the field of urban studies, fashion has been understood in two senses: as an "economic actor" and as a "social phenomenon" covering many aspects of social life (Craik, 2013). As for the city, within the framework of fashion geography, it also has been understood in two senses: as a "geographic entity" and as a "social institution." Studies on the city and fashion highlight the porosity between these two objects of study, which influence each other (Kawamura, 2004; Rocamora, 2009).

Fashion houses (as economic actors) seem to actively contribute to urban branding and to the strengthening of the city's competitiveness (Crewe & Beaverstock, 1998). By drawing in cultural capital, the fashion houses are likely to attract "creative classes" (Florida, 2002; Lazzaretti, 2013; Vicari, 2010) and to contribute to the revitalization and "touristification" of urban territories (Mommaas, 2004). From a theoretical point of view, the city is considered here as a social institution. The issue of the city's representation and the development of tourist imaginaries was extensively explored by such scholars as Jansson and Power (2010), who have analyzed the way in which global cities may benefit (from an economic and symbolic point of view) and from the urban images and myths created and conveyed by fashion houses. From a spatial perspective, they appear to have the ability to change the geography of the city.

As indicated by M. Paris (in this book), there has been a paradigm-shift in the spatial behavior of luxury actors and, by extension, of fashion houses. Traditionally located in city centers, in the last decade these actors have tended to settle in areas that have been historically remote from the tourist circuits. Confronted with increasing economic and media pressure and with globalized competitive streams, fashion houses, following the trend of other major economic groups, have since the 1980s implemented strategies to diversify their investments by integrating art and design into their fields of action.

The opening of fashion cultural foundations sponsored by fashion houses is part of a global marketing process grounded in a "Artification" strategy. The term refers to the practical aspects of the process by which people, objects, or places become creators, works, or artistic venues (Shapiro, 2004). The economic interpretation of this process suggests the existence of positive spin-offs for fashion houses: the opening of fashion-branded foundations strengthens their images, facilitating the rapprochement between the firms and the creative industries (Hagtvedt & Patrick, 2008; Kapferer, 2014), and enabling the brand to strengthen its intangible features (Jelinek, 2018).

Fashion cultural foundations seems to increase the symbolic value of the brand by enhancing its prestige, exclusivity, and *raison d'être* (Codignola & Rancati, 2016). Within this context, "art morally and aesthetically endorses fashion" (Jelinek, 2018; Kapferer, 2014, p. 376). Nevertheless, this "fashion foundation trend" is part of a wider worldwide phenomenon, since the past 30 years have been marked by a considerable increase in cultural venues following what the literature describes as "museum fever" or "museum-mania" (Guerzoni, 2014). Within the Italian context, a significant increase in the number of cultural foundations can be observed from the 2000s onwards (67% of fashion foundations were opened after that decade).

The quantitative study of fashion cultural foundations allows highlighting the major trends of luxury and fashion companies on a national level and to re-place the case of the Prada Foundation in a more specific context (Table 12.1). The analysis was conducted using data from the national inventory of corporate cultural foundations available from the online database "Italia non Profit." It is hereby noted that, among all the existing fashion foundations in Italy, only those with exhibition spaces available to the public have been considered. Among the 15 foundations analyzed are also those created by fashion designers, which bear the same name of the brand but are totally decorrelated (such as Fondazione Alda Fendi Esperimenti).

The Prada Foundation is one of the oldest Italian fashion cultural foundations: antecedented only by the Tirelli Trappetti Foundation (opened in Rome in 1986), it was the first cultural venue financed by a fashion company within the city of Milan, which is now host to 20% of such foundations. Those culturally driven fashion places are said to play a "catalytic function"

Table 12.1. Distribution of the Cultural Fashion Foundations in Italy (S. Biondo).

Analyzed Streams	Location and Periodization of the Foundations	Number of Foundations	Figures in Percent
Geographical	Metropolitan areas	13	87%
	Milan downtown	3	20%
	Rural areas	2	13%
	Total	15	N/A
Chronological	Foundations established before 1980s	1	7%
	Foundations started from 1990s to 1999	4	26%
	Foundations started from 2000s to 2009	8	53%
	Foundations started from 2010s	2	14%

by contributing to the creation of multi-stakeholder networks (Paris, 2018). The architectural component of these fashion-branded cultural places is extremely relevant: often designed by archi-stars (like Ghery, Nouvel, or Koolhaas), those venues are hypermediatized and succeed in fostering new urban economies based on tourism. These new locations can become proper destinations and may modify both the international cartography of city tourism (Gravari-Barbas & Graburn, 2011) and the tourism imaginaries (Gravari-Barbas & Graburn, 2011). Furthermore, fashion cultural foundations create new forms of tourism: creative tourism (Richards & Wilson, 2006), cultural tourism (McKercher & du Cros, 2012; Richards, 1996), and fashion tourism (Budnarowska & Marciniak, 2016; Craik, 2013) are niche market segments developed by those new fashionable "trendy places" (Maitland, 2010).

Fashion-branded foundations boost and support the creation of new relationships between tourism and "daily life" mingling the boundaries between both, the glamor and the familiar, the local and the global. However, those fashioned cultural locations are also considered active "gentrifiers" (Jensen, 2007) since the establishment of cultural foundations may entail "collateral effects" such as tourism gentrification (Pasquinelli, 2017), over-valorization of the urban context (Paris, 2018), as well as the weakening of the heterogeneity of the local economy (Evans, 2003). On the other hand, the literature insists on the positive role played by fashion-branded cultural spaces in terms of tourism attraction and urban branding, which has also consequences on the behavior of tourism entrepreneurs (hotel chains, tour operators, restaurants, and the like) within the urban framework. Those touring actors nourish fashion-oriented discourses and imaginaries about cultural foundations (and more generally about its surrounding areas), which ultimately attract new visitors and tourists.

Study Methods

The research involved the use of different methods, including interviews and text analysis of the promotional contents produced by tourism entrepreneurs. Interviews were carried out in the first trimester of 2022 in Milan. The "narrative research" method was applied using the biographical interviewing technique (Moen, 2006). The sample consists of 32 entrepreneurs; the respondents were selected based on geographical and chronological criteria. They were Italian investors, owners of real estate located in the SouPra district, who had published short-term rental offers on the Airbnb platform in the post-Prada Foundation opening period in 2015. It is hereby specified that, in all instances, the interviewed investors are independent and not associated with the Prada brand. The entrepreneurs were contacted via the AirBnb platform. The interviews were conducted by telephone or via Zoom. The respondents were asked to answer open-ended questions essentially oriented toward their personal life path and their choices in terms of real estate investment(s). The answers were transcribed *verbatim*. The interviews were coded by grouping codes according to three research axes: one, the influence (perceived or factual) of the opening of the Prada Foundation on the choice of the location of the real estate investment; two, the techniques used by entrepreneurs to attract tourists in SouPra (and the strategies which are considered to be most effective); and, three, the way investors experience the neighborhood and their perception of the (ongoing) urban transformation. To ensure anonymity, the qualitative data expressed by the speakers have been reported in a "raw" style in this chapter. No mention of the "qualifying" elements of the interlocutors appears in the text.

The method was useful both for understanding the reasons why tourism entrepreneurs invested in SouPra and for explaining the rationale for such real estate investments in a marginal area of the city. Elements of information that are subject to different interpretations are provided in the text. In fact, as emphasized in the literature, the biographical storytelling method can bring multifaceted results that may be ambivalent (Polkinhorne, 2007). To preserve methodological rigor and to avoid the risk of subjectivity, the results were cross-referenced with textual elements produced by the interviewed investors (and other real estate entrepreneurs with similar characteristics). The textual analysis was based on 256 AirBnb ads (published after 2015) related to properties located within SouPra. The analysis of these contents, carried out manually, was referred to textual ads and enabled the exploration of ambitions and lifestyles that tourism promoters and investors wish to confer to the district. The findings of both interviews and textual analysis provide input for the definition of the term "pradization."

Founded in 2008, the American company AirBnb provides short-term housing rental through an online marketplace. The platform had a rapid success. Today it has 6 million active listings located in over 100,000 cities and towns, and counts over 4 million hosts (AirBnb, 2022). As a result of numerous tax disputes, Airbnb has been regulated by many jurisdictions, including the European ones (Gainsforth, 2019). The choice of AirBnb as a platform for the analysis of this chapter has been determined by the specificities of the observed city. In Milan, more than half of the rental flats are rented out on Airbnb. In the SouPra district, following the opening of the Foundation, the number of accommodations available on the site has literally doubled (cleanbnb.net, 2022). As will be seen in the case study, in the Milanese context, the proliferation of short-term rental apartments (specifically on AirBnb) is not only a consequence of the influx of tourists, but also a prerequisite for attracting them.

The investigations were conducted based on a preliminary hypothesis which considers that Prada designed and disseminated a specific visual/esthetic presentation of the city (linked to a particular lifestyle), which has been subsequently appropriated by private actors to enhance the tourist-value of a specific urban area (namely SouPra). Barnes, Waitt, Gill, and Gibson (2006), and Peck (2005) argue that such public–private approaches can lead to the development of new urban configurations that require the development of multilayered patterns of governance (Paris, 2018).

Southern Milan and the Foundation Prada

Over the last 20 years, due to increasing pressure from the real estate market, the southern area of the city of Milan (traditionally agricultural) has undergone a strong urbanization process. It has been expanding at the expense of the surrounding municipalities. This expansion has been facilitated, among other things, by a gradual process of decentralization of some highly specialized urban services (higher education venues or headquarters of international private companies) which have moved to the southern fringe of the city. The southern border is essentially characterized by two territorial sections: the southwestern and the southeastern areas. The former contains relevant environmental features: the network of Navigli (canals) – formerly a source of irrigation for agricultural land and a means of transport for commodities – has now become a touristic hotspot that promotes a slow-paced waterside lifestyle as well as "alternative" commercial activities ("Zero kilometer" organic food, vintage thrift shops, and more). The urban landscape (characterized by pastel-colored *maisonettes* (cottages/small houses) and old-fashioned stone bridges) contributes to a more "authentic," bucolic, and peaceful image of the city. The data in this area suggest a reduction in large-scale retail places in favor of small independent shops (Morandi & Paris, 2018). The second urban area is characterized by a large concentration of important infrastructures at national level, particularly regarding railways (regional railway, and high-speed railway to Southern Italy). The presence of mobility infrastructures and the undergoing transformations are particularly visible from Milan Porta Romana railway yard (Figure 12.1).

Heavily impacted by the phenomenon of deindustrialization, the area has faced major urban transformations. Alongside economic changes (the desire

Figure 12.1. Milan Skyline From the Prada Foundation (Scalo di Porta Romana), S. Biondo, Milano, 2022.

to create a knowledge economy based on initiatives linked to specific measures, such as the Milan Smart City program), there are also urban regeneration initiatives. In this context, the opening of the Foundation Prada in 2015 on a converted industrial site seems to have triggered a wider process of transformation that had spill-over effects on the entire district. This fashion cultural Foundation (Figure 12.2) has acted as "an active driver of urban regeneration" (Morandi & Paris, 2018, p. 86).

Characterized by an impressive architectural configuration combining 10 buildings (seven existing and three newly built structures), the 28,340 sq.m, the Foundation is the outcome of the rehabilitation of an industrial wasteland (a former distillery dating from the 1910s). Designed by the archi-star Koolhaas (in collaboration with his associates from the OMA studio) and

Figure 12.2. Architectural Style of the Prada Foundation by Remment Koolhaas (OMA Studio), S. Biondo, Milano, 2022.

entirely financed by Prada, the fashion-branded place has a multifunctional vocation. It hosts an art gallery, a theater, a cinema, bars and restaurants, offices, and a library. Due to its emblematic architecture, composed, among other things, of a gold-covered building and a 60-meter tall *Torre* (tower), the cultural foundation has become a landmark for the district and, more in general, for the southern part of the city, gradually emerging as a tourism destination (Figure 12.2). Although the site has been used by Prada to stage fashion shows, the brand policy provides for a clear division between the Foundation and the corporate business (Welter, 2019). Strongly mediatized, the location aims to become both a cultural venue and a reference point for tourism (Morandi & Paris, 2018) within the "Milanese" framework.

Although the creation of urban value specifically associated with the opening of the Foundation has not been scientifically demonstrated, the latter seems to have driven a profound urban transformation that concerned the entire district and not the spaces surrounding the Prada site (Paris, 2018). A gradual urban change that has been accompanied, among other things, by the opening of new luxury headquarters (such as that of the LVMH group), by the creation of smart neighborhoods (such as the Symbiosis district financed by the Municipality of Milan), and by the adoption of specific policies supported by the public authorities. As a result, the entire perimeter of the old railway line, located in front of the Foundation, has been qualified as an *area di trasformazione urbana* (development area) and has been integrated into the new city masterplan (Figure 12.3).

The project envisages an extensive urban regeneration that includes, among other things, the construction of the Olympic village for the Milan-Cortina 2026 Olympic Games. This is an ongoing urban transformation that can be seen with the naked eye. A simple walk through the district reveals the impetus and dynamics of the transformation. Cranes and open-air construction sites characterize the urban landscape adjacent to the Foundation. In the context of the opening of the Foundation, Prada acted as an urban marketer, creating new images for an area historically absent in the classical touristic circuits of the city of Milan, with side effects on the real estate market, as well as on the tourism industry.

A Glance at SouPra

The use of acronyms to brand neighborhoods (especially those that have been the subject of urban regeneration policies) is a very common practice in Milan (like the NoLo acronym used for the North Loreto district located in the north-east of the city or Na.Pa in the Naviglio Pavese area in the south). It is therefore no coincidence that the district in which the Foundation Prada is located has taken on the moniker of the fashion-branded building: SouPra (in full: South of Prada). This district is clearly defined (it lies to the south of

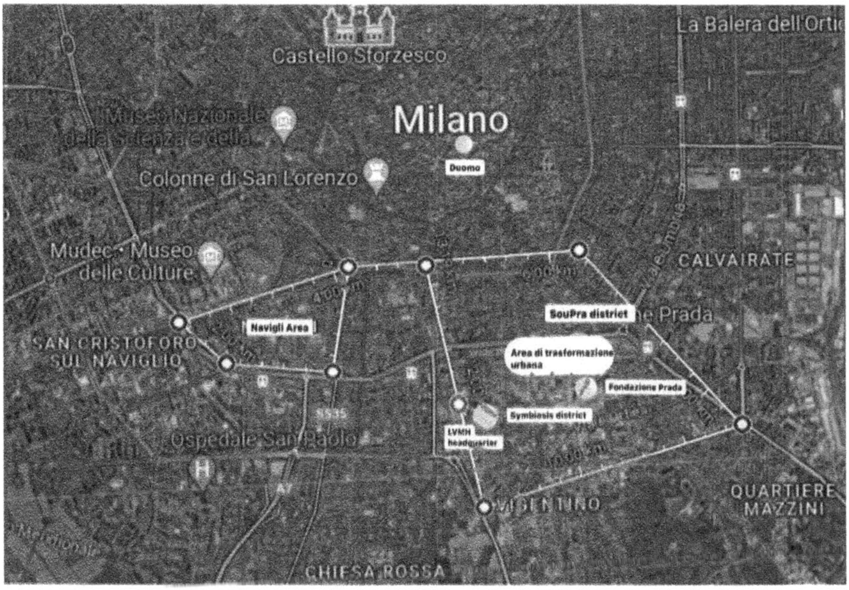

Figure 12.3. Locating the Prada Foundation and "Area di Trasformazione Urbana", S. Biondo – Based on the Map Template provided by Google Maps, 2022.

Porta Romana and extends from the Ripamonti area to Corso Lodi), covering areas of the city that were once synonymous with "difficult" suburbs. Unlike the other acronyms, which have been adopted or sponsored by the municipal authorities of Milan, the term SouPra has "bottom-up" origins. It was coined and is essentially used by local entrepreneurs who have decided to invest in the area for tourism purposes. In fact, following the opening of the Foundation, many other cultural centers, galleries, and popular local artist studios have sprung up in a few years which have transformed the area into a real tourism venue. On the artistic-cultural front, examples include Foundation ICA, the NFQ studio combining Fabio Quaranta and NERO, the Reading Room founded by Francesca Spiller, the city's first art kiosk. On the social front, there are some very popular nightclubs (Social Music City in the airport, the Magazzini Generali or the Plastic).

The naming of the district responds precisely to the vocation of increasing the attractiveness of the place, proposing a wide range of highly fashionable and cultural services specifically conceived to meet the needs of an international audience. The SouPra district has gradually begun to be populated by multifunctional places of social aggregation (such as the Madama Hostel or the Talent Garden Calabiana). The opening of the Foundation also seems to have stimulated local entrepreneurship: in the space of a few years, numerous "tourism business owners" have emerged, including individuals who, through their social networks, have been able to mobilize the necessary resources and capital in order to benefit from the (potential or real) tourism opportunities created following the launch of the Prada Foundation (Chell & Baines, 2000).

The SouPra neighborhood provides challenges for profit-driven entrepreneurs given its peripheral geography, combined with its "dangerous and degraded" reputation and its urban landscape (strongly impacted by the phenomenon of deindustrialization).

However, the attractiveness of Prada location provides relevant motives for new entrepreneurs who, through their investments, can actively contribute to the change in marginal areas from industry-based to tourism economies, creating innovative opportunities for other local businesses. The SouPra district has experienced both acquisition-driven and firm-driven models of entrepreneurship. The first mechanism concerns investments by multinationals, with the district having experienced strong development thanks to the presence of large transnational groups/brands. For example, the LVMH group and the Fastweb brand have taken over old industrial buildings in the area surrounding the Foundation to create their institutional headquarters.

The second case concerns the development of new brands (or the renewal of existing brands) linked to the development of products or services geared toward tourism consumption. Whether in the restaurant, hotel, or other sectors (such as gift shop businesses), touring services developed in SouPra are, according to the interviews conducted with local actors, not particularly affected by seasonality and are designed to remain open all year round. Among these, the Madama Hostel & Bistrot (a multipurpose hostel also acting as a cultural center), opened simultaneously with the Foundation, has become a meeting point for international tourists.

The next part of this article will focus on how tourism entrepreneurs have used the city images produced by the fashion brand to enhance and promote the urban area surrounding the Foundation to make it more attractive for tourists. In fact, Prada has been adopted as a guarantee of the quality (and creativity) of the whole SouPra district. This phenomenon is somewhat unheard of, as it goes against the evidence from the literature, which rather highlights the way in which fashion brands usually exploit the cities (and their respective urban brands and heritage assets) to enhance their own brand (Crewe & Beaverstock, 1998). Besides, it seems important to investigate the way in which the association between the Prada brand and the SouPra district is carried out and to also examine the implications of this rapprochement for the urban area and its stakeholders.

This last section focuses on tourism entrepreneurs, specifically short-term rentals investors, as well as on promotional contents associated with the rentals located within the observed district. The first part reconstructs, through the empirical material collected via the "life story" approach (Bertaux & Kohli, 1984), the specificities of these investors and the reasons that led them to invest in the area. The second part focuses on the AirBnb ads designed by entrepreneurs to attract tourists. The third part aims to analyze the intra- and interdistrict competitive dynamics in SouPra and attempts, based on research results, to define pradization.

Attracting Tourists Through the Prada Urban Brand

According to Gallione,

> The new gold hunt has already begun, and it's heading south: even beyond the Scalo di Porta Romana. It is here that, following the rhythm of the new cranes that have redesigned entire chunks of (former) suburbs, from now until the 2026 Olympics, those in search of a flat to rent as an investment will have to look to (2022).

Following the opening of the Foundation Prada, the district was branded as the new "Milanese cultural area" with alternative physical and social spaces featuring a creative dimension. The SouPra district is presented to tourists by local entrepreneurs as multidimensional, innovative, and transformative. The area responds to some typical criteria of "creative neighborhoods." Located in a postindustrial context, it benefits from the input of numerous cultural companies that intervene regularly on the territory (Bovone, Magatti, Mora, & Rovati, 2002). The interviews reveal that the entrepreneurial choices have been characterized by a prospective and profit-oriented approach within a context of urban transformation. The underlying economic model is far from the so-called "sharing economy."

Milanese Airbnb's real estate market is mainly controlled by owners who respond to a specific business model. These are multiple hosts who manage multiple offers on the e-platform. Most of the 32 interviewed actors (74%) have been able to capitalize on the momentum investing on the local real estate market before 2013. This happened just after the Milan municipality and the Prada brand reached an agreement concerning the opening of the Foundation. Competitiveness and for-profit logic were the two main aspects of the investors' choice, in a context where the risk was moderately high. The housing is increasingly used as a capital reserve (Aalbers, 2017). However, before investing, the actors concretely assessed the "set of possibilities, positive or negative, that the area seems to offer from a commercial point of view," the so-called "neighborhood risk(s)":

> When we bought the apartment, the area was deserted, or even worse: run-down and dirty. The arrival of Prada was a gamble for us: we knew

> we could count on the brand and its international reputation, but we didn't know if tourists would actually come here. The opening of the Foundation motivated us to continue with the purchase of more flats later… In those years, the real estate market in the area was accessible. (Bovone, Mazzette, & Rovati, 2005, p. 80)

Almost all the local investors are Italian, 90% of which are from Milan or have lived in the city over a long period of time (at least 10 years before the acquisition of the real estate asset). However, it is interesting to note that Milanese investors are most often based in other city districts. They are therefore physically distant from SouPra, and they used to delegate the management of the flats to intermediary actors. Most of the properties are for rental purposes only. As evoked by one of the respondents,

> As the flat is constantly rented out for weekends, I leave the keys to the housekeeper. It is rare for me to go there, and I admit that I am not a SouPra expert.

The results of the analysis also highlight the importance of networks (and digital dimension) in the development of entrepreneurship. As indicated by another interviewee, the concern about making an unfruitful investment was an underlying feeling in the beginning:

> They [referring to tourists] come for the Foundation [Prada] but then they don't necessarily want to stay here… you have to know how to narrate the neighborhood, justify it and contextualize it to be able to show them the interest of the place, the links between the Foundation and the district. At the beginning nobody came, now it's always booked up.

The touristification of the district also has quite significant impacts on the urban landscape. Following the model of the rehabilitation of the Foundation's spaces (conservation of industrial vestiges and creation of complementary new architectural assets), the entire district is being given a makeover by focusing on tangible elements. The entrepreneurs implemented a process of estheticization of the city for the sake of tourism, which results in the emergence of a unified architectural "language" and style within the district. The case study allows highlighting the process of setting up an "interior urban design" (Wilmotte, 1999). In fact, within the context of SouPra, tourism investors seem to participate (as well as local authorities) in the place-making of the city, which can lead to the clearance of identity specificities of the district (Brossat, 2018; Gainsforth, 2019). The esthetic control becomes clear when one enters the district (the streets surrounding the Foundation), providing a distinctive ambience.

The materials used to cover the façades are precious (marble or travertine), the chromatic palette of the buildings is sophisticated and luxurious (multicolored new buildings facing the Foundation). Bicycle and trolley tracks are present on every street corner within dedicated parking (BikeMi). The city offers the dream of a luxury, well-maintained and smart district, where you can move around in an eco-friendly way taking advantage of the art, fashion, benefiting from private flats offered by Milanese insiders. At a glance, SouPra organizes itself to become a proper "lifestyle destination" (Sigler & Wachsmuth, 2016) and not only a cultural district. The industrial identity of the district is specifically enhanced, narrated, and made more appealing to tourist by investors. A young entrepreneur explained how real estate offerings are increasingly adapting to tourists' desires in accordance with their vision of SouPra. As a result, a portion of the city is altered and only becomes attractive to a certain tourist target audience:

> Tourists are fascinated by the industrial past of the district, they are actively looking for loft-style accommodation in renovated buildings (or similar) … they look for authenticity and originality. In fact, the choice to rent a flat in SouPra is a statement in itself: our clients are young, cosmopolitan and trendy; they want to be seen as such.

As a matter of fact, living in the district, even if only temporarily (for a weekend) has become a sort of status symbol for tourists, thanks to the cleverly designed housing facilities made available to tourists by real estate entrepreneurs.

Locating SouPra in a Luxurious Urban Ecosystem. A report on the results of a text analysis conducted on a sample of 256 AirBnb ads related to properties can provide further insights. The ads were chosen following criteria of geographic, chronological, and linguistic order. Only ads of the apartments located in the SouPra neighborhood (defined in this chapter as the area from the Ripamonti area to Corso Lodi via Scalo di Porta Romana) were considered. The analysis is based on listings published after 2015 (date of the foundation's opening) available at the time of the research (second semester of 2022). Among the 256 ads, 32 were published by the interviewed actors. The research was based on the analysis of Italian and English texts (often the description features in both languages). Only the offerings related to apartments (not taking into account the ads related to shared rooms) were observed. This choice appeared to be representative of the local housing supply. Figure 12.5 (Inside AirBnb, accessed June 2022) suggests that within the AirBnb rental offer in SouPra, the number of apartments far exceeds the number of private rooms. Table 12.2 summarizes the information obtained from the manual analysis of the texts. Recurring terms within the texts that allowed to structure the analysis and determine the topics considered

Table 12.2. Results Specification From the Textual Analysis of the AirBnb Rental Ads (S. Biondo).

Analysis Criteria	Results Specification	Figures
Geographical	Northern area of SouPra (Scalo di Porta Romana)	70%
	Southeast area of SouPra	25%
	Southwest area of SouPra	5%
Language used	Ads in Italian only	18%
	Ads in English only	22%
	Bilingual ads (Ita/Eng)	60%
Recurring terms in ads	SouPra (naming)	0.5%
	Mention the Prada Foundation	100%
	District as a "tourist spot"	86%
	District as a "cultural hub"	55%
	Proximity to public transportation (urban mobility)	70%
	Presence of local retail units	40%

tourist-friendly by investors (proximity to public transportation, urban mobility, presence of local retail units, and the like) were examined.

Having the Prada Foundation in the district guarantees the production of an architectural statement marking the city is likely to attract tourists not only for its cultural and artistic content, but also (and above all) for its "singular and spectacular" architecture (Biau, 1991). The desire to regenerate spaces is often expressed explicitly by harmonizing urban esthetics and erasing inconsistencies in the landscape. The tourist activity affects the urban landscape in different ways, including through the standardization and disappearance of local shops and with an emergence of commercial and leisure places replacing basic/daily services (Brossat, 2018; Gralak, 2018). This renewal of local businesses is reflected in the AirBnb Ads and is considered as a lever of tourist attractiveness:

> The district has become more and more dynamic recently especially during Design Weeks, men and women Fashion Weeks and Music Week also thanks to Foundation Prada. This is the place where next winter Olympic Games will take place in few years. The area is full of bars, shops, apothecaries, and various banks (AirBnb Ad., Accessed on March 2022).

Some investors also insist on the historical and social dimension of the neighborhood (which has been clearly weakened).

> Porta Romana is a district with a rich history and Milanese traditions: old craftsmen's shops and typical street markets mix with a modern, fashionable shopping center. There are numerous venues, including typical and trendy restaurants... and at the very heart there is Foundation Prada (AirBnb Ad., Accessed on March 2022).

The more expensive available flats (classed as "super-hosts") are qualified as "fashionable," "contemporary and elegant," and are associated with a luxurious lifestyle aimed at the middle and upper classes. The advertisements mention in all cases the Prada Foundation, with the clear aim of making the accommodation more attractive to the tourist's eye. The acronym SouPra is still used less in real estate advertisements – only one of the 256 descriptions clearly refers to it. The Foundation is presented as a tourism-oriented facility in ads:

> Nice studio apartment in a typical "Old Milan" style building. In just 5 minutes on foot, you can reach one of the most active cultural centers in Milan: the Foundation Prada ... Bright flat near the Prada Museum: a unique treasure of art and culture.

It is interesting to note that in order to integrate the Foundation into tourism strategies, entrepreneurs encourage clients to visit these places alongside other heritage sites:

> Splendid loft just a few steps from Foundation Prada and three metro stops from the Duomo; both can be visited in one day.

The development of the district is progressively affecting the social geography and morphology of Milan. For the most part, tourists continue to look for accommodations in the historic center; the density of AirBnb accommodation in that area specifically illustrates this trend (Figure 12.4). However, the appeal of SouPra has led to the mild displacement of tourists also to the south of the city. The provision of AirBnB rental accommodation may reduce the tourist pressure within Milan in the foreseeable future. Figure 12.5 illustrates the density of AirBnb rentals in the southern part of Milan. It is possible to observe how, in the proximity of the Foundation, particularly in the Porta Romana area, the lodgings slightly begin to make room for themselves; however, the phenomenon is still marginal.

Intra- and Inter-district Competitive Dynamics. The analysis of the promotional content of the AirBnb platform and the responses formulated by investors during biographical interviews suggests the concept of pradization. The phenomenon can be defined as the aggregate of activities that are carried

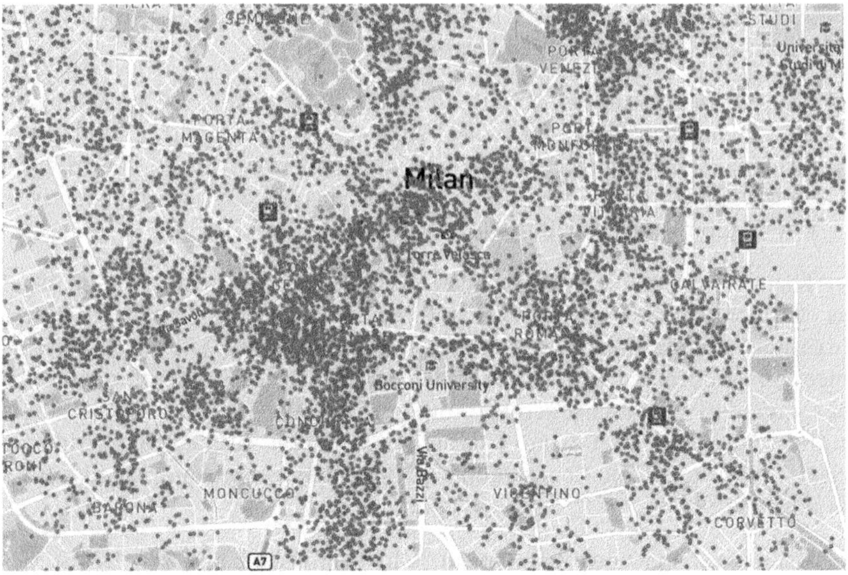

Figure 12.4. Density Map of Active Airbnb Listings in Milan, Inside AirBnb, Accessed on June 2022.

Figure 12.5. Density Map of Active Airbnb Listings in the Southern Part of Milan, Inside AirBnb, Accessed on June 2022.

out by urban entrepreneurs with the purpose of turning (through the wise use of the reputation associated with the Prada brand) a specific district from a location into a tourism-oriented destination. In this case, the opening of the Prada Foundation seems to have acted as a catalyst for the renewal of the district urban identity. "Pradization" materializes through, among others, the naming of the neighborhood with a specific label (SouPra), the reinforcement of urban communication aimed at embellishing the imagery associated with the place, and ad hoc urban initiatives (co-funded by public–private actors) to landscaping the urban environment.

Pradization intends to create a recognizable competitive identity of the SouPra district in the mind of its tourists. SouPra thereby appears to succeed in attracting a cosmopolitan class which is very demanding in terms of consumption habits. The district builds amenities considered attractive to tourists (luxury restaurants, souvenir boutiques, and more). In this context, high-end flats (which are mostly for rental purposes only) have gradually begun to appear in the SouPra area. This process has been assisted by municipal authorities who have used tourism as a strategy for economic revitalization. This is accomplished by incorporating tourism services into the re-development of the neighborhood and contributing to the esthetici-zation of the urban landscape through sophisticated street lighting systems or brand-new urban furniture (litter bins, benches), these with the aim of attracting more tourists.

To analyze the tourism phenomenon, it is necessary to take the "con-sumption phenomena" into account. Within the so-called "consumer soci-ety," cities are increasingly seen as places of consumption (Chamusca, Rio Fernandes, Carvalho, & Mendes, 2019). In the case of Milan, one can observe commercial gentrification in progress. SouPra is filled with consumer-oriented activities such as restaurants, showrooms, exhibition galleries, and entertainment/leisure venues (such as the glamor club Plastic Palace) in the residential space, thus expanding the possibilities of urban consumption. Consequently, there are knock-on effects such as gentrification with major changes in the commercial landscape, which can supply increasingly high-priced and niche products and services (Mermet & Gravari-Barbas, 2013) as well as mixed-use specialized spaces (as the fashion event place "Fabbrica Orobia"). The Foundation is acting as "a driver for urban regeneration" (Morandi & Paris, 2018, p. 86). However, the produc-tion of a spill-over effect (the creation of networks between singular places and territories) has yet to be proven and verified as well as the existence of fecund exchanges between the city and the district.

The analysis of the latter also brings out the inter- and intra-neighborhood competitive dynamics within the city of Milan. From the "outside," SouPra relates very poorly to the other districts of the city. Case studies indicate that the networks developed by tourism entrepreneurs within the area "instead of connecting, risks to become a limit for their multifaceted flows" (Morandi & Paris, 2018, p. 93). Indeed, if one considers the district "from the inside," it is possible to notice that the touring leisure amenities and/or housing services (specifically the AirBnb flats) are essentially clustered in the northern part of the area facing the Prada Foundation, close to the city metro (Figure 12.5).

The supply is relatively well-integrated in the urban context but excludes from the "new" tourism circuits the whole southern portion of the district (an area that is being regenerated but which is less in line with the urban esthetics promoted by both public and private actors). The industrial identity of the district, therefore, is clearly visible in the narrative dimension (as it feeds a precise tourist imaginary), but not in the territorial dimension insofar as industrial venues and places (wasteland, factories, or abandoned buildings) are not de facto visited by tourists. There is an incongruence between the district storytelling and the urban practices related to the latter.

Although SouPra is likely to change rapidly, it has managed both to create its own fashionable, creative, tourist-friendly identity and to provide "top-of-the-range" entertainment services. The settlement of a tourism attraction, such as the Prada Foundation in a residential district, distant from traditional tourist circuits, seems to have globally reinforced the relevance of consumer-oriented activities in the city's peripheral spaces and to have potentially encouraged a gentrification process (Chamusca et al., 2019). Although in-depth studies related to the phenomenon of residents' displacement to other districts have not been conducted within the context of Scalo di Porta Romana, the proliferation of accommodation on AirBnb has led to a loss of part of the real estate resources for residents, thus creating the premises for a gentrification. In fact, tourist-oriented short-term rentals are at the expense of long-term residential rentals. The term "tourism gentrification" is used here to describe the

> ...progressive transformation of a middle-class neighborhood into an exclusive and luxury enclave marked by the proliferation of the tourism industry ... a phenomenon that reflects the new institutional connections between local institutions, the real estate industry and the global economy. (Gotham, 2005)

In the context of peripheral economies, the impact of tourism gentrification on residents is more dramatic (Cocola-Gant, 2018) since the increase in real estate prices makes it difficult for less prosperous residents to remain in the area. This chapter is intended to initiate a preliminary prospective work on the development of the urban area; time will tell whether these are the early stages of gentrification.

CONCLUSION

The purpose of this study was to investigate the impact of the Foundation Prada on the city and more precisely on the "Scalo di Porta Romana" district in a context of touristic development of the whole area (SouPra). The analysis was carried out taking into account the point of view of tourism entrepreneurs (real estate investors offering accommodation in the area). It should be noted that the proliferation of Airbnb accommodation in the neighborhood took place in a context of a worldwide economic recession. The case study highlights how the Prada brand has been used by individual entrepreneurs to enhance the area as well as the rented accommodation, through urban branding policies. The analysis also highlights the tendency toward urban isomorphism. Local authorities, as well as private investors, contribute to the estheticization (but also the uniformization) of the city landscape. The study results highlight the risks of tourism gentrification (including both residential and commercial gentrification), which could also lead to a global homologation of urban space/landscape. This contribution provides an insight into the complexity of urban phenomena.

As for the limits, the study does not consider the way in which the fashion house Prada positions itself in relation to the appropriation/use of its brand by tourism actors. Furthermore, the question of the economic model underlying the accommodation presented on AirBnb has been treated less extensively. Further research can help to clarify the impacts of the vacancy of accommodation on the territory under crisis context (COVID-19). Lastly, it would be interesting to explore the tourists' perspective and the underlying reasons (symbolic or material) for them to seek accommodation in SouPra. Moreover, it is important to point out that the methodology used presents some criticalities. Through the narrative research technique, actors can have "distorted projections of past events" risking to partially invalidate the information exposed by the author (Polkinhorne, 2007). This study constitutes a first basis to produce more substantial evaluation work on the assessment of the territorial impacts linked to the opening of a fashion-branded cultural foundation.

Chapter 13

FASHIONING URBAN MARGINS THROUGH CULTURE-LED REGENERATION

Sandra Biondo
Université Paris 1 Panthéon-Sorbonne (EIREST), France

Abstract: This chapter investigates the importance of fashion houses in the progressive redefinition of tourism geography within a metropolitan context. The purpose is to highlight how these brands manage both to integrate marginal urban areas into the tourist circuits and to co-construct market-oriented heritage policies. Through the case of Fendi Roma and the EUR district (Rome, Italy), this chapter explores their degrees of involvement in the processes of requalification and estheticization of peripheral urban areas. The study found that the involvement of the luxury brand in Roman urban governance is symptomatic of evolutions in the political strategies pursued by public actors in their relations with private investors. **Keywords**: Contested heritage; fascism; Fendi Roma; market-oriented policies; urban regime; suburban tourism

INTRODUCTION

Traditionally, fashion brands have been located in the city centers, typically within hypertouristified urban areas (Gravari-Barbas, 2017), consistently benefiting from the economic spinoffs generated by the presence of tourists, and more specifically of "fashion tourists." The complexity of defining this notion comes from the fact that the latter is frequently associated with other types of tourism (cultural, market, or creative tourism). The term is here used to describe cases in which the choice of the destination is determined by the

Fashion and Tourism: Parallel Stories
Tourism Social Science Series, Volume 26, 215–237

Published under exclusive licence by Emerald Publishing Limited
ISSN: 1571-5043/doi:10.1108/S1571-504320230000026013

tourists' willingness to enjoy fashion-related experiences, like shopping, museums, and more (Craik, 2013). However, more recently, the literature has focused on the development of "alternative" practices of spatialization. Fashion houses gradually occupy marginal parts of the city, either on an ephemeral basis (such as through fashion shows) or permanently (through star-architecture projects). Nevertheless, it is important to point out that this phenomenon rhymes with a much broader process related to the emergence of urban peripheries as tourism spaces.

The fashion houses participate in the regeneration and touristification of marginal urban areas, taking part in the interdependent power relations of urban society. This chapter shows that the combination of private and public stakeholders' interests allows the integration of previously peripheral areas into new tourism circuits. It shows the modalities of this integration and the links between heritagization and touristification which are powered by fashion-led initiatives. The study hypothesizes that these peripheral areas are conceived as performative spaces (Potvin, 2009) where fashion houses are given the potential to spatially stage and perform their brand-identity. It demonstrates that private investors belonging to the fashion industry succeed in penetrating urban governance systems, contributing to the implementation of both market-oriented policies and urban regeneration practices focused on the enhancement of peripheral areas. It argues that public actors actively support fashion houses in this spatial dynamic, since they consider those urban spaces as important territorial assets for the development of tourism.

TOURISTIFICATION OF URBAN MARGINS

The process of touristification of urban margins has been extensively investigated, and it is somehow considered one of the most relevant trends in contemporary tourism geography (Ashworth & Page, 2011). In many cases, public authorities explicitly support policies oriented to tourism enhancement of the urban fringes through specific tools, such as mega-events (Hiller, 2000), unique and exclusive and hyperpublicized events (Hall, 1992), or flagship projects, branded (McNeill, 2009), and iconic architecture projects (Sklair, 2017), thus promoted as "exceptional" (Gravari-Barbas, 2020). These new "suburban forms of tourism" (Gravari-Barbas & Jacquot, 2013) facilitate not only the development of close connections between the centers and the urban peripheries, but also the emergence of new tourism imaginaries (Gravari-Barbas & Graburn, 2011). These evolutions raise the question of the territorial and touristic impact related to the settlement of fashion brands within the urban margins. The analysis in this chapter is based on the hypothesis that the peripheral installation of these firms generates impacts both on the local urban heritage assets and on the suburbs. The second question that can be asked is whether the phenomena observed have any effect on the tourism geography (in terms of development of new tourism circuits and/or tourist imaginaries related to the peripheries). To respond to these questions, the study works specifically on a unique and localized case study: the EUR district in Rome (Italy) and the Fendi Roma brand.

Conceived as a "quartiere-città" (a district acting as a city), the EUR district was created with the intent of reaffirming the supremacy of Italian fascist civilization over other countries of the world. Located in the southern part of the city of Rome, IX Municipio (Figure 13.2; created on the map template provided by Google Maps), the EUR was planned for the 1942 Universal Exhibition (that would later give its name to the entire E42 area) and responded to an ambitious purpose: creating a modern urban center, that would propel Rome toward the Mediterranean Sea (Quilici, 2015). This was with the aim of "bringing Rome to the sea and the sea to Rome," as Mussolini used to say (Notaro, 2000, p. 15). The construction of E42 was interrupted by the outbreak of the World War II, and it was not until the mid-1950s that a slow and disorganized transformation of the area (re)started. The core of the Universal Exposition was the fascist-era rationalist monument. Palazzo della civilità italiana (PdCI) supposed to serve as a museum and to host the Mostra della Civiltà Italiana (exhibition of Italian Civilization).

The PdCI is the most debated, least loved, but also most familiar and famous Roman monument in the modern city (Casciato & Poretti, 2002). Because of its historical connotation, it has been considered a dissonant heritage and has been difficult to reuse until recently. Designed by architects Giovanni Guerrini, Ernesto La Padula, and Mario Romano in 1937, it was inaugurated, although incomplete, in 1940. The works were progressively completed only after the World War II. However, except for occasional ephemeral events (1953 International Agricultural Fair; 1998 Bob Dylan concert), the building remained in a state of neglect for more than 70 years. This chapter focuses specifically on the process of settlement of the fashion luxury brand Fendi Roma within the PdCI in 2015. It argues that this fashion-lead initiative, powered by Fendi Roma, gave a new impetus to the entire area with a consequent increase in tourism attractiveness.

Given the regulatory environment, Italy seems to be particularly relevant: starting from 2004, there has been an increase in public–private partnerships institutionalized through specific national regulations. Within this context, this chapter examines how a contested heritage place (and more broadly, a peripheral fascist-era district) loses its marginal status and is integrated into new tourism circuits. It respectively analyzes the economic and political mechanisms that have contributed to this integration, the actors involved, the modes of action, and the impacts on tourists' perceptions. This chapter is structured around a double research question: one, to what extent the involvement of the fashion brand in urban governance is symptomatic of changes/evolutions in the strategies pursued by public actors in their relations with private investors; and, two, what territorial impact the fashion-lead initiative have on the peripheral district and on its tourist attractiveness?

Study Methods

The study is based on a mixed research method: the sources used are quantitative and qualitative. The former data were used to assess the tourist flows in the IX Municipio. The aim was to measure and qualify the gradual increase in the number of visitors and tourists in the area during the four years following the establishment of the Fendi house in the EUR district. The analysis was halted in 2019. Between 2020 and 2021, as a result of lockdown measures applied by the Italian government due to COVID-19, tourism activity\ies in the Italian peninsula were interrupted (partially or totally depending on the months). As a consequence, the Fendi museum (located in the PdCI) was fully closed to the public during this period.

The analysis was based on data provided by the Osservatorio Turistico dell'Ente Bilaterale Turismo del Lazio and the Dipartimento Trasformazione Digitale U.O. Statistica – Open Data di Roma Capitale. The qualitative data refer to the information retrieved from a series of semi-directive interviews conducted with local stakeholders between 2018 and 2021. Among these are policymakers (such as EUR Spa and IX Municipio), social actors (professionals and local associations and scholars having a "social" knowledge of the EUR district), and brand representatives (Fendi's managers, architects, and employees). For the perception of the PdCI by tourists, the reviews posted on the Tripadvisor platform in connection to the four temporary exhibitions held by the Fendi Roma brand between 2015 and 2018 were retrospectively analyzed.

The content analysis was carried out in May 2021 on a sample of 184 visitors. They were chosen on the basis of a linguistic criterion: in particular, all reviews written in nonalphanumeric characters (Latin alphabet and/or Arabic numerals) were excluded from the sample. The aim was to avoid any potential interpretative risk linked to incorrect translations. The languages of the reviews were distributed as follows: 72% Italian, 20% English, 4% French, 3% Spanish, 0.5% German, and 0.5% Portuguese. Therefore, it is important to point out that most of the reviews were made by Italians (80%). As for the reviews in English, they were produced by a rather international audience – except for the United Kingdom, tourists came mainly from the United States, Oceania, South-East Asia, and Japan.

Exploratory visits made it possible to intercept two interpretative keys proper to the PdCI: its representations and perceptions. To do this, the territory analyzed was observed not only as an urban material space (inherent to the real estate aspects), but also as an imaginary space (related to the tourist perception). Considering the demographic dynamics affecting the area (a district comparable to a Central Business District with a limited presence of households), residents were not consulted. Field research methods (in situ observations, semi-directive interviews, and informal exchanges) were also combined with a comprehensive literature review as well as with in-depth archival analysis. In particular, sources from several archives (the archives of Fendi, the Istituto Luce Cinecittà, L'Unione Cinematografica Educativa, and the database from EUR Spa) were regularly consulted between 2018 and 2021.

With regard to the exhibitions produced by Fendi Roma, particular interest was given to various components of the exhibition "Una nuova Roma. The Eur and the PdCI" held in 2015. The purpose was to assess the involvement of the fashion brand in the storytelling of the district. Despite several attempts, the inclusion of LVMH managers among the interviewees was not possible. However, it was possible to consider and analyze LVMH positions, thanks to materials such as press releases, public interviews, and fashion-branded documentaries. The main challenge was to merge these heterogeneous methods to point out the phenomenon of heritagization and touristification of marginal districts induced by fashion houses.

Case of PdCI

The first part of this chapter examines, from a diachronic perspective, the actors, and the phases of the complex negotiation inherent in the management and definition of the functional use of the PdCI (Figure 13.3). The analysis, carried out over a 10-year period (2005–2015), reveals the political-economic effects of the insertion of an actor that was external to the "Regime of Urbe" (D'Albergo & Moini, 2015) – Fendi Roma – within the Roman policy arena. The operation is concluded with a lease agreement that commits the LVMH group with a rent fixed at €240,000 per month for duration of 15 years. The purpose of this analysis was to understand if, and eventually to what extent, this process is symptomatic of changes in the strategies pursued by public actors in their relations with private investors.

The processes of heritagization adopted by the brand to rehabilitate a building considered as a "dissonant heritage" are then detailed. Fashion becomes a tool for the re-semanticization and redesigning of the building, but the nature of the operation remains exquisitely political. The information presented next come from a detailed study of journalistic sources. The contents were then cross-referenced with data provided by the Municipal archives of Roma Capitale. Observations are mainly based on the interviews implemented with managers of the Fendi Roma brand and with specialized actors (scholars and fashion-related stakeholders).

A Tripartite Political Negotiation

In Rome, the vicissitudes of the PdCI were part of a complex negotiation. The latter were regulated both by the norms on buildings of cultural interest (approved by Legislative Decree No 42/2004) and the code of cultural heritage and landscape (art. 10 of law July 6, 2002, n. 137). Those texts define the intended purpose of the building, which must aim at the "enjoyment of the community, compatible with the needs of institutional use" (art. 2 of the decree). In other words, the qualification of the building by the Italian Ministry of Cultural Heritage constrains the use of the spaces of the PdCI to only exhibition and museum purposes. The settlement of the Fendi Roma brand in the Palazzo responds only partially to these heritage constraints. This partial response was made possible by a sharp political negotiation. To assess the different stages of the negotiation, the approach developed by Savitch and Kantor (2002) was used. The latter is useful for understanding the policy streams of the urban development policy strategies within the context of private financing and management of public goods (Savitch & Kantor, 2002). Those streams may constitute the two poles of a continuum of either social or market-oriented urban development strategies, ordered by the extent of public control over them, respectively intense or lacking (Figure 13.1).

The public actors' approach can be driven by various endogenous factors (political-economic orientations and/or "urban culture"; [D'Albergo, Moini, & Pizzo, 2018]) or exogenous factors (socioeconomic conditions, regulatory framework, political-electoral outcomes). The intent is to discuss how,

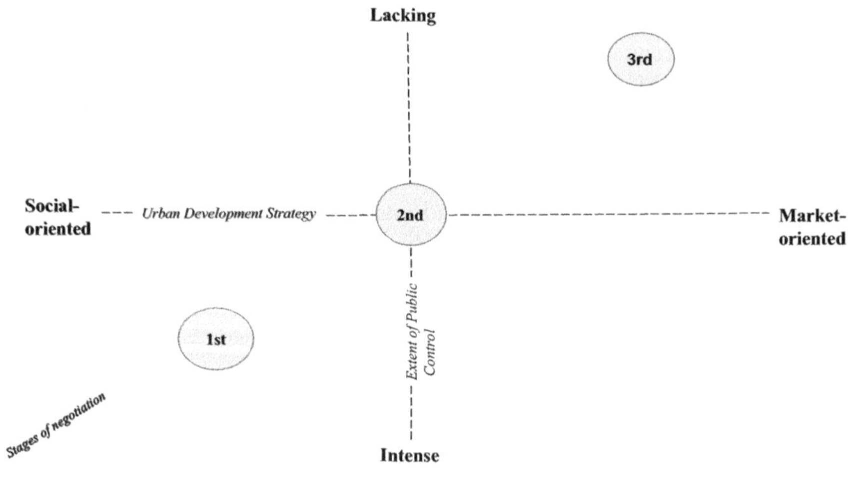

Figure 13.1. Overview of Urban Development Strategies, S. Biondo.
Source: S. Biondo's PhD thesis, 2023.

Table 13.1. Outline and Chronological Periodization of the Negotiation Stages, S. Biondo.

Stages of the Negotiation	First Stage	Second Stage	Third Stage
Timeframe	2005–2008	2009–2012	2013–2015
Municipal administration	Veltroni administration – Democratici di sinistra/Democratic Party (center-left)	Alemanno administration – Alleanza Nazionale/Il popolo delle libertà (Right)	Handover of the mandate from the Alemanno administration to the Marino administration (center-left)
Stakeholders involved	EUR SpA Ministry of Cultural Heritage	*Ibidem* *Ibidem* Fondazione Valore Italia	*Ibidem* Fendi Roma brand
Intended function of PdCI	Multifunctional National Museum (*Discoteca dello Stato*)	Permanent Exhibition of Italian Design and Made in Italy	Fendi Headquarter (*bureaux*, fur-ateliers, exhibition spaces)

Source: S. Biondo's PhD thesis, 2023.

regardless of their nature, these factors influenced and conditioned the management and the process of re-use of the PdCI. The negotiation stages are symptomatic of broader changes of the role played by political (municipal) actors within the urban regime. Table 13.1 reports a synthetic outline of the negotiation stages aimed at facilitating readers' understanding of the process.

The analysis begins in 2005 when an agreement was signed between the then Minister for Cultural Heritage and the former CEO of EUR SpA concerning the functional redefinition of the PdCI. The agreement addressed the pre-existing Convention (signed in 2001) regulating relations between EUR SpA and the Ministry of Cultural Heritage and Activities (Dipartimento per i Beni Archivistici e Librari). The use intended by the Ministry was multifunctional: the Audiovisual Museum, a national multimedia library, the audiovisual archives of the Discoteca di Stato and the offices of the Ministry were to be installed. Starting from 2006, both signatory public entities started a two-year "monumental restoration" of the building (MIC, 2005). The first part of the negotiation therefore (2005–2008) sees as main actors two public institutions interacting within a complex model of governance: unlike the other districts of Rome directly administered by Roma Capitale (the main municipality), the EUR has, since 2000, its own management entity. The EUR SpA, is a public company (90% owned by the Ministry of Economy and Finance and 10% owned by Roma Capitale). The company carries out both property management (conservation and protection of its historical, artistic, and landscape heritage) and asset management (realization of real estate and urban planning projects) of urban heritage assets.

In this case, EUR Spa is the owner of the building while the Ministry of Cultural Heritage is the designated tenant of the Palazzo, having a subaltern negotiating position. The agreement on the PdCI is part of a wider urban development project aimed at creating a new urban "centrality" for EUR, the so-called second tourist hub of Rome (Romacapitale, 2010). During this stage, corresponding to the period of the Veltroni administration (Democratici di sinistra/Democratic Party 2001–2008) the political actors seem to have followed a "social-oriented" strategy. This strategy is characterized by strong public direction and a space-planning aimed at the realization of a national museum.

The funding, as well as the actors involved, were all exclusively of public nature. In addition to the protection of the PdCI, which was matched by huge investments for the restoration of the PdCI (almost €35 million)

Figure 13.2. Locating the EUR District Within the City of Rome.

Figure 13.3. Focus on the Palazzo Della Civiltà Italiana (EUR Rome), S. Biondo, Rome, 2021.

(Repubblica, 2011), a consolidated discourse on the regeneration of the neighborhood was developed. Concrete initiatives were also implemented to revitalize the district. Among them, the new Convention Center known as "La Nuvola" was designed by Studio Fuksas and completed in 2016 and the Sea Life Roma Aquarium, a project that was never completed. However, the impacts of the 2008 economic-financial crisis on the city of Rome on the construction industry (one of the traditional "drivers" of city's growth; Sampaolo, 2018) have severely affected the regeneration plans of the EUR district. In particular, the crisis has corresponded to the general slowdown/blockage of various urban projects previously conceived for the district (like the rehabilitation of the Ligini towers of the former Ministry of Finance).

The second part of the negotiation (2009–2012) involved a third player, the Fondazione Valore Italia, a public entity founded in 2005 by the Ministry of Industry. In May 2009, the Foundation signed a new supplementary agreement for the valorization of the Palazzo della Civiltà Italiana in agreement with Italian Ministry of Cultural Heritage and Eur SpA. The building was assigned to the Fondazione Valore Italia, which was committed to the creation of a "permanent exhibition of Italian design and made in Italy." In 2011, the PdCI requalification project was publicly announced by local authorities. However, a severe spending review policy hit the Foundation, which was suppressed in 2014 pursuant to Art. 12 of legislative decree no. 95/2012 (converted into law no. 135/2012).

Over this period, corresponding to the Alemanno administration (Alleanza Nazionale/Il popolo delle libertà, 2008–2013), the EUR Spa pursued a "hybrid strategy" (Savitch & Kantor, 2002, p. 103) aimed at the implementation of a heritage policy not prejudicial to collective interests but oriented to the economic development. This phase also coincides with an awareness on the part of public authorities concerning their financial fragility (following the economic crisis). As a consequence, the economic model evolved with a stronger integration of private credit institutions within the project (that is, Cassa di Risparmio di Roma). The relationship between public and private sectors has not only evolved from a financial point of view, but also in terms of content.

The proposal of the re-functionalization of the PdCI highlighted the innovation by focusing on new exhibition technologies and the digital dimension: an ambitious program with high added value, but equally high costs. The agreement is also aimed at reinforcing the links with private stakeholders, "The project is designed to provide spaces and equipments for events and workshops for companies . . .and private actors" (Repubblica, 2011). On the other hand, the "urban planning culture" aimed at promoting a creative city environment has strongly influenced the political agenda putting culture-led urban regeneration initiatives first (Florida, 2003; Landry, 2000; Scott, 2014). The revitalization strategy adopted for the PdCI aims to attract human capital, investors, and tourists in the medium term (Vicari, 2010). Creativity is actively promoted by the public authorities and stimulated by the creative and cultural industries, which were expected to take part in the creation laboratories designed in the building (Repubblica, 2011). Due to the lack of resources, however, the project was subsequently abandoned.

As an introduction to the third part of the process, an important contextual element, the "Mafia Capitale" affair, was considered. The term indicates the existence of a collusive system between public administration officials and private companies within the city of Rome. The investigation in 2014 led to the imprisonment of some 40 suspects, including the president of Rome's city council, the head of the city's public-housing division, as well as the government of the city of Rome. Italian political science literature extensively analyzed the phenomena of corruption and the socioeconomic distortions it produces (Arnone & Iliopulos, 2005; Della Porta & Vannucci, 2007). This is critical to understand the para-political context of those years, characterized by criminal infiltration within the Roman institutional and entrepreneurial environment. The investigations related to Mafia Capitale also led to the arrest, on charges of corruption, of the former CEO of EUR Spa, which was an active promoter of the PdCI's re-qualification agreement. Even if the allegations did not concern the company EUR Spa, the Fendi's real estate transaction was highly criticized by both the press and the public. Among the reasons frequently cited were the lack of transparency in negotiations and the absence of a proper tendering procedure (Tripodi, 2013).

Fendi Roma entered the negotiations in a third phase, starting in July 2013. To ensure the completion of the work of enhancement and activation of income undertaken in previous years, EUR Spa signed a 15-year lease with the fashion brand. The execution of the transfer of use of the Palazzo was carried out without taking into account the real estate value of the asset (approximately €4.680.000 per year according the Agenzia del Territorio; Land Registry Office – Protocol no. 40379/7–2007). The fashion brand payed to the public company €2.800.000 per year for the exploitation of this heritage asset. Through this deal, the EUR Spa wanted to pursue a twofold objective. The first one was clearly oriented toward financial stability (ensuring a fixed income over a long period). The second was aimed to improve the building's installations and equipment (allowing an increase of value in the property).

The interviews revealed that further considerations had been taken into account by the managers of EUR Spa. The latter includes, among other things, the positive externalities generated by Fendi Roma (with the possibility of making the district an international fashion and touristic hub). Within this partnership, the tourism phenomenon has been equally addressed. According to the former President of the IX Municipality, the settlement of the brand "could be an opportunity to launch a fashion tourism 'route' at Eur" (IX Municipio, 2018). The arrival of the Fendi brand in the negotiations took place between two administrations, in a delicate electoral period which saw the handover of the mandate from the Alemanno administration (right) to the Marino administration (center-left/Partito democratico). However, it is important to note that, regardless of political color, a market-oriented strategy was chosen in this third phase favoring forms of urban development/heritage management with limited public control and financed exclusively by private companies. The PdCI has been leased under the "museum constraint," given its nature of "building of cultural interest." After closing the deal in 2013, the group announced the creation of an exhibition area on the first floor open to the public to "celebrate the creativity and craftsmanship of Italian genius" (Boccacci, 2013).

The purpose of public action and the use of the building do not therefore appear to be unrelated to those that inspired the previous administration (culture, creativity, and innovation). Fashion houses, key players in the cultural/creative economy (Lazzaretti, 2013), have been considered by policymakers in local development strategies that aim to promote the EUR district as a new cultural and fashion center. The major changes regard the economic model and the delegation of heritage management. The market, embodied in this case by the Fendi Roma brand, penetrates thus the political negotiation and progressively integrates the policy process. In short, with respect to the role played by politics in the urban development processes that emerged with the "regime of the Urb," the negotiations on the PdCI revealed an evolution of the public–private partnership patterns that included at first an integration and then whole participation of the Fendi Roma brand in Roman urban governance. The policy analysis showed how the sponsored policies based on a creative economy (Howkins, 2001) were legitimized, since the second stage of the negotiation, the entry of the fashion house into the political arena. Relevant in this process are the economic conditions of the Roman administration: the global economic crisis (coupled with the crisis in the real estate market and the deficit in the municipal finances) excluded the possibility of indebtedness to finance local initiatives and encouraged the arrival of external investors. Attracting capital could, in fact, permit the rehabilitation as well as the opening of the PdCI. Further, electoral changes in the negotiation period (2005–2015) facilitated the shift from a social-oriented to a market-oriented approach. However, there seems to have been no real solution of continuity within the urban policy framework.

Fendi's Initiatives Toward PdCI

On the occasion of the opening speech of the PdCI, former chairman and CEO of Fendi said "We are proud to give back to Rome and to the entire world the PdCI, a symbol of our Roman roots and of the continuous dialog between tradition and modernity, values that have always been at the very heart of Fendi" (LVMH, 2015). In this way, the brand, through its corporate channels, describes – following further renovation work – the opening of the Palazzo in 2015. An important event, but not an isolated one, as it comes in a long-standing collaboration between the municipality of Rome and fashion brand Fendi Roma. Here it is important to briefly retrace the history of the fashion house and to outline a synthetic overview of the most significant patronage initiatives carried out by the brand in collaboration with Roma Capitale.

Founded in Rome in 1925 by Adele and Edoardo Fendi with frugal means, the firm followed an upward trajectory. From the 1960s onwards, with the designation of the then young stylist Karl Lagerfeld as Creative

Director as well as with the launch of both the women's ready-to-wear collection and iconic-products, Fendi quickly gained a worldwide reputation in the fashion panorama. The brand, which was incorporated into the LVMH group at the end of 2001, crossed the $1.2 billion (€1 billion) threshold in annual sales (Reuters, 2018), with approximately 200 permanent points of sale throughout the world. However, its internationalization does not seem to have impacted its Roman identity, which has been systematically reaffirmed.

The brand's activities go far beyond clothing to include large-scale urban initiatives. The relevant participation in the restoration of the Trevi Fountain in 2013 is the first of a long series of urban patronage initiatives (Fendi for Fountains initiative in 2015 and the re-qualification of the Temple of Venus in 2018 in Rome). However, the case of the PdCI differs both in its juridical and temporal nature from other patronage actions implemented by the fashion brand within the city of Rome. In fact, the sponsorship action was not an aim in itself: it resulted in a process of temporary appropriation of the building by Fendi Roma (with a specific lease covering a period of 15 years). In order to increase and converge private funds into the protection of heritage assets, the Italian government has established since the 2000s, a comprehensive set of norms facilitating cultural patronage activities (specifically through the law n. 342 art. 38) through a system of tax relief.

The modalities of funding public goods by private actors were further clarified in 2004 with the legal establishment of two different types of donations (legislative decree 42/2004): patronage and sponsorship. Both instruments engendered a deeper involvement of private actors in the decision-making and strategic development of heritage policies, nevertheless they diverged in their form and in their effects. Patronage is a specific measure which allows private stakeholders to finance heritage restoration work(s) based on a tax deduction. On the other hand, the sponsorship system confers on the private funding entities the right to use exclusively (including for commercial purposes) the image and/or the name of the funded cultural asset(s). Although in both cases, the public authorities maintain the governance over the preservation of the heritage property, in the second case, the implications of collaboration between public and private actors are inscribed over a longer period and are more consistent.

The brand, in agreement with EUR Spa and the Italian Ministry of Cultural Heritage, was therefore able to benefit from the sponsorship legislation. It was, however, constrained by the norms on buildings of cultural interest (legislative decree 42/2004) with reference to the code of cultural heritage and landscape protection. The latter constrains the use of the spaces of the PdCI to only exhibition and museum uses. The agreement signed between the stakeholders foresaw that a part of the building would be used as a freely accessible exhibition space for events related to Italian design, art, creativity, and craftsmanship, theoretically open to all types of audience.

As a follow-up to the third negotiation stage, between 2013 and 2015, the brand has intervened on the heritage by following two main streams: the architectural one and the semiotic one. As per the first stream, Fendi Roma invested in further renovation works curated by architect Marco Costanzi, thus also covering the lighting system (designed by artist Mario Nanni). Over an 18-month period, the building was functionally rehabilitated. The PdCI hosts the brand's administrative and creative management offices (located between the second and sixth floors of the building), the exhibition gallery (on the first floor), as well as the archives (ground floor). It accommodates around 450 employees (Alaily-Mattar, Ponzini, & Thierstein, 2020, p. 98).

If one compares the architect's declarations and intentions with the size of the museum spaces, one understands how the redesigning project was intended to ultimately change the function of the place. In fact, the architectural initiative was oriented more toward the brand's staff than toward the outside public: the space in the building devoted to exhibitions is very modest, being limited to the first floor. The podium mezzanine floor is instead intended to accommodate other facilities, such as the coffee bar of the company. Costanzi's purpose was foremost to create a unique headquarters for the Fendi Rome brand, which had previously been divided into many small locations (Olsen, 2015). Apart from the first floor, the remaining floors are dedicated to internal management with a design particularly respectful of rationalist architecture (the offices consist of glass cubes): "The formal signs of the building remain the same today as they appeared over 70 years ago" (Jones & Pilat, 2020, p. 98). The building was officially inaugurated in October 2015. As per the second stream, the fashion house implemented an effort of re-semanticization of the building, which had a difficult fascist identity and was therefore considered as a "dissonant heritage" (Tunbridge & Ashworth, 1996). Analysis of the subject refers to the specific literature investigating the way in which a difficult past can be commodified for the public within a context of consumption, through "corporate heritagization." The case of the re-semanticization of the PdCI has been extensively covered by scholars (Hatherley, 2015; Jones & Pilat, 2020; Moral-Andrés, 2019).

The notion of "heritage re-semanticization" is used here to describe discursive and/or empirical practices intended to ascribe new meanings to ancient contested heritage assets. The literature suggests the risks associated with these practices, such as the re-semantization might distort the original meaning(s) (Rodríguez-Ortega, 2018) or engender processes of commodification (Torrini & Barone, 2016). As per Fendi, the practices of heritage re-semanticization included, among other things, the depoliticization of the building, its re-appropriation by the citizens, the estheticization of the architectural style, and its commodification. The "iconicity" of the Palazzo therefore implies an apolitical nature. The concept of "giving back" is also a *leitmotif*: the fashion house is (and wants to be seen as) committed to the πόλις and its citizens. Fendi Roma has also been particularly active in a long-lasting marketing campaign aimed at shifting the focus from politics to esthetics. The architectural style of the building is aligned with the style of the garments produced by the brand, both characterized by geometric and minimalistic lines. The brand identity is merged with the image of the Palazzo also from a substantial point of view. The brand has literally integrated the Palazzo's visual language into its products/advertising and sales center. The arches of the PdCI became a dominant symbol of the brand, serving as the backdrop for Fendi Roma's fashion shows (SS2022 men's collation) or for advertising campaigns (FW 2014/15 & Fendi Fall 2021 Ad Campaign) (Figure 13.4).

Faced with the challenge of functional regeneration, the fashion house adopted a specific strategy to design the representation of the building, by stressing an intentional mismatch between PdCI and its historical genesis. "For Italians and Romans, [the PdCI] hasn't any fascist significance," said the former CEO during the inaugural ceremony (Zargani, 2015). The brand strategy is thus used to define a new representation. The Palazzo is used as an "esthetic element" for commercial purposes, to the point that the charm of rationalist architecture becomes a brand to be consumed. This trend is symbolized by the use of the arches of the PdCI inside other flagship stores of

Figure 13.4. Fendi Advertising Campaign Within PdCI, S. Biondo, Fiumicino, 2021.

the brand (Palazzo Fendi in Largo Goldoni, Rome) and even outside (or the Fendi store in the Ginza district of Tokyo). The esthetic element is unconnected to the historical and social past of the building (and the district). This has the effect of producing an urban landscape with no history, a looming victim of "territorial amnesia" (ETICity, 2018, p. 261) that becomes attractive for investment, commercial initiatives, and business speculation.

Concerning the effective level of accessibility to the public, it remains constrained. Unlike what was initially negotiated with the local authorities, the museum is not accessible to the external public other than during temporary exhibitions, organized by the fashion house in accordance with the procedures and opening hours fixed by the latter. Since 2015, the year the PdCI reopened, four exhibitions have been held, respectively: Una nuova Roma: L'Eur and the PdCI in 2015; Fendi: the artisans of dreams in 2016; Giuseppe Penone: Matrice in 2017; and Fendi Studios in 2018. In the period between 2015 and 2021, the first floor of the PdCI has been de facto open to the public only 35% of the time. The assessment of the compliance with the museum's vocation as well as the accessibility to the external public remains ambivalent so far.

Fashioning the PdCI

The strategies adopted by the fashion house on the roman territory shed more light on the subject and so does the Fendi's modes of (re)production of placemaking narratives associated to EUR. These reveal contextualization of the mechanisms related to the construction of urban representations. The purpose is to demonstrate that fashion houses participate in the production and the implementation of city-branding policies through tourism marketing strategies. The discussion reveals how the brand has acted as a catalyst for tourism development in the EUR district, as well as how tourist perceptions and imaginaries are shaped before or after visiting the PdCI or the EUR. The information is derived from interviews conducted with policymakers, Fendi Roma brand managers, and stakeholders (exhibition curators and academics). Observations are mainly based on the reviews provided by the Tripadvisor platform. The information was cross-referenced with data provided by the Osservatorio Turistico dell'Ente Bilaterale Turismo del Lazio and the Dipartimento Trasformazione Digitale U.O. Statistica – Open Data di Roma Capitale.

"Una nuova Roma" – Enhancing the EUR District through Place-making Narratives. With the creation of the Ente EUR, since the 1950s, the district has assumed a function that is essentially financial and administrative, with the presence of numerous banks and private enterprises. The district is also an important hub for museums, hosting, for instance, the Museum of Roman

Civilization and the National Museum of Popular Arts and Traditions. Mainly inhabited by the middle-upper class, the district has never been considered as a tourism attraction. Somehow, the history of the PdCI is emblematic of some trends common to the entire district: a long period of neglect followed by fragmentary and heterogeneous actions of re-functionalization and development (Quilici, 2015).

Because of its particular architecture, the PdCI has been the target of representations (movies or events) that have emphasized or modified its appearance over the decades. The representation of the building – and more globally of the district – has experienced an evolution. From an abandoned and decaying space (as represented by movie directors in the 1960s – R. Rossellini, M. Antonioni, and F. Fellini), the PdCI became a location aimed at hosting fashion shows and cultural events, including Giorgio Armani – the "One Night Only Event" (2013); and live concert "Renaissance-Anima Mundi" (2020) by Accademia di Santa Cecilia. Since then, the building has been highly mediatized, becoming the core of the marketing campaigns of the Fendi Roma brand. Regardless of the format (film or advertising campaign), representation is particularly effective in this case because it contributes to shaping the tourism imaginaries and building a cultural perception of the place (Figure 13.4).

Fendi actively contributed to the production of a proper "tourism destination image." In fact, the firm actively developed marketing campaigns (and digital initiatives) to modify the "beliefs, ideas and impressions that visitors might have of the PdCI place and/or of the EUR destination" (Crompton, 1979; Lopes, 2011, p. 307). The brand's purpose seems to have been facilitated by the morphological characteristics of the neighborhood. As movie director, Fellini has repeatedly stated "EUR is a very congenial district for those who professionally represent images" (D'Amato & Petti, 2008, p. 31). In this sense, the mediatization of the EUR district and the PdCI has gradually contributed not only to the creation of a collective and shared representation of the latter, but also to the comprehension of its transformation.

Upon its installation, the fashion house endeavored to be a proactive player in the production of both a renewed placemaking narrative related to EUR and an unprecedented sense of place associated with the PdCI. Through the first exhibition held within the building in 2015 entitled "Una Nuova Roma. L'Eur and the Palazzo della Civiltà Italiana," Fendi suggested a completely revised storytelling of the whole district. The analysis of the contents of the temporary exhibition (coordinated by the Sovrintendenza Capitolina ai Beni Culturali and Roma Capitale) allows a deeper understanding of this fashion-led urban narrative. Launched with the aim of showing, through an artistic, figurative, photographic, and filmic device, the evolution of the district and of the PdCI from a diachronic perspective, the exhibition embodies the fashion house's willingness to "rewrite the past."

Crucial to the exhibition project is the idea of EUR as "quartiere-città" (a district acting as a city). The genesis of the term "New Rome," used in the title of the exhibition, dates back to the Fascist period. It derives from a speech by the politician Giuseppe Borrelli De Andreis who, at the inauguration of the E42, said "What is about to be created is not a new satellite, but a new star, as great as the old one, not simply a quarter of Rome, but a new Rome, a modern one with the same characters of monumentality and universality to perform the imperial function she has today" (Borrelli De Andreis, 1942; Notaro, 2000). Interestingly, Fendi Roma decided to employ the same terminology as Borrelli De Andreis rather than use the notion of "new tourist hub," which was more widely accepted by the former municipal administration (and EUR SpA).

Furthermore, from a substantive point of view, through the temporary exhibitions held in the building, the fashion house revitalized the PdCI's Mussolinian vocation to host ephemeral and spectacular events: mega, unique, and exclusive events (Hall, 1992), capable of promoting the place and the administration that managed it "by enhancing its reputation outside its own borders" (Montanari, 2002, p. 760). However, it is important to stress the difference between the two urban projects. While the (Fascist) museum embodied an "authoritarian, often mono-vocal voice of truth" (Calinao & Lin, 2017, p. 215) to avoid controversial and discordant topics, the fashion house integrates them into the creative process and its heritage. In this case, Fendi Roma realized an unprecedented process by transforming the PdCI into a visitor-centered forum, offering heterogeneous socio-political-cultural interpretations of the complex history of the district (Melchior, 2011).

Through the exhibition, the brand specifically produced a storytelling mainly based on cultural and creative policies, trying to socially (re)construct (and renew) the sense of the place: the way in which the PdCI was "interpreted, narrated, perceived, felt, understood and imagined" by tourists (Gieryn, 2000, p. 465). The comparison between the two monographic exhibitions on the EUR district, held the same year in the city of Rome, is emblematic in this regard.

The exhibition, sponsored by the City of Rome, entitled "Esposizione Universale Roma. Dal Fascismo agli anni '60" (curated by Professor V. Vidotto in 2015) insisted on the Fascist genesis of a piece of the city (from the urban-planning point of view). The exhibition powered by Fendi was mainly focused on urban cultural creativity. As indicated by the architect Carlo Lococo, the exhibition co-curator, during an interview of this study in September 2021, the aim of the exhibition was to produce a placemaking narrative shifting from the common imaginaries related to the district: "We wanted to narrate an urban project characterized not only by gray, austere, rationalist architecture but also by fantastic artistic initiatives that had been

Figure 13.5. "Hand in Hand" Fendi Exhibition at PdCI, S. Biondo, Rome, 2021.

proposed by designers at the Universal Exposition in 1942. A new story for an ancient building."

At a global level, the case of the PdCI and the Fendi's project of temporary exhibitions and performances allows one to study "from the inside" the dynamics of intradistrict competitiveness. The cultural offer is in fact in competition with that of the two other museums – also from the Fascist era – located in the EUR district. Inscribed within a local competitive framework, Fendi adopted a form of fashion museology, displaying immersive experiential contents – usually in a digital format – to reach new audiences (Melchior & Svensson, 2014) and differentiate itself from other museum institutions (Figure 13.5). The brand's strategy may effectively attract tourists, leading to increasing tourism in the EUR district.

Attracting Tourists through "the Fendi Factor". The case of the PdCI is an example of a territorial revitalization policy carried out by a fashion house, Fendi Roma, which succeeded in stimulating the attractiveness of a residential and not tourism-oriented district, the EUR. Despite its limitations, the strategy developed by the brand around the Palazzo has reached its purpose insofar as the visibility of the district has increased. Just after the inauguration of the PdCI by Fendi Roma and the launch of the exhibition "Una nuova Roma. L'Eur and the PdCI" in 2015, the IX municipio exceeded significantly more than 1 million visits with an increase of 17% compared to the previous year (EBTL, 2015). However, these figures must be relativized, as they are intertwined with the kick-off of the Expo 2015 world exhibition held in Milan, which had a trickle-down effect on tourism throughout the peninsula. Nonetheless, the positive trend in the increase of tourist flows continues to strengthen in the following years, especially in conjunction with the events and exhibitions organized by the Fendi Roma brand.

According to the data provided by the Osservatorio Turistico, the annual attendance figures for the IX Municipio between 2016 and 2018 (the year of the "Fendi Studios" exhibition) have continued to rise, from 1,399,089 to 1,508,572 visitors. These data make it possible to evaluate the territorial impacts of the rehabilitation of the PdCI (the fashion house). Fashion as an exhibitor acts as a catalyst for the development of tourism in the EUR district. In fact, in terms of absolute values, the months in which the museum was open correspond to those in which there were the highest number of visitors within the district (EBTL, 2018). Further, the percentage variation between the number of tourists present in the IX municipality between 2015 (the year in which the museum was opened) and 2018 (the last year in which statistic data are available) was significantly positive (11.6%).

From the interviews, a consensus emerged about the explanatory causes that led to the increase in the number of tourists in the neighborhood. The "Fendi factor" (as qualified by the former Chairman of EUR Spa) has been the determining component for attracting new tourists (especially international ones) to the area. In tandem with these preliminary results, there is also the media coverage. Both the real estate transaction inherent to PdCI and the Fendi exhibitions "have been received quite positively by the press" (Jones & Pilat, 2020, p. 79).

As regards the study of the perception of the PdCI by tourists (and more broadly by visitors), it is interesting to note that the terms "fascist" or "Mussolinian" appear only sporadically. In just 10% of cases, visitors seem in to have acquired the descriptive figures and imaginaries sponsored by the fashion house. The esthetic and stylistic elements of the building are largely enhanced, as is its rationalist architecture (simple, clean, clear forms, geometric lines for grandiose effects, and luminous arches). The monument is considered as iconic as the Colosseum. Fendi's initiatives are positively evaluated. Some visitors even speak of a "temple of fashion," others openly express their gratitude to the brand: "The Fendi fashion house deserves all the gratitude of Italians for having restored this building to its splendor, which until recently had been left in absolute disrepair" (Tripadvisor, 2016).

The critical dimension previously mentioned is absent in this case. The most surprising element, however, regards the recurring use of the notion of the PdCI's photogenicity considered "nice to take photos" and/or "Instagrammable." Some users even use the term "photopportunity." Further analysis on the causal relationship between the branding process of the PdCI initiated by Fendi Roma and the behavior (and photographic practices) of visitors would be appropriate. However, the results of similar case studies in the literature have demonstrated the strong correlation between social media and the development of photogenic tourism destinations (Cunningham, 2021; Siegel, Tussyadiah, & Scarles, 2019). This tendency has enhanced the power of user-generated content and influencer/brandmarketing (Sormaz & Ruoss, 2020). The PdCI's representation on digital platforms requires (re)consideration of the role of social media in the transformation of this building and its perception.

A key role in the touristification practices of the place by the firm Fendi Roma has also been played by social networks. The latter systematically used by the brand to disseminate an image of the PdCI and attract new visitors/customers. In 2017, for example, the fashion house launched an Instagram page entitled @Fisforfendi, devoted to brand marketing. The approach is resolutely promotional, and the contents include most of the time the PdCI as a glamorous background for (more or less explicit) advertisements. Through the creation of Fendi hashtag (#Fisforfendi) invites visitors to be proactive in the creation of content with the Palazzo as its setting, thus increasing its popularity, especially among young people. In this case, the enhancement and virtual promotion of the place was accompanied by a concrete artistic-performative action: the same year the fashion house asked the Russian artist Pokras Lampas (Arsenij Pyženkov) to paint on the roof of the PdCI a calligraphy in yellow on a black backdrop depicting several words having the letter "F" as initial. The art, the most extensive work ever done in Italy (Lella, 2017), coupled with the digital initiative, promotes a process of estheticization, showcasing and commodifying the Palazzo which becomes an integral part of the brand identity. However, this represents a complex identity linked to a "fluid geography" (Monnet, 2015) that goes beyond the perimeter of the EUR district.

The "Romanity" claimed and promoted by the brand – which in 2013 has permanently included the term "Rome" in its logo – is associated with an ideal-typical territory with fluctuating boundaries. The historical significance is concealed in favor of a comprehensive heritage appreciation of the urban sites that have been turned into heritage by the brand. Fendi Roma has the arduous task of weaving "fil rouge" between fashion-branded urban places. This includes Palazzo Fendi a majestic 17th-century building located in Rome's fashion district (Quadrilatero della moda) and the PdCI. The list also includes places that have been patronized (like the Trevi Fountain, the Temple of Venus), each of which has its own style and history.

To provide an overall narrative coherence, the fashion house appeals to an estheticized, fashionable imaginary of the city, systematically mentioning urban beauty in the broadest sense of the word "la grande bellezza," regarded as "universal" and worldwide. This narrative is also found in the institutional statements fostered by the Fendi group. An example is the statement of the CEO of the group, Serge Brunschwi, on the occasion of the "The Dawn of Romanity" event (Haute Couture FW 2019/2020):

> Bringing our culture to Rome is the best way to celebrate Karl Lagerfeld, Fendi and its city, a unique opportunity to express our roots, bold creativity and the highest savoir-faire, which have always been part of the House's DNA. Rome … is a magical place, perfectly representing the values of Fendi, its tradition and its history. I am also very proud of the restoration of heritage assets in Rome, thus continuing to support cultural heritage, not only of Rome and Italy, but of the whole world. (Klein, 2019)

The Fendi initiative is also part of a wider policy. In fact, the touristification process has been warmly encouraged by local authorities through specific local policies. The PdCI has become a valuable heritage asset of the Roman metropolis. Tourism development is the goal of EUR Spa which encouraged the holding of major artistic events to attract new audiences (the International Contemporary Art Fair "Roma Arte in Nuvola," the National Fair "Più libri, più liberi," and more). As stated by the manager of the company during the study interview conducted in November 2021:

> …the purpose is to establish EUR as a tourist destination complementary to Rome. A very new culture-oriented touring destination … It is one of the rare places in Rome capable of accommodating large-scale international events such as the G20. To succeed, the involvement of private stakeholders is mandatory.

Within this context, the fashion house is considered by policymakers as an important player for the development of a culture-led tourism policy.

CONCLUSION

This chapter evaluates how the settlement of a fashion house in a peripheral urban area and the transformation of a contested heritage asset into a fashionable exhibition space impacted the development of the Roman tourism circuit. In this sense, the PdCI case is useful to illustrate both the mechanisms of production of public–private partnerships within the framework of urban policies and the specificities of fashion-led urban regeneration initiatives. It illustrates that the involvement of fashion houses in urban governance can facilitate the shift from a social-oriented to a market-oriented approach without entrenching solutions of continuity in the existing urban regime.

At a broader level, the phenomenon also implies an evolution in the strategies pursued by public actors in their relations with private investors.

In terms of effects on urban heritage, the actions of Fendi Roma contribute to the production of a branded and estheticized environment that seems to be a victim of "territorial and historical amnesia" (ETICity, 2018, p. 271). Although the heritage assets remain the property of the public authorities, luxury brands, acquire a strong autonomy both in the management and rehabilitation of the sites, and in the production of specific placemaking narratives that can influence tourism imaginaries. The case study allows one to analyze the complexity of the process of heritagization initiated by the firm Fendi Roma, stressing both its limits/contradictions, and its territorial effects in terms of touristification. In fact, the observed fashion-led project also had impacts on the tourism attractiveness of the whole district. The case shows that, considering the museum vocation of the brand and the constraints imposed by the public authorities, the "tourism component" had (willy-nilly) to be progressively integrated into the scope of the fashion house.

The limitations of the study concern both the analyzed stakeholders and the geographical scope. More studies are needed to comprehend the point of view of the locals and traders. This allows one to understand if and how they have experienced the change in the district. Not many studies have been conducted on the evolution of the EUR since 2015. More globally, the question that can be asked is if the studied phenomena are specific to the city of Rome or can be observed in other metropolises. The analysis of the case of the Prada Foundation in Milan seems to provide similar findings to those exposed in this piece (Paris, 2020). A systematic comparative study might be useful to understand the extent of the phenomenon. The effects on the surrounding areas could also have been documented, whether the heritagization of the PdCI provoke a desire to estheticize nearby spaces. The study also opens the door to more in-depth reflections on the financial dimension of the phenomenon on the process of heritage-capitalization of the part of fashion houses.

Concerning the implications for future research, the analysis opens new perspectives on the processes related to the spatial diversification of tourism, insisting on the role that fashion houses can play in these evolutions. On a broader scale, it also makes it possible to question the level of implication of multinational corporations (such as LVMH) within territorial policies implemented by single brands. A closer study of the interrelation between those two actors would make it possible to understand the entrepreneurial logic underlying the processes of peripheral touristification (the overall increase in the number of tourists in the area).

Chapter 14

FASHION AND TOURISM GO OFF-THE-BEATEN-TRACKS

Maria Gravari-Barbas
Paris 1 Panthéon-Sorbonne University, France

Abstract: Since the end of the twentieth century a movement has been observed, both in geography of tourism and in fashion, spreading to districts located on the outskirts of cities. This is the case of Château Rouge, located in the 18th arrondissement of Paris. For years considered as a "no-go-zone," the district is now experiencing parallel phenomena of "off-the-beaten-tracks" tourism and fashion development. This chapter analyzes the processes and actors behind the expansion of the tourism perimeter and the diversification of fashion venues, as well as the implications of these developments for the city of Paris. **Keywords**: Paris; Château-Rouge; Goutte d'or; tourism off-the-beaten-tracks; fashion cities; ethnic areas

INTRODUCTION

Since their emergence as modern social, cultural, and economic phenomena, tourism and fashion have characterized predominantly Paris, compared with other European metropolises (Williams, 1982). Today, Paris still is one of the "big four" cities of fashion (Rabbiosi, 2015; Wubs et al., 2020), and remains a major world urban tourism destination (Freytag & Bauder, 2018; Pappalepore & Gravari-Barbas, 2022).

The geographical distribution of tourism and fashion in Paris is precise, circumscribed, and long-established. On the one hand, the tourism places in Paris are concentrated around the Ile de la Cité, along the Seine, and the Rue de Rivoli main axis, extending through the Champs Elysées to the Arc du Triomphe. The Latin Quarter, the Champ de Mars, and the Eiffel Tower are the main poles of mass tourism on the left bank, while Montmartre

Fashion and Tourism: Parallel Stories
Tourism Social Science Series, Volume 26, 239–257

Published under exclusive licence by Emerald Publishing Limited
ISSN: 1571-5043/doi:10.1108/S1571-504320230000026014

represents the tourism magnet of the Parisian right bank. A small number of tourism "satellites" (the Père Lachaise Cemetery or the Park of La Villette) contribute to a certain diffusion of otherwise highly concentrated tourism areas. The "Central Tourism District" (Bauder, 2015; Duhamel & Knafou, 2007) in Paris emerged geographically at the end of the nineteenth century and evolved slowly throughout the twentieth and beginning of the twenty-first century (Figure 14.1).

On the other hand, the geographical distribution of Parisian fashion is also very circumscribed (APUR, 2016; Rocamora, 2009). Fashion houses are located on the north bank, close to the places of consumption that are the major department stores and the Faubourg Saint-Honoré street. From the 1950s onwards, the *Maisons de Haute Couture* have been concentrated in and around the "Golden Triangle," formed by the Avenues of Champs Elysées, Georges V, and Montaigne. The geographical distribution of the Fashion Week main spots (located mainly in the 1st, 8th, and 16th districts) is close to the *Maisons de Haute Couture*. Tourism (most luxury hotels are in the 8th district) and accessibility (the need of going from one place to another easily) explain these spatial patterns. The *façonniers* (the person who make the patterns for the garments) have also been historically located around the Sentier neighborhood (APUR, 2016; Montagné-Villette, 1990). For several decades, the geographical distribution of fashion has not changed much: the Sentier is still the *façonniers'* place, and the Faubourg Saint Honoré or the Avenue Montaigne remains the most *chic* places (Figure 14.1).

However, today fashion is more dispersed because it is more diversified; it has spread to Les Halles, Bastille, and Saint Michel for the mass consumption, and while Avenue Montaigne remains the main spot for Haute couture; Saint Sulpice or Saint-Germain also emerge as places for more expensive ready-to-wear products. For several reasons, including technological and financial changes, the geography of fashion in Paris is becoming more complex, creating new urban polarities, in areas that were not previously related to fashion. The geographical distribution of tourism in Paris is also experiencing changes. If these do not shift the main mass tourism patterns, they certainly reflect the desires of tourists, mainly repeaters (Freytag, 2008), to go "off-the-beaten-tracks."

Sometimes, it is precisely the fashion-related activities that attract tourism, since they produce new creative *loci* (Capone & Lazzeretti, 2016; Kalbaska et al., 2018; Lazzaretti, Capone, & Casadei, 2017), attractive for more adventurous tourists. This is the case of the area of Château Rouge and adjacent Goutte d'Or, located in the 18th district of Paris, which have evolved over the last few years from a "no-go-zone" (Gravari-Barbas, 2017c) to an "off-the-beaten-tracks" destination (Gravari-Barbas & Delaplace, 2015). The recent development of an emerging fashion district, and the installation of young fashion designers, because of initiatives by the Parisian

Figure 14.1. Tourism Areas and Fashion Places in Paris.
Source: M. Gravari-Barbas.

public authorities to develop this economic sector, contributed to this evolution.

This chapter examines the parallel stories of fashion and tourism in the Chateau Rouge/Goutte d'Or district by exploring their joint development dynamics. Who are the actors that initiated this double process of touristification and fashionability? Do the fashion actors contribute to the tourism development of the district? Conversely, do the tourism actors contribute to the fashion development of the area, and do they profit from its new fashion identity? What changes have allowed Château Rouge (whose image is in total contrast to the Parisian stereotype for tourism and fashion) to emerge as a tourism destination today? Further, how have these developments impacted the nature of the area, in terms of (tourism) gentrification (Gravari-Barbas & Guinand, 2017)?

This chapter addresses these questions using a set of methodologies: one, bibliographical analysis of the off-the-beaten-tracks literature, more specifically in the case of Paris; two, analysis of the content provided for the Chateau Rouge/Goutte d'Or areas in the Parisian guidebooks (published for English, German, and French speakers); three, *in situ* observation carried out during six fieldworks between 2020 and 2022 (covering the architectural and urban characteristics of the area and their visible changes; everyday life patterns; the behavior of tourists; and the visible changes due to gentrification); four, four additional visits proposed by tourist guides (three visits with Bastina, an "alternative tourism" visit provider; and one visit with Trips AirbnB); and, five, interviews of a number of fashion stakeholders established in the area which included the director of the *École de la Maille* in Paris; three local guides; six owners of local fashion businesses; the director of a nongovernmental organization specialized on off-the-beaten-tracks visits in the area.

OFF-THE-BEATEN-TRACKS TOURISM

The tourism literature has paid limited attention to the spatial aspects of tourism (Delaplace & Gravari-Barbas, 2016). However, a priori nontouristic places can allow one to follow emerging territorial, cultural, social, and tourism processes. These happen under the combined action of public demand, including tourists who wish to get out of the "tourist bubbles" (Judd, 1999) of mass tourism, and the offer of "marginal" or "ordinary" territories that seek to further develop tourism. These forces are particularly important in touristically hyperpolarized places, inducing urban conflicts and tensions (such as in Venice, Barcelona, or Paris), making it necessary to go beyond the established tourism perimeters.

The growth of "alternative" tourism practices (Cohen, 1987) and products is highlighted by several urban and researchers, in Paris (Gravari-Barbas, 2017; Vivant, 2010), London (Maitland & Newman, 2004; Pappalepore et al., 2010), or Berlin (Füller & Michel, 2014; Novy & Huning, 2008). For several decades, the "mass" model of tourism has been strongly challenged by more composite, diversified, segmented, and even individualized offers.

Tourism has not escaped the changes brought about by globalization, metropolization, individuation, and hybridization of tastes. Renewed attention is thus paid to the everyday, to the ordinary, to the contextualization of the stay, to social interactions, and to "authentic" experiences (Andersson, 2007; Pine & Gilmore, 1998), as evidenced by the development of Couchsurfing (Priskin & Sprakel, 2008), the phenomenon of greeters (Sallet-Lavorel, 2003), or the development of a whole range of homestay practices and activities.

New tourism offers are multiplying, meeting the demands and imaginaries of tourists, renewing the system (its practices, actors, spaces, temporalities, and forms). Alternative tourism (Butler, 1990, 1992), participatory tourism (Tosun, 2005), slow tourism (Fullagar & Markwell, 2012), creative tourism (Richards & Wilson, 2006), and suburban tourism (Gravari-Barbas & Jacquot, 2013) are some of the terms that refer to these tourism approaches. They create new relations between center(s) and periphery(ies), tourism and everyday life, exotic and familiar, and the near and the far. Tourism categories are becoming blurred, uncertain, and are produced and consumed in contexts that are much more difficult to define, describe, and quantify than in the past. They are certainly much more porous, less circumscribed in time and space.

The evolution of tourism challenges the existing demarcation lines between defined tourism places and others, between tourism sights and every day, ordinary places (Condevaux, Gravari-Barbas, & Guinand, 2021).

Urban economist Robert Maitland's (2008) research in London (more specifically in Islington, Bankside, and Spitalfields) has highlighted the attractiveness of "everyday places" (including deprived and marginal areas) to both domestic and international tourists. Maitland refers to these places as "heterogeneous," as opposed to tourism enclaves or ghettos. While a tourism precinct is "clean" and rather controlled, a heterogeneous tourist space is "hard to classify," with blurred boundaries; it is a multipurpose space in which a wide range of activities and populations can be found. Tourism facilities coexist with businesses, public and private institutions, and housing; tourists mingle with locals. Heterogeneous spaces are stages on which transitional identities are performed alongside the everyday practices of residents, passersby, and workers (Edensor, 2001, p. 64, cited in Maitland, 2010).

Maitland summarizes the interacting forces that, when synergized, help produce what he calls

"creativity clusters" or "cool places" with – interacting "creatives" – a high concentration of creative industries and "creative" visitors (Florida, 2002; Maitland, 2007, 2010; Vivant, 2007).

– an image of an uncontrolled, unexpected, and unplanned place to explore, which emanates from a combination of features of the built environment (historic buildings, industrial architecture);

- a perception of "authenticity" and spontaneous, noncommercial everydayness (expressed through the existence of independent stores as opposed to chain stores);
- a perception of "safe danger": a feeling of "marginality", associated with the presence of trendy and fashionable populations, bars and stores, which contribute to create a feeling of safety;
- cultural diversity, including ethnic restaurants and stores;
- the certainty of distinction: places reserved for the adventurous few, not enclaves open to mass tourism, manifesting in visitors a sense of being in a "village" and sharing the authenticity of the place with others (Maitland, 2010).

Château-Rouge, an Off-The-Beaten-Tracks Destination

Although it is at an earlier stage of touristification than the already fashionable areas of Islington, Bankside, and Spitalfields were at when studied by Maitland (2008), Château Rouge/Goutte d'Or is emerging as a similar off-the-beaten-tracks area of Paris. Located 10 minutes from one of the most iconic Parisian sights, Montmartre, Château Rouge opens up a window to a totally different world (Bouly de Lesdain, 1999). The African area of Paris is swarming with people, ethnic shops, African beauty boutiques, and open-air markets with unique products hard to find elsewhere in Paris. According to Kévi Donat, the guide who organizes the *Le Paris Noir* (Black Paris) tours (Boukhris, 2017), Château Rouge is a crossroads of cultures and races, "a place of passage and commerce for the African community" (Bruschi, 2017). It is teeming with people and shops that are crossroads of cultures and crossbreeding for the African community. Over time, the district was originally shaped by the various waves of immigration that decided to settle down in the area and start small businesses (Figure 14.2).

In 2015, shortly after the Paris terrorist attacks, the journalist Nolan Peterson created a huge controversy by presenting on Fox News a map with the "No-Go-Zones" in Paris: zones where nonmuslims and police could not enter. Château Rouge was indicated as one of these areas. Though the TV channel publicly apologized for this, the report was symptomatic of the negative image of the area, seen as dangerous and uncontrolled, and to be avoided during the night.

Château Rouge is one of the poorest Parisian districts (Chabrol, 2011). It is also an area in which multiple cultures form a melting pot, with a strong sense of heritage, connected to the West African and Caribbean populations. These cultures came together to either buy or sell products that are desired by the different cultures that are living in this area. They are aspiring to a strong social commitment to bring people together from all parts of the world, to help the area grow and improve.

Figure 14.2. Traditional African Shops, Château Rouge.
Source: The author 2021.

As one of the most affordable areas of Paris, gentrification phenomena have been observed recently (Bacqué & Fijalkow, 2006). The area attracts residents in search of an alternative Parisian living. The newcomers are attracted by the popular side of the neighborhood: the affordable bistros, the village spirit, and the cosmopolitan ambiance. Creativity also plays an important role in the recent evolutions of the area. The neighborhood welcomes young emerging designers who are opening their businesses in this area and have different market opportunities and various benefits. According to the founder of the Cocobohème design brand and a lifelong resident "When you move to Château-Rouge, there is a little militancy and a lot of tolerance" (Bruschi, 2006).

Gentrification is not spontaneous: it comes because of the urban renovation projects initiated by the city of Paris and the French state (Baqué, 2005; Chabrol, 2011). For some scholars, the implementation of the urban renovation projects in the area can be qualified as neocolonialism (Kipfer, 2015). Renovation does not however globally concern the entire area. Further, gentrification processes affect some areas and leave others untouched, creating a contrasted mosaic (Kipfer, 2015) of the residential space.

The opening of several trendy bars tends to create a new destination for young Parisians. Starting in the 2010s, tourists began to appreciate the neighborhood charms, and to settle in its tourism accommodation properties. This is mainly due to Airbnb rather than to the few, small, and aging local hotels. The proximity of Montmartre plays a determinant role in the choice of accommodation in the area.

However, Château Rouge is only starting to be quoted in some travel guides. Nine different guidebooks were analyzed (in German, French, and English) in 2021. In the German and English guidebooks, there is not any mention of the neighborhood, and in the maps of Paris provided in the books, Château Rouge is not even included. Furthermore, the 18th district is simply cut out. The only guidebooks that mention Château Rouge are French guidebooks. They however have very little to say about the neighborhood. In the Michelin *Guide Vert,* there is a warning regarding the safety: "Take a guided tour of the neighborhood with l'ICI Leon. Be careful with your personal belongings: security conditions are not optimal in this area." Compared to other Parisian locations, the text about Château Rouge is very short:

> This dynamic and creative district has kept a village feel despite the rehabilitation policy carried out since the 1980s. It is home to a multitude of shops: stalls overflowing with exotic fruits and vegetables, stalls of colorful African fabrics, tailors, jewelry stores, halal butcher shops, etc. that take you on a journey from the Maghreb to black Africa.

The guide also mentions the newly created fashion district of Château Rouge, located within the Goutte-d'Or area: "Clothing, accessories and design have taken over the rue des Gardes on the initiative of the City of Paris and the federation of women's ready-to-wear clothing, and the designers easily show their workshops" (Guide Vert, 2019, p. 18).

In the book section related to Goutte d'Or, there is only one line dedicated to the textile industry which is then condensed to only the Rue des Gardes. The guidebooks mostly reference the food market rather than the fashion aspect. *Lonely Planet* mentions Goutte d'Or beyond its food stalls, saying that little Africa is also worth a shopping trip. It gives information about the shopping area of Château Rouge and offers recommendations regarding the stores such as Maison Château Rouge. It also mentions Rue des Gardes, which it explicitly says has been dubbed the "Rue de la Mode" (Fashion Street). Government initiatives contributed to the creation of an off-the-beaten-tracks fashion area located distinctively away from the historic fashion locations in Paris. Château Rouge is therefore becoming an off-the-beaten-tracks area for both tourism and fashion.

Redesigning the Fashion Geography of Paris

The Rue de la mode refers to an urban operation started in 2000 when 10 spaces on the Rue des Gardes were provided with attractive rent to young fashion creators to rehabilitate the local commercial spaces. Since the 2000s, the city council has indeed been working on the area's urban renewal, part of which is based on its fashion identity. After Rue des Gardes, the 18th district's local authorities developed Rue Myrha, offering preferential leases to attract fashion businesses that relate to the area's identity. The project, aiming at the economic development and enhancement of the region's image, was launched in 2011, and the association *Pôle de la Goutte d'Or de la Mode et du Design* (Center of the Goutte d'Or for Fashion and Design) was created by several professionals in the neighborhood (Délégation à la Politique de la Ville et à l'Intégration, 2013).

It is important to stress that the initiatives take place in an area that was, until recently, one of the most dilapidated in Paris and one of the capital's main pockets of poverty. In 2015, an arson attack on a rundown building caused the death of six adults and two children on the Rue Myrha, which currently hosts the hippest businesses in the area. This tragedy has been added to the list of events and incidents that give the neighborhood a negative reputation. In 2015, the unemployment rate in the area stood at 21%. In addition, the explosion of drug trafficking and insecurity in the 1990s earned Rue Myrha the nickname of "death row." A study conducted in 1997 by the association Espoir Goutte d'Or described it as "one of the main crack markets in eastern Paris."

The Goutte d'Or was the first Parisian neighborhood to become a *zone de sécurité prioritaire* (priority security zone) in 2012, and then a *quartier de reconquête républicaine* (neighborhood of republican reconquest) in 2019. These two initiatives aimed to ensure a reinforced police presence to fight against drug trafficking, delinquency, and communalism. Despite these measures, an important potential was also detected by the local and state authorities, concerning the possibilities of developing an original fashion district. In the Goutte d'Or, the concentration of companies and brands in the textile sector, run mainly by professionals from sub-Saharan Africa and the Maghreb, appears to be an essential feature of the neighborhood's economic structure. A very large number of businesses are present in the neighborhood. However, the situation of young creators is often fragile. Besides, several activities are primarily part of the informal economy based on particularly precarious immigrant populations. In addition, there are other handicaps, linked to insufficient qualifications, lack of equipment and suitable premises, and a lack of overall visibility.

Faced with these observations, the City of Paris launched a diagnostic in 2010–2011. A preoperational study was then conducted by consulting firms at the request of the *Délégation à la Politique de la Ville et à l'Intégration* and the Ateliers de Paris of the Economic Development, Employment and Higher Education Department. This initiative should be put into perspective with a previous operation initiated in the neighborhood, demonstrating the long-term nature of public intervention in this sector. In 2000, 10 premises on the ground floors of buildings on Rue des Gardes were made available to young fashion and accessories designers at attractive rents.

In August 2011, many professionals from various components of the fashion sectors present in the district formed an association "to jointly develop new markets, both local and export, and to participate in various collective projects aimed at improving the productivity and competitiveness of member companies," as stated in its statutes. The association, *Les Gouttes d'Or de la Mode et du Design* participates, in connection with the local development team and the group of consultants, in the elaboration of a multi-year action program which had defined the development modalities of the sector: the animation of the network; the structuring and the pooling of tools and services; the organization of training, with the aim of answering to the needs of qualifications and of developing the competences of the professionals; and the creation of tools and devices of communication, promotion, and event. Luc Dognin, a bag maker and leather designer awarded with the "Fabriqué à Paris" label insisted on the importance of the association *Les Gouttes d'Or de La Mode et du Design* for the development of the area (Dognin, personal communication, 2021).

The project of structuring the industry refers to social, economic, and urban issues and is part of a dynamic process that articulates several scales. First, it is part of urban renewal logic, linking economic development and neighborhood redevelopment. These measures also seek to support project leaders in creating businesses and reaching the most vulnerable populations, working in dilapidated and unsuitable premises, insufficiently qualified, and whose activities are most often in the informal sector. Finally, these actions are part of a broader logic of territorial marketing, of promoting the Goutte-d'Or district's brand image to facilitate its influence. Therefore, if one of the objectives remains the opening of the network toward other partners beyond the borders of the district, the stake today is first of all the consolidation and development of associative dynamics and the creation of the industry's economic structure, to pass from an economy of niche to that of cluster (Figure 14.3).

Thus, the multiplication of these innovative businesses in Rue Myrha owes nothing to chance: they were carefully selected by the city council. As early as the 1980s, the latter used its right of preemption to redevelop the street. The City of Paris owns nearly half of the area (18 buildings). According to the Mayor of the 18th district, every time the city rehabilitated a building, it tried to install in its ground floor a brand that would make the street more dynamic (Musca, 2020).

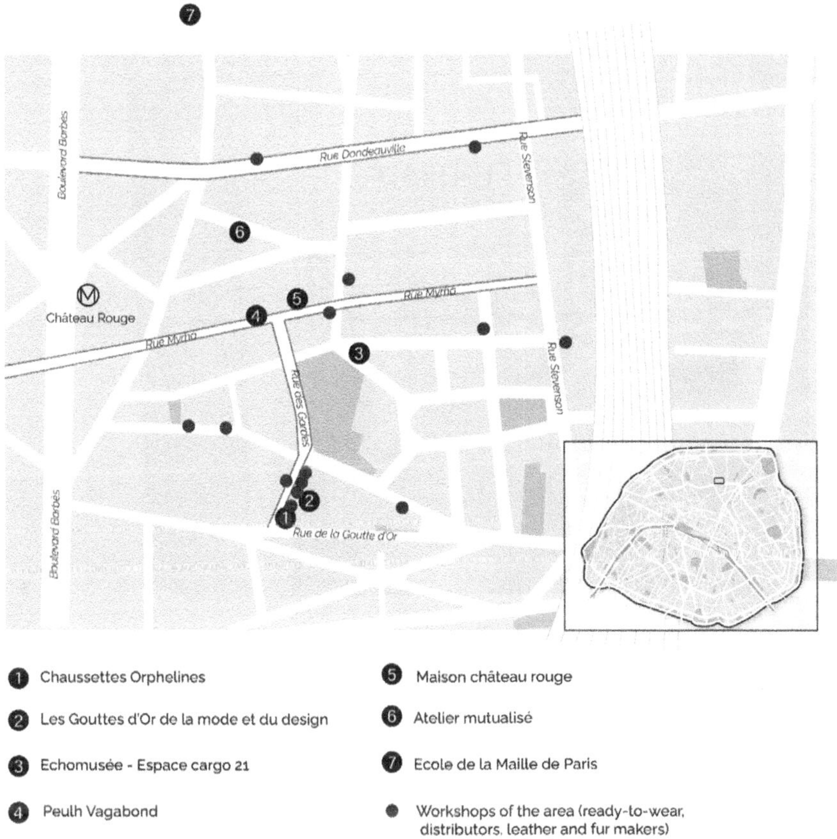

Figure 14.3. The Château-Rouge/Goutte d'Or Fashion Area.
Source: M. Gravari-Barbas.

The fashion shops are located in a specific area of the neighborhood: the area around Rue Myrha, Rue des Gardes, and Rue Doudeauville. It is an evolving fashion scene, particularly in the area of batik and wax fabrics, which are an important attraction for this unique Parisian area. In addition, some of the brands symbolize the meeting point between several cultures and draw inspiration from the melting pot of the neighborhood, combining African and French heritage in a contemporary spirit creating something new and unique.

Some initiatives are emblematic of the changes in the area (Musca, 2020). For example, the shop Peulh Vagabond, located at 48 Rue Myrha offers high-end clothing made from traditional African fabrics. Since its foundation in 2016, the brand has had the opportunity to dress Beyoncé on two different occasions.

Figure 14.4. Maison Château Rouge. © M.Gravari-Barbas.
Source: Gravari-Barbas (2021).

Maison Château Rouge (Figure 14.4) is the most iconic success story of the street transformation. Launched in 2015, it offers pop clothing and objects, mixing African crafts and Parisian streetwear. The Maison wants to reflect the dual culture of its creator, Youssouf Fofana, born in Seine-Saint-Denis and son of Senegalese immigrants. After collaborations with La Redoute and Monoprix, the brand partnered with Nike in November 2019 to create a pair of Air Jordans. The success has been overwhelming. The fact that the young designer was invited to accompany French President Emmanuel Macron on his African tour in November 2017, as well as to participate in the dinner of great designers organized at the presidential palace in March 2018 for the opening of Fashion Week is symptomatic of the consecration of the designer and his brand born in Château Rouge. Fofana's contribution to the Air Jordan "I Mid Fearless" series "deepens his contribution to Afrocentric fashion from the 18th arrondissement, the heart of Parisian street culture" (Maison Château Rouge).

The story of Maison Château Rouge begins in 2015, when Youssouf Fofana, employee at a social economy bank, with half of his salary he purchases fabrics on Rue Myrha and, with the other half, he had 100 pieces produced in a workshop in the Paris district of Sentier (Guillaume, 2018). In 2015, Fofana registered the brand Maison Château Rouge, created the commercial site, and launched the Instagram account fed by a series of photos of friends taken in the neighborhood. The story was immediately relayed by blogs, then by the American site The Huffington Post. The context is positive: at the same time, the Fondation Cartier exhibits "Beauté Congo," an art show which traces the creative spirit of the Democratic Republic of the Congo. The first orders for the Maison came from Japan and the United States. Today, it is a well-establish brand, still located at Château Rouge but with national and international reputation.

Sawa Basket is a store selling sneakers made in Africa opened on Rue Myrha in 2011. The shopkeeper insisted on the fact that the neighborhood has been changing in the last few years, and that there is a sense of new momentum, a "breath of new life." This point came up many times with various people (personal communications, 2021). Several interviewees (Sawa Basket, Maison Château Rouge) insisted on the mutual help between the stores on the street, and the role of the *Pôle de la Goutte d'Or de la Mode et du Design*. An example of shared services in the area is seen at the *Atelier Mutualisé* (shared workshop), where new designers have the possibility to work. Thanks to the conditions created by the City of Paris, the district attracts designers who were not already located at the area. This is the case of the shop and workshop of Marcia de Carvalho, *Chaussettes Orphélines* (Orpheline Socks), where everything done and sold is recycled from socks (personal communication, 2021).

Véronique Dupérier, the director of the *École de Maille de Paris* (Paris Knitting School), the first and only fashion school dedicated to knitwear in France, was founded in the neighborhood in 2011. She too confirmed that the neighborhood is slowly changing. A notable change was the rise, in the last few years, of an associative field: young people with ecological concerns moving in. She and the school have close ties with the town hall. The students participate in international competitions, one of them even winning the Woolmark and Adidas design competition, which granted her the opportunity to create a product with them. Others go on to work with high-end fashion houses such as Kenzo, Nina Ricci, or Sonia Rykiel, indicating a link to high end and international fashion through this school situated in Château Rouge. According to her, Château Rouge is full of creative effervescence, with many printed fabrics available and people creating. Château Rouge is a place on the move, though things are not always easy; it is not a wealthy neighborhood, and people there sometimes experience hard times.

The development of the fashion district at Chateau Rouge required a considerable engagement from the City of Paris and the national government. The challenge goes far beyond fashion: in the Goutte d'Or there are many people without regular papers. The development of the local fashion activity sector is a way for them to enter the working environment. It coincides with the general trend in French society where more and more people are concerned with ethical consumption and the idea of buying ethical products made in a workshop. In its own way, corporate social responsibility becomes crucial here. These developments add to the strengths of Château Rouge, encapsulated in the following quote by Maison Château Rouge's Youssouf Fofana:

> ...there has always been an emulation in this neighborhood, with the African tailors and dressmakers, the designers Xuly Bët and Sakina M'Sa, not to mention the dense network of associations. Today, people want authenticity, so they turn to less well-known districts (Chahine, 2020; translation by the author).

Among the different initiatives by the City of Paris, it is essential to mention the label *Fabriqué à Paris*. In the six years of its existence, the label was given to several creators of the area, thus contributing its notoriety as an emerging fashion district.

Blend with Tourism: Tourism initiatives are recent in the area, mainly starting at the beginning of the twenty-first century. They are the result of alternative approaches of various stakeholders, not necessarily from the tourism industry. They are mostly locals and founders of nongovernmental organizations, offering off-the-beaten-tracks visits. Today, Paris is the home to a large number of nongovernmental organizations or private companies that have various objectives: from fair tourism and solidarity, or the sharing economy, to initiatives that are more tractable in market economic models. What they all have in common, however, is the shift in the geography of tourism in Paris and the attention given to the marginal tourism areas of the capital.

In Château Rouge, most of the proposed tours offer the possibility to visit everyday places such as ethnic shops, mainly for cosmetic products, wax or African fabrics, and local food. No monuments or other major sites are visited, only ordinary places of the everyday life of the guides who usually live in the area. This is the case of Siby Mahamadou, who left Mali in the 2000s some 10 years earlier, driven by poverty. He founded a development association that helps the inhabitants of his village near Kayes, in the west of the country. He offers a visit called "Little Mali," presenting the places of everyday life of recent Mali immigrants.

The visits start with a warning to the visitors: the fact that they are in an area in which they must remain careful. All visitors are French, and most of them from Paris or the Ile-de-France region (Chabrol, 2013) as Château Rouge is not yet an international destination. However, some visits are offered in English, mainly to special groups. Visitors are invited to be discreet with pictures and to keep their bags closed. During the visits, tourists encounter street vendors, and haranguing the group is frequent. Sometimes there are also reactions from locals who feel uncomfortable by the cameras of the visitors. The context is different than in the more touristic areas of the city, where the tourists have been part of the city's landscape for more than two centuries.

The example of the visits proposed in Château Rouge/Goutte d'Or by Bastina Voyages is particularly interesting. This company proposes solidarity and fair tourism products located "around the corner," offering "ordinary" places as well as districts considered dangerous, by reversing the paradigm of their dangerousness or liminality (Figure 14.5). The tour guides are named *passeurs de culture* (transmitters of culture) which refers to migrants or people with an immigrant background. These "in-betweens" are bearers of a cultural universe and a living heritage that is often underestimated, and they tell the stories of places where they have been welcomed and in which they live and work. The aim is to avoid the otherization of individuals (Chapuis & Jacquot, 2014), through their exoticization.

The walks proposed in the Chateau Rouge neighborhood show the Paris of the Malians through their living and social spaces. The aim is to "turn around the paradoxical situation of knowing Malians in Mali but not here, even though the Paris region is the primary receptive basin for Malian immigration in France" (S. Buljat interview with Gravari-Barbas, 2015). More generally, about 20 "transmitters of culture" on different urban routes

Figure 14.5. A "Fashion Mix" Visit. © M.Gravari-Barbas.

Source: Gravari-Barbas (2021).

and themes "tell" their city to visitors. The personalities met along these routes are as important as the "physical" urban walks, which are nourished by the personal background of these guides. The tour is thus fed as much by the local heritage as by the personality and cultural universe of the "transmitters of culture." To carry out the visits, a certain "territorial legitimacy" is required from the "transmitters." Stefan Buljat, director of Bastina Voyages, expresses it as follows:

> We didn't ask people who live in Montreuil to take a walk in the 13th arrondissement in Paris, because our idea is that a person creates an intimate social and cultural link with the neighborhood where he or she lives. We wanted to show what it means to live in this neighborhood according to one's own life path.

According to Buljat, the urban walk offers a time of encounter that represents a founding part of alternative tourism, as it means that the guides are not interchangeable from one commune to another (they are not tour guides).

The visits are based on the assumption that today's tourists are not only interested in getting to know the city in its historical, architectural, or monumental attributes, but they also want to know something about the history, background, and culture of the person accompanying them. Therefore, it is not only presenting the museums and historical buildings but also the more unusual places such as a hairdresser's salon, a "sape" store or a traditional pharmacopeia, a place of worship in a garage or a place of work in a garment factory, a café where old migrants gather. According to Buljat, "Each emblematic place, each atmosphere, invites exchange, each urban interstice represents the cultural heritage of a migration."

A dozen walks are now proposed through places that may seem unusual, locations where the know-how of the inhabitants is visible. Food and handicrafts are two themes that can facilitate intercultural interpretation during the stroll. However, it is important to understand the intangible cultural heritage of migrations in its entirety: the knowledge and skills, the cultural and social practices, the rites and beliefs, the events that nourish the walker's purpose, the empathy toward the guide, and finally his or her integration in the host territory.

The walks in places off-the-beaten-tracks were realized within the framework of a European project, "Migrantour," which brought together several European cities. This project, which lasted 20 months between 2014 and 2015, consisted in working on places and themes that could highlight these migrations, be it African-Asian-American or intra-European.

Understandably, in Château-Rouge/Goutte d'Or, off-the-beaten-tracks tourism meets fashion: Several visits offered in the area specifically target the very particular fashion mix of Chateau Rouge. This is the case for the

"Fashion Mix à la Goutte d'Or" tour, one of the visits offered by Bastina. It is marketed as: "A Fashion Mix stroll outside the walls" in an old district of Paris:

> ...to meet the craftsmen, tailors, mechanics, *sapeurs* (designers) who, one day, crossed the ocean, the mountains and the desert to come to the capital of France. Their impulses and inspirations create the trends of the Parisian Fashion every day. They make visible the participation of immigrants in the French couture and ready-to-wear (clothing) and highlight their contributions to the inventiveness, beauty and French elegance (hair, fabrics, style and creation ...

This is linked to the movement of the "sapeurs" which refers to the Society of Atmosphere and Elegant People (better known by the acronym SAPE), a cultural and social movement originating in the Republic of the Congo, more precisely from the Lari ethnic group. This movement is compared to dandyism. Its followers, known as "sapeurs," dress in the finest fashion houses and practice "sapologie," the art of being well "dressed."

Fashion visits to Château Rouge are also offered via the tourism experience service of Airbnb Trips, "African Fashion in the city," organized by Chayet Chiénin and Adama Anotho. They work together, as editor-in-chief and artistic director, for a new digital platform on African fashion, "Nothing But the Wax." The goal is

> ...to show Parisians and travelers that Paris is not only the capital of fashion, but also a capital of African fashion, and that the neighborhood of Château-Rouge, which often has a negative image, is really changing, becoming gentrified. (Pellissier, 2017)

Different styles of African fabrics (wax, bogolan, bazin, dashiki) are presented during the visit. Tourists visit traditional and modern stores in the area (like Holland Textile) they purchase Senegalese clothing at the most famous boutiques (such as "African beautiful"), before finishing the visit at the trendy Maison Château-Rouge.

CONCLUSION

Château Rouge/Goutte d'or offers a striking example of a parallel evolution between the phenomena of fashion and tourism. The beginning of a development of visits to the neighborhood, essentially by Parisians and people from the Ile-de-France region with an ethnological view of their own city, makes it difficult to speak of touristification in the neighborhood. This only concerns a niche market and remains almost invisible for international tourism. For national tourism, the neighborhood still suffers from an image of danger, communitarianism, and even fundamentalism. This is confirmed by the analysis of guidebooks: national guidebooks insist on the dangerous character of the district, while international guidebooks completely erase this district from the Parisian map. This indeed confirms the fact that the neighborhood is not part of the mass tourist universe of Paris. However, changes are clearly visible, both from "local" visitors, attracted by the cosmopolitan character of the neighborhood, as well as from tourists looking for an alternative image of Paris, or from international tourist of African descent.

Tourism in Chateau Rouge/Goutte d'Or is undoubtedly off-the-beaten-tracks tourism. The same is true for fashion: far from the fashion districts established in Paris since the nineteenth century, Château Rouge/Goutte d'Or offers a fashion that draws its roots from the Africanity of the neighborhood. Today, numerous shops selling traditional African fabrics remain open, and continue to be sources of inspiration alongside an increasing trend of young designers who are attracted to the neighborhood. These up-and-coming designers revisit the codes of African clothing and fabrics in a new and original way.

These developments are not spontaneous: France and the City of Paris have been trying for many years, through urban renewal projects, to combat what is considered as the communitarianism character of the neighborhood by means of urban renewal projects likely to attract a new population. The resulting urban gentrification (although less visible in Château Rouge than in other nearby Parisian districts, particularly the 19th one) contributes to the settlement of residents from higher social strata. They are attracted by the same shops, bars, and cafés as the tourists who visit the neighborhood (Gravari-Barbas & Guinand, 2017). The conjunction of the two trends (the installation of new residents and tourism seeking an alternative product, far from the clichés of mass tourism) is changing the character of the neighborhood.

In the context of a very tense real estate market in Paris, it is foreseeable that gentrification trends will continue in the years to come. One can also anticipate an interest on the part of more and more discerning tourists for more original and off-the-beaten-tracks urban tourism products. This is accompanied by the offer of service providers, both from the tourism industry and, more often than not, from the nonprofit sector. Notably, the installation of shops and fashion designers (half spontaneous, half provoked by the public authorities), undoubtedly contributes to the development of tourism in the district. As has been shown, most tourist visits highlight the fashion designers in the neighborhood.

Tourism certainly benefits from the existence of the fashion businesses, showcasing both the cosmopolitan character and the Africanity of the neighborhood, as well as "authentic" Parisian designers producing in synergy with the place. Fashion designers also benefit indirectly from tourism and visits to the neighborhood, less in terms of direct consumption than through the change in image that their presence induces. Château Rouge/Goutte d'Or is thus a particularly interesting case for the analysis of parallel developments between fashion and tourism.

FASHIONING FORWARD

Chapter 15

THE FUTURE OF FASHION HYPE AND DROPS

Collaboration, Events, and Destination Experiences

Daniel William Mackenzie Wright
University of Central Lancashire, UK

Abstract: Today, collaborative fashion approaches are a popular method of reimaging and positioning in contested markets. Fashion collaborations see brands, designers, artists, and companies come together, offering consumers new, alternative products. While shopping continues to be a popular leisure and touristic activity, it is becoming comparable across cities. At present, scholars and practitioners have paid scant attention to collaborative fashion consumption (Botsman & Rogers, 2010). This chapter considers how destinations should become involved with fashion collaborations and drop culture from the offset, establishing specific events for tourists to experience. Ultimately, changing the culture and behavior of shopping tourists to one of event experience and not solely product ownership. **Keywords**: Fashion; event tourism; drop culture; collaborations; sustainability; destination

INTRODUCTION

I shop therefore I am.

–Barbara Kruger

According to Shahbandeh (2021), the global apparel market is projected to grow in value from $1.5 trillion in 2020 to around $2.25 trillion by 2025. The global e-commerce fashion market value stands at around $759.5 billion,

Fashion and Tourism: Parallel Stories
Tourism Social Science Series, Volume 26, 261–282

ISSN: 1571-5043/doi:10.1108/S1571-504320230000026015

with apparel, accessories, and footwear as the number one sector in the world. With the 7.18% compounded annual growth of online fashion, the next 5 years could see the e-commerce industry pass the $1.0 trillion mark (Orendorff, 2021).

The business of fashion is more than just big; it is massive, and it is growing. However, attitudes and behaviors toward fashion consumption and engagement are evolving. As people move further into the 21st century, the premise of this chapter suggests that the industry will be more about emotional attachment, loyalty, and excitement toward fashion labels and brands. Unlike the fast approach driven by seasons (Bhardwaj & Fairhurst, 2010), in the future, "consumers will increasingly expect and demand an emphasis on sustainability from fashion brands" (Granskog, Lobis, & Magnus, 2020). Thus, brand love and loyalty will become increasingly dependent on the sustainability attributes that a brand enables or builds with its consumers. However, the fashion industry is complex and varied, and with the impact of social media, innovative approaches are driving consumer interest.

Today, brand collaborations, product hype, based on the concept of scarcity, and drop culture are all leading to novel approaches. Approaches which brands are looking toward as a means of establishing new methods of generating interest, excitement, and desire on behalf of consumers. However, drop culture, hype, and scarcity is not just about fashion items being released; it is a way of thinking, behaving and can center on community and importantly consumer ideology. Consequently, an opportunity is emerging for the future of fashion. One which can bring continued success not only for fashion brands (big and small) but also for destinations by attracting new consumers.

Traditionally, the leisure activity of retail and fashion was carried out in physical stores; today the online market offers a predominantly central role, from buying, selling, and showcasing perspectives. The online marketplace has had both positive and negative impacts for stakeholders and will continue to do so in the future. However, many global destinations and cities promote themselves as fashion capitals and use fashion to attract tourists. As noted, the retail industry is likely to see significant growth in the coming years, and while online shopping has seen continued growth, this does not mean the end of high street retail.

This chapter explores how destinations can take advantage of new fashion trends. It explores how (tourism and leisure) destinations can become an increasingly central part (fashion) of the consumers experiences by promoting themselves as the "place for dropping" of collaborative fashion products and experiences. By presenting innovative and original discussions exploring the potential for destinations to start collaborating with (international and local) fashion brands and other organizations use the method of driving tourism (domestically and internationally), similarly to the method of event tourism. Thus, the chapter considers how the future of drop culture could evolve and not only challenge but change the behaviors of consumers, moving from a more common fast fashion style to a desirable, experience-based approach.

Study Methods

This chapter offers novel exploration into how organizations within fashion collaborate with other industries and how the tourism industry and destinations could play a more active role going forward. A convenient research approach to data collection and analysis was applied in this theoretical chapter. The sources examined were selected due to the direct relevance they have to the topic under examination. Applying a more pragmatic research approach provided a framework that embraces different views, both constructivist and positivist. The philosophical approach of pragmatism can be viewed as the philosophical partner to the mixed method approach to research, one which recognizes the strengths and weaknesses of both qualitative and quantitative methods (Maxcy, 2003).

The pragmatic philosophical approach embraces multidisciplinary studies and ensures a more holistic consideration to social conditions are embraced. This study considers the potential growth of fashion tourism, taking a futures consideration. As noted by Lee (2012), future research is often seen as multidisciplinary, as the methodological approach often draws on data from a range of sciences. Likewise, Leigh, Webster, and Ivanov (2013, p. 3) identify how "authors strive to predict through the use of drivers and understanding current trends." Thus, to build its discussions and draw conclusion from them, the chapter examines qualitative and quantitative information.

To proceed, the extrapolation method which observes the development and growth of trends over time (Thompson, 1979) was applied. Using this method, the study was able to consider relevant past and current trends and how they could advance in the future (Yeoman, 2012; Yeoman & Mars, 2012). Consequently, research findings are based on the examination of refined information and models from secondary sources and or published material/reports.

CONSUMER EXPERIENCES, COLLABORATION, AND EVENTS

Millennials are dominating the market, fashion trends are constantly evolving, and new, alternative, and sustainable brands are introduced, as creators reach global markets. As a result, recent years have seen fashion brands collaborating with high-end designers and retailers. As Ismailjee (2020) recognizes, luxury retailers are becoming more open to the concept of making their brands more accessible to a wider demographic audience through the idea of collaborating with more mainstream and high street giants, doing so with the aim of increasing sales and engagement. Likewise, Baron (2018) notes that luxury designers are increasingly moving into streetwear tactics as a means of remaining relevant to younger consumers. This is achieved through the creation of exclusive product collections and limited-edition ranges generated by brand partnerships to realize the increasing demand for "newness," something more common with Generation Z consumers.

"Collaborations have become a clear and feasible marketing strategy for fashion brands to remain relevant in an ever-growing consumer market where millennials seem to be dominating" (Ismailjee, 2020). Recently collaborative works have seen a significant increase in the fashion industry, with big luxury designer brands working with streetwear brands. As noted by Kloster (2020), the fashion industry in 2020 found its own key to virality with unlikely designer pairings, with collaborative business models becoming the focus for fashion brands. According to Burton (2005), collaboration stands for cooperation, teamwork, and combined effort. It is a strategy to maximize company profits by working together with similar or different businesses. Collaboration can be defined as people working together on nonroutine cognitive work, and this can be linked to activities such as behavior, work habits, culture, management, and business goals and value (Cannell, 2005).

Jang's (2006, p. 119) research identified three types/classifications. One, *coproduct* refers to the development of a new product with a unique attraction by hybriding, a promotional effect by joining enterprises with the designer. These new products are used in sale promotion and publicity by selling only limited editions for a brief period. However, if this collaboration is successful, the company will continue to search for other partners.

Two, *cobranding*, which means more than a mere joining of promotion. Many new shopping malls and fashion designers are included in this area. Here, creating contemporary brands so that fashion brands can expand into new business areas (and make up for the weaker business practices) by sharing their strong points with others. Three, *comarketing* focuses on maximizing the cooperation effect in order to increase sales and decrease the marketing cost. To achieve comarketing, the companies' targets are ideally the same, with a goal to increase recognition of each brand by sharing the target audience the key concept is to increase and strengthen communications while limiting costs.

In Jang's research of the larger percentage (and more popular), collaborative approach was the coproduct development within the fashion industry (the study included 27 cases of fashion collaboration in South Korea). Collaboration strategies performed well as they reduced marketing costs, expanded business boundaries, created new consumer groups, and offered effective publicity and the opportunity for establishing new products. Significantly, collaboration styles change over time and the fashion industry is one of the most popular collaboration partners alongside other industries because its categories offer greater variety in fashion codes. Also, fashion is continuously evolving with its surroundings and its values are always changing (Jang, 2006). Due to this, industries pursue collaborations with fashion brands as it can add to the creative aspects of their own image (and products). Thus, fashion brand collaboration is not limited to working with other fashion labels, and more commonly cross-industry collaboration is increasingly popular. The collaboration can cross not just product collaboration (such as bringing two clothing brands together), but can operate when considering product development, production, promotion, sales, and distribution.

With the internet also comes greater collaboration between offline and online brands (as not all industries, businesses, and locations operate online). Fashion brands are increasingly collaborating with musicians, sports brands, car manufactures, food labels, social media influencers, entertainment industries, and much more. The potential of collaborating and establishing fashion that is unique allows companies to stand out, as they have new and exciting products they can bring to market. In so doing, it provides companies with the opportunity to generate excitement around their brand. One method to drive desirability is around the idea of uniqueness, potentially promoting fashion as art.

A quick internet search of fashion collaborations brings a myriad list of articles exploring the rich history of companies coming together with streetwear brands such as Nike, Adidas, Supreme and the more luxury designers such as Gucci, Dior, or Ralph Lauren (there are far too many to be named). Table 15.1 provides five examples showcasing the range of industries, brands, and iconic individuals who have come together to produce collaborative fashion apparel. The examples display the range of different industries that collaborate in fashion, from sport, music, street artists, and entertainment. They offer an insight into more recent iconic collaborations, but many others could have been included to highlight the range and variety of collaborations that have and continue to work together.

Fashion as Art

> And what about art? It can be defined as the ability, through visual, verbal, gestural, and musical means, to objectify one's experience of the world: to show and tell, through an eloquent shorthand, how it feels to be alive. And of course, a work of art can also be a potential commodity, a vessel of financial speculation and exchange. (Kruger, 1993, p. 6)

Table 15.1. Examples of Fashion Collaborations.

Example	Brands	Description
1	Juventus × Palace × Adidas partnership	Italian football team, alongside Adidas released a 4th kit in collaboration with skateboard brand Palace. The announcement came out of nowhere. The Juventus Instagram account posted photos of the team warming up before a game against Genoa in November 2019. The collection was released at Palace store locations and web store and adidas.com, as well as Juventus stores and juventus.com (Chin, 2019).
2	KAWS × Nike Air Jordan	Brooklyn-born, world-renowned athlete Michael Jordan and Brooklyn-based, world-renowned artist KAWS in collab with Nike. The Jordan × KAWS capsule collection celebrates two iconoclasts. It recognizes that behind every game-changer lies the desire to master one's craft. And, ultimately, it honors the larger-than-life ingenuity of MJ and KAWS (Nike News, 2017).
3	Supreme × Fender Stratocaster Guitar	"Supreme's Fall/Winter 2017 collection also saw the skate imprint collaborate with Fender on an all-white Stratocaster – save for a red box logo, of course. Also included were a Supreme-branded strap, case and picks. Supreme turned to DJ Quik, who was filmed strumming it and then proclaiming that "there are kids that are gonna pick up this guitar and change the world with it" (Richardson, 2020).
4	Disney × Gucci collection	To celebrate Chinese New Year and welcome in the year of the Rat, Gucci launched a capsule collection paying homage to the world's most famous rodent, Mickey Mouse. The carefree unisex capsule (the third collaboration between Walt Disney and the Italian

Table 15.1. *(Continued)*

Example	Brands	Description
		powerhouse) offered a dedicated range of exclusive items humorously playing around with Gucci's double-G motifs and Disney's iconic mouse (Truscott & Chilton, 2020).
5	McLaren × Belstaff	McLaren is the maker of some of the most advanced supercars in the world. Belstaff is a producer of fine clothes targeting adventure-seeking customers. The two British brands came together to create a new "capsule" collection. The clothing line was designed to be as functional as possible (Kalagi, 2021)

Joanne Entwistle states that fashion is about bodies, produced, promoted, and worn, and the body must be dressed in most social encounters. One dresses every day, and life cannot be separated from the living body and from its social existence. In this context, if fashion is art, it moves away from the traditional dominant place in "high culture" and begins to circulate within other cultural realms and meanings around consumption, popular culture, and the more everyday existence that people experience. This renewal, the updated nature of (mass) fashion renders the debate more complex. "The evanescence of fashion and the lastingness of art is the real sticking point" (Geczy & Karaminas, 2013, pp. 2–3, 6).

Can fashion be art? Scholars have explored this subject, and while it is beyond the scope of this chapter to provide an answer to this debate, it is useful to consider such a question. The chapter is highlighting the potential of fashion and clothes to hold higher value and thus become more adored by their owners, thus making fashion less disposable and more of a commodity of desire, and this could prove pivotal in attaining greater levels of sustainable consumption.

Traditionally, art is defined and categorized within the realms of "high culture" and art refers to visual forms of creativity such as painting or sculpture, but it can also refer to music and dance. In each case, it is an expression or application of human creativity, skill, and imagination, and to be appreciated for their beauty and or emotional prowess and power. Thus, fashion art might not be placed within the categories of original "high culture."

As Miller (2007) suggests, like art, clothes can provide the subject of historical research (as can traditional art forms). While Miller (2007) provides a more philosophical exploration of fashion as art, the conclusion offered suggests clothes can be regarded in two ways: One, from their functional use, keeping people warm, used for various jobs, offering erotic appeal, and being adorning and two, clothes can be regarded as "beautiful objects of aesthetic contemplation by disregarding the 'concept' under which they fall and therefore ignoring their functional dimension. They could be (as indeed they are) objects of admiration in a museum" (Miller, 2007, p. 39). However, recent fashion collaborations have even seen them come together, where clothing focused on utility also offers a sense of artistic novelty and uniqueness (be it through the collaboration of brands or the design and artistic nature of the clothing itself).

Berges (2017) explores fashion as a true art form and suggests it should be seen as a perfect marriage of utility, creativity, and communication. While recognizing that historically, fashion has not been elevated to the heights and stature of music, sculpture, architecture, and painting. Berges suggests, it is one of the purest expressions of art because it is art lived by all, daily. Berges recalls the work and art performance of Marina Abramović and how the fashion designer creates artwork that requires another person for its completion, here suggesting the individual who wears it. This individual wearing the art fashion is conversing with the designer and the audience (others who see them wearing their clothes). Fashion is to be a manifestation of human art and communication and it supports people individually to artistically communicate "who we are, who we want to be, where we are going, and where we have been" (2017). Herein lies the complexity of fashion. Clothes cannot be grouped and classified in one context. Today, fashion brands work with artists, and put art on clothing.

According to Geczy and Karaminas (2013), the 20th century saw fashion becoming a central focus for many artists as they began to understand the provocative power of clothing in creating identity and establishing their work as global brands. An example to consider here is the streetwear brand Supreme. "Supreme isn't the first commercial venture to enlist artists to create merchandise, but it is the first to offer the artists' merchandise at a regular price" (Jebbia, KAWS O'Brien, & Bondaroff, 2010, p. 10). McCormick (Supreme, 2020) suggests that Supreme has become far more sustainable and significant than other players because of their uncanny understanding of the artist's role in defining the visuals by which they navigate the world and self. He goes on to note that Haring (a New York artist whose pop art emerged from graffiti subculture in the 1980s, recognized for his pop shop selling T-shirts with art) had been worn by many in the art world and that the commercialization of his work into apparel would only end up hurting his position in the art market. However, Haring suggested that the use of commercial projects enabled him to reach millions of people who otherwise would not have been reached, leaving him as an unknown artist. According to Haring, "I assumed after all that the point of making art was to communicate and contribute to culture" (Supreme, 2020, p. 10). Supreme create artistic fashion in collaboration with various artists (offering opportunities to showcase their work). Offering an avenue to get artistic work not only out into the visual playground of fashion, but also offering such products in accessible and affordable ways, unlike the traditional approach, where limited and expensive works aimed at the privileged few is often the case.

McCormick continues by suggesting, "this democracy of terms as a new kind of art making, and the place that aesthetics as well as subcultural meaning can have within this genre, is as endemic to the history of Supreme as it is to its ongoing modus operandi" (Supreme, 2020, pp. 10–13). Going on to note,

> As an art critic with a proclivity for art's cross-pollination with popular culture and the dumb luck of knowing Supreme since its commercially inauspicious start, I must admit that art has always been my principle and paramount entry point into the brand. I'd like to close with something that is sure to piss everyone off that wears supreme: You can think all you want about what you're representing, kids. But you're wearing art. (Supreme, 2020, p. 13)

According to Karl Lagerfeld, "art is art. Fashion is fashion" (Geczy & Karaminas, 2013, p. 23). But it was Andy Warhol who proved that the two can exist together. Warhol asked the question, what is art, and philosopher Arthur Danto (1997) concluded, "anything can be art," but this does not suggest everything is art. Andy Warhol realized that in the corporate world (of art), it was going to become very tough for the single artist in his studio to compete. The pop artist realized that in the future, art was going to move away from its more traditionalist ideas, as there was no more nature to imitate. In the future, art would become indistinguishably linked with commerce, but this does not need to mean that art would need to betray its spirit (Jebbia et al., 2010, p. 8).

The discussions around fashion as art will likely continue, and maybe the quote offered by Bucchianeri (2011) that art is in the eye of the beholder, and therefore people will have their own interpretations, emphasizes the complexity of this discussion. Not surprisingly then, when considering the value of art, Agnes Martin noted, art's value is down to the observer (Laing, 2015). American art dealer Jeffrey Loria once said, "The real value of art is not always revealed by the price set upon it" (Tellis, 2018). If fashion (or at least some forms of it) can be received as art, then its value and significance is placed at those who deem it worthy. Like art, if fashion can hold greater value, then consumers will hold the pieces they own in greater esteem. In time, this could play a significant role in moving society beyond the fast, disposable consumption approach, to a place where fashion items (clothes and accessories) become more valuable. Not only as a primary purchase, but also the resell value (just like more traditional pieces of art), where second-hand items continue to hold a means of desirability beyond the original body (person) that displayed it. Collaborative approaches in fashion, where different artists and industry come together can lead to more desirable items, as witnessed by many international fashion brands, from streetwear brands like Nike and Supreme to high-end brands like Prada and Moschino. Collaborating with artists and other industries can generate interest and hype, and position fashion in greater regard (beyond the fashion industry itself). "The art we wear and live with is the art we become. Art – fashion and otherwise – reflects who we are and who we aspire to be" (Berges, 2017).

Fashion Hypes and Drop Culture

"Hype culture is a term used to describe a generation obsessed with finding the next big thing. It is a culture bent on excitement and adrenaline – almost to the point of self-exhaustion" (Paul Gravette, 2021). As noted by Morency (2018) "high-end brands are implementing Supreme-style 'drops' to better connect with young consumers who crave newness at the speed of Instagram." Drop culture can be defined as the limited release of merchandise, often as a marketing technique by streetwear fashion brands.

"Drop culture is the thinking, behavior, and community surrounding it" (Dictionary, 2021). The drop marketing model originally appeared around the 1980s and was driven by sneaker brands such as Nike and Adidas. The aim was to generate hype and excitement around the release of a new product. The premise was that on a certain day, at a particular time, the brand would release a limited-edition product. Merchandise would be dropped (released) in a brick-and-mortar store, and once sold out, it was gone for good. It was from here that the drop culture grew, and the thrill was very much entwined to the idea of product scarcity. "Drop culture grew around the thrill of the drop. The lines, the frantic shopping, the anticipation of future drops, the reselling of out-of-stock goods – these all make up the culture" (Dictionary, 2021). Again, Supreme offers a good example of how more recently this concept has grown.

> With my eye on Supreme, I noticed that it seemed to be more than a store, it had at least some qualities of a cult. The store would close for installations, just like an art gallery, and then reopen with new merchandise, just like a gallery. But unlike a gallery, Supreme had long lines of customers waiting to get in, and they would even camp out overnight. I eventually learned that there was something analogous to art sales going on here; the cats in the queue were there to get

> limited-edition merchandise. But I couldn't recall anyone ever camping out for the release of a lithograph. (Jebbia et al., 2010, p. 8)

According to Alter, "If you want to create a scarcity frenzy, and your brand has a strong following, all you need to do is release a large number of different products, but very few of each one" (Fowler, 2018). The question here, is releasing fewer products within a specific range, as bad as fast fashion, where copious amounts of the same product is mass produced and sold? The concept of hype and drop culture has its critics. One issue is around the idea of people becoming addicted to getting an item from the "next" drop. Of course, with hype and interest around fashion brands, one which a consumer has become ideologically attached to, could lead to issues around fashion addiction. However, shopping, and fast fashion are also open to consumer addiction.

Further, there is a negative stigma that comes with the idea of getting excitement for fashion hypes and drops, the idea that people will wait for hours (even days) in queues for the next release of items. But the value these consumers are putting toward a product is arguably different, as these consumers are seen to be buying into a culture and an identity. Potentially more so than consumers who shop for clothes that are practical (some of which come at a much higher cost than the clothes that are dropped by companies such as Nike and Supreme), and at times they offer lower product quality, and resell value. As stressed by Bozinoski (2020), pessimists will ridicule, but there is no denying that currently hype is a winning strategy for both brands and resellers alike. Thus, brands should recognize the power of drop and hype approaches and target consumers' ideological desires to build greater brand association. As noted by Piana (Binkley, 2021), 2020 served as an "accelerator of relationship permission," where customers became more interested in brands they relate to. If consumers feel an affiliation toward the brand, then they could be willing to wait for the right clothing items, ideally consuming less (a more sustainable approach), but also consuming and purchasing products they desire. Ideally, over time, this could lead to more sustainable consumption patterns by shoppers, as the "less is more" approach is valued higher than fast fashion and disposable fashion.

Fashion Sustainability

> And in an era that will be remembered forever for greed, hubris, and excess, this rebel business had been marked by its classical values. Supreme is about value. It gives its customers good value. It makes things to last, not to be consumed and cast aside. Its clothes have great style and flash but they are also designed for utility, economy, and longevity. Supreme mirrors the values that one often associated with

> the optimism of youth and that one hopes will stick around for once. (Jebbia et al., 2010, p. 11)

As environmental challenges continue to confront society, the idea of sustainable fashion production and consumption continues to be explored by several scholars (Black & Anderson, 2010; Fletcher, 2008). Terms often applied to sustainable fashion include "eco fashion" and "ethical fashion." The former is defined as garments designed and produced to increase benefits for people and society while reducing negative environmental effects (Ochoa, 2010). The latter entails clothing manufactured with high regard for fair trade principles and environmental standards in the production process (Joergens, 2006). These two types focus on the design and production process, while sustainable fashion refers to clothing designed, produced, (re-)used, and disposed in a way that is aligned with the concept of sustainable development (Stanszus & Iran, 2015).

Sustainability is not just about the production of clothing, but also the usage and postusage of them, especially that consumers play a significant role in the sustainability of fashion, much to consumer intentions, behaviors, and habits (Iran & Schrader, 2017). Significantly, consumers play a major role in decreasing the harmful effects of fashion consumption on the environment (Niinimäki, 2010). Consumers do this when choosing which fashion product to purchase, how to use and maintain products (repairing, laundry, and lifetime usage) and what to do if they decide to dispose it. Iran and Schrader (2017) explore the concept of collaborative fashion consumption, which focuses on consumer behavior once in ownership of clothing. The study explores how the sharing economy concept could be applied to fashion. Here, emphasis is on ideas such as sharing, renting, leasing, lending, swapping, gifting, and the second-hand concept (as a means to reduce environmental impacts from greater design, production, and consumption of new clothing).

Fashion has a long way to go before it can establish an industry which is sustainable at all levels, from production, distribution, consumption, usage and maintenance, and the postusage stage. However, if clothing and fashion are to become sustainable, the "less is more" concept should be embraced. Brands should focus on generating less clothes with greater quality (in material) and with higher levels of desirability (through collaborations, hype, artistic ventures, and scarcity). Ultimately, developing higher levels of interest, where items retain value, like art, and thus resell also becomes an important part of the cycle.

Fashion should move beyond the perishable and disposable nature it has become. Therefore, fashion brands should consider creating more desirable products for consumers which have a longer shelf-life. After all, if they do not, they might eventually go out of business all the same. Recent reports have pointed toward such scenarios. Adegeest (2021) suggests that, with sustainability agendas on the rise of consumer concerns, ethical fashion choices could see businesses (like Zara, H&M, and Primark) facing steep revenue declines. Likewise, Gosden (2021) notes, growing awareness of environmental impacts of "fast fashion" could see sales of cheap clothing dropping by as much as 30% in the next five to 10 years. Consequently, fashion brands and the industry need to play a more active role in the sustainable design and production of clothing and aim to adapt to changing consumer attitudes – where more attractive clothes are created which are desired by consumers.

Event Tourism, Shopping, and Destinations

Fashion tourism can be defined as the phenomenon whereby people travel to and stay in places outside their usual environment to enjoy, experience, and consume fashion. The phenomenon, that is, fashion tourism is categorized in various forms, from fashion travel, fashion knowledge (current and historic), and shopping tourism. The latter is "a contemporary form of tourism fostered by individuals for whom purchasing goods outside of their usual environment is a determining factor in their decision to travel" (UNWTO, 2014, p. 13).

Regardless of the terminology, the idea centralizes around the concept of tourists visiting or traveling (nationally or internationally) for the purposes of fashion viewing or purchase. This could be seen as a niche market, as tourists seek to fulfill various needs, wants, and desires around fashion (clothing, footwear, accessories, and knowledge enhancement). Visiting other destinations for fashion also offers the potential for learning new skills and ideas around fashion and how culture can reflect the creativity, innovation of host locations. The current and historical element here is significant, as tourists can be interested in exploring the more historical nature of clothing or driven to engage with more current fashion trends, such as visiting fashion weeks, with more traditionally popular cities being Paris, London, New York, and Milan. More recently, shopping festivals (or trade fairs) are created by destinations to increase tourist interests in destination and to drive economic growth, through the promotion of offering superior quality products and services from respective host cultures. Destinations are and will continue benefiting from this new trend; South Africa and Miami Beach International Fashion Week are recent examples.

Beyond the specific fashion tourism experience is the reality that shopping is often viewed as a component to travel, which can form a significant or smaller part of leisure and business travel trips. As suggested by Timothy (2005), shopping is one of the most common motivations for cross-border travel and tourists often identify it as a principal activity. Butler (1991) simply identified two categories for the relationship between tourism and shopping: that shopping is the primary purpose of the tourist trip and that it is carried out as a subordinate activity. Thus, for some shopping is an afterthought, while others travel to destinations specifically for shopping purposes, seeking out alternative and novel opportunities (Choi, Law, & Heo, 2017). Hsieh and Chang (2006) note the value of shopping as a "means of experiencing a local culture" (Hsieh & Chang, 2006, p. 3).

Shopping as a touristic activity has even been recognized as a driver to other leisure activities, with some scholars suggesting that shopping opportunities are among the major driving forces when selecting destinations (Saayman & Saayman, 2012; Timothy, 2005). As noted by Jansen-Verbeke (1998), shopping opportunities within destinations can provide a competitive advantage for countries and regions in combination with other attractions. As with famous fashion events, many destinations have developed into well-known tourist shopping locations, some have purposefully established themselves in this image, while others have specific products or stores that offer something unique to tourists (Begley, 1999; Kreiner, 1996; Riegler, 1999). Timothy (2005) notes that shopping was (and continues to be) seen as such a significant economic activity that destinations adopted policy initiatives and promotional campaigns. Destinations such as Hong Kong, Thailand, Singapore, and Dubai are commonly associated with such practices. These destinations have seen several associations developed by private organizations and public agencies (and quasi-government groups) to actively manage the touristic shopping activities by promoting through various media channels (Timothy, 2005). Such destinations have established an identity as shopping cities and or destinations.

While shopping might not be the primary motivation to all destinations, it is recognized as a universal tourism activity that can add to the overall attractiveness of almost every region in the world (Page, 1992; Reisinger & Turner, 2002). As Butler (1991) noted, there are boundless innate and individual motivational drivers for shopping, be it self-esteem, indulgence, prestige, nostalgia, vanity, seeking authentic products and materials or for economic savings. For some tourists, seeking novelty and alternative shopping experiences is an important factor. In a globalized world, where many city landscapes are overcrowded with the same brands and shops, novelty seeking is increasingly more important, but also difficult to locate.

According to Crompton (1979), novelty seeking is the need to be involved in something new, different, alternative, something outside of the ordinary range of activities. As standardization and globalization become common for consumers, seeking novel and unique shopping opportunities become more complex, something identified in the 20th century by Page (1995). Today, this trend is an ever-increasing reality for many global cities. However, if standardization is a pattern, how do destinations stand out from the crowd? How can they offer uniqueness? Can the current trends around fashion collaborations be a way forward for destinations? Cities and towns should consider how they can further promote fashion tourism in their destinations.

Events, Festivals, and Destination Identity

This section explores the wide, varied nature of definitions and categories of events. What is important is how the literature recognizes the value of events to destinations as a means for developing, promoting, and attracting tourists. "Events are an important motivator of tourism, and figure prominently in the development and marketing plans of most destinations." Further suggesting that, from a tourism industry perspective in line with DMOs, events are highly valuable attractions, as well as catalysts, animators, place marketers, and image-makers (Getz, 2008, p. 403). Chalkely and Essex (1999) discuss how communities and organizations globally display common desires to stage events as a means to stimulating economic growth. Events are seen as a platform to building and or reviving the brand image of cities (Robertson & Guerrier, 1998), organizations (Javalgi, Traylor, Gross, & Lampman, 1994; Pope & Voges, 2000), and products (Gorse, Chadwick, & Burton, 2010). Webber (2004) states that events can be staged to raise money and awareness. From a demand perspective, scholars suggest that events, like other leisure, symbolic, and experience goods, have become increasingly valuable for individuals (Lash & Urry, 1994; Nazreth, 2007; Pine & Gilmore, 1999).

In the past, events were more associated with the upkeep of cultural-heritage values, but in more contemporary societies, events can be staged for a myriad of purposes and desires. Richards (2010) suggested that in todays' world, events share an omnipresence globally, arguably seen as a current state of "hyper-festivitiy." MacLeod (2006) described the "placeless festivals." Here the association of the event (or festival) is not to a particular community, instead the event represents shared interests and ideals or staged for commercial purposes. This was recognized by Getz (1994), who suggested that commercialization will detract from celebration and entertainment will replace the inherent meaning of celebrations, especially when festivals and events are purposefully created and marketed as attractions. Of course, the concepts of "placeless festivals" has its critics, where the abundance of such events are seen as diminishing the meaningfulness of more traditional and heritage-based events to meaningless tourist spectacles (MacLeod, 2006).

Boorstin (1961) criticized "pseudo-events" as media driven creations and suggested that they bring the irrelevant to real life. This has left scholars questioning the motives of postmodern tourists, who are less interested in the real and genuine, but more in the imitations of the real (Rojek, 1993; Urry, 2002). However, not all events (and festivals) are rooted in the culture and heritage of the place in which they take place. According to MacLeod (2006, p. 222), "if postmodern society is characterized by the dislocation of people from their temporal and spatial identities, then it may be argued that the postmodern condition is that of placelessness." If the question is one of authentic experiences, then as noted by Cohen (1988), authenticity is not an absolute attribute of objects and places; rather it can be recognized as a socially constructed phenomenon. Thus, authenticity is ever-changing and emerging over time, a forever evolving system of representation instead of a fixed setting of ideas and objects. Massey (1994) likewise notes that the idea of authenticity of place suggests that places are static and timeless, instead, place identities are unfixed, contested, and multiple.

Today, societies and the individuals operate and fluctuate between differing cultural structures, be it dominant, high (elite), popular, sub, and counterculture. For many today, the idea of sense of place and feeling connected to a place is potentially diminishing (at least from a heritage perspective). This was identified by Relph (1976), who suggested that mass communication, mass culture, big business, powerful central authority, and the economic system all played a role in the individual loss of feeling toward an authentic relationship with place.

Aligning the discussions around events and festivals allows for variety and opportunity. Fashion and fashion events are not always "culturally relative" or "place sensitive" and can be staged anywhere. In a world of collaboration potential, the opportunities are arguably endless and varied. In as much, destinations could stage events that offer collaborations where the focus is solely on local culture, to ones where globalized visions (collaborations) are presented, or offering a mixture of local and international ideas, a blending of cultural realities through collaborative works.

Future Event Drops

> Taste literally dictates the technique of our bodies. It is a social orientation that shows us our place in the world. What we love, what we hate, what "works" for us, is inevitably a combo of where we've come from, and where we think we're going. Taste is not an object, but a process: a series of framings and refinements which lead to one's particular image of perfection. And because everything is, to some degree, subsumed by fashion, even our images of perfection are up for grabs, changing constantly, mutating from one hotness to another. Quality might be said to be the end product of the process of taste: the essence that's left after the acid test: the nectar of resolution that becomes exemplary. (Kruger, 1993, pp. 8–9)

According to Wong (2019), the concept of brand collaborations is not new to the fashion industry. Collaborations have proven to be a reliable method to increase brand awareness, experiment with new product ranges, and reach new customers. Significantly, they are also demonstrating their ability to become an extremely effective method in accelerating more sustainable practices across the industry. As Wong (2019) suggests, sustainable brand collaborations can lead to knowledge-sharing opportunities between businesses, whereby expert pioneering brands can support and work with companies in the fashion industry. The creative industries, from (small to large) fashion brands to (well-known and smaller) artists (be it musicians, painters, photographers, sculptors, illustrators, gamers, and graphic designers) are operating in saturated and competitive markets. "Brands are struggling to get coverage on traditional media these days, so they have to do things to stand out on social media and cut through all the noise" (van Elven, 2018). Social media and online influencers have and continue to play a key role in driving drop culture.

Working in collaboration with other brands can provide added exposure and strength. Collaborations do not need to be kept within the same industry. Bringing different artistic cultures and industries together can be a powerful tool for generating original ideas. Teaming up with others is about brand management and consumer awareness. Collaborations should generate hype around products being released. Fashion brands can come together with (local, national, and international) artists and designers and other industries and businesses (such as pop-culture, sport, entertainment, food and beverage, automobile and tech). The value of collaboration means that it does not need to only consist of two parties, but it can draw in many different industries, personnel, and stakeholders. Importantly, collaboration approaches offer opportunities not just for large fashion companies, and popular industries (beyond fashion), but also to smaller local companies, artists, and fashion labels.

The collaboration, hype, and drop approach can be used on international and local levels as an opportunity to drive brand and consumer interest. It is here where destinations of any size can become more involved. As noted earlier, the online market has transformed the accessibility, distribution, and promotion of fashion. However, physical locations continue to be attractive to (tourism and leisure) consumers, and this is where destinations should look to get involved in the current fashion movement. For example, Palace Skateboards joined forces with Belgium beer brand Stella Artois to launch all-new Palace Artois pubs in London and New York. The collaboration saw the two brands working together (for the second time) to transform two famous pubs, London's Blue Post and New York's Vig Bar, into special edition bar spaces to promote a new Stella Artois × Palace collaboration, which included a unique range of "barware" items and apparel (Pajkovic, 2021). The pubs opened for three days from Tuesday August 24 to Friday August 27 at The Blue Posts in Soho and Wednesday August 25 to Thursday August 26 at Vig Bar in New York. In doing so, generating not only interest by increasing visitor numbers.

The consumption of fashion can take place at any physical location, and it is not limited to retail shops and outlets. People purchase fashion from all sorts of physical locations, from open markets, sports stadiums, events, museums, cafes, pop-up locations, and much more. This vast range makes the opportunity so varied for different locations to become more involved in collaborative fashion event drops. Significantly, for destinations and locations where clothing drops occur, there is an opportunity to make more from the occasion, turning it into more of an event, where consumers can get closer to the brand, the artist and anyone for that matter, who is part of the collaboration. Destinations should be looking into opportunities in which they can be part of the collaborative fashion trend, where hype is also generated around the destination and or a specific "drop event," with the intention of driving consumer interest (and ideally visitation) in the direction of the destination.

Figure 15.1 offers a model presenting the process/cycle of discussions presented in this chapter. The latter sections of the model, "managing the

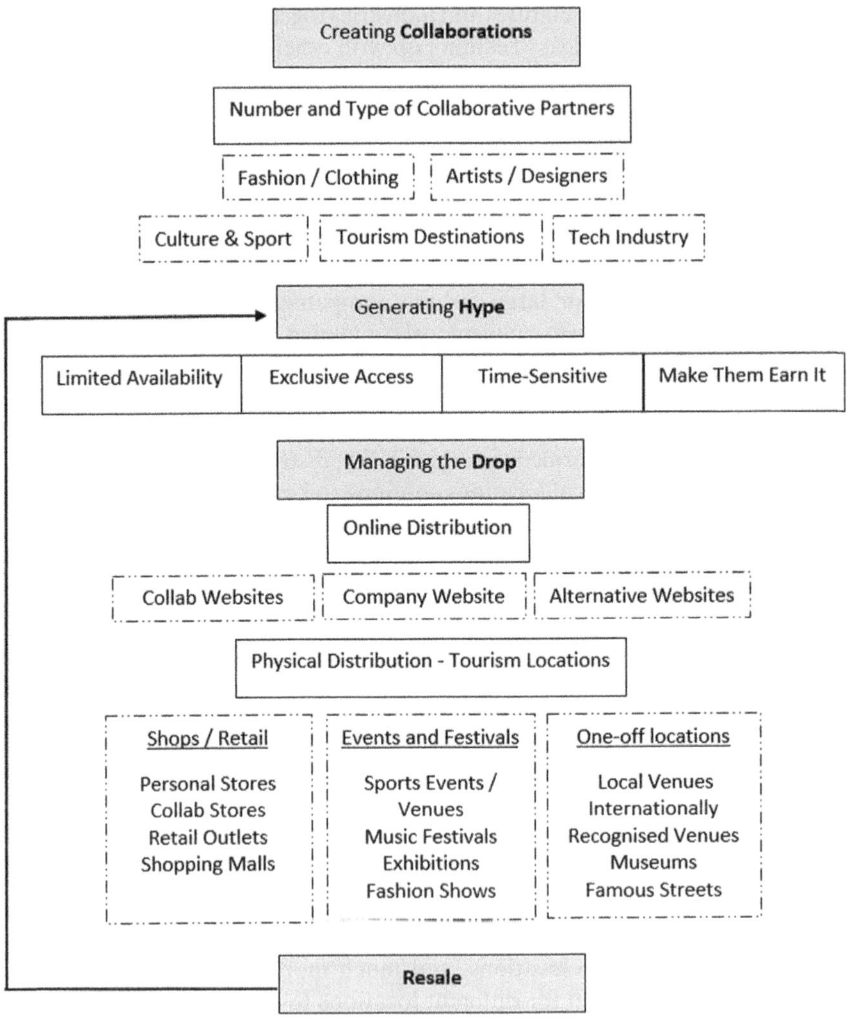

Figure 15.1. Management Model for Future Fashion.

drop" and the "physical locations," are where destinations (cities and towns) and shopping sites are often more likely to be involved (when not purchasing online). However, it is argued that destinations need to get involved in the initial stages of collaboration. If destinations are integrated at the start of the collaboration, then they can have more involvement in the other (later) stages. For example, generating hype, here, marketing and promoting the destination alongside the collaborative partner(s). From here, the destinations can also be actively involved in the physical locations in which the drops take place. Therefore, they would begin to embrace their role and engagement in future fashion drops, becoming an integral part of the entire process, and in so doing distinguishing the potential of collaborative engagements with the fashion industry and beyond. The scope and potential ranges significantly from small localized collaborative fashion events to destinations building identities around fashion and using collaborative methods to enhance their image. Stakeholders who can benefit from the fusion of different industries through fashion collaborations could set themselves apart, offering uniqueness to consumers, be it niche markets to more mainstream audiences.

In the future, the retail landscape within destinations will need to consider how they can offer alternative and unique opportunities to consumers in what is becoming a competitive and saturated market. Collaboration and events offer the opportunity to penetrate the fashion markets in new and exciting ways. Such an approach could be increasingly valuable for emerging fashion brands and artists looking to compete. Likewise, less-known destinations looking to generate local visitation with a focus on fashion events could consider the collaboration, hype, and drop approach by making use of local brands, artists, and physical spaces, putting on specific events to showcase (drop) collaborative products.

Brands are applying the hype concept to build interest and excitement around new clothing products, to appeal to new (younger and older) consumers and to encourage brand loyalty. New ideological approaches are being considered. Fashion brands are increasingly promoting themselves as more than mere items of clothing by selling a brand identity, one which the consumer will want to associate themselves to. Thus, creating clothing that consumers will want to cherish, feel proud of owning and displaying on their person. The significance of approach is its potential to move consumers away from the fast fashion concept to something more sustainable, here, focusing on the concept of experience, brining consumers closer to the brands, and not just emphasizing the value of product ownership. Ultimately, brands can drive consumers' desires away from the central objective of product ownership toward one driven by experience.

Fundamentally, the concept should continue to be based on product scarcity and limited availability. As noted, the limitation of products is part of the culture and allure for consumers, where scarcity is deemed to generate greater demand and the got-to-have-it mentality. However, rather than being a playground for the rich and elite, the idea of "drop events" allows for greater consumer inclusion through the offering of experiences. Today, some of the "hottest drops" are often managed around membership-only events (available via physical and digital locations). Membership to brands comes with privileges, and exclusive access is one of these. This creates a sense of community among the brands' followers. Membership and "being in the know" is important because product drops are time-sensitive, as products are often (depending on the level of hype and interest) sold out within seconds of being released (at least online) and within hours when released in physical stores. However, consumers are likely to value the product more if they feel like they have earned it.

At present, fast fashion and mass production devalues the quality and importance consumers place on products. If society aims to move toward more sustainable methods, then increasing the value in the products consumers own should be seen as important. If products are more appreciated, consumers will have to work for their purchase. Limited and scarce items are more difficult for consumers to get their hands on. All these tactics are important in generating hype, and significantly generating a culture and identity around the brand. Consumers buy into the identity and excitement that comes with the brand and the hype new collaborations generate. Destinations should consider their role in shifting consumer desires beyond ownership, toward experience via the use of "drop events."

CONCLUSION

This chapter considers the important relationship between tourism and shopping and, significantly, how future consumers could continue to seek novel and original shopping experiences. Today's consumers are more attached to the brands that they associate with, and this is arguably going to become stronger and more apparent in the future. Today's fashion trends are witnessing growing collaborative designs, where companies, artists, and fashion brands come together to create clothing that is desirable and unique. In so doing, brands draw in wider interest from consumers, as collaborations are based on an idea that there will be limited stock available.

The limited stock concept is around the idea of product scarcity, and consequently, consumers who are interested in such items show greater levels of desirability as the opportunity to own products is harder to come by. Companies and brands build "hype" around the items that will be released. Then comes "the drop," the moment of sale, and this can be online or in-store. Due to limited stock availability and limited access to the physical stores, not everyone is able to purchase the products. This often generates resale opportunities (in the short and long term), which can come at inflated costs depending on the desirability (level of hype) of the product on behalf of consumers.

This emerging and powerful approach to fashion is driven by streetwear culture. However, it is drawing in big brands and organizations through novel collaborations. Importantly, the idea of collaboration can operate on small and larger scales, both locally and internationally. Therein lies the potential for destinations, the opportunity to become part of the collaborations, and not only as the locations where products "drop" but to consider their role in overall process. Toffler (1970, p. 226) predicted, individuals would "begin to collect experiences as consciously and passionately as they once collected things." Destinations should consider their role in providing experiences for individuals via fashion events and/or festivals. This way, they can extend the hype beyond the product, and more toward the experience. There is an opportunity, on both large and small-scale levels, for brands, designers, artists, retailers, and destinations to come together and to create clothing that is desirable and valuable to consumers while also generating novel selling/shopping experiences alongside them. New opportunities can arise for destinations which want to get involved with the hype, be part of the collaborative ideas and to reconsider the value of "the drop," where experience is just as valuable as the purchasing and ownership of the products. If brands want to entice consumers and develop stronger brand affiliation, then, when dropping new clothing products, destinations should consider greater use of social events and the stakeholders involved.

As this chapter demonstrates, if fashion wants to move away from the fast-consumerist approach, the industry needs to consider the value consumers put of the brands and the products they own. Collaborative fashion, where clothes become pieces of art, could lead to changing consumers' attitudes and behaviors. The industry should look to reeducate consumers into owning less, but of more value. Alongside this, fashion brands could seek to place more value on the experience of shopping and engaging with brands rather than ownership. This includes offering novel events and festivals to bring consumers closer to the brands and the collaborative artists involved, moving more toward the consumption of fashion experiences, with less emphasis on the consumption of products.

This theoretical study explored the potential relationship between fashion collaborations and the potential role for greater involvement by tourism destinations and events. Future research should continue to explore cases where collaborations have included destinations (such as the Palace examples discussed earlier), and to examine the resulting impacts for destinations (and collaborative partners) and the benefits for all stakeholders (including the consumers). As consumers seek uniqueness in fashion related tourism, destinations should begin to consider their role in the current collaborative approaches, one which appeals to the younger generations through thoughtful collaborations, to further appeal to consumers across the diverse landscape of commodity, art, and fashion. A limitation to this research is the ability to consider the diverse and multifaceted nature of fashion itself, let alone the complex nature of collaborations. In this chapter, the focus has been on streetwear and more high-end brands, as they have played a significant role in driving the concept forward. Future research should look to alternative shopping markets/groups and, likewise, consider how the ideas covered here could be applied to other areas of fashion, tourism, and consumers.

"And I must say that I never felt like the old guy there, shopping among kids who could be my kids. Supreme is youth fashion, it is street fashion, but there's something – I hate to say – transcendental about it" (Jebbia et al., 2010, p. 8).

BIBLIOGRAPHY

Aaker, D. (1991). *Managing brand equity: Capitalizing on the value of a brand name.* New York, NY: Free Press.

Aaker, J. (1997). Dimensions of brand personality. *Journal of Marketing Research, 34*(3), 347–356. doi:10.2307/3151897

Aalbers, M. (2017). The variegate financialization of house. *International Journal of Urban and Regional Research*, 542–544. doi:10.1111/1468-2427.12522

Abidin, C. (2018). *Internet celebrity: Understanding fame online.* Bingley: Emerald Publishing Limited.

Abrams, A. (2015). *Why are fashion blockbusters more popular than art exhibitions and what can we do about it? ArtNet News.* Retrieved from https://news.artnet.com/market/savage-beauty-matisse-cut-outs-curator-art-fashion-blockbuster-exhibition-324701

Abriat, S. (2018, November). *La croisière s'amuse.* L'Officiel. Paris: ditions Jalou.

Acuti, D., Mazzoli, V., Donvito, R., & Chan, P. (2018). An Instagram content analysis for city branding in London and Florence. *Journal of Global Fashion Marketing, 9*(3), 185–204. doi:10.1080/20932685.2018.1463859

Adegeest, D. (2021, June 8). *Consumer backlash could dent fast fashion companies' profits.* Fashion United. Retrieved from https://fashionunited.uk/news/fashion/consumer-backlash-could-dent-fast-fashion-companies-profits/2021041454975

AirBnb. (2022, July 1). *About us.* Retrieved from https://news.airbnb.com/about-us/

Airlines, A. (2018). *Profile.* Retrieved from https://en.about.aegeanair.com/company/profile/

Alac, P. (2002). *The Bikini: A cultural history.* New York, NY: Parkstone Press.

Alaily-Mattar, N., Ponzini, D., & Thierstein, A. (2020). *About star architecture: Reflecting on cities in Europe.* London: Springer.

Alananzeh, O. A., Jawabreh, O., Al Mahmoud, A., & Hamada, R. (2018). The impact of customer relationship management on tourist satisfaction: The case of Radisson Blue Resort in Aqaba city. *Journal of Environmental Management & Tourism, 9.2*(26), 227–240. doi:10.14505//jemt.v9.2(26).02

Alimin, N. (2016). Masjid Raya Sumatra Barat Sebagai Simbol Persatuan Muslim di Sumatra Barat [Grand mosque architecture as the symbol of Muslim community in West Sumatra]. *INVENSI – Indonesian Journal of Fine Arts and Cultural Research, 1*(1), 80–89. doi:10.24821/invensi.v1i1.1605

Almanach de l'étranger à Paris: Guide pratique. (1867). Paris. p. 69.

Almatourism. (2018). Fashion between heritage and tourism. *Almatourism – Journal of Tourism, Culture and Territorial Development.* Retrieved from https://almatourism.unibo.it/issue/view/745

Amatulli, C., De Angelis, M., Pino, G., & Guido, G. (2020). An investigation of unsustainable luxury: How guilt drives negative word-of-mouth. *International Journal of Research in Marketing, 37*(4), 821–836. doi:10.1016/j.ijresmar.2020.03.005

Andersson, T. (2007). The tourist in the experience economy. *Scandinavian Journal of Hospitality and Tourism*, *7*(1), 46–58. doi:10.1080/15022250701224035

Andriotis, K. (2010). Heterotopic erotic oases: The public nude beach experience. *Annals of Tourism Research*, *37*(4), 1076–1096. doi:10.1016/j.annals.2010.04.003

Anholt, S. (2005). Some important distinctions in place branding. *Place Branding*, *1*(2), 116–121. doi:10.1057/palgrave.pb.5990011

APUR. (2016). *La mode et le design à Paris*. Paris: Métiers/événements/lieux.

Arendt, H. (1968). *Illuminations*. New York, NY: Schocken Books.

Armitage, J., & Roberts, J. (2016). *Critical luxury studies: Art, design, media*. Edinburgh: Edinburgh University Press.

Armondi, S., & Di Vita, S. (2018). *Milan: Productions, spatial patterns and urban change*. London & New York, NY: Routledge.

Arnone, M., & Iliopulos, E. (2005). *La corruzione costa. Effetti economici, istituzionali e sociali*. Milano: Vita & pensiero.

Arnoud, E., & Thompson, C. (2005). Consumer culture theory (CCT): Twenty years of research. *Journal of Consumer Research*, *4*(31), 868–882.

Arya, R. (2021). Cultural appropriation: What it is and why it matters? *Sociology Compass*, *15*(10), 1–11. doi:10.1111/soc4.12923

Ashworth, G., & Page, J. (2011). Urban tourism research: Recent progress and current paradoxes. *Progress in Tourism Management*, *32*(1), 1–15. doi:10.1016/j.tourman.2010.02.002

Athens Partnership. (2021, June 29). *Athens tourism partnership*. Retrieved from http://athenspartnership.org/athens-tourism-partnership/

Atsız, O., & Seyitoğlu, F. (2023). A netnography approach on the daily local-guided shopping tour experiences of travellers: An unexplored facet of the sharing economy. *Journal of Vacation Marketing*, *29*(1), 103–118. doi:10.1177/13567667221078248

Aubusson et Kugelmann. (1843). *Le Guide officiel de Paris*. Paris: Renseignements officiels et d'utilité journalière pour l'étranger comme pour l'habitant de la capitale.

Aulia, T., & Alfansyah, M. (2019). Strategi hubungan masyarakat pemerintah kota Tangerang dalam upaya mengembangkan publikasi tempat wisata kampung batik kembang mayang melalui media sosial Instagram [Public Relations Strategy of the Tangerang City Government in an Effort to Develop Publication of Tourist Attractions in Kampung Batik Kembang Mayang through Instagram]. *PANTAREI*, *3*(04).

Aux Galeries Lafayette. (1910a). *Accueil parfumé, chromolithographie*.

Aux Galeries Lafayette. (1910b). *Panorama de Montmartre pris de la Terrasse du Magasin des Galeries Lafayette*.

Aux Galeries Lafayette. (1919). *Aux Galeries Lafayette, atterrissage de Védrine*.

Aux Galeries Lafayette. (1925). Pavillon "La Maîtrise" des Galeries Lafayette, Paris, 1925.

Aux Galeries Lafayette. (1931). Plan de l'Exposition colonial internationale, Paris.

Avantie, A. (2022, April 4). *Anne Avantie Desainer Kebaya terbaik asal Semarang*. Retrieved from http://seputarsemarang.com/anne-avantie/

Avenel, G. (1894, July 25). Les grands magasins. *Revue des deux mondes*. p. 334.

Bacqué, M. (2005). *Projets urbains en quartiers anciens*. La Goutte d'Or, South End, report for PUCA. p. 239.

Bacqué, M. H., & Fijalkow, Y. (2006). En attendant la gentrification: Discours et politiques à la goutte d'or (1982–2000). *Presses de Sciences P. Sociétés Contemporaines*, *3*(63), 63–83. doi:10.3917/soco.063.0063

Bada, O. (2013). *The emerging role of fashion tourism and the need for a development strategy in Lagos, Nigeria (Undergraduate)*. Centria University of Applied Sciences.

Bae, S. Y., & Yeu, M. (2022). Herding behaviors in family travel decision-making in mothers' online communities: A netnographic approach. *Journal of Tourism and Cultural Change*, *20*(6), 756–773. doi:10.1080/14766825.2021.1992414

Bain & Company. (2021). Il mercato del turismo di alta gamma. Contributo diretto e indiretto, competitor e pieno potenziale. Retrieved from https://altagamma.it/download/Il-Mercato-del-turismo-di-alta-gamma-Bain-&-Company.pdf

Bakker, M. (2005). *Luxury and tailor-made holidays, travel and tourism analyst*. Mintel International Group Ltd.

Balducci, A., Fedeli, V., & Curci, F. (2017). Post-metropolitan territories. In *Looking for a new urbanity*. London: Routledge. doi:10.4324/9781315625300

Baranowski, S. (2007). *Strenght through joy. Consumerism and Mass Tourism in the Third Reich*. Cambridge: Cambridge University Press.

Barbery-Coulon, L. (2012). *Les saintes huiles (solaires). LeMonde*. Retrieved from https://www.lemonde.fr/m-styles/article/2012/06/29/les-saintes-huiles-solaires_1726479_4497319.html

Barbon, N. (1690). *A discourse of trade*. London: Tho. Milbourn.

Barnard, M. (1996). *The Function of fashion and clothing*. Fashion as Communication.

Barnes, L. (2013). Fashion marketing. *Textile Progress*, *45*(2–3), 182–207. doi:10.1080/00405167.2013.868677

Barnes, K., Waitt, G., Gill, N., & Gibson, C. (2006). Community and nostalgia in urban revitalization: A critique of urban village and creative class strategies. *Australian Geographer*, *37*(3), 335–354. doi:10.1080/00049180600954773

Baron, K. (2018, June 10). Digging into drop culture: Evolving a roaring retail ritual. Forbes. Retrieved from https://www.forbes.com/sites/katiebaron/2018/10/29/digging-into-drop-culture-evolving-a-booming-retail-ritual/?sh=68c0e88477d8

Barrère, C., & Santagata, W. (2005). La mode: Une économie de la créativité et du patrimoine, à l'heure du marché. *La Documentation Française*.

Barthes, R. (1973). *Système de la mode*. Paris: Éd. Du Seuil.

Barthes, R. (2020). Fashion photography. In M. Barnard (Ed.), *Fashion theory* (2nd ed., pp. 119–121). London: Routledge. doi:10.4324/9781315099620

Bastina. (n.d.). Brochure. Retrived from http://www.bastina.fr/voyage/paris-18eme/fashion-mix-a-la-goutte-d-or.html

Bauder, M. (2015). Affinage du Central Tourist District de Paris grâce au données de repérage GPS et à l'analyse SIG. *ViaTourism Review*, *8*. doi:10.4000/viatourism.1614

Bauer, A. (2005). Definitional anxieties. *Anthropology News*, *46*(9), 27. doi:10.1525/an.2005.46.9.27

Baum, T., & Hai, N. (2019). Applying sustainable employment principles in the tourism industry: Righting human rights wrongs? *Tourism Recreation Research, 44*(3), 371–381. doi:10.1080/02508281.2019.1624407

BCG and Altagamma. (2021). *The 8th true-luxury global consumer insight.* Boston Consulting Group.

Beard, N. (2011). Defining the fashion city: Fashion capital or style centre? In *Fashion forward* (pp. 219–232). Brill. doi:10.1163/9781848880016_018

Begley, L. (1999). Shopping: London, cheaper and chicer. *Travel and Leisure, 29*(2), 42–51.

Belfanti, C. (2014). *Histoire culturelle de la mode.* Paris: Éditions du Regard.

Bellaïche, J. M., Kluz, M., Mei-Pochtler, A., & Wiederin, E. (2012). *Luxe Redux: Raising the bar for selling of luxuries.* Boston, MA: Boston Consulting Group.

Bellini, N., & Pasquinelli, C. (2016). Urban brandscape as value ecosystem: The cultural destination strategy of fashion brands. *Place Branding and Public Diplomacy, 12*(1), 5–16. doi:10.1057/pb.2015.21

Bell, C., & Lyall, L. (2005). 'I was here': Pixilated evidence. In *The media and the tourist imagination* (pp. 149–156). London; New York, NY: Routledge.

Bellman, R., & Zadeh, L. (1970). *Decision-making in a fuzzy environment.* Washington, DC: National Aeronautics and Space Administration.

Benjamin, W. (1931/1996). Little history of photography. In M. Jennings, H. Eiland, & G. Smith (Eds.), *Walter Benjamin, selected writings* (Vol. 2, pp. 1927–1934). Cambridge, MA & London: The Belknap Press of Harvard University Press.

Benjamin, W. (1935). *Paris, the capital of the nineteenth century in Benjamin, W. 1999. The Arcades Project* [Trans by Howard Eiland and Kevin McLaughlin] Cambridge, Massachusetts and London: The Belknap Press of Harvard University Press.

Benjamin, W. (1935/1968). The work of art in the age of mechanical reproduction. In H. Arendt (Ed.), *Illuminations.* New York, NY: Schocken Books.

Benjamin, W. (1939/2006). On some Motifs in Baudelaire. In H. Eiland & M. Jennings (Eds.), *Walter Benjamin, selected writings* (Vol. 4, pp. 1938–1940). Cambridge, MA: Harvard University Press.

Bennett, J. (2014). Our bodies, our selfies: The feminist photo revolution. Time Magazine. Retrieved from https://time.com/3099103/feminist-selfies-uglyfeminists-iwokeuplikedis

Benur, A., & Bramwell, B. (2015). Tourism product development and product diversification in destinations. *Tourism Management, 50*, 213–224. doi:10.1016/j.tourman.2015.02.005

Berdet, M. (2013). *Fantasmagories du capital: L'invention de la ville-marchandise.* Paris: La Découverte.

Berg, M. (2005). *Luxury and pleasure in eighteenth-century Britain.* Oxford: Oxford University Press.

Berg, M., & Eger, E. (2003). *Luxury in the eighteenth century, debates, desires and delectable goods.* London: Palgrave Macmillan.

Berges, G. (2017, June 09). Defense of fashion as a true art form. Observer. Retrieved from https://observer.com/2017/06/fashion-true-art-form/

Berliner, D. (2020). *Losing culture.* New Brunswick, NJ: Rutgers University Press.

Berrino, A. (2011). *Storia del turismo in Italia.* Bologna, Italy: Il Mulino.

Berry, L. (2000). Cultivating service brand equity. *Journal of the Academy of Marketing Science*, *28*, 128–137. doi:10.1177/0092070300281012

Berry, C. (2016). Luxury: A dialectic of desire? In J. Armitage & J. Roberts (Eds.), *Critical luxury studies: Art, design, media*. Edinburgh: Edinburgh University Press.

Bertaux, D., & Kohli, M. (1984). The life story approach: A continental view. *Annual Review of Sociology*, *10*(1), 215–237.

Bhardwaj, V., & Fairhurst, A. (2010). Fast fashion: Response to changes in the fashionIndustry. *The International Review of Retail, Distribution and Consumer Research*, *20*(1), 165–173. doi:10.1080/09593960903498300

Biau, V. (1991). Biau Véronique. Innovations architecturales. Logiques de recherche, logiques d'action. In *Villes en parallèle*, Acteurs et chercheurs dans la ville. (n°17–18, avril 1991, pp. 282–289). doi:10.3406/vilpa.1991.1146 Retrieved from www.persee.fr/doc/vilpa_0242-2794_1991_num_17_1_1146

Bide, B. (2020). London leads the world: The reinvention of London fashion in the aftermath of the Second World War. *Fashion Theory*, *24*(3), 349–369. doi:10.1080/1362704X.2020.1732015

Binet, F., Coste-Manière, I., Decombes, C., Grasselli, Y., Ouedermi, D., & Ramchandani, M. (2019). Fast fashion, fashion brands and sustainable consumption. In *Fast fashion and sustainable consumption* (pp. 19–35). doi:10.1007/978-981-13-1268-7_2

Binkley, C. (2019, July 25). *Saint-Laurent incident underlines environmental cots of fashion shows. Vogue Business*. Retrieved from https://www.voguebusiness.com/fashion/saint-laurent-resort-mens-spring-summer-2020-malibu

Binkley, C. (2021, September 15). *The future of physical retail*. Vogue Business. Retrieved from https://www.voguebusiness.com/consumers/the-future-of-physical-retail

Biondo, S. (2021). Fashion stories in Rome: Place-making narratives within fashion branded city guides. In *Fashion communication: Proceedings of the FACTUM 21 conference* (pp. 321–337). Springer International Publishing. doi:10.1007/978-3-030-81321-5_24

Black, S., & Anderson, S. (2010). Making sustainability fashionable: Profile of the Danish fashion company noir. Fashion practice. *The Journal of Design Creative Process & the Fashion Industry*, *2*(1), 121–128. doi:10.2752/175693810X12640026716555

Blanks, T. (2015, May 11). Christian Dior. Resort 2016. Review. Vogue Runway. Retrieved from https://www.vogue.com/fashion-shows/resort-2016/christian-dior

Blaszczyk, R. (2008). *Producing fashion: Commerce, culture, and consumers*. Philadelphia, PA: University of Pennsylvania Press.

Blick, S., & Tekippe, R. (2005). *Art and architecture of late Medieval Pilgrimage in Northern Europe and the British Isles: Texts*. Leiden-Boston: Brill.

Blue Magazine. (2019). *The other side of Mykonos*. Retrieved from https://en.aegeanair.com/travel-information/on-board/blue-magazine/blue-79/. Accessed on June 29, 2021.

Blumer, H. (1969). Fashion: From class differentiation to collective selection. *The Sociological Quarterly*, *10*(3), 275–291.

Boccacci, P. (2013, July 18). *Il "colosseo quadrato" al gruppo Fendi-Arnault: A Roma l'ultimo colpo del re del lusso francese*. Retrieved from https://roma.repubblica.it/cronaca/2013/07/18/news/cos_il_colosseo_quadrato_sar_la_vetrina_della_moda-63205525/

Boehlke, H. L. (2008). *Nation as fashion in new order Indonesia, 1967–1998*. Minneapolis, MN: University of Minnesota.

Bô, D., Guével, M., & Lellouche, R. (2019). Brand culture: La cohérence des marques en question. Dunod.

Böhme, H. (2014). *Fetishism and culture. A different theory of modernity*. In A. Galt (Trans.), Boston, MA and Berlin: De Gruyter

Boime, A. (1979). Les hommes d'affaires et les arts en France au XIXème siècle. *Actes de la Recherche en Sciences Sociales*, *28*(1), 57–75.

Bookman, S. (2014). Brands and urban life: Specialty coffee, consumers, and the co-creation of urban café sociality. *Space and Culture*, *17*(1), 85–99. doi:10.1177/1206331213493853

Boorstin, D. (1961). *The image: A guide to pseudo-events in America*. New York, NY: Vintage.

Boston Consulting Group. (2021). *Il turista di alta gamma: Comportamenti e percezione dell'Italia*. Retrieved from https://altagamma.it/turismo-bcg/

Botsman, R., & Rogers, R. (2010). *What's mine is yours*. London: Collins.

Boukhris, L. (2017). The Black Paris project: The production and reception of a counter-hegemonic tourism narrative in postcolonial Paris. *Journal of Sustainable Tourism*, *25*(5), 684–702. doi:10.1080/09669582.2017.1291651

Bouly de Lesdain, S. (1999). Château Rouge, une centralité africaine à Paris. *Ethnologie française, Presses Universitaires de France*, *XXIX*(1), 86–99.

Bouneau, C. (2007). La promotion de l'économie touristique, levier de la politique d'aménagement du territoire en France des années 1950 aux années 1980. *Entreprises et Histoire*, *47*(2), 93. doi:10.3917/eh.047.0093

Bovone, L., Magatti, M., Mora, E., & Rovati, G. (2002). *Intraprendere cultura: Rinnovare la città*. Milano: Franco Angeli.

Bovone, L., Mazzette, A., & Rovati, G. (2005). *Effervescenze urbane*. Milano: FrancoAngeli.

Bozinoski, M. (2020, June 09). Hype-notized. Vogue. Retrieved from https://www.vogue.pt./english-version-hype-culture-vogue

Branch, J. D. (2007). Postmodern consumption and the high-fidelity audio microculture. In *Consumer culture theory*. Emerald Publishing Limited. doi:10.1016/S0885-2111(06)11004-2

Branch, J. D (2011). Postmodern consumption and the high-fidelity audio microculture. In R. W. Belk & J. F. Sherry (Eds.), *Consumer culture theory. Research in consumer behavior* (Vol. 11, pp. 79–99). Emerald Publishing Limited. doi:10.1016/S0885-2111(06)11004-2

Braun, V., & Clarke, V. (2012). Thematic analysis. In H. Cooper, P. M. Camic, D. L. Long, A. T. Panter, D. Rindskopf, & K. Sher (Eds.), *APA handbook of research methods in psychology*, (Vol. 2, pp. 57–71). Research designs: Quantitative, qualitative, neuropsychological, and biological. Washington, DC: American Psychological Association. doi:10.1037/13620-004

Brennan, Z. (2016). *The bag you are not allowed to buy*. Retrieved from https://www.dailymail.co.uk/femail/article-3556882/The-bag-not-allowed-buy-covetable-snooty-stores-sell-list-happened-sent-ordinary-women-ask-Hermes-handbag.html

Breward, C. (2004). *Fashioning London: Clothing and the modern metropolis*. Berg Pub Limited.

Breward, C., & Gilbert, D. (2006). *Fashion's world cities*. London: Berg Publisher.

Briciu, V. A. (2013). Differences between place branding and destination branding for local brand strategy development. *Bulletin of the Transilvania University of Braşov, Series VII: Social Sciences and Law*, (1), (pp. 9–14).

Brida, J. G., Gómez, D. M., & Segarra, V. (2020). On the empirical relationship between tourism and economic growth. *Tourism Management*, *81*, 104131. doi: 10.1016/j.tourman.2020.104131

Brooks, G., Drenten, J., & Piskorski, M. J. (2021). Influencer celebrification: How social media influencers acquire celebrity capital. *Journal of Advertising*, *50*(5), 528–547. doi:10.1080/00913367.2021.1977737

Brossat, I. (2018). AirBnb: La ville uberisée. Montreuil: Éditions la ville brulée.

Broughton, K., & Beggs, B. (2007). Leisure satisfaction of older adults. *Activities, Adaptation & Aging*, *31*(1), 1–18. doi:10.1300/J016v31n01_01

Bruhn, M., Schoenmüller, V., Schäfer, D., & Heinrich, D. (2012). Brand authenticity: Towards a deeper understanding of its conceptualization and measurement. *Advances in Consumer Research*, *40*.

Brunel, C., & Porret, K. (2019, June 12). Croisières culturelles, L'Express.

Bruschi, M. A. (2017, March 24). *Une visite dans l'hyper-populaire quartier de Château-Rouge*. Grazia. Retrieved from https://www.grazia.fr/lifestyle/carnet-adresse/une-visite-dans-lhyper-populaire-quartier-de-chateau-rouge-175444.html#item=1

Brydges, T., & Sjöholm, J. (2019). Becoming a personal style blogger: Changing configurations and spatialities of aesthetic labour in the fashion industry. *International Journal of Cultural Studies*, *22*(1), 119–139. doi:10.1177/1367877917752404

Bucchianeri, E. A. (2011). *Brushstrokes of a Gadfly*. New York, NY: Batalha.

Buchanan, T. (1983). Toward an understanding of variability in satisfactions within activities. *Journal of Leisure Research*, *15*(1), 39–51. doi:10.1080/00222216.1983.11969539

Buckley, R. (2003). Adventure tourism and the clothing, fashion and entertainment industries. *Journal of Ecotourism*, *2*(2), 126–134. doi:10.1080/14724040308668139

Budnarowska, C., & Marciniak, R. (2016). Fashion, tourism and the creative industries. In P. Long & N. Morpeth (Eds.), *Tourism and the creative industries: Theories, policies and practice* (pp. 69–87). London and New York, NY: Routledge. doi:10.4324/9781315735870

Buhalis, D. (2020). Technology in tourism-from information communication technologies to eTourism and smart tourism towards ambient intelligence tourism: A perspective article. *Tourism Review*, *75*(1), 267–272. doi:10.1108/TR-06-2019-0258

Buhalis, D., & Law, R. (2008). Progress in information technology and tourism management: 20 years on and 10 years after the Internet—The state of eTourism research. *Tourism Management*, *29*(4), 609–623. doi:10.1016/j.tourman.2008.01.005

Burton, B. (2005). How to define a collaboration strategy that drives business value. Gartner.

Butler, R. (1990). Alternative tourism: Pious hope or Trojan horse? *Journal of Travel Research*, *28*(3), 40–45. doi:10.1080/10261133.1989.10559086

Butler, R. (1991). West Edmonton Mall as a tourist attraction. *Canadian Geographer, 35*(3), 287–295. doi:10.1111/j.1541-0064.1991.tb01103.x

Butler, R. (1992). Alternative tourism: The thin edge of the wedge. In V. L. Smith (Ed.), *Tourism alternatives: Potentials and problems in the development of tourism* (pp. 31–46). Philadelphia, PA: University of Pennsylvania Press.

Butler, R. (2014, May). Addressing seasonality in tourism: The development of a prototype. In *Paper pesented at the Punta del Este Conference*.

Cai, L. (2002). Cooperative branding for rural destinations. *Annals of Tourism Research, 29*(3), 720–742. doi:10.1016/S0160-7383(01)00080-9

Calinao, D. (2020). Catwalks and cloisters: A semiotic analysis of fashion shows in built heritage. *Social Semiotics, 1–17*. doi:10.1080/10350330.2020.1788821

Calinao, D., & Lin, H. (2017). The cultural tourism potential of a fashion-related exhibition–the case of Alexander McQueen: Savage Beauty at the Victoria and Albert Museum. *Journal of Heritage Tourism, 12*(2), 204–217. doi:10.1080/1743873X.2016.1206550

Campbell, S. (2022, April 14). *What is the best social media platform for influencer marketing in 2022?* Retrieved from https://thesmallbusinessblog.net/best-social-media-platform-for-influencer-marketing/

Cannell, L. (2005). Creating a collaboration strategy: Aligning Solutions to Business Needs, Collaboration Loop's Spring 2005 Web seminar, Collaboration Technologies Conference April.

Cantoni, L. (2020). Digital transformation, tourism and cultural heritage. In M. Gravari Barbas (Ed.), *A research agenda for heritage tourism* (pp. 235–252). Cheltenham: Edward Elgar Publishing. doi:10.4337/9781789903522.00025

Cantoni, L., Cominelli, F., Kalbaska, N., Ornati, M., Sádaba, T., & SanMiguel, P. (2020). Fashion communication research: A way ahead. *Studies in Communication Sciences, 20*(1), 121–125. doi:10.24434/j.scoms.2020.01.011

Capart, J. (1932). *Le temple des muses, Bruxelles, Musées royaux d'art et d'histoire* (p. 127).

Capone, F., & Lazzeretti, L. (2016). Fashion and city branding: An analysis of the perception of Florence as a fashion city. *Journal of Global Fashion Marketing, 7*(3), 166–180. doi:10.1080/20932685.2016.1166715

Caracalla, J.-P. (1989). *Le Roman du Printemps: Histoire d'un grand magasin* (p. 167). Paris: Denoël.

Carlisle, S., Kunc, M., Jones, E., & Tiffin, S. (2013). Supporting innovation for tourism development through multi-stakeholder approaches: Experiences from Africa. *Tourism Management, 35*, 59–69. doi:10.1016/j.tourman.2012.05.010

Cartner-Morley, J. (2018, May 29). Louis Vuitton's cruise show: Sculptural silhouettes and iconoclasm. The Guardian. Retrieved from https://www.theguardian.com/fashion/2018/may/29/louis-vuitton-cruise-show-sculptural-silhouettes-iconoclasm

Casais, B., & Gomes, L. R. (2022). Fashion bloggers' discourse on brands under corporate crisis: A netnographic research in Portugal. *Journal of Fashion Marketing and Management: International Journal, 26*(3), 420–435. doi:10.1108/JFMM-09-2020-0206

Casciato, M., & Poretti, S. (2002). *Ll Palazzo della Civiltà Italiana: Architettura e costruzione del Colosseo Quadrato*. Milano: Federico Motta.

Cater, C. (2006). Looking the part: The relationship between adventure tourism and the outdoor fashion industry. In *Taking tourism to the limits* (pp. 179–188). Routledge. doi:10.1016/B978-0-08-044644-8.50017-5

Caves, R. (2000). *Creative industries: Contacts between art and commerce*. Cambridge, MA: Harvard University Press.

Cayla, J., & Arnould, E. J. (2008). A cultural approach to branding in the global marketplace. *Journal of International Marketing*, *16*(4), 86–112. doi:10.1509/jimk.16.4.86

Cazes, G. (1997). Le tourisme urbain. *L'urbanisme*, *296*, 48–53.

Cerisola, S. (2018). Creativity and local economic development: The role of synergy among different talents. *Papers in Regional Science*, *97*(2), 199–215. doi:10.1111/pirs.12254

Chabrol, M. (2011). De nouvelles formes de gentrification? Dynamiques résidentielles et commerciales dans le quartier de Château-Rouge (Paris), Unpublished PhD thesis. University of Poitiers. Retrieved from https://tel.archives-ouvertes.fr/tel-00658852

Chabrol, M. translated by Waine, O. (2013). Château Rouge: A "Little Africa" in Paris? The users and usages of a migrant commercial centrality. Metropolitics. Retrieved from https://metropolitics.org/Chateau-Rouge-a-Little-Africa-in-Paris.html

Chahine, V. (2017, May 20). *La collection croisière se doit d'être un spectacle fantastique*. M Le Magazine du Monde. Retrieved from https://www.lemonde.fr/m-mode/article/2017/05/25/la-collection-croisiere-se-doit-d-etre-un-spectacle-fantastique_5133820_4497335.html

Chahine, V. (2020, March 13). *La mode métissée de Château Rouge*. Les Echos. Retrieved from https://www.lesechos.fr/weekend/mode-beaute/la-mode-metissee-de-chateau-rouge-1213968

Chalkely, B., & Essex, S. (1999). Urban development through hosting international events: A history of the Olympic Game. *Planning Perspectives*, *14*(4), 369–394. doi:10.1080/026654399364184

Chambers, E. (1997). *Tourism and culture: An applied perspective*. Albany: SUNY Press.

Chambers, E. (2009). *Native tours: The anthropology of travel and tourism*. Long Grove, IL: Waveland Press.

Chamusca, P., Rio Fernandes, J., Carvalho, L., & Mendes, T. (2019). The role of Airbnb creating a "new"-old city centre: Facts, problems and controversies in Porto. *Boletín de la Asociación de Geógrafos Españoles*, *83*, 1–30.

Chan, A., Alexandri, M., & Tresna, P. (2019). Place brand experience of Bandung City as UNESCO's creative city network in city economy development. *Review of Integrative Business and Economics Research*, *8*, 225–238.

Chaney, D. (1983). The department store as a cultural form. *Theory, Culture & Society*, *1*(3), 22–31. doi:10.1177/026327648300100303

Chapuis, A., & Jacquot, S. (2014). Le touriste, le migrant et la fable cosmopolite Mettre en tourisme les présences migratoires à Paris. Homme & Migrations. *Le Paris des Migrants*, *1308*, 75–84. doi:10.4000/hommesmigrations.2999

Chatriot, A., & Chessel, M. (2006). *L'histoire de la distribution: Un chantier inachevé. Histoire, économie et société* (pp. 67–82). Paris: Armand Colin. doi:10.3917/hes.061.0067

Chell, E., & Baines, S. (2000). Networking, entrepreneurship and microbusiness. *Entrepreneurship & Regional Development*, *12*, 195–215. doi:10.1080/089856200413464

Chetioui, Y., Benlafqih, H., & Lebdaoui, H. (2020). How fashion influencers contribute to consumers' purchase intention. *Journal of Fashion Marketing and Management: International Journal*, *24*(3), 361–380. doi:10.1108/JFMM-08-2019-0157

Childs, M., & Jung, E. (2018, January). Modern product placement: An understanding of consumers' responses to fashion brand advertisements featuring a destination In *International textile and apparel association annual conference proceedings*. Iowa State University Digital Press.

Chin, M. (2019, September 17). *Palace's Juventus x Adidas Football collab is dropping this week*. Hypebeast. Retrieved from https://hypebeast.com/2019/11/palace-skateboards-winter-2019-week-six-drop-list-juventus-adidas-football-collaboration

Choi, J., & Kim, M. (2019). Sneakerhead brand community netnography: An exploratory research. *Fashion, Style & Popular Culture*, *6*(2), 141–158. doi:10.1386/fspc.6.2.141_1

Choi, M., Law, R., & Heo, C. (2017). An investigation of the perceived value of shopping tourism. *Journal of Travel Research*, *57*(7), 962–980. doi:10.1177/0047287517726170

Christopher, M., Payne, A., & Ballantyne, D. (2013). *Relationship marketing*. Routledge. doi:10.4324/9780080516042

Clean BnB. (2022, January 3). *Airbnb Milano: Più della metà degli appartamenti affittabili è su Airbnb*. Cleanbnb.net. Retrieved from https://www.cleanbnb.net/airbnb-milano/

Coccia, E., & Grau, D. (2018). *Le Musée transitoire: Sur 10 Corso Como*. Klincksieck.

Cocola-Gant, A. (2018). Struggling with the leisure class: Tourism, gentrification and displacement. PhD Thesis| School of Geography and Planning. Cardiff: Cardiff University.

Codignola, F., & Rancati, E. (2016). The blending of luxury fashion brands and contemporary art: A global strategy for value creation. In A. Vecchi & C. Buckley (Eds.), *Handbook of research on global fashion management and merchandising* (pp. 50–76). Hershey, PA: IGI Global. doi:10.4018/978-1-5225-0110-7.ch003

Coëffé, V., & Morice, J. (2019). *Du grand magasin au «grand» site touristique ou le paradigme des Galeries Lafayette Haussmann (Paris)*. EspacesTemps.net.

Coëffé, V., & Morice, J. (2020). The Parisian department store as a paradigmatic place for interactions between tourism and shopping: The production of a heterotopia, Belgeo. *Revue Belge de Geographie*, *1*.

Cohen, E. (1979). A Phenomenology of tourist experiences. *Sociology, the Journal of the British Sociological Association*, *13*(2), 179–201. doi:10.1177/003803857901300203

Cohen, E. (1987). Alternative tourism. A critique. *Tourism Recreation Research*, *12*(2), 13–18. doi:10.1080/02508281.1987.11014508

Cohen, E. (1988). Authenticity and commoditization in tourism. *Annals of Tourism Research*, *15*, 371–386. doi:10.1016/0160-7383(88)90028-X

Comune di Milano. (2018). *Imposta di soggiorno: Numero complessivo delle strutture ricettive*. Retrieved from https://dati.comune.milano.it/dataset/ds477-imposta-di-soggiorno-numero-complessivo-strutture-ricettive. Accessed on August 28, 2023.

Comune di Milano. (2021). *Imposta di soggiorno: Numero complessivo delle strutture ricettive*. Retrieved from https://dati.comune.milano.it/dataset/ds477-imposta-di-soggiorno-numero-complessivo-strutture-ricettive. Accessed on August 28, 2023.

Conchoy, F. (2011). *De la curiosité. L'art de la séduction marchande*. Paris, Armand Colin.

Condevaux, A., Gravari-Barbas, M., & Guinand, S. (2021). *Tourism dynamics in everyday places: Before and after tourism*. Oxon; New York, NY: Routledge.

Conlin, J. (2000). Le 'Musée de marchandises' the origins of the Musée Cognacq-Jay. *Journal of the History of Collections*, *12*(2), 193–202. doi:10.1093/jhc/12.2.193

Connell, J. (1994). Repositioning Forte Hotels Portfolio. *English Tourist Board Insights*, *5*, 43–51.

Connell, J. (2013). Contemporary medical tourism: Conceptualisation, culture and commodification. *Tourism Management*, *34*, 1–13. doi:10.1016/j.tourman.2012.05.009

Conty, H. (1863). Guide pratique de l'étranger dans Paris et ses environs: Paris en poche, Paris, Faure (p. 184).

Corbin, A. (2018). *Le territoire du vide: L'Occident et le désir de rivage*. Paris: Flammarion.

Corneo, G., & Jeanne, O. (1999). Segmented communication and fashionable behavior. *Journal of Economic Behavior & Organization*, *39*(4), 371–385. doi:10.1016/S0167-2681(99)00046-3

Correia, A., Kozak, M., & Kim, S. (2019). Investigation of luxury values in shopping tourism using a fuzzy-set approach. *Journal of Travel Research*, *58*(1), 77–91. doi:10.1177/0047287517741005

Costantini, V. (2018, June 17). Eur, «Sea life» è ancora un cantiere: L'acquario mai aperto compie 10 anni. Roma.corriere.it. Retrieved from https://roma.corriere.it/notizie/cronaca/18_giugno_17/dorso-rm-4-testocorriere-web-roma-5a1bd400-718c-11e8-8802-e09859fdb268.shtml

Craik, J. (2013). Fashion, tourism and global culture. In R. Root, S. Black, H. Thomas, A. Rocamora, J. Entwistle, & A. de la Haye (Eds.), *The handbook of fashion studies* (pp. 364–380). London: Bloomsbury Academic.

Crane, D., & Bovone, L. (2006). Approaches to material culture: The sociology of fashion and clothing. *Poetics*, *34*, 319–333. doi:10.1016/j.poetic.2006.10.002

Crash Magazine. (2021, June 18). Dior Cruise 2022. Crash Magazine. Retrieved from https://www.crash.fr/dior-cruise-2022/

Crewe, L. (2000). Geographies of retailing and consumption. *Progress in Human Geography*, *24*(2), 275–290. doi:10.1191/030913200670386318

Crewe, L. (2017). *The geographies of fashion: Consumption, space, and value*. London: Bloomsbury Publishing.

Crewe, L., & Beaverstock, J. (1998). Fashioning the city: Culture of consumption in the contemporary. *Geoforum*, *29*, 287–308. doi:10.1016/S0016-7185(98)00015-3

Crompton, J. (1979). Motivations for pleasure vacation. *Annals of Tourism Research*, *6*(4), 408–224. doi:10.1016/0160-7383(79)90004-5

Crouch, D., & Lübbren, N. (2003). *Visual culture and tourism*. New York, NY: Bloomsbury USA Academic.

Cui, Y., Thrash, T., Shkeyrov, R., & Varga, P. (2020). Inspiration in the creative process. *Encyclopedia of Creativity*, *1*, 660–666. doi:10.1016/B978-0-12-809324-5.23840-6

Cunningham, M. (2021). *Social spaces, tourism, instagrammability, and authenticity: The phenomenon of eccentric and aesthetic cosmopolitan-style coffee shops in Chiang Mai, Thailand*. William & Mary Scholar works.

D'Albergo, E., Moini, G., & Pizzo, B. (2018). Il negoziato sullo stadio dell'AS ROMA: Elementi di discontinuità nel regime urbano. In A. Coppola & G. Punziano (Eds.), *Roma in transizione: Governo, strategie, metabolismi e quadri di vita di una metropoli* (pp. 183–193). Roma: Planum Publisher.

D'Amato, A., & Petti, D. (2008). *Lady ASL: La casta della sanità: Fatti e misfatti*. Roma: Editori Riuniti.

D'Albergo, E., & Moini, G. (2015). *Il regime dell'urbe. Politica, economia e potere a Roma*. Roma: Carrocci.

Dallabona, A. (2017). The challenges of luxury fashion flagship hotels: The case of Maison Moschino. *Critical Studies in Fashion & Beauty*, *8*(2), 219–237. doi:10.1386/csfb.8.2.219_1

Danto, A. (1997). *After the end of art*. Princeton, NJ: Princeton University Press.

Davis, F. (1994). *Fashion, culture and indentity*. Chicago, IL: University of Chicago Press.

De Andia, B. (2006). *Les cathédrales du commerce parisien: Grands magasins et enseignes*. Action Artistique Ville Paris.

De Ascaniis, S., & Cantoni, L. (2022). *Handbook on heritage, sustainable tourism and digital media*. Edward Elgar Publishing. doi:10.4337/9781788970082

De Ascaniis, S., & Gretzel, U. (2013). Communicative functions of online travel review titles: A pragmatic and linguistic investigation of destination and attraction OTR titles. *Studies in Communication Sciences*, *13*(2), 156–165. doi:10.1016/j.scoms.2013.11.001

De Perthuis, K., & Findlay, R. (2019). How fashion travels: The fashionable ideal in the age of Instagram. *Fashion Theory*, *23*(2), 219–242. doi:10.1080/1362704X.2019.1567062

DeAcetis, J. (2021). *The Fastest Ferrari menswear style from the Spring 2022 collections*. Forbes. Retrieved from www.forbes.com/sites/josephdeacetis/2021/07/10/the-fastest-ferrari-menswear-style-from-the-spring-2022-collections/

Dedet, F., & Simon, P. (2019, November 21). Carnets de Croisière. Les Echos -Série Limitée.

Deeb-Swihart, J., Polack, C., Gilbert, E., & Essa, I. (2017). Selfie-presentation in everyday life: A large-scale characterization of selfie contexts on Instagram. *Proceedings of the International AAAI Conference on Web and Social Media*, *11*(1), 42–51.

Deeny, G. (2021, June 21). *Maria Grazia Chiuri on her metaphysical-mode Cruise Collection for Dior*. Fashion Magazine. Retrieved from https://ww.fashionnetwork.com/news/Maria-grazia-chiuri-on-her-metaphysical-mode-cruise-collection-for-dior,1311743.html

Delaplace, M., & Gravari-Barbas, M. (2016). Aux marges du tourisme: Utopies et réalités du tourisme hors des sentiers battus. *Via Tourism Review*, *9*. doi:10.4000/viatourism.417

Délégation à la Politique de la ville et à l'Intégration. (2013). Les fiches d'expérience de Pôle Ressources: Développer la filière mode et design à la Goutte-d'Or. Retrieved from http://i.ville.gouv.fr/index.php/reference/9006/les-fiches-d-experience-du-pole-ressources-developper-la-filiere-mode-et-design-a-la-goutte-d-or

Della Porta, D., & Vannucci, A. (2007). *Mani impunite. Vecchia e nuova corruzione in Italia*. Roma: Laterza.

Demirović, D., & Pivac, T. (2013). Belgrade (Serbia) as an alternative site or city of fashion tourism. *European Researcher*, *12*(2), 2882–2891.

Deng, Z., Benckendorff, P., & Wang, J. (2022). From interaction to relationship: Rethinking parasocial phenomena in travel live streaming. *Tourism Management*, *93*, 104583. doi:10.1016/j.tourman.2022.104583

Denis, G., & Reali, M. (2017, June 02). *Quand la mode part en croisière*. Paris: Les Echos Week-End.

Denissa, L., Widodo, P., Adisasmito, N., & Piliang, Y. (2015). Public Engagement and the making of Carnaval's Place at Jember Fashion Carnaval. *Procedia-Social and Behavioral Sciences*, *184*, 95–103. doi:10.1016/j.sbspro.2015.05.061

Di Giangirolamo, G. (2018). The State Funding programme for Haute Couture in Paris – Defending and promoting a Tradition (1952–1960). In D. Calanca (Ed.), *The fashion, culture and society notebook 2018*. Pearson Italia.

Di Giangirolamo, G. (2020). *Istituzioni della moda. Interventi tra pubblico e privato in Italia e Francia (1945–1965)*. Bruno Mondadori.

Di Giangirolamo, G., & Mariotti, A. (2021). Fashion and tourism in transition. *ZoneModa Journal*, *11*(2), V–VIII. doi:10.6092/issn.2611-0563/14013

Dictionary. (2021, June 08). *Drop culture*. Dictionary. Retrieved from https://www.dictionary.com/e/fashion/drop-culture/

Diderich, J. (2019, April 30). *Dior Cruise 2020*. WWD. Retrieved from https://wwd.com/runway/resort-2020/all/christian-dior/review

Diderich, J. (2020, July 22). *Dior Cruise 2021*. WWD. Retrieved from https://wwd.com/runway/resort-2021/all/christian-dior/review/

Diderich, J. (2021, June 17). *Dior Cruise 2022*. WWD. Retrieved from https://wwd.com/runway/resort-2022/all/christian-dior/review/

Dinhopl, A., & Gretzel, U. (2015). Changing practices/new technologies: Photos and videos on vacation. In I. Tussyadiah & A. Inversini (Eds.), *Information and communication technologies in tourism 2015* (pp. 777–788). Berlin: Springer Verlag. doi:10.1007/978-3-319-14343-9_56

Dinhopl, A., & Gretzel, U. (2016). Selfie-taking as touristic looking. *Annals of Tourism Research*, *57*, 126–139. doi:10.1016/j.annals.2015.12.015

Dion, D., & Arnould, E. (2011). Retail luxury strategy: Assembling charisma through art and magic. *Journal of Retailing*, *87*(4), 502–520. doi:10.1016/j.jretai.2011.09.001

Dirion, P. (1926). *La deuxième exposition d'art ancien à la Samaritaine, La Renaissance de l'art français et des industries du luxe* (p. 294). May.

Dolivo, N. (2019, May 10). *Contes d'effets*. Elle.

Dubois, B., & Duquesne, P. (1993). The market for luxury goods: Income versus culture. *European Journal of Marketing*. doi:10.1108/03090569310024530

Duffy, B. E., & Hund, E. (2015). "Having it all" on social media: Entrepreneurial femininity and self-branding among fashion bloggers. *Social Media + Society*, *1*(2). doi:10.1177/2056305115604337

Duhamel, P., & Knafou, R. (2007). Le tourisme dans la centralité parisienne. La métropole parisienne. *Centralités, inégalités, proximités*, 39–64.

Dupuis, M. (2018, June 08). *Hymne au réalisme magique*. Madame Figaro. Retrieved from https://www.pressreader.com/france/madame-figaro/20180608/281522226783837

EBTL. (2015). *Rapporto annuale – Roma – Distribuzione degli arrivi e delle presenze negli alberghi per Municipi*. Roma: EBTL Press.

EBTL. (2016). *Rapporto annuale – Roma – Distribuzione degli arrivi e delle presenze negli alberghi per Municipi*. Roma: EBTL Press.

EBTL. (2017). *Rapporto annuale – Roma – Distribuzione degli arrivi e delle presenze negli alberghi per Municipi*. Roma: EBTL Press.

EBTL. (2018). *Rapporto annuale – Roma – Distribuzione degli arrivi e delle presenze negli alberghi per Municipi*. Roma: EBTL Press.

Eco, U. (s.d., probably 1971). L'abito parla il monaco. *Psicologia del vestire. Novara*. Co Gritti S.P.A.

Edensor, T. (2001). Performing tourism, staging tourism, (re)producing tourist space and practice. *Tourist Studies*, *1*, 59–81. doi:10.1177/146879760100100104

Eiland, H. (Trans.). (2006). *On Hashish. Walter Benjamin*. Cambridge, MA & London: The Belknap Press of Harvard University Press.

Eiland, H., & McLaughlin, K. (2002). *The arcades project*. Cambridge, MA and London: The Belknap Press of Harvard University Press. Trans. from Rolf Tiedemann, R. (1983). Walter Benjamin, Das Passagen-Werk. Frankfurt, Germany: Suhrkamp.

Elbanna, A. R. (2009). Actor-network theory in ICT research. *International Journal of Actor-Network Theory and Technological Innovation*, *1*(3), 1–14. doi:10.4018/jantti.2009070101

Elias, N., & Dunning, E. (1986–1994). Sport et civilization. La violence maîtrisée, Paris, Fayard.

Entwistle, J., & Rocamora, A. (2006). The field of fashion materialized: A study of London Fashion Week. *Sociology*, *40*(4), 735–751. doi:10.1177/003803850606

Enzensberger, H. (1996). A theory of tourism. *New German Critique*, *68*, 117–135.

ETICity. (2018). Paesaggi storici urbani in cambiamento: Il caso di Ostiense. In A. Coppola & G. Punziano (Eds.), *Roma in transizione* (pp. 261–274). Roma: Planum Publisher.

Euromonitor International. (2021, June 29). *Fashion Friday: Global Apparel in 2019 and beyond*. Retrieved from https://blog.euromonitor.com/podcast/fashion-friday-global-apparel-in-2019-and-beyond/

Evans, G. (2003). Hard-branding the cultural city – From Prado to Prada. *International Journal of Urban and Regional Research*, *27*(2), 417–440. doi:10.1111/1468-2427.00455

Farsani, N. T., & Jamshidi, H. M. (2021). An investigation of the positive impacts of traditional fashion tourism. *Journal of Policy Research in Tourism, Leisure and Events*, *13*(3), 298–313. doi:10.1080/19407963.2020.1808004

Fashion United. (2021). *Global fashion industry statistics*. Fashion United. Retrieved from https://fashionunited.com/global-fashion-industry-statistics

Faure, E. (2019, May 02). *Dior célèbre le "made in Africa"*. Le Figaro. Retrieved from https://www.lefigaro.fr/style/la-croisiere-dior-celebre-le-made-in-africa-20190501

Faure, E. (2020, July 24). A mes yeux, rien ne saurait remplacer un vrai défilé. Interview de Maria Grazia Chiuri. Le Figaro.

Femenia-Serra, F., Gretzel, U., & Alzua-Sorzabal, A. (2022). Instagram travel influencers in# quarantine: Communicative practices and roles during COVID-19. *Tourism Management*, *89*, 104454. doi:10.1016/j.tourman.2021.104454

Ferrero-Regis, T., & Lindquist, M. (2020). *Staging the fashion show and its spaces* (Vol. 1). Staging Fashion: The Fashion Show and Its Spaces.

Fiano, F. (2017, September 15). *Nuvola di Fuksas, Eur spa deve pagare altri 53 milioni di euro*. Roma.corriere.it. Retrieved from https://roma.corriere.it/notizie/cronaca/17_settembre_14/nuvola-fuksas-eur-deve-pagare-altri-53-milioni-euro-857abea0-9987-11e7-a6df-3caa5bfe0dde.shtml

Financial Times. (2022). *Loss of Chinese tourists forces Europe's luxury retailers to rethink*. Retrieved from https://www.ft.com/content/f1cefbbc-fa3b-403f-b04c-d59060ed92e2

Fitzgerald, F. (1934). *Tender is the night*. Harrap's.

Fletcher, K. (2008). *Sustainable fashion and textiles. Design journeys*. London: Earthscan.

Florek, M. (2005). The country brand as a new challenge for Poland. *Place Branding*, *1*, 205–214. doi:10.1057/palgrave.pb.5990021

Florida, R. (2002). *The rise of the creative class and how it's transforming work, leisure, community and everyday life*. New York, NY: Basic Books.

Florida, R. (2003). Cities and the creative class. *City & Community*, *2*(1), 3–19. doi:10.1111/1540-6040.00034

Flugel, J. (1930). *The psychology of clothes*. London: Hogarth.

Foucault, M. (1967/2008). Of other spaces. In L. de Cauter & M. Dehaene (Eds., Trans.), *Heterotopia and the city: Public space in a postcivil society*. New York, NY and London: Routledge.

Fournier, S., & Alvarez, C. (2012). Brands as relationship partners: Warmth, competence, and in-between. *Journal of Consumer Psychology*, *22*(2), 177–185. doi:10.1016/j.jcps.2011.10.003

Fournier, S., & Alvarez, C. (2019). How brands acquire cultural meaning. *Journal of Consumer Psychology*, *29*(3), 519–534. doi:10.1002/jcpy.1119

Fowler, D. (2018, June 09). Streetwear brands are using scarcity and social media hype to supercharge the traditional supply-and-demand model – And fuelling a remarkably lucrative resale industry in the process. BBC. Retrieved from https://www.bbc.com/worklife/article/20180205-the-hype-machine-streetwear-and-the-business-of-scarcity

Freytag, T. (2008). Making a difference: Tourist practices of repeat visitors in the city of Paris. *Social Geography Discussions*, *4*(1). doi:10.5194/sgd-4-1-2008

Freytag, T., & Bauder, M. (2018). Bottom-up touristification and urban transformations in Paris. *Tourism Geographies*, *20*(3). Tourism and urban planning in European cities: Overtourism, Placemaking and Heritage, 443–460. doi:10.1080/14616688.2018.1454504

Friedman, V. (2015, November 18). *Embracing French art and fashion as a counter-attack*. New York Times.

Frisch, T., Sommer, C., Stoltenberg, L., & Stors, N. (2019). *Tourism and everyday life in the contemporary city*. London: Routledge.

Frochot, I., & Batat, W. (2013). *Marketing and designing the tourist experience*. Oxford: Goodfellow Publishers Ltd.

Fuchs, M., Fossgard, K., Stensland, S., & Chekalina, T. (2021). Creativity and innovation in nature-based tourism: A critical reflection and empirical assessment. In *Nordic perspectives on nature-based tourism* (pp. 175–193). Edward Elgar Publishing. doi:10.4337/9781789904031.00022

Fullagar, S., & Markwell, K. (2012). *Slow tourism: Experiences and mobilities*. Channel View Publications. doi:10.21832/9781845412821

Füller, H., & Michel, B. (2014). 'Stop being a tourist!' New Dynamics of urban tourism in Berlin-Kreuzberg. *International Journal of Urban and Regional Research*, *38*(4), 1304–1318. doi:10.1111/1468-2427.12124

Fung, J., MacAusland, C., & Chang Mazza, G. (2012). *Louis Vuitton and the Traveling Chinese Consumer*. Retrieved from https://knowledge.wharton.upenn.edu/article/louis-vuitton-and-the-traveling-chinese-consumer/

Fuster, L. F. (1967). *Teoría y técnica del turismo*. Madrid: Editora Nacional.

Gainsforth, S. (2019). *Airbnb città merce: Storie di resistenza alla gentrificazione digitale*. Roma: Derive Approdi.

Gallione, A. (2022, January 5). *Scalo Romana, oltre città studi e a sud della Bocconi: Ecco i quartieri di Milano dove la casa diventa un affare*. Repubblica. Retrieved from https://milano.repubblica.it/cronaca/2022/01/05/news/scalo_romana_oltre_citta_studi_e_a_sud_della_bocconi_ecco_i_quartieri_di_milano_dove_la_casa_diventa_un_affare-332668895/

García, J. A., Gómez, M., & Molina, A. (2012). A destination-branding model: An empirical analysis based on stakeholders. *Tourism Management*, *33*(3), 646–661. doi:10.1016/j.tourman.2011.07.006

Garrabos, M. (2018, May 31). *Le défilé Gucci enflamme les Alyscamps*. Arles Info. Retrieved from https://www.arles-info.fr/2018/05/31/le-defile-gucci-enflamme-les-alyscamps/

Gartner, W. (1993). Image formation process, communication and channel systems. In M. Uysal & D. Fesenmaier (Eds.), *Tourism marketing* (pp. 191–215). New York, NY: The Hawotrh Press Inc.

Garuda, M. (2020). *Indonesian ministry of finance bulletin on iWareBatik initiative*. Retrieved from https://matagaruda.org/2020/09/27/iwarebatik-cara-anak-muda-menjaga-warisan-budaya/

Geczy, A., & Karaminas, V. (2013). *Fashion and art*. London: Berg.

Getz, D. (1994). Event tourism and the authenticity dilemma. In W. Theobald (Ed.), *Global tourism: The next decade* (pp. 313–329). Oxford: Butterworth-Heinemann.

Getz, D. (2008). Event tourism: Definition, evolution, and research. *Tourism Management*, *29*, 403–428. doi:10.1016/j.tourman.2007.07.017

Ghidouche, K., & Ghidouche, F. (2019). Community-based ecotourism for preventing overtourism and tourismophobia: Algerian associations' viewpoints. *Worldwide Hospitality and Tourism Themes*, *11*(5), 516–531. doi:10.1108/WHATT-06-2019-0035

Gholamhosseinzadeh, M., Chapuis, J., & Lehu, J. (2021). Tourism netnography: How travel bloggers influence destination image. *Tourism Recreation Research*, 1–17. doi:10.1080/02508281.2021.1911274

Gibson, E., & Firth, B. (2005). *The original million dollar mermaid: The Annette Kellerman Story*. Sydney: Allen & Unwin.

Gieryn, T. (2000). A space for place in sociology. *Annual Review of Sociology*, *26*(1), 463–496. doi:10.1146/annurev.soc.26.1.463

Giffard, P. (1882). *Paris sous la Troisième République, Les grands bazars* (pp. 12–14). Paris: Paris sous la Troisième République.

Gilbert, D. (2000). Urban outfitting: The city and the spaces of fashion culture. In S. Bruzzi & P. Church-Gibson (Eds.), *Fashion cultures* (pp. 7–24). London: Routledge.

Gilbert, D. (2006). From Paris to Shanghai: The changing geographies of fashion's world cities. In C. Breward & D. Gilbert (Eds.), *Fashion's world cities*. Berg. doi:10.2752/9780857854117

Gilbert, D. (2019). *Paris, New York, London, Milan: Paris and a world order of fashion capitals* (pp. 73–91). Paris: Capital of Fashion.

Gilbert, D., & Casadei, P. (2020). The hunting of the fashion city: Rethinking the relationship between fashion and the urban in the twenty-first century. *Fashion Theory*, *24*(3), 393–408. doi:10.1080/1362704X.2020.1732023

Gillespie, K. (2019). *What the ideal Instagram influencer looks like*. Retrieved from https://www.papermag.com/the-face-of-influence-2639356208.html

Giusti, N. (2009). Introduzione allo studio della moda. *Il Mulino*.

Glaser, B. (1978). *Theoretical sensitivity: Advances in the methodology of grounded theory*. Mill Valley: Sociology Press.

Gnoth, J. (2007). The structure of destination brands: Leveraging values. *Tourism Analysis*, *12*(5–6), 345–358. doi:10.3727/108354207783227939

Godart, F. (2010a). *Sociologie de la mode*. Paris: Editions la Découverte.

Godart, F. (2010b). *Sociologie de la mode*. La Découverte.

Godey, B., Pederzoli, D., Aiello, G., Donvito, R., Chan, P., Oh, H., … Weitz, B. (2010). Interactions between Country of Origin (COO) and brand on consumer behaviour: An international research investigation on luxury brands in 7 Countries. *Marketing Trends-Venezia*, 1–23.

Goerner, D. (1986). *Woven structure and design. Part 1: Single cloth construction*. Wira Technology Group.

Goffman, E. (1959/1990). Front and back regions of everyday life. In Goffman, E. (Ed.), *The presentation of self in everyday life*. Harmondsworth: Penguin.

Goodrum, A. (2009). True Brits? Authoring national identity in Anglo-Japanese fashion exports. *Fashion Theory: The Journal of Dress, Body & Culture*, *13*(4), 461–480. doi:10.2752/175174109X467486

Google. (2014). *The 2014 Traveler's Road to Decision. Think with Google*. Retrieved from www.thinkwithgoogle.com/consumer-insights/consumer-trends/2014-travelers-road-to-decision/

Gopaldas, A. (2016). Therapy. *Consumption, Markets and Culture*, *19*(3), 264–268. doi:10.1080/10253866.2015.1096070

Gorse, S., Chadwick, S., & Burton, N. (2010). Entrepreneurship through sports marketing: A case analysis of Red Bull in Sport. *Journal of Sponsorship*, *3*(4), 348–357.

Gorsuch, A., & Koenker, D. (2006). *Turizm: The Russian and East European tourist under capitalism and socialism*. Ithaca, NY: Cornell University Press.

Gosden, E. (2021, June 8). *Why fast fashion could be set for go-slow*. The Times. Retrieved from https://www.thetimes.co.uk/article/why-fast-fashion-could-be-set-for-go-slow-3vf580cgm

Goss, J. (1993). The "magic of the mall": An analysis of form, function, and meaning in the contemporary retail-built environment. *Annals of the Association of American Geographers*, *83*(1), 18–47. doi:10.1111/j.1467-8306.1993.tb01921.x

Gotham, K. (2005). Tourism gentrification: The case of New Orleans' vieux carré (French Quarter). *Urban Studies*, *42*(7), 1099–1121.

Govers, R., Go, F., & Kumar, K. (2007). Promoting tourism destination image. *Journal of Travel Research*, *46*(1), 15–23. doi:10.1177/0047287507302374

Graburn, N. (2001/2010). Secular ritual: A general theory of tourism. In S. B. Gmelch & A. Kaul (Eds.), *Tourists and tourism: A reader*. Long Grove, IL: Waveland Press.

Gralak, K. (2018). *Tourism gentrification as a symptom of an unsustainable development* (pp. 197–212). Problemy Zarzadzania.

Granskog, A., Lobis, M., & Magnus, K. (2020, February 3). *The future of sustainable fashion*. Mckinsey. Retrieved from https://www.mckinsey.com/industries/retail/our-insights/the-future-of-sustainable-fashion

Gravari-Barbas, M. (2009). La «ville festive» ou construire la ville contemporaine par l'événement. (The 'Festival City': Urban events and contemporary city building). *Bulletin de l'Association de Geographes Français*, *86*(3), 279–290. doi:10.3406/bagf.2009.2673

Gravari-Barbas, M. (2015). Interview with S. Burjat, Téoros (online). *34*, 1–2. Accessed on August 9, 2022.

Gravari-Barbas, M. (2017a). Architecture, musées, tourisme. La guerre des marques. *Revista de Arquitectura*, *20*(1), 102–114. doi:10.14718/RevArq.2010.20.1.1573

Gravari-Barbas, M. (2017b). Super-gentrification and hyper-tourismification in Le Marais, Paris. In M. Gravari-Barbas & S. Guinand (Eds.), *Tourism and gentrification in contemporary metropolises. International perspectives* (pp. 1–21). London: Routledge.

Gravari-Barbas, M. (2017c). Tourisme de marges, marges du tourisme. Lieux ordinaires et "no-go zones" à l'épreuve du tourisme. [Tourism at the margins, margins of tourism. Ordinary places and "no-go zones" challenged by tourism]. Bulletin de l'association de géographes français. *Géographies*, *94*(3), 400–418. doi:10.4000/bagf.2097

Gravari-Barbas, M. (2019). What makes Paris being Paris? Stereotypes, simulacra and tourism imaginaries. *Journal of Tourism and Cultural Change*, *17*(1), 27–41. doi:10.1080/14766825.2019.1560765

Gravari-Barbas, M. (2020). Star architecture and the boundaries of tourism: The case of Paris. In N. Alaily-Mattar, D. Ponzini, & A. Thierstein (Eds.), *About star architecture: Reflecting on cities in Europe* (pp. 203–226). New York, NY: Springer.

Gravari-Barbas, M., & Delaplace, M. (2015). Le tourisme urbain 'hors des sentiers battus'. Coulisses, interstices et nouveaux territoires urbains. *Téoros*, *34*, 1–2.

Gravari-Barbas, M., & Graburn, N. (2011). Imagined landscapes of tourism. *Journal of Tourism and Cultural Change (JTCC)*, *9*(3), 159–166. doi:10.1080/14766825.2011.640490

Gravari-Barbas, M., & Graburn, N. (2012). Tourist imaginaries. Via. *Tourism Review*, (1). doi:10.4000/viatourism.1188

Gravari-Barbas, M., & Guinand, S. (2017). *Tourism and gentrification in contemporary metropolises. International perspectives*. London: Routledge/Taylor and Francis.

Gravari-Barbas, M., & Jacquot, S. (2013). Patrimoine, tourisme et développement en banlieue. *Les Cahiers de l'IAU (Institut d'aménagement et d'urbanisme)*, *167*, 65–67.

Gravari-Barbas, M., & Renard-Delautre, C. (2015). *Stararchitecture(s): Figures d'architectes et espace urbain*. Paris: Editions l'Harmanattan.

Gravette, P. (2021, June 9). *Hype culture and the power of branding*. Paul Gravette. Retrieved from https://www.paulgravette.com/blog-1/hype-culture-and-the-power-of-branding

Gregory, D. (1994). *Geographical imaginations*. Oxford: Blackwell.

Gretzel, U. (2018). Influencer marketing in travel and tourism. In M. Sigala & U. Gretzel (Eds.), *Advances in social media for travel, tourism and hospitality: New perspectives, practice and cases* (pp. 147–156). New York, NY: Routledge. doi:10.4324/9781315565736

Gretzel, U. (2022). The perpetual traveler–hypermobility in a connected world. In R. Llamas & R. Belk (Eds.), *The routledge handbook of digital consumption* (pp. 351–361). New York, NY: Routledge. doi:10.4324/9781003317524

Gretzel, U., Fuchs, M., Baggio, R., Hoepken, W., Law, R., Neidhardt, J., & Xiang, Z. (2020). e-Tourism beyond COVID-19: A call for transformative research. *Information Technology & Tourism*, *22*, 187–203. doi:10.1007/s40558-020-00181-3

Gretzel, U., & Yoo, K. (2008). Use and impact of online travel reviews. In *Information and communication technologies in tourism 2008* (pp. 35–46). Vienna: Springer. doi:10.1007/978-3-211-77280-5_4

Guerreiro, C., Viegas, M., & Guerreiro, M. (2019). Social networks and digital influencers: Their role in customer decision journey in tourism. *Journal of Spatial and Organizational Dynamics*, *7*(3), 240–260.

Guerzoni, G. (2014). Designing Museums in the 21st century. A matter of responsibility. In G. Guerzoni (Ed.), *Museums on the Map 1995–2012* (pp. 15–85). Torino: Allemandi.

Guide de l'étranger dans Paris et ses environs: Illustré de 130 gravures sur bois d'après les dessins de A. de Bar, H. Clerget, Deroy, G. Doré, Lancelot, Marie, Thérond, Thiollet. (1874). (Paris, Hôtel du Louvre).

Guide général dans Paris pour 1855 suivi d'une visite à l'Exposition. (1855). (p. 121). Paris: Wiesener.

Guilbault, L. (2016, September 7). *Paris Unveils 'La Mode Aime Paris' Campaign*. Women's Wear Daily.

Guillaume, H. (2018, April 18). De Château Rouge à l'Élysée, le succès fulgurant de Youssouf Fofana. Madame Figaro. Retrieved from https://madame.lefigaro.fr/style/maison-chateau-rouge-son-succes-lui-ouvre-les-portes-de-lelysee-190418-148307

Gumbrecht, H. (2004). *Production of presence, what meaning cannot convey*. Stanford, CA: Stanford University Press.

Hadi, D. (2022). *Danar Hadi World*. Retrieved from https://danarhadibatik.com/id/danar-hadi-world

Hagtvedt, H., & Patrick, V. (2008). Art and the brand: The role of visual art in enhancing brand 'extendibility. *Journal of Consumer Psychology*, *18*(3), 212–222. doi:10.1016/j.jcps.2008.04.010

Hall, C. (1992). *Hallmark tourist events: Impact, management and planning*. New York, NY: Halsted Press.

Hall, C. (2019). Constructing sustainable tourism development: The 2030 agenda and the managerial ecology of sustainable tourism. *Journal of Sustainable Tourism*, *27*(7), 1044–1060. doi:10.1080/09669582.2018.1560456

Hall-Duncan, N. (2022). *Fashion photography. Love to know*. Retrieved from https://fashion-history.lovetoknow.com/fashion-clothing-industry/fashion-photography

Halwani, L. (2021). The rise of inconspicuous consumption. *Luxury Research Journal*, *2*(1/2), 48–69. doi:10.1080/0267257X.2014.989890

Hancok, C. (2003). *Paris et Londres au XIXème siècle – Représentations dans les guides et récits de voyage*. Paris: CNRS Publisher.

Hann, M. (2013). *Symbol, pattern and symmetry*. London: Bloomsbury Publishing.

Hansen, K. (2004). The world in dress: Anthropological perspectives on clothing, fashion, and culture. *Annual Review of Anthropology*, *33*, 369–392. doi:10.1146/annurev.anthro.33.070203.143805

Haqi, F., & Pandangwati, S. (2020). Mayoral leadership in shaping urban beautification in Surabaya and aspects influencing its capacity. *EMARA: Indonesian Journal of Architecture*, *6*(2), 94–104. doi:10.29080/eija.v6i2.1035

Hardy, A., Dolnicar, S., & Vorobjovas-Pinta, O. (2021). The formation and functioning of the Airbnb neo-tribe. Exploring peer-to-peer accommodation host groups. *Tourism Management Perspectives*, *37*. doi:10.1016/j.tmp.2020.100760

Harvey, D. (2013). *Rebel cities: From the Right to the city to the urban revolution*. London & New York, NY: Verso Books.

Hatherley, O. (2015, March 3). *Fendi vidi vici: When fashion flirts with fascism. Architectural-review.com*. Retrieved from https://www.architectural-review.com/essays/fendi-vidi-vici-when-fashion-flirts-with-fascism

Heidegger, M. (1949/1971). The thing. In: Hofstadter, A. (Trans.). *Poetry, language, thought*. New York, NY: Harper & Row.

Heilbrunn, B. (2018). *Médi(t)ations Marchandes*. Le Bord de L'eau.

Heim, H., Ferrero-Regis, T., & Payne, A. (2021). Independent fashion designers in the elusive fashion city. *Urban Studies*, *58*(10), 2004–2022. doi:10.1177/0042098020930937

Heine, K., & Atwal, G. (2022). Growing luxury brands through culture-driven innovation. *Strategic Change*, *31*(5), 533–543. doi:10.1002/jsc.2524

Henderson-Smith, B. (2003). *From booth to shop to shopping mall: Continuities in consumer spaces from 1650 to 2000, PhD thesis*. doi:10.25904/1912/1420

Hengky, S. (2015). Beneficial images: Batik handicraft tourism in Yogyakarta, Indonesia. *Business and Economic Ressearch*, 11–23. doi:10.5296/ber.v5i1.6760

Hepburn, S. (2000). The cloth of barbaric pagans: Tourism, identity, and modernity in Nepal. *Fashion Theory*, *4*(3), 275–299. doi:10.2752/136270400778995453

Hernandez, A. (2018, May 31). Gucci Cruise 2019 fashion show in Arles. See Provence. Retrieved from https://www.seeprovence.com/news/gucci-cruise-2019-presented-in-arles-arles-716392

Hiller, H. (2000). Mega-Events, urban, boosterism and growth strategies, an analysis of the objectives and legitimations of the Cap Town 2004 Olympic Bid. *International Journal of Urban and Regional Research*, *24*(2), 439–458. doi:10.1111/1468-2427.00256

Holt, D. (2003). What becomes an icon most. *Harvard Business Review*, *81*(3), 43–49.

Holt, D. (2016). Branding in the age of social media. *Harvard Business Review*, *94*(3), 40–50.

Holt, D., & Cameron, D. (2010). *Cultural strategy: Using innovative ideologies to build breakthrough brands*. Oxford: Oxford University Press.

Horlent, L., Salemme, M., Herrero, N., & Roseman, S. (2015). Finis terrae: The end-of-the-world imaginary in Tierra del fuego (Argentina). In *The tourist imaginary and pilgrimages to the edges of the world* (pp. 179–205). Multilingual Matters/Channel View Publications. doi:10.21832/9781845415242-010

Howkins, J. (2001). *The creative economy: How people make money from ideas*. London: Allen Lane.

Hsieh, A., & Chang, J. (2006). Shopping and tourist night markets in Taiwan. *Tourism Management*, *27*(1), 138–145. doi:10.1016/j.tourman.2004.06.017

Hunt, M. (1972). *Competition in the major home appliance industry, 1960–70*. Graduate School of Business Administration, Harvard University. Unpublished doctoral dissertation.

Idenstadt, S. (2016). The spaces of shopping: A historical overview. In *Deborah C. Andrews, shopping. material culture perspectives* (p. 16). University of Delaware Press.

Ijaouane, V., & Kapferer, J. (2012). Developing luxury brands within luxury groups – Synergies without Dilution? *Marketing Review St. Gallen*, *29*(1), 24–29. doi:10.1007/s11621-012-0107-8

Inglis, F. (2000). *The delicious history of the holiday*. London: Routledge.

Inversini, A., Xiang, Z., & Fesenmaier, D. (2015).New media in travel and tourism communication. Toward a new paradigm. In *Communication and technology* (pp. 497–512). Berlin, München, Boston, MA: De Gruyter Mouton. doi:10.1515/9783110271355-029

Iran, S., & Schrader, U. (2017). Collaboarative fashion consumption and its environmental effects. *Journal of Fashion Marketing and Management*, *21*(4), 468–482. doi:10.1108/JFMM-09-2016-0086

Iraqi, F. (2020, January 20). *How Marrakesh became the destination of choice for celebrities. The Africa Report*. Retrieved from https://www.theafricareport.com/22393/how-marrakesh-became-the-destination-of-choice-for-celebrities

Iredale, J. (2017, May 12). *Dior Cruise 2018. WWD*. Retrieved from https://wwd.com/runway/resort-2018/los-angeles/christian-dior/review/

Isaad, T. (2018, August 24). Le tourisme mode, un nouveau filon pour faire rayonner la jeune création française? *FashionNetwork*. Retrieved from https://fr.fashionnetwork.com/news/Le-tourisme-mode-un-nouveau-filon-pourfaire-rayonner-la-jeune-creation-francaise-,1007078.html

Ismailjee, S. (2020, June 08). Stronger together: The rise of the fashion brand collaboration. The Industry. Retrieved from https://www.theindustry.fashion/stronger-together-rise-fashion-brand-collaboration/

iWareBatik. (2020a). iWareBatik official homepage. Retrieved from www.iwarebatik.org

iWareBatik. (2020b). *Android app store*. Retrieved from https://play.google.com/store/apps/details?id=org.iwarebatik.mobileapp. Accessed on May 28, 2022.

iWareBatik. (2020c). ios app store. Retrieved from https://apps.apple.com/ch/app/iwarebatik/id1506929306?l=en. Accessed on May 28, 2022.

iWareBatik. (2020d). Rangkiang West Sumatra motif. Retrieved from https://www.iwarebatik.org/en-rangkiang/. Accessed on February 17, 2022.

iWareBatik (2021). *Digital technologies in promoting inclusive growth: iWareBatik user experience events in cooperation with 997 participants from 33 universities across Indonesia*. Retrieved from https://www.iwarebatik.org/digital-technologies-in-promoting-inclusive-growth-iwarebatik-user-experience-events-in-cooperation-with-33-universities-across-indonesia

IX Municipio, F. P. (2018, 18 March). Semi-directed interview conducted as part of the PhD researches. (Biondo, S. Interviewer).

Jamal, T., & Getz, D. (1995). Collaboration theory and community tourism planning. *Annals of Tourism Research*, *22*(1), 186–204. doi:10.1016/0160-7383(94)00067-3

James, H. (2016). *The American (1877)*. Read Books Ltd.

Jang, E. (2006). An analysis on cases of fashion collaboration strategy. *Journal of Fashion Business*, *10*(6), 110–121.

Jansen-Verbeke, M. (1998). The synergism between shopping and tourism. In W. F. Theobold (Ed.), *Global tourism* (2nd ed., pp. 428–446). Oxford: ButterworthHeinemann.

Jansson, J., & Power, D. (2010). Fashioning a global city: Global city brand channels in the fashion and design industries. *Regional Studies*, *44*(7), 889–904. doi:10.1080/00343400903401584

Javalgi, R., Traylor, R., Gross, A., & Lampman, E. (1994). Awareness of sponsorship and corporate image: An empirical investigation. *Journal of Advertising*, *23*(4), 47–58. doi:10.1080/00913367.1943.10673458

Jawabreh, O., Jahmani, A., Khaleefah, Q., Alshatnawi, E., & Abdelrazaqe, H. (2020). Customer expectation in five star hotels in aqaba special economic zone authority (ASEZA). *International Journal of Innovation, Creativity and Change*, *11*(4), 417–438.

Jebbia, J., KAWSO'Brien, G., & Bondaroff, A. (2010). *Supreme: Downtown New York Skate culture*. New York, NY: Rizzoli International Publications.

Jégouzo, L. (2019). *L'évolution de la politique publique du tourisme en France. Mondes Du Tourisme*. doi:10.4000/tourisme.2193

Jelinek, J. (2018). Art as strategic branding tool for luxury brands. *The Journal of Product and Brand Management*, *27*(3), 294–307. doi:10.1108/JPBM-01-2017-1408

Jennings, M. (2006). *Walter Benjamin, the writer of modern life, essays on Charles Baudelaire*. Cambridge, MA & London: The Belknap Press of Harvard University Press.

Jensen, R. (2001). *The dream society: How the coming shift from information to imagination will transform your business*. New York, NY: Mc Grow Hill.

Jensen, O. (2007). Culture Stories: Understanding cultural urban branding. *Planning Theory*, *6*, 211–236. doi:10.1177/1473095207082032

Jenson, W. (2013). *The new selfie: Feet. The Hollywood Reporter*. Retrieved from https://www.hollywoodreporter.com/lifestyle/style/new-selfie-feet-660461/

Jiang, M., Green, R. J., Henley, T. B., & Masten, W. G. (2009). Acculturation in relation to the acquisition of a second language. *Journal of Multilingual and Multicultural Development*, *30*(6), 481–492. doi:10.1080/01434630903147898

Jin, S. V., & Ryu, E. (2020). Instagram fashionistas, luxury visual image strategies and vanity. *The Journal of Product and Brand Management*, *29*(3), 355–368. doi:10.1108/JPBM-08-2018-1987

Joergens, C. (2006). Ethical fashion: Myth or future trend? *Journal of Fashion Marketing and Management*, *10*(3), 360–371. doi:10.1108/13612020610679321

Johnson, P. (2013, March 26). *10 definitions of 'luxury travel' from within the industry. A Luxury travel blog*. Retrieved from https://www.aluxurytravelblog.com/2013/03/26/so-what-is-luxury-travel/

Jonathan, C., & Tarigan, R. (2016). The effects of e-tourism to the development of tourism sector in Indonesia. *CommIT (Communication and Information Technology) Journal*, *10*(2), 59. doi:10.21512/commit.v10i2.1669

Jones, K., & Pilat, S. (2020). *The Routledge companion to Italian Fascist architecture*. New York, NY: Routledge.

Jorif, S. (2020, August). *Miss Dior, interview de Maria Grazia Chiuri*. Vogue Paris.

Jung, E. J., & Childs, M. L. (2018). Modern product placement: An understanding of consumers' responses to fashion brand advertisements featuring a destination. In *International Textile and Apparel Association Annual Conference Proceedings* (Vol. 75, No. 1). Iowa State University Digital Press

Judd, D. (1999). Constructing the tourist Bubble. In D.-R. Judd & S.-S. Fainstein (Eds.), *The tourist city* (pp. 35–53). New Haven, CT: Yale University Press.

Jung, E., & Childs, M. (2020). Destination as product placement: An advertising strategy to impact beliefs and behavioral intentions. *Journal of International Consumer Marketing*, *32*(3), 178–193.

Jung Jung, H., Lee, Y., Kim, H., & Yang, H. (2014). Impacts of country images on luxury fashion brand: Facilitating with the brand resonance model. *Journal of Fashion Marketing and Management*, *18*(2), 187–205. doi:10.1108/JFMM-10-2013-0113

Kadam, A., Ambegaonkar, O., & Deshmukh, R. (2021). *Luxury travel market. Global Opportunity Analysis and Industry Forecast, 2021–2027*. Allied Market Research.

Kadam, A., & Deshmukh, R. (2019). *Luxury travel market size, share & growth*. Industry Report, 2019-2026. Allied Market Research. Retrieved from https://www.alliedmarketresearch.com/luxury-travel-market/

Kalagi, P. (2021, September 17). *7 collabs between carmakers and luxe fashion labels on our radar*. Lifestyleasia. Retrieved from https://www.lifestyleasia.com/ind/gear/motoring/luxury-fashion-collaborations-with-car-brands/

Kalbaska, N., Ramírez, E. A., & Cantoni, L. (2018). The role of tourism destinations within the presence of fashion weeks. *Almatourism – Journal of Tourism, Culture and Territorial Development*, *9*(9), 87–114. doi:10.6092/issn.2036-5195/7245

Kalbaska, N., Sádaba, T., & Cantoni, L. (2018). Fashion communication: Between tradition and digital transformation. *Studies in Communication Sciences*, *18*(2), 269–285. doi:10.24434/j.scoms.2018.02.005

Kalbaska, N., Sádaba, T., Cominelli, F., & Cantoni, L. (2019). Fashion communication: Between tradition and future digital developments. Proceedings of the FACTUM 19 conference, Ascona, Switzerland. Cham: Springer. doi:10.1007/978-3-030-15436-3

Kapferer, J. (2007). *Les marques, capital de l'entreprise*. Paris: Editions d'Organisation.

Kapferer, J. (2011). Paris as a brand. In K. Dinnie (Ed.), *City branding* (pp. 184–189). London: Palgrave Macmillan. doi:10.1057/9780230294790_25

Kapferer, J. (2012). Abundant rarity: The key to luxury growth. *Business Horizons*, *55*(5), 453–462. doi:10.1016/j.bushor.2012.04.002

Kapferer, J. (2014). The artification of luxury: From artisans to artists. *Business Horizons*, *57*(3), 371–380. doi:10.1016/j.bushor.2013.12.007

Kapferer, J., & Laurent, G. (1992). *La sensibilité aux marques: Marchés sans marques, marchés à marques*.

Karamalak, O., Kalbaska, N., & Cantoni, L. (2021). What do hashtags afford in digital fashion communication? An exploratory study on Gucci-related hashtags on Twitter and Instagram. *Semiotica*, *243*, 325–351. doi:10.1515/sem-2019-0114

Katemliadis, I., & Papatheodorou, A. (2021). The Importance of tourism for the Greek economy: Traits and development. In V. Vlachos, A. Bitzenis, & B. Sergi (Eds.), *Modeling economic growth in contemporary Greece* (pp. 263–279). Bingley: Emerald Publishing Limited. doi:10.1108/978-1-80071-122-820211019

Kaufmann, J. (2007). *Corpi di donna, sguardi di uomo. Sociologia del seno nudo*. Milan: Raffaello Cortina.

Kavaratzis, M. (2012). From "necessary evil" to necessity: Stakeholders' involvement in place branding. *Journal of Place Management and Development*, *5*(1), 7–19. doi:10.1108/17538331211209013

Kawamura, Y. (2004). *Fashion-ology: An introduction to fashion studies*. London: Bloomsbury USA Academic.

Kawamura, Y. (2018). *Fashion-ology: An introduction to fashion studies*. London: Bloomsbury Publishing.

Kedzior, R., Allen, D., & Schroeder, J. (2016). The selfie phenomenon – Consumer identities in the social media marketplace. *European Journal of Marketing*, *50*(9/10), 1767–1772. doi:10.1108/EJM-06-2016-0363

Kennedy-Eden, H., & Gretzel, U. (2021). My heritage in my pocket: Mobile device and app use by genealogy tourists. *Information Technology & Tourism*, *23*(3), 327–350. doi:10.1007/s40558-021-00206-5

Kim, D., Baek, E., & Choo, H. (2017). The effect of self-presentation and self-expression attitude on selfie behavior in SNS. *Fashion & Textile Research Journal*, *19*(6), 701–711. doi:10.5805/SFTI.2017.19.6.701

Kipfer, S. (2016). Neocolonial urbanism? La renovation urbaine in Paris. *Antipode*, *48*(3), 603–625. doi:10.1111/anti.12193

Kirilenko, A., & Stepchenkova, S. (2018). Tourism research from its inception to present day: Subject area, geography, and gender distributions. *PLoS One*, *13*(11). doi:10.1371/journal.pone.0206820

Klein, A. (2019). *Fendi's haute couture show in Rome will pay a moving tribute to Karl Lagerfeld*. Vogue.fr. Retrieved from https://www.vogue.fr/fashion/article/fendis-haute-couture-show-in-rome-will-pay-a-moving-tribute-to-karl-lagerfeld

Kloster, C. (2020, January 20). *The 9 most viral fashion collaborations of 2020, L'Officiel USA*. Retrieved from https://www.lofficielusa.com/fashion/fashion-designer-collaborations-2020-prada-adidas-yeezy-gap

Knoll, S. (2008). *Cross-Business synergies: A typology of cross-business synergies and a midrange theory of continuous growth synergy realization*. Gabler. doi:10.1007/978-3-8349-9687-9

Koenker, D. (2017). *Club Red: Vacation travel and the Soviet dream*. Ithaca, NY: Cornell University Press.

Kovesi, C. (2016). The aura of luxury: Cultivating the believing faithful from the age of saints to the age of luxury brands. doi:10.1080/20511817.2016.1232468

Kozinets, R. (2019). *Netnography: The essential guide to qualitative social media research*. London: Sage.

Kozinets, R. (2020). E-tourism research, cultural understanding, and netnography. In Z. Xiang, M. Fuchs, U. Gretzel, & W. Höpken (Eds.), *Handbook of e-Tourism* (pp. 1–16). Singapore: Springer International Publishing. doi:10.1007/978-3-030-05324-6_43-1

Kozinets, R., & Gretzel, U. (2022). Netnography. In D. Buhalis (Ed.), *Encyclopedia of tourism marketing and management*. Northampton, MA: Edward Elgar Publishing. doi:10.4337/9781800377486.netnography

Kreiner, J. (1996). Piccadilly is the place to get royaled up about shopping. *Insight*, *12*(2), 42–43.

Kretz, G. (2012). Consuming branded Stories: A netnography of fashion and luxury Blog consumption. In Z. Gürhan-Canli, C. Otnes, & R. Zhu (Eds.), *North American advances in consumer research* (Vol. 40, pp. 1057–1058). Duluth, MN: Association for Consumer Research.

Kruger, B. (1993). *Remote control: Power, cultures, and the world of Appearances*. Electronic Publishing Services.

Kurkdjian, S. (2019). *The cultural value of parisian couture* (pp. 141–152). Paris: Capital of Fashion.

Kurkdjian, S. (2020). Paris as the capital of fashion, 1858–1939: An inquiry. *Fashion Theory*, *24*(3), 371–391. doi:10.1080/1362704X.2020.1732022

Kurkdjian, S. (2021). *Géopolitique de la mode: Vers de nouveaux modèles?* Paris: Le Cavalier Bleu. doi:10.3917/lcb.kurkd.2021.01

Kusumaningrum, T. (2018). *Jelajah Arsitektur Lamin Suku Dayak Kenyah [the discovery of Lamin architecture of Dayak Kenyah Tribe]*. Indonesia: Ministry of Education and Culture.

Kusumasondjaja, S. (2020). Exploring the role of visual aesthetics and presentation modality in luxury fashion brand communication on Instagram. *Journal of Fashion Marketing and Management: International Journal*, *24*(1), 15–31. doi:10.1108/JFMM-02-2019-0019

Lacoeuilhe, J. (2000). L'attachement à la marque: Proposition d'une échelle de mesure. *Recherche et Applications en Marketing*, *15*(4), 61–77. doi:10.1177/076737010001500

Laing, O. (2015, June 09). *Agnes Martin: The artist mystic who disappeared into the desert*. The Guardian. Retrieved from https://www.theguardian.com/artanddesign/2015/may/22/agnes-martin-the-artist-mystic-who-disappeared-into-the-desert

Laing, J., & Frost, W. (2013). Using fashion exhibitions to reimagine destination image: An interview with Karen Quinlan, Director, Bendigo Art Gallery. In K. Williams, J. Laing, & W. Frost (Eds.), *Fashion, design and events* (pp. 162–174). Routledge.

Landry, C. (2000). *The creative city: A toolkit for urban innovators*. London: Earthscan.

Landry, C. (2008). *The creative city: A toolkit for urban innovators*. London: Dunston House.

Larique, B. (2007). Les débuts et déboires de l'organisation officielle du tourisme en France: L'expérience malheureuse de l'Office National du Tourisme (1910–1935). *Entreprises et Histoire*, *47*(2), 73. doi:10.3917/eh.047.0073

Lash, S., & Urry, J. (1993). *Economies of signs and spaces*. London: Sage.

Lazzaretti, L. (2013). *Creative industries and innovation in Europe*. Abingdon: Routledge.

Lazzeretti, L., Capone, F., & Casadei, P. (2017). The role of fashion for tourism: An analysis of Florence as a manufacturing fashion city and beyond. In *Tourism in the city: Towards an integrative agenda on urban tourism* (pp. 207–220). doi:10.1007/978-3-319-26877-4_14

Leaver, T., Highfield, T., & Abidin, C. (2020). *Instagram: Visual social media cultures*. Cambridge: Polity Press.

Lee, M. (2012). *Knowing our future: The startling case for futurology*. Oxford: Infinite Ideas Limited.

Leigh, J., Webster, C., & Ivanov, S. (2013). *Future tourism: Political, social and economic challenges (Advances in tourism) Oxon*. Routledge.

Leitch, L. (2017, May 5). Chanel. Resort 2018. Review. Vogue Runway. Retrieved from https://www.vogue.com/fashion-shows/resort-2018/chanel

Lella, S. (2017, August 3). Il graffito-poesia sul tetto del quartier generale Fendi. Vogue.it. Retrieved from https://www.vogue.it/news/vogue-arte/2017/08/03/graffito-poesia-sul-tetto-del-quartier-generale-fendi

Lemarchand, N. (2011). Nouvelles approches, nouveaux sujets en géographie du commerce. Une géographie renouvelée par l'analyse culturelle. *Géographie et Cultures*, 77, 9–24. doi:10.4000/gc.703

Les Grands Magasins du Louvre. (1900). *Chefs d'œuvre du Musée du Louvre*.

Les Grands Magasins du Louvre. (1914). *Visite des souverains anglais*.

Les Grands Magasins du Louvre. (1919). *Souvenir des Fêtes de la Victoire*.

Les Grands Magasins du Louvre. (1936). *Leur rôle dans la vie nationale, sociale et économique de 1855 à 1936*.

Les Grands Magasins du Louvre. (1938). *Paris, Visite de LL. MM. le Roi et la Reine d'Angleterre*. Décoration de la Façade des Grands Magasins du Louvre.

Les Magasins du Bon Marché. (1900a). *L'Exposition et Paris. Guide illustré du Bon Marché, 175 gravures, 9 cartes en couleurs*.

Les Magasins du Bon Marché. (1900b). *Le Pavillon du Bon Marché* (p. 36).

Les Magasins du Bon Marché. (1900c). *Interprètes dans toutes les langues*. Maison A. Boucicaut.

Les Magasins du Bon Marché. (1910). *Les modes de Paris depuis Louis XVI d'après les documents de la Bibliothèque Nationale pour la période de 1860 à 1910* (p. 67).

Les Magasins du Bon Marché. (1925). *Le Pavillon "Pomone" à l'Exposition des Arts décoratifs 1925.*

Leslie, E. (1999). Souvenirs and forgetting: Walter Benjamin's Memory-Work. In M. Kwint, C. Breward, & J. Aynsley (Eds.), *Material memories.* Oxford, U.K: Berg.

Lever, M. W., Elliot, S., & Joppe, M. (2021). Exploring destination advocacy behavior in a virtual travel community. *Journal of Travel & Tourism Marketing, 38*(5), 431–443. doi:10.1080/10548408.2021.1940421

Lewis, C., Kerr, G., & Burgess, L. (2013). A critical assessment of the role of fashion in influencing the travel decision and destination choice. *International Journal of Tourism Policy 1, 5*(1–2), 4–18.

Lewis, C., Kerr, G., & Burgess, L. (2019). Positioning a destination as fashionable: The destination fashion conditioning framework. *Tourism Management, 72,* 209–219. doi:10.1016/j.tourman.2018.12.004

Liberato, P., Mendes, B., Liberato, D., & Alén, E. (2022). Fashion Weeks as a Driver of sustainable development in tourism destinations: The case of Portugal fashion. In *Advances in Tourism, Technology and Systems: Selected Papers from ICOTTS 2021* (Vol. 1, pp. 645–658). Singapore. Springer Nature Singapore. doi:10.1007/978-981-19-1040-1_53

Lichrou, M., O'malley, L., & Patterson, M. (2010). Narratives of a tourism destination: Local particularities and their implications for place marketing and branding. *Place Branding and Public Diplomacy, 6,* 134–144. doi:10.1057/pb.2010.10

Ling, W., Lorusso, M., & Reinach, S. (2019). Critical studies in global fashion. *Zone Moda Journal, 9*(2), 5–16. doi:10.6092/issn.2611-0563/10066

Lipovetsky, G. ([1987], 1991). *L'empire de l'ephemère: La mode et son destin dans les sociétés modernes.* Paris: Gallimard.

Lipovetsky, G., & Roux, E. (2003). *Le luxe éternel.* Paris: Gallimard.

Lipovetsky, G., & Serroy, J. (2013). L'esthétisation du monde. Vivre à l'âge du capitalisme artiste. Gallimard.

Litirell, M., Baizerman, S., Kean, R., Gahring, S., Niemeyer, S., Reilly, R., & Stout, J. (1994). Souvenirs and tourism Styles. *Journal of Travel Research, 33*(1), 3–11. doi:10.1177/004728759403300101

Liu, T., Liu, S., & Rahman, I. (2022). International anime tourists' experiences: A netnography of popular Japanese anime tourism destinations. *Asia Pacific Journal of Tourism Research, 27*(2), 135–156. doi:10.1080/10941665.2021.1998163

Liu, R., & Suh, A. (2017). Self-branding on social media: An analysis of style bloggers on Instagram. *Procedia Computer Science, 124,* 12–20. doi:10.1016/j.procs.2017.12.124

Löfgren, O. (1999). *On Holiday. A history of vacationing.* Berkeley, CA: University of California Press.

Logan, A. (2015). Netnography: Observing and interacting with celebrity in the digital world. *Celebrity Studies, 6*(3), 378–381. doi:10.1080/19392397.2015.1062652

Lopes, S. (2011). Destination image: Origins, developments and implications. *Journal of Tourism and Cultural Heritage*, *9*(2), 305–315. doi:10.25145/j.pasos.2011.09.027

Loureiro, S. M. C., Serra, J., & Guerreiro, J. (2019). How fashion brands engage on social media: A netnography approach. *Journal of Promotion Management*, *25*(3), 367–378. doi:10.1080/10496491.2019.1557815

Lu, S. (2019). *Fashion homepage*. Retrieved from https://shenglufashion.com/2020/08/03/wto-reports-world-textiles-and-apparel-trade-in-2019/. Accessed on April 4, 2022.

Lue, C., Crompton, J., & Stewart, W. (1996). Evidence of cumulative attraction in multidestination recreational trip decisions. *Journal of Travel Research*, *35*(1), 41–49. doi:10.1177/004728759603500107

Lukács, G. (1971). *History and class consciousness, studies in Marxist Dialectics*. Cambridge, MA: The MIT Press.

Lussault, M. (2017). *Hyper-lieux. Les nouvelles géographies de la mondialisation*. Média Diffusion.

LVMH. (2015, November 4). *Fendi inaugurates new headquarters in Rome. Lvmh.com*. Retrieved from https://www.lvmh.com/news-documents/news/fendi-inaugurates-new-headquarters-in-rome/

Lynch, K. (1960). *The image of the city*. Cambridge, MA: MIT Press.

Lysikova, O. (2012). Fashions in tourism: The views of Russian tourists and experts. In *Field Guide to Case Study Research in Tourism, Hospitality and Leisure (Advances in Culture, Tourism and Hospitality Research*. (Vol. 6, pp. 195–204). Bingley: Emerald Publishing Limited. doi:10.1108/S1871-3173(2012)0000006012

Macalister-Smith, T. (2015). *Destinationwear Takes Flight. Year-round demand for beach-friendly wardrobes has driven the growth of the swimwear market and the emergence of a new category of luxury destinationwear*. Business of Fashion. Retrieved from https://www.businessoffashion.com/articles/luxury/destinationwear-takes-flight

MacCannell, D. (1973). Staged authenticity: Arrangements of social space in tourist settings. *The American Journal of Sociology*, *79*(3), 589–603.

MacCannell, D. (1976). *The tourist: A new theory of the leisure class*. Berkeley, CA: University of California Press.

Machado, A. (2008). Archives de Paris: Les Grands Magasins du Louvre, Archives d'entreprise (1855-967); V14S1 à 158.

MacLeod, N. (2006). The placeless festival: Identity and place in the post-modern festival. In D. Picard & M. Robinson (Eds.), *Festivals, tourism, and social change: Remaking worlds* (pp. 222–237). Clevedon: Channel View Publications. doi:10.21832/9781845410490-015

Maisey, S. (2018, June 3). *The concept of cruise collection explained*. UAE News. Retrieved from https://www.thenationalnews.com/lifestyle/fashion/the-concept-of-the-cruise-collection-explained-1.736522

Maison Château Rouge. (s.d.). *Air Jordan and Maison Château Rouge*. Nike. Retrieved from https://www.nike.com/launch/t/air-jordan-1-mid-fearless-maison-chateau-rouge

Maitland, R. (2007). Tourists, the creative class and distinctive areas in major cities: The roles of visitors and residents in developing new tourism areas. In R. Greg, & J. Wilson (Eds.), *Tourism, creativity and development*. London: Routledge.

Maitland, R. (2008). Conviviality and everyday life: The Appeal of new areas of London for visitors. *International Journal of Tourism Research*, *10*(1), 15–25. doi:10.1002/jtr.621

Maitland, R. (2010). Everyday life as a creative experience in cities. *International Journal of Culture, Tourism and Hospitality*, *4*(3), 176–185. doi:10.1108/17506181011067574

Maitland, R., & Newman, P. (2004). Developing metropolitan tourism on the fringe of central London. *International Journal of Tourism Research*, *6*, 339–348.

Malagina, A. (2018). *Adiwastra tiga negeri [the Batik of three Kingdom, textile heritage masterpiece]*. Jakarta: National Geography of Indonesia.

Maninggar, N., Hudalah, D., Sutriadi, R., & Firman, T. (2018). Low-tech industry, regional innovation system and inter-actor collaboration in Indonesia: The case of the Pekalongan batik industry. *Asia Pacific Viewpoint*, *59*(3), 249–264. doi:10.1111/apv.12193

Marchetti, L. (2016). *La mode exposée. Penser la mode par l'exposition*. Head.

Marchiori, E., & Cantoni, L. (2011). The online reputation construct: Does it matter for the tourism domain? A literature review on destinations' online reputation. *Information Technology & Tourism*, *13*(3), 139–159. doi:10.3727/109830512X13283928066715

Martawardaja, S. (2019). *Pengaruh Brand Image Galeri Dian Pelangi Terhadap Minat Berkunjung Ke Kota Pekalongan [the influence of Dian Pelangi's brand image gallery on interest to visit Pekalongan city]*. Jakarta: Sekolah Tinggi Pariwisata Trisakti.

Marti, C. (2019). *Les médiations culturelles des marques: Une quête d'autorité* (Vol. 1). ISTE Group.

Martin, A. (1890). *Les étapes d'un touriste en France: Paris, promenades dans les 20 arrondissements*. Paris.

Martinez, J. G. (2007). Selling avant-garde: How Antwerp became a fashion capital (1990–2002). *Urban Studies*, *44*(12), 2449–2464.

Marx, K. (1867, 1885, 1894). *Capital* (*Volume 1, 2, & 3*). London: Penguin.

Marzel, S. (2017). Contexte mercantile, sociabilité et œuvre d'art, COnTEXTES, 19.

Masdari, F., & Hosseini Sarvari, S. (2021). The aesthetics of Instagram: Exploring the aesthetics of visual and semantic aspects of Instagram. *Journal of Cyberspace Studies*, *5*(1), 59–78. doi:10.22059/jcss.2021.325552.1060

Massey, D. (1994). *Space, place and Gender*. Cambridge: Polity.

Massi, M., & Turrini, A. (2020). When fashion Meets art: The artification of luxury fashion brands. In *The artification of luxury fashion brands* (pp. 1–32). Cham: Palgrave Pivot. doi:10.1007/978-3-030-26121-4_1

Maxcy, S. (2003). Pragmatic threads in mixed methods research in the social sciences: The search for multiple modes of inquiry and the end of philosophy of formalism. In A. Tashakkori & C. Teddlie (Eds.), *Handbook of mixed methods in social behaviour research* (pp. 51–90). London: Sage Publications.

Mazzali-Lurati, S., & Cantoni, L. (2006). Photography: Semiotics. In K. Brown (Ed.), *Encyclopedia of language & linguistics* (2nd ed., pp. 569–571). Elsevier. doi:10.1016/B0-08-044854-2/01437-1

McCracken, G. (1989). Who is the celebrity endorser? Cultural foundations of the endorsement process. *Journal of Consumer Research, 16*(3), 310–321. doi:10.1086/209217

McFarlane, A., & Samsioe, E. (2020). # 50+ fashion Instagram influencers: Cognitive age and aesthetic digital labours. *Journal of Fashion Marketing and Management: International Journal, 24*(3), 399–413. doi:10.1108/JFMM-08-2019-0177

McKercher, B., & du Cros, H. (2012). *Cultural tourism: The partnership between tourism and cultural heritage management*. New York, NY: Routledge.

McKinsey (2020). *A perspective for the luxury-goods industry during—and after—coronavirus*. McKinsey. Retrieved from https://www.mckinsey.com/industries/retail/our-insights/a-perspective-for-the-luxury-goods-industry-during-and-after-coronavirus

McNeill, D. (2009). *The global architect: Firms, fame and urban form*. New York, NY: Routledge.

McQuarrie, E. F., Miller, J., & Phillips, B. J. (2013). The megaphone effect: Taste and audience in fashion blogging. *Journal of Consumer Research, 40*(1), 136–158. doi:10.1086/669042

Meilich, O. (2019). Strategic groups maps: Review, synthesis, and guidelines. *Journal of Strategy and Management, 12*(4), 447–463. doi:10.1108/JSMA-03-2019-0046

Melchior, M. (2011). *Fashion museology: Identifying and contesting fashion in museums*. Oxford: Mansfield College.

Melchior, M., & Svensson, B. (2014). *Fashion and museums: Theory and practice*. London: Bloomsbury Publishing.

Mermet, A., & Gravari-Barbas, M. (2013). Commerce et patrimoine. In *L'exemple du Marais à Paris* (pp. 56–67). Les Annales de la Recherche Urbaine.

Metropolitan Museum of Art. (2018). 1,659,647 Visitors to Costume Institute's Heavenly Bodies Show at Met Fifth Avenue and Met Cloisters Make It the Most Visited Exhibition in The Met's History. Met Museum. Retrieved from www.metmuseum.org/press/news/2018/heavenly-bodies-most-visited-exhibition

MIC. (2005, December 1). *Palazzo della civiltà italiana all'EUR: Firmato l'accordo per il rilancio*. Beniculturali.it. Retrieved from https://www.beniculturali.it/comunicato/Palazzo-della-civilta-italiana-all-eur-firmato-l-accordo-per-il-rilancio

MIC. (2011, 14 February). Presentazione del Progetto di riqualificazione del Palazzo della Civiltà Italiana all'EUR. Beniculturali.it. Retrieved from https://www.beniculturali.it/comunicato/presentazione-del-progetto-di-riqualificazione-del-Palazzo-della-civilta-italiana-all-eur

Michaud, Y. (2013). Paris, Stock, Le Nouveau Luxe.

Michault, J. (2017, November). Voyage au bout du luxe. L'Officiel.

Michel, G. (2022). *Au coeur de la marque-4e éd.: Les clés du management des marques*. Paris: Dunod.

Michelin Le Guide Vert Paris. (2020). *Paris: 75 Idées de promenades*. Paris: Travel House Media.

Miles, S. (2010). *Spaces for consumption pleasure and placelessness in the post-industrial city*. Los Angeles, CA: SAGE.

Miller, M. (1987). The Bon Marché: Bourgeois Culture and the Department Store, 1869–1920, Paris, Armand Colin.

Miller, S. (2007). Fashion as art; is fashion art? Fashion theory. *The Journal of Dress, Body and Culture*, *11*(1), 25–40. doi:10.2752/136270407779934551

Milleret, G. (2015). *Haute couture: Histoire de l'industrie de la création: Des précurseurs à nos jours*. Editions Eyrolles.

Miotto, G., & Vilajoana-Alejandre, S. (2019). Gender equality: A tool for legitimacy in the fast fashion industry. *Harvard – Deusto Business Review*, *VIII*(2), 134–147. doi:10.3926/hdbr.244

Moen, T. (2006). Reflections on the narrative research approach. *International Journal of Qualitative Methods*, *5*(4), 56–69. doi:10.1177/160940690600500405

Mohd Yasin, N., Nasser Noor, M., & Mohamad, O. (2007). Does image of country-of-origin matter to brand equity? *The Journal of Product and Brand Management*, *16*(1), 38–48. doi:10.1108/10610420710731142

MOI-Ministry of Industry. (2020). Through OVOP, Ministry of Industry encourages SMEs to leverage on products based on local wisdom. Retrieved from https://www.industry.co.id/read/77279/lewat-ovop-kemenperin-dorong-ikm-hasilkan-produk-berbasis-kearifan-lokal

Mommaas, H. (2004). Cultural clusters and the post-industrial city: Towards the remapping of urban cultural policy. *Urban Studies*, *41*, 507–532. doi:10.1080/0042098042000178663

Monnet, J. (2015). Pour une géographie du fluide et du flou. *Acta Geographica*, *2*, 89–94.

Monneyron, F. (2017). *Sociologie de la mode*. Paris: Presses Universitaires de France.

Montagné-Vilette, S. (1990). *Le Sentier, un espace ambigu*. Paris: Masson.

Montanari, A. (2002). Grandi eventi, marketing urbano e realizzazione di nuovi spazi turistici. *Bollettino della società geografica italiana*, *XII*(VII), 760.

Moral-Andrés, F. (2019). (*21*, pp. 254–259). The definition of an urban and global icon. Public-private strategies for the regeneration of the Museum "Palazzo della Civiltà Italiana", Rome. Revista de Arquitectura, Pamplona. doi:10.15581/014.21.138-155

Morandi, C., & Paris, M. (2018). Forms of urban change: Nodes of knowledge-based networks as drivers of new metropolitan patterns in Southern Milan. In S. Armondi & S. Di Vita (Eds.), *Milan: Productions, spatial patterns and urban change* (pp. 84–96). New York, NY: Routledge.

Morency, C. (2018, September 16). *Is Luxury's love affair with 'drops' more than marketing? Business of fashion*. Retrieved from https://www.businessoffashion.com/articles/luxury/is-luxurys-love-affair-with-supreme-style-drops-more-than-marketing-moncler-burberry-off-white-celine

Moret, F. (1992). Images de Paris dans les guides touristiques en 1900. *Le Mouvement Social*, *160*, 79–98.

Morgan, N., Pritchard, A., & Piggott, R. (2002). New Zealand, 100% pure. The creation of a powerful niche destination brand. *Journal of Brand Management*, *9*, 335–354. doi:10.1057/palgrave.bm.2540082

Morgan, N., Pritchard, A., & Pride, R. (2011). *Destination brands: Managing place reputation*. Routledge.

Morrison, A., & Anderson, D. (2002, June). Destination branding. Paper presented at the Missouri Association of Convention and Visitor Bureau Annual Meeting, Lake of the Ozarks, MO.

Motahar, P., Tavakoli, R., & Mura, P. (2021). Social media influencers' visual framing of Iran on YouTube. *Tourism Recreation Research*, 1–13. doi:10.1080/02508281.2021.2014252

MTEC-Ministry of Tourism and Creative Economy. (2016). *Indonesia's Haute couture fashion designers' Galleries in Jakarta.* Retrieved from https://www.indonesia.travel/id/id/ide-liburan/indonesia-s-haute-couture-fashion-designers-galleries-in-jakarta

MTEC-Ministry of Tourism and Creative Economy. (2020). *Indonesian creative cities directory.* Retrieved from https://kotakreatif.kemenparekraf.go.id/direktori-kota-kreatif/

MTEC-Ministry of Tourism and Creative Economy. (2021a). Ministry of Tourism and Creative Economy to promote creative sector through fashion heritage events. Retrieved from https://kemenparekraf.go.id/berita/Siaran-Pers%3A-Bantu-Pemasaran-UMKM-Batik%2C-Menparekraf-Dukung-Gelaran-Busana-Gantari-di-Candi-Prambanan

MTEC-Ministry of Tourism and Creative Economy. (2021b). *Textile heritage, the source of Indonesian creative economy.* Retrieved from https://kemenparekraf.go.id/ragam-ekonomi-kreatif/Kain_Nusantara%2C-Sumber-Inspirasi-Ekonomi-Kreatif-Indonesia

Murphy, P., Pritchard, M., & Smith, B. (2000). The destination product and its impact on traveller perceptions. *Tourism Management*, *21*(1), 43–52. doi:10.1016/S0261-5177(99)00080-1

Musca, H. (2020, December 12). *Rue Myrha, la grande transformation d'un faubourg malfamé de Paris.* Le Figaro. Retrieved from https://www.lefigaro.fr/actualite-france/rue-myrha-la-grande-transformation-d-un-faubourg-malfame-de-paris-20201212

Mustafa, H. (2001). Ruins and spectacles: Fashion and city life in contemporary Senegal. *Journal of Contemporary African Art*, *15*(1), 47–53. doi:10.1215/10757163-15-1-47

Nancy, J. (2002 [original edition 1999]). *La città lontana.* Verona: Ombre Corte.

Natale, R. (2020, July 26). *Dior parades in Lecce under the lights with the rhythm of 'pizzica'. Italiani.* Retrieved from https://www.italiani.it/dior-parades-in-lecce-under-the-lights-with-the-rhythm-of-pizzica/

Nayak, L., & Mishra, S. (2016). Prospect of bamboo as a renewable textile fiber, historical overview, labeling, controversies and regulation. *Fashion and Textiles*, *3*(1), 1–23. doi:10.1186/s40691-015-0054-5

Nazreth, L. (2007). *The leisure economy: How changing demographics, economics and Generational Attitudes will Reshape our Lives and our industries.* Ontario: John Wiley and Sons, Canada Ltd.

Ngwira, C., & Kankhuni, Z. (2018). What attracts tourists to a destination? Is it attractions? *African Journal of Hospitality, Tourism and Leisure*, *7*(1), 1–19.

Niinimäki, K., Peters, G., Dahlbo, H., Perry, P., Rissanen, T., & Gwilt, A. (2020). The environmental price of fast fashion. *Nature Reviews Earth & Environment*, *1*(4), 189–200. doi:10.1038/s43017-020-0054-x

Nike News. (2017, September 17). *Jordan x KAWS Capsule.* Nike. Retrieved from https://news.nike.com/news/kaws-jordan-4

Nobile, T., Kalbaska, N., de Oliveira, R., & Cantoni, L. (2021). Digital fashion competences: A longitudinal study. In *Fashion communication: Proceedings of the FACTUM 21 conference*, Pamplona, Spain (pp. 17–28). Cham: Springer International Publishing. doi:10.1007/978-3-030-81321-5_2

Nobile, T., Noris, A., Kalbaska, N., & Cantoni, L. (2021). A review of digital fashion research: Before and beyond communication and marketing. *International Journal of Fashion Design, Technology and Education*, *14*(3), 293–301. doi:10.1080/17543266.2021.1931476

Noris, A., & Cantoni, L. (2022). Digital fashion communication: An (Inter) cultural perspective. In *Digital fashion communication* (pp. 1–147). Brill. doi:10.1163/9789004523555

Noris, A., Nobile, T. H., Kalbaska, N., & Cantoni, L. (2021). Digital fashion: A systematic literature review. A perspective on marketing and communication. *Journal of Global Fashion Marketing*, *12*(1), 32–46. doi:10.1080/20932685.2020.1835522

Notaro, A. (2000). Exhibiting the New Mussolinian City: Memories of empire in the World Exhibition of Rome (EUR). *Geojournal*, *51*, 15–22. doi:10.1023/A:1010893010920

Novy, J., & Huning, S. (2008). New Tourism (Areas) in the 'New Berlin'. In R. Maitland et P. Newman (dir.), World Tourism Cities. Developing Tourism Off the Beaten Track, Londres, Routledge.

Numéro (2021, June 17). *Comment l'artiste Grecque Christiana Soulou a-t-elle créé les dessins pour le défilé Dior Cruise 2022? Numéro*. Retrieved from https://www.numero.com/fr/fashion-week/defile-dior-cruise-2022-athenes-peintre-christiana-soulou-femmes-myhologie

Ochoa, L. (2010). Will 'eco-fashion' take off? A survey of potential customers of organic cotton clothes in London. *AD-Minister*, *16*, 118–131.

Olsen, K. (2015, May 31). *Fendi moves its headquarters to Rome's Palazzo della Civiltà Italiana*. Architecturaldigest.com. Retrieved from https://www.architecturaldigest.com/story/fendi-rome-headquarters-article

Orendorff, A. (2021, September 17). *10 trends styling 2021's ecommerce fashion industry: Growth + data in online apparel & accessories market*. Common Thread Co. Retrieved from https://commonthreadco.com/blogs/coachs-corner/fashion-ecommerce-industry-trends

Ostberg, J. (2011). The mythological aspects of country-of-origin: The case of the Swedishness of Swedish fashion. *Journal of Global Fashion Marketing*, *2*(4), 223–234. doi:10.1080/20932685.2011.10593100

Owen-Jones, J. (2019, May 6). *Rural Moroccan women contribute to the Dior's Cruise 2020 show. Morocco World News*. Retrieved from https://www.moroccoworldnews.com/2019/05/272388/rural-moroccan-women-dior-show

Page, S. (1992). Managing tourism in a small historic city. *Town and Country Planning*, *61*(7/8), 208–211.

Page, S. (1995). *Urban tourism*. London: Routledge.

Paivio, A. (1971). Imagery and language. In *Imagery* (pp. 7–32). Cambridge, MA: Academic Press.

Pajkovic, N. (2021, March 3). Palace teams up with Stella Artois to open 'Palace Artois' Pubs. Trend Hunter. Retrieved from https://www.trendhunter.com/trends/palace-artois-pubs

Paladini, A. (2018). *Tra Stato e parastato* (pp. 1925–1978). L'Ente Nazionale Artigianato e Piccole Industrie.

Pappalepore, I., & Gravari-Barbas, M. (2022). Tales from two cities: COVID-19 and the localisation of tourism in London and Paris. *International Journal of Tourism Cities*, *8*(4), 983–999. doi:10.1108/IJTC-09-2021-0199

Pappalepore, I., Maitland, R., & Smith, A. (2010). Exploring urban creativity: Visitor experiences of Spitalfields London. *Tourism Culture & Communication*, *10*(3), 217–230. doi:10.3727/109830410X12910355180946

Paravantes, M. (2021, June 16). *Greece in the spotlight for Dior Cruise collection show*. Greek Tavel Pages. Retrieved from https://news.gtp.gr/2021/06/16/greece-in-the-spotlight-for-dior-cruise-collection-show

Paris, M. (2018). *Making prestigious places. How luxury influences the transformation of cities*. New York, NY and London: Routledge.

Paris, M. (2020). Luxury as Driver for new urban Identities in Milan: Spatial practices, geographies and Open Questions. In L. Rajendran & D. Odeleye (Eds.), *Mediated identities in the futures of place* (pp. 211–231). Springer. doi:10.1007/978-3-030-06237-8_12

Paris, M., & Balducci, A. (2019). *Practicing a polycentric (post) metropolis. A dialogue about the milan urban Region*. Inplanning-AESOP.

Paris, C. M., & Pietschnig, J. (2015). "But first, let me take a selfie": Personality traits as predictors of travel selfie taking and sharing behaviors. Travel and Tourism Research Association: Advancing Tourism Research Globally. 1.

Park, K. W., Reisinger, Y., & Noh, E. H. (2009). Luxury shopping in tourism. *International Journal of Tourism Research*, *12*, 164–178. doi:10.1002/jtr.744

Parville, M., & Montémont, A. (1867). *Exposition universelle de 1867: Guide universel et complet de l'étranger dans*. Paris.

Pasdermadjian, H. (1949). *Le Grand Magasin. Son origine, son évolution, son avenir*. Paris: Dunod.

Pasquinelli, C. (2013). *The economic geography of brand associations*. CIND Research Papers. Uppsala: Uppsala University.

Pasquinelli, C. (2014). Branding as urban collective strategy making. The formation of Newcastle Gateshead's organisational identity. *Urban Studies*, *51*(4), 727–743. doi:10.1177/0042098013493025

Pasquinelli, C. (2017). The cultural branding Matrix: Framing the relation between cultural institutions and city branding. In A. Campelo (Ed.), *Handbook on place branding and marketing* (pp. 41–55). Cheltenham: Edward Elgar. doi:10.4337/9781784718602.00012

Patchett, M., & Williams, N. (2021). Geographies of fashion and style: Setting the scene. *GeoHumanities*, *7*(1), 198–216. doi:10.1080/2373566X.2021.1925138

Patterson, A., & Ashman, R. (2020). Getting up-close and personal with influencers: The promises and pitfalls of intimate netnography. In R. Kozinets & R. Gambetti (Eds.), *Netnography unlimited* (pp. 241–248). New York, NY: Routledge. doi:10.4324/9781003001430

Peck, J. (2005). Struggling with the creative class. *International Journal of Urban and Regional Research*, *29*(4), 740–770. doi:10.1111/j.1468-2427.2005.00620.x

Pedroni, M. (2022). Two decades of fashion blogging and influencing: A critical overview. *Fashion Theory*, 1–32. doi:10.1080/1362704X.2021.2017213

Pellissier, P. (2017, March 17). *On a testé: Une visite guidée autour du wax à Château-Rouge*. Grazia. Retrieved from https://www.grazia.fr/dossiers/afrique-activisme-black-power/on-a-teste-une-visite-guidee-autour-du-wax-a-chateau-rouge-176196.html#item=1

Peres, A., & Friel, M. (2019). Futourism: New maps for the travel industry. EGEA spa.

Permatasari, P. (2016). Les Villages du Batik sur L'île Madura comme Un Moyen du Developpement de la Region Touristique. A Master thesis presented by IREST – Université de Paris 1 Panthéon-Sorbonne, France.

Permatasari, P. A. (2022). *iWareBatik: Digital information system for enhancing Batik learning in the framework of heritage preservation and sustainable tourism*. Doctoral thesis, Universita della Svizzera italiana. Retrieved from https://susi.usi.ch/global/documents/320917. Accessed on August 23, 2023.

Permatasari, P., & Cantoni, L. (2019a). Indonesian tourism and batik: An online map. *E-Review of Tourism Research*, *16*(2/3).

Permatasari, P., & Cantoni, L. (2019b). Mapping mobile apps on Batik: A journey across heritage and fashion. In *Fashion communication in the digital age: FACTUM 19 fashion communication conference, Ascona, Switzerland*. July 21–26, 2019 (pp. 166–178). Springer International Publishing. doi:10.1007/978-3-030-15436-3_15

Permatasari, P. A., & Kalbaska, N. (2022). Digital technologies for communicating fashion heritage. In S. De Ascaniis & L. Cantoni (Eds.), *Heritage, tourism, and technology*. Lugano: Università della Svizzera italiana. Retrieved from https://www.e-elgar.com/shop/gbp/handbook-on-heritage-sustainabletourism-and-digital-media-9781788970075.h

Permatasari, P., Ningrum, F., Uriawan, W., & Cantoni, L. (2023). More than words. Evaluating iWareBatik digital technologies in the perspective of heritage tourism. In *Combining modern communication methods with heritage education*. IGI Global Publishing. doi:10.4018/978-1-6684-6217-1

Perrot, P. (1981). *Les Dessus et les dessous de la bourgeoisie, une histoire du vêtement au XIXe siècle*. Paris: Arthème Fayard.

Pesonen, J. (2020). Management and leadership for digital transformation in tourism. *Handbook of e-Tourism*, 1–34. doi:10.1007/978-3-030-05324-6_68-1

Phelps, N. (2017, May 12). Christian Dior. Resort 2018. Review. Vogue Runway. Retrieved from https://www.vogue.com/fashion-shows/resort-2018/christian-dior

Phelps, N. (2020, July 22). Christian Dior. Resort 2021. Review. Vogue Runway. Retrieved from https://www.vogue.com/fashion-shows/resort-2021/christian-dior

Picon-Lefebvre, V. (2013). Hyper Paris des touristes, le Printemps et les Galeries Lafayette. In M. Gravari-Barbas, & E. Fagnoni (Eds.), *Métropolisation et tourisme* (pp. 130–143). Paris, Belin: Comment le tourisme redessine.

Pike, S. (2005). Tourism destination branding complexity. *The Journal of Product and Brand Management*, *14*(4), 258–259. doi:10.1108/10610420510609267

Pike, A. (2011). Placing brands and branding: A socio-spatial biography of Newcastle Brown Ale. *Transactions of the Institute of British Geographers*, *36*(2), 206–222. doi:10.1111/j.1475-5661.2011.00425.x

Pinchera, V., & Rinallo, D. (2019). Marketplace icon: The fashion show. *Consumption, Markets and Culture*, *24*(5), 479–491. doi:10.1080/10253866.2019.1703699

Pinchera, V., & Rinallo, D. (2020). The emergence of Italy as a fashion country: Nation branding and collective meaning creation at Florence's fashion shows (1951–1965). *Business History*, *62*(1), 151–178. doi:10.1080/00076791.2017.1332593

Pinchera, V., & Rinallo, D. (2021). Marketplace icon: The fashion show. *Consumption, Markets and Culture*, *24*(5), 479–491. doi:10.1080/10253866.2019.1703699

Pine, B., & Gilmore, J. (1999). *The experience economy: Work is theatre and every business a stage*. Boston, MA: Harvard Business School Press.

Pine, B. J., II, & Gilmore, J. H. (1998). Welcome to the experience economy. juillet-août. *Harvard Business Review*. Retrieved from https://hbr.org/1998/07/welcome-to-the-experience-economy

Pine, J., II, James, H., & Gilmore, J. (1998, July-August). Welcome to the experience economy. Harvard Business Review. Retrieved from https://hbr.org/1998/07/welcome-to-the-experience-economy

Pistilli, O. (2018). The heritage-creativity Interplay. How fashion designers are reinventing heritage as modern design: The French case. *Zone Moda Journal*, *8*(1), 77–95. doi:10.6092/issn.2611-0563/8223

Plog, S. (1974). Why destination areas rise and fall in Popularity In *Cornell hotel and restaurant administration quarterly*. Ithaca, NY: The Center for Hospitality Research at Cornell University. doi:10.1177/00108804014230

Polkinghorne, D. (2007). Validity Issues in narrative research. *Qualitative Inquiry*, *13*(4), 471–486. doi:10.1177/1077800406297670

Pope, N., & Voges, K. (2000). The impact of sport sponsorship activities, corporate image, and prior use on consumer purchase intention. *Sport Marketing Quarterly*, *9*(2), 96–102.

Porter, M. (1980). *Competitive strategy: Techniques for analyzing industries and competitors*. New York, NY: The Free Press.

Potvin, J. (2009). *The places and spaces of fashion, 1800–2007*. New York, NY: Routledge.

Poulston, J. (2009). Working conditions in hospitality: Employees' views of the dissatisfactory hygiene factors. *Journal of Quality Assurance in Hospitality & Tourism*, *10*(1), 23–43. doi:10.1080/15280080902716993

Pozzo, R., Filippetti, A., Paolucci, M., & Virgili, V. (2020). What does cultural innovation stand for? Dimensions, processes, outcomes of a new innovation category. *Science and Public Policy*, *47*(3), 425–433. doi:10.1093/scipol/scaa023

Prideaux, B., & Cooper, C. (2003). Marketing and destination growth: A symbiotic relationship or simple coincidence? *Journal of Vacation Marketing*, *9*(1), 35–51. doi:10.1177/135676670200900103

Pritchard, A., & Morgan, N. (2005). 'On location' Re (viewing) bodies of fashion and places of desire. *Tourist Studies*, *5*(3), 283–302. doi:10.1177/1468797605070338

Pynchon, T. (1973). *Gravity's Rainbow*. London: Penguin.

Quilici, V. (2015). *Eur. Città di fondazione*. Roma: De Luca.

Quinn, B. (2003). *The fashion of architecture*. Oxford: Berg Publishers.

Qu, H., Kim, L., & Im, H. (2011). A model of destination branding: Integrating the concepts of the branding and destination image. *Tourism Management*, *32*(3), 465–476. doi:10.1016/j.tourman.2010.03.014

Rabbiosi, C. (2015). *Renewing a historical legacy: Tourism, leisure shopping and urban branding in Paris. Cities* (pp. 195–203). doi:10.1016/j.cities.2014.07.001

Rabkin, E. (2020, June 09). *Will coronavirus kill hype culture as we know it? High Snobiety*. Retrieved from https://www.highsnobiety.com/p/will-coronavirus-kill-hype-culture/

Rahman, K., & Cherrier, H. (2010). Galloping through the global brandscape: Consumers in a branded reality. *Advances in Consumer Research*, *37*(1), 420–427.

Ramirez, R., Mukherjee, M., Vezzoli, S., & Kramer, A. M. (2015). Scenarios as a scholarly methodology to produce "interesting research". *Futures*, *71*, 70–87. doi:10.1016/j.futures.2015.06.006

Ramos-Serrano, M., & Martínez-García, Á. (2016). Personal style bloggers: The most popular visual composition principles and themes on Instagram. *Observatorio*, *10*(2), 89–109. doi:10.15847/obsOBS1022016947

Rastegar, R., Zarezadeh, Z., & Gretzel, U. (2021). World heritage and social justice: Insights from the inscription of Yazd, Iran. *Journal of Sustainable Tourism*, *29*(2–3), 521–540. doi:10.1080/09669582.2020.1782925

Reid, E., & Duffy, K. (2018). A netnographic sensibility: Developing the netnographic/social listening boundaries. *Journal of Marketing Management*, *34*(3–4), 263–286. doi:10.1080/0267257X.2018.1450282

Reisinger, Y., & Turner, L. (2002). The determination of shopping satisfaction of Japanese tourists visiting Hawaii and the Gold Coast compared. *Journal of Travel Research*, *41*(2), 167–176. doi:10.1177/004728702237417

Relph, E. (1976). *Place and placelessness*. London: Pion.

Repubblica, L. (2011, February 5). *Colosseo Quadrato, lavori finiti: Il Palazzo -museo aprirà nel 2012. Repubblica*. Retrieved from https://roma.repubblica.it/cronaca/2011/02/15/news/colosseo_quadrato_lavori_finiti_il_Palazzo-museo_aprir_nel_2012-12493607/

Reuters. (2018, February 20). *LVMH taps Dior's Brunschwig to lead luxury brand Fendi*. Reuters.com. Retrieved from https://www.reuters.com/article/lvmh-fendi/lvmh-taps-diors-brunschwig-to-lead-luxury-brand-fendi-idINKCN1G41G5

Rexroth, T. (1972). *Walter Benjamin, Über Haschisch*. Frankfurt: Suhrkamp Verlag.

Richards, G. (1996). *Cultural tourism in Europe*. Oxon: CAB International.

Richards, G. (2010). Leisure in the Network Society: From pseudo events to hyper-festivity. Inaugural address given at the public acceptance of the appointment of Professor in Leisure Studies at Tilburg University, 8 October.

Richards, G. (2014). *Tourism Trends: The Convergence of culture and tourism*. The Netherlands: Academy for leisure NHTV. University of Applied Sciences.

Richards, G. (2019). Creative tourism: Opportunities for smaller places? *Tourism & Management Studies*, *15*(1), 7–10. doi:10.18089/tms.2019.15SI01

Richardson, M. (2020, September 17). *The supreme universe: The 25 best supreme collaborators*. Grailed. Retrieved from https://www.grailed.com/drycleanonly/best-supreme-collabs

Richards, G., & Wilson, J. (2006a). Developing creativity in tourist experiences: A solution to the serial reproduction of culture? *Tourism Management*, *27*(6), 1209–1223. doi:10.1016/j.tourman.2005.06.002

Richards, G., & Wilson, J. (2006b). Developing creativity in tourist experiences: A solution to the serial reproduction of culture? *Tourism Management*, *27*(6), 1209–1223. doi:10.1016/j.tourman.2005.06.002

Richards, G., & Wilson, J. (2007). *Tourism, creativity and development*. Routledge. doi:10.4324/9780203933695

Ricketson, S. (2017). Rights on the Border: The Berne Convention and Neighbouring rights. In R. L. Okediji (Ed.), *Copyright law and age of limitations and exceptions*. Cambridge University Press. doi:10.1017/9781316450901.014

Rickly-Boyd, J. (2012). Authenticity & Aura, A Benjaminian approach to tourism. *Annals of Tourism Research*, *30*(1), 269–289. doi:10.1016/j.annals.2011.05.003

Riegler, S. (1999). The new capital of cutting edge. *Travel and Leisure*, *29*(6), 142–146.

Riello, G. (2012). *La moda. Una storia dal Medioevo a oggi*. Roma; Bari: Laterza.

Rintamäki, T., Kuusela, H., & Mitronen, L. (2007). Identifying competitive customer value propositions in retailing. *Managing Service Quality: International Journal*, *17*(6), 621–634. doi:10.1108/09604520710834975

Rishika, A. (2020, August 14). An Ode to Puglia: How Dior's Cruise Show Celebrates Italian Craftmanship, Another Mag. Retrieved from https://www.anothermag.com/fashion-beauty/12702/dior-latest-cruise-2021-show-lecce-puglia-full-collection-maria-grazia-chiuri

Roach-Higgins, M., Eicher, J., & Kim, K. J. (1995). *Dress and identity*. New York City: Fairchild Publications.

Roberts, J., & Armitage, J. (2018). Luxury. From the idea to reality of prestigious places. In M. Paris (Ed.), *Making Prestigious Places: How luxury influences the transformation of the city* (pp. 23–34). London: Routledge.

Roberts, J., & Armitage, J. (2020). The third realm of luxury: Conceptualizing the connections between real places and imaginary spaces. Bloomsbury. Retrieved from https://www.bloomsburycollections.com/book/the-third-realm-of-luxury-connecting-real-places-and-imaginary-spaces/ch1-the-third-realm-of-luxury-conceptualizing-the-connections-between-real-places-and-imaginary-spaces

Robertson, M., & Guerrier, Y. (1998). Events as entrepreneurial displays: Saville, Barcelona and Madrid. In D. Tyler, Y. Guerrier, & M. Robertson (Eds.), *Managing tourism in cities* (pp. 215–228). Chichester: John Wiley and Sons.

Rocamora, A. (2009). *Fashioning the city: Paris, fashion and the media*. London: Bloomsbury Publishing.

Rocamora, A. (2013). Personal fashion blogs: Screens and mirrors in digital self-portraits. In S. Bruzzi & P. Church Gibson (Eds.), *Fashion cultures revisited* (pp. 112–127). London: Routledge. doi:10.2752/175174111X13115179149794

Rocamora, A. (2017). Mediatization and digital media in the field of fashion. *Fashion Theory*, *21*(5), 505–522.

Roche, D. (2020, September). *Esquisse- Maria Grazia Chiuri. Numéro*. Retrieved from https://www.numero.com/en/fashion-0/interview-with-maria-grazia-chiuri-young-people-see-onlythe-artistic-side-to-fashion

Rodríguez-Ortega, N. (2018). Canon, value, and cultural heritage: New processes of assigning value in the Postdigital Realm. *Multimodal Technologies and Interact*, *2*(25), 1–13. doi:10.3390/mti2020025

Rodzi, N., Zaki, S., & Subli, S. (2013). Between tourism and intangible cultural heritage. *Procedia-Social and Behavioral Sciences*, *85*, 411–420. doi:10.1016/j.sbspro.2013.08.370

Rojek, C. (1993). *Ways of escape: Modern transformations in leisure and travel*. London: Macmillan.

Romacapitale (2010, June 5). *Roma si apre ad un nuovo sistema di offerta turistica. Internal Conference Report*. Rome: Università Luiss Guido Carli.

Roncayolo, M. (1996). *Les grammaire d'une ville. Essais sur la genèse des structures urbaines à Marseille*. Paris: Editions de l'Ecole des Hautes Etudes en Sciences Sociales.

Roux, E. (1991). Comment se positionnent les marques de luxe? *Revue Française de Marketing*, *132/133*(3), 111–118.

Ruoss, E., & Alfarè, L. (2013). Challenging Hit and Run tourism in cultural heritage sites. In *Proceedings of the International Conference on Sustainable Heritage Management*, 525–235.

Saayman, M., & Saayman, A. (2012). Shopping tourism or tourists shopping? A case study of South Africa's African Tourism Market. *Tourism Economics*, *18*(6), 1313–1329. doi:10.5367/te.2012.0169

Sádaba, T., Kalbaska, N., Cominelli, F., Cantoni, L., & Torregrosa Puig, M. (2021). Fashion communication. In *Proceedings of the FACTUM 21 conference, Pamplona, Spain*. Cham, Springer. doi:10.1007/978-3-030-81321-5

Sádaba, T., LaFata, V., & Torres, A. (2020). Cultural appropriation in the digital Context: A Comparative study between two fashion Cases. In *International conference on human-computer interaction* (pp. 504–520). Cham: Springer. doi: 10.1007/978-3-030-50341-3_38

Saillard, O. (2019). *Le bouquin de la mode*. Paris: Robert Laffont.

Salazar, N., & Graburn, N. (2014). *Tourism imaginaries: Anthropological approaches*. Berghahn Books.

Sallet-Lavorel, H. (2003). *Pour un tourisme participatif en Île-de-France. Encourager le rapprochement entre touristes et visiteurs, Report presented to the IAURIF*, Paris: Institut d'aménagement et d'urbanisme de la région Ile-de-France).

Sampaolo, S. (2018). Tra rendita e nuove logiche di sviluppo: processi adattativi e reattivi. In A. Coppola & G. Punziano (Eds.), *Roma in transizione: governo, strategie, metabolismi e quadri di vita di una metropoli* (pp. 153–166). Roma: Planum Publisher.

Sampaolo, S., & Punziano, G. (2018). Tra rendita e nuove logiche di sviluppo: Processi adattativi e reattivi. In *Roma in transizione: Governo, strategie, metabolismi e quadri di vita di una metropoli by A. Coppola* (pp. 153–166). Roma: Planum Publisher.

Sanderson, R. (2018, February 8). *Chiara Ferragni — The Italian influencer who built a global brand*. Financial Times. Retrieved from https://www.ft.com/content/9adce87c-2879-11e9-a5ab-ff8ef2b976c7

SanMiguel, P. (2020). *Influencer Marketing. Conecta tu marca con tu públic*. Madrid: LID Editorial Empresarial.

SanMiguel, P., Guercini, S., & Sádaba, T. (2018). The impact of attitudes towards influencers amongst millennial fashion buyers. *Studies in Communication Sciences*, *18*(2), 439–460. doi:10.24434/j.scoms.2018.02.016

Santoso, I. (2019). Batik: Object and tourist attraction. In *3rd international seminar on tourism (ISOT 2018)* (pp. 314–317). Atlantis Press.

Sapori, M. (2010). *Rose bertin*. Paris, Perrin: La couturière de Marie Antoinette.

Saroso, D., & Fauzi, F. (2013). The OVOP approach to improve SMEs business performance: Indonesia's experience. *GSTF Journal on Business Review*, *2*(3).

Sassen, S. (1991). *The global city*. New York, NY, London, Tokyo, Princeton, NJ: Princeton University Press.

Savage, M. (1995/2000). Walter Benjamin's urban Thought, A critical analysis. In M. Crang & N. Thrift (Eds.), *Thinking space*. New York, NY and London: Routledge. doi:10.1068/d130201

Savitch, H., & Kantor, P. (2002). *Cities in the international market place: The political economy of urban development in north America and in western europe*. Princeton, NJ: Princeton University Press.

Scaraboto, D., & Fischer, E. (2013). Frustrated fatshionistas: An institutional theory perspective on consumer quests for greater choice in mainstream markets. *Journal of Consumer Research*, *39*(6), 1234–1257. doi:10.1086/668298

Schmidt, C. (2012). *The swimsuit: Fashion from poolside to catwalk*. London: Berg.

Schrader, U. (2001). *Konsumentenakzeptanz Eigentumsersetzender Dienstleistungen. Konzeption und Empirische Analyse*. Frankfurt am Main: Lang.

Schroeder, J., Borgerson, J., & Wu, Z. (2016). A brand culture perspective on global brands. In D. Riley, J. Singh, & C. Blankson (Eds.), *The Routledge companion to contemporary brand management*. Oxon; New York, NY: Routledge.

Schroeder, S., Cornicelli, L., Fulton, D., & Merchant, S. (2019). The influence of motivation versus experience on recreation satisfaction: How appreciative-versus achievement-oriented recreation experience preferences relate to hunter satisfaction. *Journal of Leisure Research*, *50*(2), 107–131. doi: 10.1080/00222216.2018.1557502

Schuett, M. (1993). Refining measures of adventure recreation involvement. *Leisure Sciences*, *15*(3), 205–216. doi:10.1080/01490409309513200

Schwarz, K. (2021). "Gazing" and "performing": Travel photography and online self-presentation. *Tourist Studies*, *21*(2), 260–277. doi:10.1177/1468797620985789

Scott, A. (2014). Beyond the creative city: Cognitive-cultural capitalism and the new urbanism. *Regional Studies*, *24*(4), 565–578. doi:10.1080/00343404.2014.891010

Semmens, K. (2005). Seeing Hitler's Germany. In *Tourism in the Third Reich*. London: Palgrave Macmillan.

Sentenac, P. (1925, August). *Le Pavillon de Primavera, La Renaissance d l'art français et des industries de luxe* (pp. 370–373).

Shahbandeh, M. (2021, September 17). *Global Apparel Market – Statistics & Facts. Statista*. Retrieved from https://www.statista.com/topics/5091/apparel-market-worldwide/

Shand, P. (2002). Scenes from the colonial catwalk: Cultural appropriation, intellectual property rights, and fashion. *Cultural Analysis*, *3*(2002), 47–88.

Shao, J., & Gretzel, U. (2011). Social media created the Chinese Backpacker Star. In W. Frost, G. Croy, J. Laing, & S. Beeton (Eds.), *Proceedings of the international tourism and media conference*. Melbourne, Australia: La Trobe University and Monash University.

Shapiro, R. (2004). *Qu'est-ce que l'artification? Paris*: XVII Congrès de l'Association française de sociologie, HalSHS.Cnrs.

Sherman, L. (2017, May 12). *Dior goes West. The business of fashion*. Retrieved from https://www.businessoffashion.com/reviews/fashion-week/christian-dior-goes-west/

Shetty, K., & Fitzsimmons, J. (2022). The effect of brand personality congruence, brand attachment and brand love on loyalty among HENRY's in the luxury branding sector. *Journal of Fashion Marketing and Management*, *26*(1), 21–35. doi:10.1108/JFMM-09-2020-0208

Shimul, A., & Phau, I. (2022). Luxury brand attachment: Predictors, moderators and consequences. *International Journal of Consumer Studies*, *46*(6), 2466–2487. doi: 10.1111/ijcs.12799

Sianipar, K., Gunardi, G., & Rustiyanti, S. (2015). Makna Seni Ukiran Gorga Pada Rumah Adat Batak [Meanings of Gorga wood carvings on Batak traditional house]. *Pandjajaran University*, *25*(3), 227–235.

Siegel, L., Tussyadiah, I., & Scarles, C. (2019). Does social media help or hurt destinations? A qualitative case study. *E-Review of Tourism Research*, *17*(4), 5–12. doi:10.1016/j.jdmm.2023.100765

Siegel, L., Tussyadiah, I., & Scarles, C. (2022). Cyber-physical traveler performances and Instagram travel photography as ideal impression management. *Current Issues in Tourism*, 1–25. doi:10.1080/13683500.2022.2086451

Sigler, T., & Wachsmuth, D. (2016). Transnational gentrification: Globalisation and neighborhood change in Panama's Casco Antiguo. *Urban Studies*, *53*(4), 705–722. doi:10.1177/0042098014568070

Sikarskie, A. G. (2016). *Textile collections: Preservation, access, curation, and interpretation in the digital age*. Lanham, MD: Rowman & Littlefield.

Simas, T., Oliveira, S., & Cano-Hila, A. (2021). Tourismophobia or touristification? An analysis of the impacts of tourism in Poblenou, Barcelona. *Ambiente Construído*, *21*, 117–131. doi:10.1590/s1678-86212021000300541

Simmel, G. (1908/1997). Excursus on the sociology of the senses. In P. David, D. P. Frisby, & M. Featherstone, (Eds.), *Simmel on culture: Selected writings*. London: Sage Publications.

Simmel, G. (1994). *La mode. Philosophie de la modernité*. Paris: Payot.

Singer, S. (2018, May 25). Christian Dior. Resort 2019. Review. Vogue Runway. Retrieved from https://www.vogue.com/fashion-shows/resort-2019/christian-dior

Skivko, M. (2013). Fashion metaphors for the city, the discourse of urban repre-sentation by fashion phenomenon. *The Journal of Urbanism*, *27*(2), 1–5. doi:10.1186/s40410-016-0051-z

Skivko, M. (2016). Touring the fashion: Branding the city. *Journal of Consumer Culture*, *16*(2), 432–446. doi:10.1177/1469540516635806

Skivko, M. (2017). *Fashion in the city and the city in fashion: Urban representation in fashion magazines. PhD thesis. School of philosophy*. Weimar: Bauhaus-Universität Weimar.

Sklair, L. (2017). *The icon project: Architecture, cities, and capitalist globalization*. Oxford: Oxford University Press.

Skov, L., Skjold, E., Moeran, B., Larsen, F., & Csaba, F. (2009). The fashion show as an art form. In *Creative Encounters*, 2–37.

Slowinska, M. A. (2014). *Art/commerce: The convergence of art and marketing in contemporary culture*. Transcript Verlag.

Smith, V. (1977, 1989, 2012). *Hosts and guests: The anthropology of tourism*. University of Pennsylvania Press.

Smith, S. (2015). A sense of place: Place, culture and tourism. *Tourism Recreation Research*, *40*(2), 220–233. doi:10.1080/02508281.2015.1049814

Smith, S. (2018). Instagram abroad: Performance, consumption and colonial narrative in tourism. *Postcolonial Studies*, *21*(2), 172–191. doi:10.1080/13688790.2018.1461173

Soedigdo, D., Harysakti, A., & Usop, T. B. (2014). Elemen-elemen pendorong kearifan lokal pada arsitektur nusantara [Local Wisdom Elements on Indonesian traditional Architecture]. *Jurnal Perspektif Arsitektur*, *9*(1).

Sombart, W. (1913). *Luxury and capitalism*. Ann Harbor, MI: University of Michigan Press. 1967. Trans. from Sombart, W. (1913). Luxus und Kapitalismus. Munich and Leipzig, Germany: Verlag von Duncker & Humblot, 1912.

Sormaz, A., & Ruoss, E. (2020). *Social Media to balance tourism flow in Natural Heritage destinations. Heritage, Tourism and Hospitality International Conference HTHIC2020 Preceedings* (pp. 15–28). Switzerland: Mendrisio.

Sorrieu, F. (19th century). *Grands Magasins du Louvre Les plus vastes du monde, décliné en français, anglais et espagnols*. Musée Carnavalet.

Specht, J. (2014). *Architectural tourism: Building for urban travel destinations*. Springer. doi:10.1007/978-3-658-06024-4

Spode, H. (2010). La recherche historique sur le tourisme. Vers une nouvelle approche. *Mondes du Tourisme*, *2*, 4–18. doi:10.4000/tourisme.267

Stanszus, L., & Iran, S. (2015). Sustainable fashion. In S. Idowu, N. Capaldi, M. Fifka, L. Zu, & R. Schmidpeter (Eds.), *Dictionary of corporate social responsibility* (pp. 514 515). Cham: Springer.

Stark, G. (2018). *The fashion show: History, theory and practice*. London: Bloomsbury Publishing.

Statista (2021). *Real fashion consumer spending per capita forecast in Greece 2010–2025*. Retrieved from https://www.statista.com/forecasts/1157197/real-fashion-consumer-spending-per-capita-forecast-in-greece

Statistic, I. N. B. (2015). *Statistic data of Indonesian tribes*. Retrieved from https://www.bps.go.id/news/2015/11/18/127/mengulik-data-suku-diindonesia.html

Steele, V. (2017). *Paris fashion: A cultural history*. London: Bloomsbury Publishing.

Štefko, R., & Steffek, V. (2018). Key issues in slow fashion: Current challenges and future perspectives. *Sustainability*, *10*(7), 2270. doi:10.3390/su10072270

Stoppard, L. (2020, March 3). Everyone's a curator now. New York Times.

Strähle, J. (2018). *Fashion & music*. Springer. doi:10.1007/978-981-10-5637-6

Studium-Louvre (1925). (p. 355). Paris: Guide de l'exposition.

Sullivan, P., Gallarza, M., Fayos, T., & Calderon, H. (2015). Do Fashion Involvement, Shopping Motivations, Cognitive and Affective Destination Involvement, and Demographics Affect Tourists' Trip Length? An Empirical Study in the City of Valencia (Spain). In *The 18th International Conference on Research in the Distributive Trades of the European Association for Education and Research in Commercial Distribution*, Rennes, France.

Sumarto, R., Sumartono, S., Muluk, M., & Nuh, M. (2020). Penta-Helix and Quintuple-Helix in the management of tourism villages in Yogyakarta City. *Australasian Accounting, Business and Finance Journal*, *14*(1), 46–57. doi:10.14453/aabfj.v14i1.5

Supreme. (2020). *Supreme*. New York, NY: Phaidon Press.

Sustainable Travel. (n.d.). *Carbon footprint of tourism*. Sustainable Travel. Retrieved from https://sustainabletravel.org/issues/carbon-footprint-tourism

Svendsen, L. (2006). *Fashion: A philosophy*. London: Reaktion.

Swanson, K., & Everett, J. (2013). Emerging fashion: Berlin fashion week. In *Fashion, design and events* (pp. 177–190). London; New York, NY: Routledge.

Syfret, W. (2016, May 7). *Was the Chanel Cruise show actually good for Cuba? i-D Magazine*. Retrieved from https://i-d.vice.com/en/article/8xg75k/was-the-chanel-cruise-show-actually-good-for-cuba

Tavakoli, R., & Mura, P. (2015). 'Journeys in Second Life'–Iranian Muslim women's behaviour in virtual tourist destinations. *Tourism Management*, *46*, 398–407. doi:10.1016/j.tourman.2014.07.015

Tellis, S. (2018, June 09). David Hockney's painting, which was auctioned for $90.3 mn, was initially sold for $18,000, Economic Times. Retrieved from https://economictimes.indiatimes.com/magazines/panache/david-hockneys-painting-which-was-auctioned-for-90-3-mn-was-initially-sold-for-18000/articleshow/66930948.cms?from=mdr

Thakor, M., & Kohli, C. (1996). Brand origin: Conceptualization and review. *Journal of Consumer Marketing*, *13*(3), 27–42. doi:10.1108/07363769610147929

Thawley, D. (2018, July 6). *Why you need to Add Arles to your travel bucket list*. Vogue. Retrieved from https://www.vogue.co.uk/article/arles-france-things-to-do

The British Council. (2021). The British fashion industry calls on government for support. Retrieved from https://www.britishfashioncouncil.co.uk/bfcnews/4325/The-British-Fashion-Industry-Calls-on-Government-for-Support

The Business of Fashion. (2017, May 26). *The business of Cruise: Go big or go home. The Business of Fashion*. Retrieved from https://www.businessoffashion.com/articles/luxury/when-it-comes-to-cruise-go-big-or-go-home

Thompson, A. (1979). *Understanding Futurology: An introduction to futures study*. Devon: David & Charles Publishing.

Thorndike, E. (1920). A constant error in psychological ratings. *Journal of Applied Psychology*, *4*(1), 25–29. Washington, DC: American Psychological Association.

Thrash, T., & Elliot, A. (2003). Inspiration as a psychological construct. *Journal of Personality and Social Psychology*, *84*(4), 871–889. doi:10.1037/0022-3514.84.4.871

Thrash, T., & Elliot, A. (2004). Inspiration: Core characteristics, component processes, antecedents, and function. *Journal of Personality and Social Psychology*, *87*(6), 957–973. doi:10.1037/0022-3514.87.6.957

Thrift, N. (2004). Intensities of feeling: Towards a spatial politics of affect. *Geografiska Annaler, Series B: Human Geography*, *86*(1), 57–78. doi:10.1111/j.0435-3684.2004.00154.x

Timothy, D. (2005). Shopping tourism, retailing, and leisure, Clevedon: Channel view.

Tirta, I. (2022). *Iwan Tirta brand history*. Retrieved from https://www.iwantirtabatik.com/content/83-the-history

Tinsley, H., & Tinsley, D. (1986). A theory of the attributes, benefits, and causes of leisure experience. *Leisure Sciences*, *8*(1), 1–45. doi:10.1080/01490408609513056

Titton, M. (2015). Fashionable personae: Self-identity and enactments of fashion narratives in fashion blogs. *Fashion Theory*, *19*(2), 201–220. doi:10.2752/175174115X14168357992391

Toffler, A. (1970). *Future shock*. New York, NY: Random House Inc.

Toposophy (2018). *Trends shaping visitor demand in 2018: Focus on Athens*. Retrieved from https://www.aia.gr/media/workshop/workshop18/presentations/02_Trends-shaping-visitor-demand-2018-Focus_on-Athens.pdf

Torrini, C., & Barone, T. (2016). Branding & the city. In I. Pezzini & C. A. de Oliveira (Eds.), *Roma in divenire tra identità e conflitti – Collana semiotica* (pp. 313–344). Roma: Edizioni Nuova Cultura.

Tosun, C. (2005). Stages in the emergence of a participatory tourism development approach in the developing world. *Geoforum*, *36*(3), 333–352. doi:10.1016/j.geoforum.2004.06.003

Triani, G. (1988). *Pelle di luna, pelle di sole. Nascita e storia della civiltà balneare 1700–1946*. Venice, Italy: Marsilio.

TripAdvisor (2021). *Palazzo della Civiltà Italiana – Tourist Comments. Tripadvisor.com*. Retrieved from https://www.tripadvisor.com/ShowUserReviews-g187791-d5614708-r433517190-Palazzo_della_Civilta_Italiana-Rome_Lazio.html

Tripodi, A. (2013). *Eur spa cede a Lvmh il Palazzo della Civiltà, scoppia la polemica. Isole24 ore*. Retrieved from www.ediliziaeterritorio.ilsole24ore.com/art/progetti-e-concorsi/2013-07-19/cede-lvmh-Palazzo-civilta-084105.php?uuid=AbLC7YFI

Trubert-Tollu, C., Tétart-Vittu, F., & Martin-Hattembourg, J. (2017). *La maison worth: Naissance de la haute couture, 1858–1954*. Bibliothèque des arts.

Truscott, K., & Chilton, J. (2020, September 17). *5 of the best pieces from the disney X Gucci collection. Harpers Bazaar Arabia*. Retrieved from https://www.harpersbazaararabia.com/fashion/featured-news/disney-x-gucci-collaboration

Tseëlon, E. (2001). Fashion research and its discontents. *Fashion Theory*, *5*(4), 435–451. doi:10.2752/136270401778998864

Tseëlon, E. (2015). *Erving Goffman. Thinking through fashion: A guide to key theorists* (Vol. 149).

Tunbridge, J., & Ashworth, G. (1996). *Dissonant heritage. The management of the past as a resource in conflict*. Chichester: Wiley.

Tungate, M. (2012). *Fashion brands: Branding style from Armani to Zara*. Kogan Page Publishers.

Turner, V. (1969). Liminality and communitas, *The ritual process: Structure and anti-structure*. Chicago, IL: Aldine Publishing.

Turner, V. (1977). Variations on a theme of liminality. In S. Moore & B. Myerhoff (Eds.), *Secular ritual*. Assen, The Netherlands: Van Gorcum.

Turner, E., & Turner, V. (1978). Image and Pilgrimage in Christian culture, *Anthropological perspectives*. New York, NY: Columbia University Press.

UNESCO. (2009). *Indonesian batik*. Paris: UNESCO. Retrieved from https://ich.unesco.org/en/RL/indonesian-batik-00170

UNESCO. (2012). *Noken multifunctional knotted or woven bag, handcraft of the people of Papua*. Paris: UNESCO. Retrieved from https://ich.unesco.org/en/USL/noken-multifunctional-knotted-or-woven-bag-handcraft-of-the-people-of-papua-00619

UNESCO. (2019). *The UNESCO 2003 convention for the safeguarding of the intangible cultural heritage: Opportunities for indigenous peoples.* Paris: UNESCO. Retrieved from http://www.unesco.org/new/en/unesco-liaison-office-in-new-york/about-this-office/single-view/news/the_unesco_2003_convention_for_the_safeguarding_of_the_intan/

UNWTO. (2014). *Global Report on shopping tourism.* Spain: UNWTO.

UNWTO. (2020). *World tourism Barometer Statistical Annex 16(4).* Spain: UNWTO.

Urbain, J. (1996). *Sur la plage.* Paris, France: Payot.

Urry, J. (1990). *The tourist gaze: Leisure and travel in contemporary societies.* Sage.

Urry, J. (2002). *The tourist gaze.* London: Sage.

Urry, J., & Larsen, J. (2011). *The tourist gaze 3.0.* London: Sage.

Usui, R. (2021). Feral animals as a tourism attraction: Characterizing tourists' experiences with rabbits on Ōkunoshima Island in Hiroshima, Japan. *Current Issues in Tourism, 25*(16), 2615–2630. doi:10.1080/13683500.2021.1978950

Vaill, A. (1999). *Everybody was so young: Gerald and Sara Murphy: A Lost Generation Love story.* New York, NY: Broadway Books.

Vajda, J. (2006). Paris en huit jours. À la découverte de la ville à travers les guides, les journaux pour touristes et les récits de voyage, 1855–1937. *Societes and Representations, 1*(21), 255–273.

Valette-Florence, R., & Valette-Florence, P. (2020). Effects of emotions and brand personality on consumer commitment, via the mediating effects of brand trust and attachment. *Recherche et Applications en Marketing, 35*(1), 84–110. doi:10.1177/205157072090

Vallée, I. (2013). Nouvelle tendance: Le tourisme de mode, 26 August, Veilletourisme.ca.

Vamplew, W. (2021). *Games people played: A global history of sports.* London: Reaktion Books.

Van Elven, M. (2018, January 20). *The business of hype: Why so many fashion brands are now doing "product drops".* Fashion United. Retrieved from https://fashionunited.uk/news/retail/the-business-of-hype-why-so-many-fashion-brands-are-now-doing-product-drops/2018101739501

Van Gennep, A. (1960). *The Rites of Passage, 1909* [trans. Monika B. Vizedom, Gabrielle L. Caffee] Chicago, IL: University of Chicago Press. Translated from Van Gennep, A. (1909). Les rites de passage. Paris: Émile Nourry.

Varey, R. J., & Ballantyne, D. (2006). Relationship marketing and the challenge of dialogical interaction. *Journal of Relationship Marketing, 4*(3), 11–28. doi:10.1300/J366v04n03_02

Veillon, D. (1990). Le théâtre de la mode. Vingtième Siècle. *Revue D'histoire, 28*(1), 118–120. doi:10.3406/xxs.1990.2307

Veillon, D. (2002). Fashion under the occupation. *Berg.* doi:10.1093/es/khg035

Verheyde, P. (1993). *Les Galeries Lafayette 1899-1955: Histoire économique d'un grand magasin.* Etudes et Documents, Volume V, Comité pour l'Histoire économique et financière de la France, Paris, Imprimerie nationale.

Vezina, B. (2019). Curbing cultural appropriation in the fashion industry with intellectual property. *Wipo Magazine*, (4), 9–14.

Vicari, S. (2010). *Brand building: The creative city. A critical look at current concepts and practices.* Firenze: Firenze University Press.

Visit Morocco. (2019, April 29). Marrakech, chosen by Dior for its next Cruise Fashion Show on April 29, 2019. Visit Morocco. Retrieved from https://www.visitmorocco.com/en/blog/marrakech-chosen-dior-its-next-cruise-fashion-show-april-29-2019

Vivant, E. (2007). Les événements off: De la résistance à la mise en scène de la ville creative. *Géocarrefour*, *82*(3), 131–140. doi:10.4000/geocarrefour.2188

Vivant, E. (2010). The (re)Making of Paris as a Bohemian place? *Progress in Planning*, *74*(3), 107–152. doi:10.1016/j.progress.2010.05.002

Viveiros de Castro, E. (2014). *Cannibal metaphysics, for a post-structural anthropology*. Minneapolis, MN: Univocal Publishing.

Vlassi, E., & Papatheodorou, A. (2021). Towards a method to assess the role of online marketing Campaigns in the airline – Airport – Destination authority triangular business relationship: The case of Athens Tourism Partnership. In A. Graham, N. Adler, M. H. Niemeier, O. Betancor, P. A. Antunes, V. Bilotkach, ... G. Martini (Eds.), *Air transport and regional development policies* (pp. 227–239). Oxford: Routledge. doi:10.4324/9781003092070

Vlassi, E., & Papatheodorou, A. (2022). Destination Brand Image Co-Creation: User Generated Content VS Destination Generated Content. The case of Athens, ICSIMAT. Chios, 17-21 July 2019.

Vogue Business. (2019). *Greece's luxury market shows signs of recovery*. Retrieved from https://www.voguebusiness.com/consumers/greece-luxury-market-recovery-louis-vuitton-dior

Vogue Greece. (2019a, July 1). Rastoni. *Vogue*, 152–169.

Vogue Greece. (2019b, 1 August). FlashBack. Vogue, 102–125.

Vogue Greece. (2019c, 1 August). (pp. 134–147). A little more summertime. Vogue.

Vogue Greece. (2019d, 1 July). (pp. 178–215). Θάλασσα. Vogue.

Vogue Runway. (2011, June 08). *Louis Vuitton*. Resort 2012. Review. Vogue Runway. Retrieved from https://www.vogue.com/fashion-shows/resort-2012/louis-vuitton

Vota, G. (1954). *I sessant'anni del Touring Club Italiano*. Milan: Touring.

Walton, J. (2000). *The British seaside. Holidays and resorts in the twentieth century*. Manchester: Manchester University Press.

Wang, C. (2019). Building a network for preserving intangible cultural heritage through education: A study of Indonesian batik. *International Journal of Art and Design Education*, *38*(2), 398–415. doi:10.1111/jade.12200

Wang, Q. (2019, June 08). *Brand collaboration: Good for business, good for sustainability*. Common Objective. Retrieved from https://www.commonobjective.co/article/brand-collaboration-good-for-business-good-for-sustainability

Webber, D. (2004). Understanding charity fundraiser events. *International Journal of Nonprofit and Voluntary Sector Marketing*, *9*(2), 122–134. doi:10.1002/nvsm.239

Webster, K. (2013). Creating wow in the fashion industry: Reflecting on the experience of Melbourne Fashion Festival. In K. M. Williams, J. Laing, & W. Frost (Eds.), *Fashion, design marketing and events* (pp. 118–130). New York, NY: Routledge.

Weidenfeld, A., Butler, R., & Williams, A. (2011). The role of clustering, cooperation and complementarities in the visitor attraction sector. *Current Issues in Tourism*, *14*(7), 595–629. doi:10.1080/13683500.2010.517312

Welter, A. (2019). Modern patronage. Fashion for art. Cultureshifts.net. Retrieved from https://cultureshifts.net/en/modern-patronage-fashion-for-art/

Wigglesworth, R. (2010). Architecture and textiles (Master's thesis). New Zealand: Unitec Institute of Technology.

Williams, R. (1982). *Dream worlds: Mass consumption in late nineteenth-century France*. Berkeley, CA: University of California Press.

Wilmotte, J. (1999). *Architecture intérieur des villes – Interior urban design*. Paris: Le Moniteur.

Wissinger, E. (2015). *This year's model: Fashion, media, and the making of Glamour*. New York, NY: NYU Press.

Wong, Q. (2019, December 3). *Brand collaboration: Good for business, good for sustainability*. Retrieved from https://www.commonobjective.co/article/brand-collaboration-good-for-business-good-for-sustainability

World Bank. (2019). *How much do our wardrobes cost to the environment? World Bank*. Retrieved from https://www.worldbank.org/en/news/feature/2019/09/23/costo-moda-medio-ambiente

World Tourism Organization and Netflix. (2021). *Cultural Affinity and screen tourism – The case of internet entertainment services*. Madrid: UNWTO. doi:10.18111/9789284422838

WTTC. (2019). *Economic Impact Reports*. World Travel & Tourism Council. Retrieved from https://wttc.org/research/economic-impact

WTTC. (2021). *Travel and tourism economic impact 2018*. London: WTTC.

Wubs, B., Lavanga, M., & Janssens, A. (2020). Letter from the Editors: The Past and present of fashion cities. *Fashion Theory*, *24*(3), 319–324. doi:10.1080/1362704X.2020.1732012

Wu, M., & Pearce, P. (2014). Chinese recreational vehicle users in Australia: A netnographic study of tourist motivation. *Tourism Management*, *43*, 22–35.

Yasin, N., Noor, M., & Mohamed, O. (2007). Does Image of country-of-origin matter to brand equity? *The Journal of Product and Brand Management*, *16*(1), 38–48. doi:10.1108/10610420710731142

Yeoman, I. (2012). *2050 – Tomorrow's tourism*. Bristol: Channel View Publications.

Yeoman, I., & Mars, M. (2012). Robots, men and sex tourism. *Futures*, *44*, 365–371. doi:10.1016/j.futures.2011.11.004

Yotka, S. (2017, May 3). *Chanel brings Ancient Greece to Paris for Resort 2018*. Vogue. Retrieved from https://www.vogue.com/article/chanel-resort-2018-fashion-show

Yousaf, S., Razzaq, A., & Fan, X. (2021). Understanding tourists' motivations to launch a boycott on social media: A case study of the# BoycottMurree campaign in Pakistan. *Journal of Vacation Marketing*, *27*(4), 479–495.

Zargani, L. (2015). *Fendi's New Roman Headquarters*. WWD. Retrieved from https://wwd.com/fashion-news/designer-luxury/fendi-roman-headquarters-10127820/

Zelinsky, W. (2004). Globalization reconsidered: The historical geography of modern western male attire. *Journal of Cultural Geography*, *22*(1), 83–134. doi:10.1080/08873630409478248

Zhang, J. (2020). *Temples of high style: The 7 most exotic fashion show locations worldwide*. Retrieved from https://www.prestigeonline.com/my/style/fashion/exotic-fashion-show-locations-worldwide/

Zocchetti, V. (2019, January 25). Croisière, un défilé majeur? Madame Figaro.

Zola, E. (2009). *Au Bonheur des Dames*. Paris: Larousse.

Zuelow, E. (2015). *A history of modern tourism*. London: Bloomsbury Publishing.

INDEX